FLIGHT CADET

Flight Cadet

Royal Air Force College Cranwell

RUTHERFORD M. HANCOCK

The Pentland Press
Edinburgh – Cambridge – Durham – USA

First published in 1996 by
The Pentland Press Ltd
1 Hutton Close
South Church
Bishop Auckland
Durham

ISBN 1-85821-414-9

Typeset by Carnegie Publishing, 18 Maynard St, Preston
Printed and bound by Bookcraft (Bath) Ltd

To Betty, my darling wife

Contents

List of Illustrations

Illustration Credits

i. The Sport and General Press Agency Ltd, 4 Racquet Court, Fleet Street, London: 5

ii Air Officer Commanding & Commandant RAF College: 13, 14, 21

iii Photochrom: 16, 17, 18

iv Van Hallan Press & General Photographic Agency, 1 Hibernia Road, Hounslow, Middlesex: 31, 32

v *Illustrated*, 189 High Holborn, London: 33, 35

vi Air Ministry, Photographic Reproduction Branch: 34

vii Gale & Polden Ltd: 38, 39

viii The Chapel Studios, 51 Chapel Street, Aberdeen: 40

ix Polyphoto: front cover

x Pat Rooney: 25

xi The Author: 1–4, 6–12, 15, 19, 20, 23, 24, 26–30, 36, 37

xii Unknown Flight Cadet photographer: 21

High Flight

Oh, I have slipped the surly bonds of earth
And danced the skies on laughter-silvered wings;
Sunward I've climbed, and joined the tumbling mirth
Of sun–split clouds . . . and done a hundred things
You have not dreamed of . . . wheeled and soared and
    swung

High in the sunlit silence. Hov'ring there,
I've chased the shouting wind along, and flung
My eager craft through footless halls of air.
Up, up the long, delirious, burning blue
I've topped the windswept heights with ease and grace

Where never lark, or even eagle flew.
And, while with silent, lifting mind I've trod
The high untrespassed sanctity of space,
Put out my hand, and touched the face of God.

John Gillespie Magee, Jr.

Foreword

by Air Marshal Sir Richard B. Bolt, KBE, CB, DFC, AFC, RNZAF – New Zealand Chief of Defence Staff, NZ Defence Forces 1976–81

WITH SO MANY THOUSANDS of New Zealand airmen having served in air operations during World War II it was not surprising that many lads of the author's generation were attracted to an Air Force life and fired with enthusiasm to fly. But this book owes nothing to daring wartime exploits or even dramatic peacetime adventures or achievements beyond the normal. It is simply the personal record and human story of a transition from very inexperienced Air Training Corps cadet in New Zealand to professional Air Force officer and pilot via that most highly respected of all Air Force training establishments on the other side of the world – the RAF College at Cranwell.

I can only remember Rutherford Hancock as 'Hank' – tall, slim, athletic and keen – but as one who served with the RAF in war and then was lucky enough to continue through a rather lengthy career of my own, I can readily identify with many of the memories, activities and thoughts which 'Hank' has so faithfully recorded from training days as he progressed along the full length of his learning curve as a Flight Cadet. I therefore feel pleased and privileged to be invited to write this short foreword.

As a personnel staff officer myself in the Air Force Headquarters of 1950–1, I can clearly recall when Hank Hancock made his bid and was selected as one of the first two New Zealanders to attend the RAF College in the postwar years. It was an important 'first' for the RNZAF and all those who were to attend subsequently. Many achieved high office. All would, I think, agree that Hank's experiences at Cranwell still have relevance today. Despite dramatic changes and advances in military aviation since those times, the personal challenges to be faced in the process of becoming a military pilot and professional service officer have not changed all that much. New Zealanders may no longer go to Cranwell with an RNZAF career in view, but the Cranwell training patterns significantly influenced those developed to meet New Zealand's own modern Air Force needs at home. Certainly the standards, values and traditions which Hank remembers being taught in the fifties remain as vital elements in the professionalism which today's Air Forces demand.

But this book is so much more than an account of training at Cranwell. There are the now old fashioned charms of official travel across the world by sea, the delights of a young man from remote New Zealand in discovering so many aspects of the British and European scenes – and not least, in discovering his wife to be. I have no doubt it will all be read with pleasure and some nostalgia by those who have themselves been through Air Force training systems of the past. It will also deserve the attention of any young persons contemplating Air Force flying careers of their own.

Introduction

MARSHAL PETAIN, FRENCH SOLDIER AND POLITICIAN, once said, 'To write one's memoirs is to speak ill of everybody except oneself.' In writing about my personal experiences as a Flight Cadet at the Royal Air Force College Cranwell, I hope that nobody will accuse me of that!

Ron Chippindale and I were fortunate to be the first two members of the Royal New Zealand Air Force to attend the College, part of a group of fifteen from the RNZAF who were to graduate from Cranwell during the period 1951–64. We have therefore found ourselves filling a unique place in the history of the RNZAF and the College.

My story is an attempt to record in an informal way how I became interested in aviation and was selected for the longest established air academy in the world, what happened before my training began and during other leave periods, and the many interesting (to me) and sometimes traumatic experiences I had while learning to fly at Cranwell.

Some events have been transposed a little in time to make a more coherent text, but the record is as accurate as my notes, research and memory can make it.

Acknowledgements

I WISH TO ACKNOWLEDGE the assistance of the following in writing this book (and apologise if I have inadvertently omitted anyone or anything):

RAF College *Journal*, June 1951–November 1954.
RAF College *List of Graduates*, 5 February 1920–18 December 1962, and the *Supplement to the List of Graduates*, 30 July 1963–16 March 1973.
The Air Force List and *The Royal Air Force Retired List*, HMSO.
The History of Royal Air Force Cranwell, by Gp. Capt. E.B. Haslam, MA, FRHistS, 1982, HMSO.
The Royal Air Force Review, March and April 1952, February 1953.
Illustrated, 11 and 18 July 1953.
Esquire, 1951.
The Times Survey of British Aviation, 1952 and 1953.
Personnel Management Centre, RAF Innsworth, Ministry of Defence.
Public Relations, Headquarters New Zealand Defence Force.
Air Secretary, Royal Pakistan Air Force.
Mrs Jean M. Buckberry, ALA, RAF College Librarian and Archivist; Ron Chippindale; Jim C. Brown; John N. Baber; Lindsay J. Rollo; my wife, children and sisters.
My mother for keeping 193 of my Cranwell letters, 1951–3.
My flying log books, cuttings from publications/newspapers etc.

R.M. Hancock
Wellington, N.Z.
August 1996

CHAPTER I

The Preparation

THE BOX was kept at the rear of the top shelf of the airing cupboard beside the coal-fired range in our kitchen. Mum had placed it there so that I couldn't reach it, even when standing on a chair. I was about eight years old and wasn't allowed to touch it.

One of my cousins, Keith Skinner, had given me the box and its contents after a visit to our family. He'd made a 25 inch wing-span rubber powered free flight model aeroplane called the Swift and flown it several times in the park near his home in Dunedin, New Zealand. He'd then decided his interests lay elsewhere, put the model in a cardboard box and given it to me.

Dad and I flew the Swift on the Temuka golf course across the road from our house, but the plane crashed on landing, breaking its balsa propeller. Mum said I was too young for such things and put the Swift in the airing cupboard. I loved the sweet smell of the dope on the model, warmed by the hot water tank in the cupboard, and wanted to repair the propeller and fly the plane, but Mum was adamant – I had to be older to do that.

I'd been born at Temuka, a small town near the coast in the South Island of New Zealand on the south-eastern part of the Canterbury Plains. The area was one of mixed farms and good fishing rivers that stretched to the Southern Alps in the west and New Zealand's highest mountain. Near Temuka in 1903, an inventor farmer called Richard William Pearse had made the world's first flight in a self-powered heavier-than-air machine of his design, though not a controlled flight as achieved by the Wright brothers about nine months later. Twelve miles south of Temuka was the port and city of Timaru, the birthplace of Marshal of the Royal Air Force The Rt. Hon. The Lord Elworthy of Timaru, KG, GCB, CBE, DSO, LVO, DFC, AFC, KStJ, MA.

Dad, one of two chemists at Temuka, worked long hours to build up his business, later expanding by becoming an optician and photographic dealer and processor. He married Dora Skinner and in due course my sisters Beverley, Heather and Lyndall were born. Mum wanted names that were distinctive and uncommon for those days.

When I was born, Dad thought of calling me Selwyn after the pioneer Anglican bishop in New Zealand, Bishop Augustus Selwyn, but Mum decided

I'd be christened Rutherford Moncrieff. The Rutherford came from the name of the renowned Presbyterian minister and social reformer, the Rev. Dr Rutherford Waddell, MA, who for forty years had been minister at St Andrew's Church in the city of Dunedin where Mum had grown up. He'd been like a beloved uncle to her and had died a week before I was born. I don't think Mum was aware that Rutherford in Old English meant, 'the river crossing made of red stones'. Moncrieff was just a Scottish name Mum fancied. Little did she know what problems I'd have with these names!

Dad's father had an Anglican background and came as a boy from the Cotswold area of Gloucestershire, England, to Christchurch, New Zealand. As a result, Dad became a chorister in Christchurch Cathedral and was educated at the Cathedral Grammar School and then at the prestigious public school, Christ's College. Mum's father was the Rev. James Skinner, MA, from Rothiemay in Banffshire, Scotland. He'd graduated from Aberdeen University and, in 1874, been ordained and inducted into the Presbyterian parish of the gold-rush town of Waitahuna in Central Otago, New Zealand. With Mum having a strong manse background and Dad having become a nominal Anglican, my sisters and I were brought up as Presbyterians.

Before he married, Dad smoked a pipe, said 'damn' when provoked, and had the occasional beer. Needless to say, Mum was 'dead agin' such things. She persuaded him to stop drinking, but failed with the swearing and pipe smoking. Dad was banished to outside the house when he lit his pipe. Mum then made sure that I didn't follow in Dad's footsteps in these respects. At the tender age of eleven, I was taken to meetings of the Band of Hope and, with other youngsters, signed a pledge of abstinence from alcohol. I privately tried smoking my father's pipes, but they tasted so revolting I soon gave them up.

In due course Beverley and Heather went off to board at a secondary school in Timaru while Lyndall and I went to the Temuka District Primary School. I drifted through school and, without too much effort, topped my class in Standard 4. Miss Heenan, my teacher that year, had a hard time controlling the unruly elements in her class and on one occasion retreated behind the portable blackboard in tears. I was strapped on another occasion.

During World War II, Temuka was honoured by a visit of His Excellency The Governor General, Marshal of the Royal Air Force The Rt. Hon. Sir Cyril Newall, OM, GCB. All the local organisations were to march from the main street to meet the Governor General at the War Memorial in the Domain and, as Dad was in the Home Guard and the parade seemed to me to be a lot of fun, I persuaded him to let me march with him. As this was my first experience of marching and I was rather small, I had great difficulty in keeping in step. When the Governor General inspected the parade he stopped in front of me, shook my hand and asked, 'What do you do in the

Home Guard?' 'I'm a Message Boy,' I answered. The Governor General smiled and moved on.

(I later read that Sir Cyril Newall was considered to be one of the 'old school' and had made a celebrated *faux pas* during a speech in New Zealand by referring to 'boys of the Navy, men of the Army and gentlemen of the Air Force'. He also earned the ire of an Air Force audience on some other occasion when he began his address with 'Officers and their ladies, NCOs and their wives, airmen and their women . . .')

With better secondary schooling at Timaru, Mum was keen for the family to shift there. Lyndall could then become a day pupil instead of a boarder at secondary school. Beverley and Heather by that time were in Dunedin doing nursing and kindergarten training respectively, so were unaffected by the proposed shift. Mum's main reason for shifting, however, was that she felt that underground water at Temuka was adversely affecting her health. A water diviner confirmed Mum's suspicions that underground streams joined below our sitting-room. Dad, of course, didn't want to move as his business was in Temuka. Mum went ahead anyway and, with her own money, bought a substantial house in Timaru after the water diviner had pronounced it bone dry. So at age eleven, I moved with my family to Timaru, and Dad commuted between Timaru and Temuka for the next eleven years or so until he sold his business and retired.

I had the choice of going to several primary schools in Timaru, but decided on Waimataitai School because it had a good reputation and Paul Barnes, a friend I'd known in Temuka, was going there. Waimataitai had some five hundred pupils, the boys and girls being in separate classrooms.

Form 1 at Waimataitai was quite a revelation for me. Not only were the other pupils ahead of me in most studies, but we had Bill Pickard as our teacher. I found myself caught up by this excellent teacher and worked harder than I'd ever worked before. Mum called Mr Pickard a 'slave-driver'. He encouraged me in my handwriting. I'm partially ambidextrous, but left-handed for writing. A teacher at Temuka had tried to make me a right hander until Dad had objected, so my handwriting had never been very regular. Mr Pickard helped me write with my left hand below the line so my fingers didn't smudge the ink from my pen. With others in the class I was soon entering national handwriting competitions, but I didn't win a prize.

I found that I excelled in history and geography projects. Many hours were spent researching the subjects, doing illustrations and reproducing maps. Mr Pickard kept my project books for several years as examples to other pupils until I eventually asked for the books to be returned. I also enjoyed wood-working and was in the group that went to the Timaru Technical College for the subject and found Mr Lamb, the woodwork instructor, to be a first rate teacher. Mental arithmetic was never my strong point, but Mr Pickard gave me a good understanding of things mathematical. At the end of the year I was surprised to finish as high as third in my class.

At last, Mum decided I could have the Swift model aeroplane. Dad built a workbench for me in a shed on our property. I soon repaired the Swift and flew it successfully. I spent hours with that model and learned a lot about aerodynamics and aircraft construction. I began building model aircraft – as far as my pocket money would allow.

Scale display models were carved out of solid balsa or redwood – a Hawker Typhoon, an Empire Flying Boat, and Jean Batten's record breaker Percival Gull – before I built several small rubber powered flying models – the 18 inch wing-span Eaglet spar model, the 19 inch wing-span Ranger pusher canard, the 20 inch wing-span Sportster and a 15 inch wing-span scale Moth Minor. Next came several 'chuck' gliders, the 36 inch wing-span Zephyr sailplane and the 21 inch wing-span Thistledown rubber powered indoor model. The latter was very light and fragile, being covered with a microfilm created by pouring a special dope mixture onto water and then carefully transferring the resulting film onto the wings, body and even the built-up propeller. The model was attached by a thread to a pole and flew slowly around it for several minutes.

I discovered that one of my classmates, Arthur Macaulay, had similar interests and had progressed to competing in the New Zealand Model Aeroplane Championships, as well as overseas with Wakefield Class rubber powered models. We spent a lot of our spare time talking about model aeroplanes.

At Temuka I'd joined the Life Boys, the junior section of the Boys' Brigade. Soon after shifting to Timaru, I was able to move into No. 3 Company of the Boys' Brigade which met at Trinity Presbyterian Church. I thoroughly enjoyed the Boys' Brigade camps, gymnastics and other activities, and eventually became the Colour Sergeant of my Company. Mum took the family, however, to Chalmers Presbyterian Church as it was nearest to our home. At Sunday School I won the gold medal for being dux. The teacher in my final year there, Miss Ronaldson, was the sister-in-law of 'Dogs' Kemshed, an elder of the church and the Deputy Principal of Timaru Boys' High School. I was to meet up with them both in later years.

My final year at Waimataitai in 'Beefy' Robertson's class was also a period of great development for me. Paul Barnes and I sat at the same desk and we used to fool around a bit, but I was the one who got caught and moved to the far side of the room for the remainder of the year. I was taught amongst other things the basics of singing and encouraged to sit for a secondary school bursary, which I didn't get – exams not being my forte. I had stiff competition from Warwick Byrom and Keith Miller. On several occasions Warwick and I had to go to the Form 2 girls' class, show them our project books and tell them how we went about researching the projects. This was most embarrassing, particularly when one or two of the girls got a crush on me and kept intercepting me on my way home from school, but speaking in front of a lot of strangers was good experience. That year, I again finished third in my class.

The next year I commenced my secondary schooling at the Timaru Boys' High School, which was well known as a 'rugby union' school and for its many academic and sporting heroes. The latter included the great Jack Lovelock, MA, MRCP (Lond), a Rhodes Scholar who'd won the 1,500 metres race at the 1936 Berlin Olympic Games in world record time. The orientation for new boys at the school included viewing Lovelock's medals in the library and, in the school grounds, the oak tree that Hitler had given him.

I found that there were school songs and traditions to get used to, such as new boys being ducked in the rain barrel behind the gymnasium, and no one (except sissies) wearing togs in the outdoor swimming pool. There was Assembly each morning and pupils moved every hour to the room of their particular teacher. Woe betide a pupil who lost his way and ended up in the wrong class! 'Foot' Tait headed an impressive array of masters, some of whom had been there almost all their working lives – 'Dogs' Kemshed, 'Buster' Moore, 'Wuzzie' Wilson, 'Bull' Ledingham, 'Cash' Hind and 'Chimp' Murray (who later murdered his wife). The school was certainly a different world from Waimataitai. I was up against some really brainy people – duxes from many primary schools – and made a hash of the initial examinations, so ending up in Form 3C, the lowest of the low.

I eventually settled down and came top of Form 3C, moved up to Form 4B, came top of that, passed School Certificate and went into Form 5A. University Entrance was another big hurdle, but I passed in my specialist subjects of English, History and Geography.

In Form 3, I was a member of the Gym Team. George Hilland, the ex-Royal Navy physical education master, wanted me to continue gymnastics in Form 4, but I was more interested in athletics. I was keen on the sprints and jumps and achieved some modest success in these. Mr Hilland encouraged me to change from the Scissors style in the high jump to the Western Roll or the Eastern Cutoff. I played rugby like most pupils at the School, but felt I didn't have the right build for the game. The other major sport of cricket didn't interest me as I always seemed to be put on some far-flung part of the field rather than amongst the real action.

The Timaru Boys' High School was not a well endowed school so performed Gilbert and Sullivan operas to raise money and give pupils some exposure to the magic of comic opera. I thoroughly enjoyed being in the chorus for HMS Pinafore and The Pirates of Penzance, and then being one of the gentlemen of Japan in The Mikado.

By coincidence, the Germans surrendered on my birthday, 8 May, and the

Japanese some three months later, so ending World War II. There were great celebrations at Timaru on both occasions with huge bonfires on Caroline Bay and marches along the main street. School children were included in the marches and there was much hilarity, particularly when one of the bands in the parade played 'Colonel Bogey' and a slightly drunken man standing on a shop veranda played the same tune on a trombone, but several beats behind the band.

Mum wanted me to play the piano like my sisters, so I became the unwilling pupil of Miss Rudge during my Form 2 year. I felt the piano exercises were mainly for the good of my soul. What I really wanted to do was to play the bagpipes, so in Form 3 at Timaru Boys' High School I joined the Pipe Band. I had first to learn the chanter and went each week for lessons from Duncan Cormack, pipe major of the Timaru Highland Pipe Band. Two years later, I was allowed to start on the bagpipes and, after passing a test, commenced playing in the band. This was great fun, much better than being in the School's Army Cadets, who seemed to do drill and rush around with rifles all the time. The small group of Air Training Corps Cadets at the School did more interesting things, but for the time being I wanted to play the bagpipes. The Pipe Band was always winning the School's annual drill competition and from time to time played on public occasions. One year, despite not having full highland dress, I entered the Timaru piping competitions. I practised so hard beforehand that in the competition I soon became 'blown' (where my lips wouldn't provide an effective seal on the mouthpiece), and I could only manage third place in one of the E Grade events.

At the time I went from Sunday School to Bible Class, Mum became unhappy with our minister when he made it clear that he was not averse to drinking alcohol and he preached a sermon encouraging young people to do the same. A number of people walked out of the church during the sermon. As a result, Mum took the family to Trinity Church where the minister had similar views to her own.

This move seemed to have advantages in it for me because I saw for the first time Margaret Hornsey, daughter of the Session Clerk. She tossed her honey blond, shoulder length hair most effectively and wore court shoes, which seemed to me to be very sophisticated for a schoolgirl at the end of the War. When I found that Mr Hornsey was my Bible Class leader and that Margaret was in the ballroom dancing class I attended at Miss Dorothy Thwaite's Dancing Academy, I thought I was made! During my last two years at school, Margaret and I went to a number of school and church dances, and I was allowed to drive her in my parent's Chevrolet car. She and I, along with thirty-nine other young people, became communicant members of the church. When Margaret joined the church choir, so did I. My motivation was obviously not the best, but I did learn to sing in parts and can still sing some parts today.

In my workshop, I put a lot of time into doing aeromodelling, fretwork and metalwork, and making a coffee table and electrical gadgets. I subscribed to the *Aeromodeller* magazine, joined the Timaru Model Aeroplane Club, wrote to model aeroplane firms in New Zealand, England and the United States and imported model aeroplane books, kits and X-Acto tools. Purchasing overseas currency through official channels was almost impossible in those days, so I resorted to buying United States dollars from the young Mormon missionaries who'd recently come to the Timaru area. I'd all the R.H. Warring books on *Airfoil Sections, Design of Wakefield Models, Rubber Motors, Airscrews,* and *Nomographs for the Aeromodeller,* in addition to B.H. Winston's *Gas Model Plane Construction,* P.R. Payne's *Model Sailplane Design,* L.G. Temple's *Model Sailplanes,* the Model Aeronautical Press's *Design for Aeromodellers,* and L.H. Sparey and C.A. Rippon's *Model Aeroplane Manual.*

The Ron Warring 48 inch wing-span Aeolus high performance pod and boom sailplane I made was a big success. I also built the English KeilKraft 21 inch wing-span Phantom control-line model and flew it in the prototype class of the New Zealand Model Aeroplane Championships at Christchurch, gaining a minor placing with it. Another control-line model was Cyril Shaw's 28 inch wing-span Dervish stunt model. I even converted to control-line my old Swift rubber powered free flight model. I also built the American Frank Zaic's 50 inch wing-span Sailwing flying wing glider (Fig. 1), and the 50 inch wing-span Banshee high performance pylon, sports model.

These activities taxed my meagre pocket money to the limits, especially as the Phantom, Dervish and Banshee models required motors. I decided to work for a fortnight during the Christmas holidays to earn enough money for an English made ED Competition Special 1.5 cc diesel motor. I became a car cleaner at Dominion Motors, the big car firm on the main street of Timaru. The hours were long and the work strenuous, particularly when I had to prepare for resale a farmer's car in which dogs had been carried and that'd never been cleaned since purchase. At the end of the fortnight, the manager of Dominion Motors asked me to stay on, so I worked there another week. The extra money helped me later to buy a second model aeroplane motor, an English made Mills 1.3 cc diesel.

During my last two years at school I began wondering what I'd do when I left school. Warwick Byrom invited me to accompany him to various work places on educational visits arranged by his father. We had a great time inspecting factories and businesses, but neither Warwick nor I could see ourselves working in such places. The new principal at school, Mr M.A. Bull, MA (affectionately known as 'Maybull') had a series of top businessmen from banks, insurances, retailers, and manufacturers give pupils lectures at the

Figure 1. Author at Timaru, New Zealand, with the framework of his 50 inch wing-span Sailwing flying wing model glider, designed by the American Frank Zaic, 1950.

morning Assembly on careers in their particular spheres. The information just seemed to indicate that there was a world beyond the school for which we were totally unprepared.

I didn't want to follow my father's footsteps and become a chemist, or work in a garage, and I saw no career in playing the bagpipes, but I was interested in model aeroplanes and flying and the Air Force seemed to be an extension of that interest. I really needed to know something about the Air Force.

An aero pageant was to be held at Saltwater Creek aerodrome at Timaru and I wanted to see it. Mum wasn't at all keen because it was on a Sunday, and Sundays were for going to church and rest. She eventually said I could go to just the afternoon part of the pageant. I was thrilled by the many types of light aircraft present, particularly the barnstorming acts of the Tiger Moth pilots who pretended they were drunk in charge of their planes and touched one wheel and then the other on the grass as they flew by in opposite directions to each other. The highlight was the formation aerobatics of three Harvards from Royal New Zealand Air Force Station Wigram, near the city of Christchurch. They flew so low I thought I could see every rivet on their undersides. The noise was terrific and the spectacle most exciting. I decided to be a pilot – but I'd never been up in an aeroplane.

I solved this by going to Saltwater Creek one Saturday and paying NZ 10s. for a ten minute joy ride in the front cockpit of a yellow Tiger Moth flown by Mr L.G. Mitchell, the Chief Flying Instructor of the South Canterbury Aero Club. The engine noise, the smell of dope and oil, the cold and wind in the open cockpit, the shouted instructions through a primitive voice tube from the pilot in the rear cockpit, gravity forces and the bumpy air conditions scarcely put me off.

Then Sqn. Ldr. Bob McKay, AFC, flew the only jet fighter in the Royal New Zealand Air Force, a Gloster Meteor Mark IV, over the principal cities of New Zealand. He put on a magnificent display of aerobatics over Timaru, doing low level steep turns above Timaru Boys' High School, then vertical climbs that seemed to go on for ever followed by wing overs, loops and barrel rolls. Flying like that was definitely what I wanted to do!

My next step was to persuade my parents to let me join No. 15 Squadron of the Air Training Corps at Timaru. They agreed that this would give me good experience and help me decide what I should do on leaving school. They also allowed me to leave the Boys' Brigade so I'd not become over committed with too many out of school activities.

So in my Form 6B year, I joined the Air Training Corps, an event that was to change my life. What I didn't know was that my old school teacher, Bill the 'slave-driver' Pickard, was the Squadron Commander! He was a Flight Lieutenant in the Air Force Reserve and wore an Efficiency Decoration. At my interview, he asked me why I wanted to join the ATC. (See Appendix I for abbreviations and expressions.) When I said I was thinking of becoming a pilot in the Air Force, he replied, 'Cranwell is the place for you.' I'd no idea what he was talking about, but he immediately took me in hand and showed me a pre-War brochure of a place called the Royal Air Force College, Cranwell. There were pictures of an impressive looking building that had a tower in the centre with a dome on top, rather like the Capitol Building in Washington DC. Other photos showed cadets doing drill, physical training in rather long shorts and swimming in a tiled indoor pool.

Flt. Lt. Pickard told me that a cadetship scheme was being set up so that RNZAF members could go to Cranwell. He didn't know much about it, but said he'd find out more for me. I went home and told my parents what was probably a rather garbled story. The prospect of me going to Britain hardly seemed real and they didn't comment much. I tried to locate Cranwell on a map. The brochure had said it was in Lincolnshire, but where exactly? I found a place called Cranfield, but it was a civilian college of aeronautics and wasn't in Lincolnshire.

True to his word, Flt. Lt. Pickard found out that candidates for the two year eight month course at Cranwell needed to have University Entrance in maths and physics, be aged 17½ to 19 and be physically fit. I didn't have the maths and physics so this was rather daunting.

On becoming principal of Timaru Boys' High School, 'Maybull' had told parents that he'd visit their homes if they wanted to have discussions about their sons. Mum immediately invited Mr Bull to our place, told him about my interest in Cranwell and asked for his advice. He carefully inspected the model aeroplanes and other things in my workshop, said he was most impressed and advised that I should try and pass University Entrance maths and physics in my final year at school. So in Form 6A when my contemporaries were relaxing a bit and enjoying being the élite of the school, I was hard at work studying maths and physics with pupils a year below me. I had a lot to catch up on as I'd previously done only basic maths and no physics at all. At the end of the year, much to my relief, I was accredited with University Entrance maths and physics and gained my Higher School Certificate.

I found the ATC was still very much influenced by World War II. There were magazines available full of Pilot Officer Prune and 'careless talk costs lives', aircraft recognition, developments in aircraft and so on. The wartime manuals on navigation, level bombing theory and weapons didn't seem to be relevant any more. I was put into uniform, taught some rifle drill, given lectures on aviation topics and generally had a good time. Flt. Lt. Pickard bent the rules a little by giving me a travel allowance for the wear and tear on my bicycle, even though I lived just within the required minimum distance for the payment of an allowance. I volunteered to go to an ATC camp at

Figure 2. John Brazier, Chief Flying Instructor South Canterbury Aero Club, and Author with de Havilland Tiger Moth 82A at Timaru, New Zealand, 1950.

the stores depot of RNZAF Weedons near Christchurch, and lived in a tent for a week with three other cadets from Timaru. Visits were made to No. 1 Flying Training School at nearby RNZAF Station Wigram so we could clamber over the Harvards and other aircraft, and inspect the many interesting things to be seen there.

Midway through my Form 6A year, the RNZAF advertised Flying Scholarships of 30 hours flying training free of charge with local aero clubs. Arthur Macaulay, Jim Park and I applied and, after rigorous medical examinations, were all accepted.

For the next three months I dressed in ATC uniform on Saturday mornings and biked to Saltwater Creek aerodrome to fly Tiger Moths with John Brazier, who'd become the Chief Flying Instructor of the South Canterbury Aero Club even though he lived a hundred miles away at Christchurch (Fig. 2). He used to fly to Timaru each Saturday morning, weather permitting, to do instructing for the Club. On many occasions I was disappointed when he couldn't come because of bad weather or business pressures. Eventually, Harry Wigley, the founding Managing Director of Mount Cook Airline, became my instructor.

The de Havilland 82A Tiger Moth was a great aircraft to fly, being light

on the controls and reasonably forgiving when one did the wrong thing. The
Gipsy Major engine was started by swinging the propeller. To see past the
engine, the pilot had to lean out into the slip-stream or weave the aircraft.
John Brazier in the front cockpit would shout down the communications
tube to me, '65, not 75.' The plane seemed to climb and descend at 65
m.p.h., fly straight and level at about 95 m.p.h., and stall at 45 m.p.h. Stalling,
spinning and aerobatics was something my stomach wasn't prepared for and
I felt decidedly queasy on several occasions. This discomfort somehow didn't
relate to the glamorous image I had of flying.

I applied for a Cranwell cadetship. The RAF and the RNZAF (See
Appendix II) were both offering cadetships and permanent commissions on
successful graduation from Cranwell. I expressed a preference for an RAF
cadetship. Harry Wigley wrote a reference for me saying that I'd 7 hours 15
minutes flying time on Tiger Moths, hadn't had time to go solo though I
was close to doing so, and was of average flying ability. This and other
supporting documentation was sent to Air Department in the capital city of
Wellington. After what seemed an age, I was invited to go to Wellington
for two days of selection interviews and tests. I decided to wear my ATC
uniform, and was the only one of the fifteen or so boys who assembled at
Air Department to be in uniform.

We underwent a modified form of the group selection methods developed
in Britain by the War Office Selection Board during World War II. These
comprised written tests (intelligence, general knowledge, personal inventory
and 'projection' tests), and indoor group tests (discussions, planning tasks,
individual situations, chairmanship exercises and lecturettes). There were no
practical outdoor tests at that time. A medical examination and individual
interview concluded the procedures. The latter was in front of the full
selection team, headed by the Air Member for Personnel, Air Cdre. S.
Wallingford, CB, CBE. The psychologist, Sqn. Ldr. W.C.J. Williams, BA,
DipEd, asked me:

'How do you think you got on in the tests?'

'I left about two and a half pages of questions undone in one test,' I replied.

'Perhaps the questions were getting harder,' he said.

I'd brought a photo album with me and was asked what was in it. I showed
the selection team photos of my model aeroplanes, and was most embarrassed
when they continued looking through the album at family and other photos.

Back home again in Timaru, I became a friend of the postman. At last a
letter arrived for me:

Dear Sir,
     I am pleased to advise you that you have been selected for enlistment
in the Royal New Zealand Air Force and appointment to a cadetship at
the Royal Air Force College, Cranwell.

It is requested that within seven days you advise this Department (P3) whether or not you are prepared to accept this appointment. Further details concerning your enlistment will be forwarded when available.

Yours faithfully,
(L.T. Armstrong)
Flight Lieutenant
for AIR SECRETARY

I rushed to show Mum the letter. She read it carefully and didn't say anything. Full of enthusiasm, I said, 'What do you think? Don't you think it's great!' She smiled weakly and mumbled something about it was very nice, if that was what I wanted.

I didn't realise until afterwards that she was probably thinking about her only son being on the other side of the world for three years, beginning a career that could be dangerous, and being subject to all sorts of temptations that might take me away from the way of life she hoped I would follow. No doubt she remembered that in her youth she'd planned a trip to Britain, but arrangements had been cancelled when her chaperon was found to be a secret drinker. Like so many parents, I think she felt that I was far too young to leave home and needed to show a lot more responsibility before doing so. Though New Zealand born, she, like many of the older generation New Zealanders, had always referred to Britain as 'home'. Eventually I think she was glad that I was getting an opportunity to go 'home'.

Dad read the letter and just accepted the inevitable that I was going to be an Air Force pilot. I felt some disappointment, however, that I'd missed out on an RAF cadetship. The RAF seemed to me to offer far more opportunities than the RNZAF because it was bigger and had the latest types of aircraft.

The next two months went by in a flash. There was so much to do! I'd been away for short holidays by myself, but never overseas or for so long. Mum looked at our suitcases and decided I'd need to take a small suitcase and an overnight bag, but she'd have to buy me a large suitcase and a trunk. She was concerned the bags might be stolen so I painted the trunk and suitcases with a large red cross on each side and my initials in the middle of the lids. Mum tried to get me to think what I would need overseas, but my mind was in a whirl and I was quite pleased when she decided how many pairs of socks etc. I should take. I ended up taking far too much.

There were my friends to see – John Ashwell from across the road; my classmates Paul Barnes, Warwick Byrom, Geoff Hamilton, Alf Pollard and John Sinclair; Jack Mehlhopt in the ATC and Colin Westoby of the Timaru Model Aeroplane Club. Then there was Flt. Lt. Pickard and, of course, Margaret Hornsey. Uncle Jack Skinner invited me to Dunedin to see relatives before I departed. He'd had an adventurous life and been in Britain during

World War I, so was able to pass on all sorts of useful tips to me. He drove me to his country house at Lake Wanaka for a few days and very generously gave me NZ £100 to spend in Britain. My parents had already arranged with the Bank of New Zealand in London for me to draw from a deposit of NZ£100 that they'd made, so I felt I was well provided for. I had to get clearance from the Department of Labour and Employment to leave New Zealand as I was liable for compulsory military training. The clearance arrived just before I left New Zealand. Miss Annie McLean, an elderly, almost blind friend visiting Mum, peered shortsightedly at my model aeroplanes and said, much to my amusement, that I had a great talent. She'd lived in England for many years and advised me not to drawl my words like the word 'yes', as the English spoke with a very clipped accent.

'Dogs' Kemshed asked me to pass on his regards to Sam Elworthy, a Group Captain at RAF Tangmere, should I run into him. He said he'd tutored Sam before Sam had left South Canterbury to further his education in England. (I never did run into Gp. Capt. Elworthy, but years later as ACM Sir Charles Elworthy, he laid the foundation stone of Trenchard Hall at Cranwell.)

The Timaru Boys' High School journal, *The Timaruvian*, recorded that I'd won a Cranwell cadetship, and somehow the news reached the Mayor of Timaru who wrote to me:

Dear Rutherford,

Pardon the use of your Christian name but we feel that we could not let you slip quietly away from Timaru without a word of farewell. I heard about you only today, and I am indeed proud of your achievement. To be selected for Cranwell College is an honour which will be treasured by your parents and rightly so. I am proud of your grit and determination and have no hesitation in saying that further honours will shower thick upon you.

When overseas remember your old ATC unit, your School, your town and your family above all.

Timaru has been honoured by your selection, likewise Temuka. That you may enjoy health and success is the wish of

Yours sincerely
W.L. Richards.

This very nice and unexpected letter seemed to sum up all the good wishes given me. I thought that the 'further honours will shower thick upon you' was a bit much and highly unlikely, but it all added to an exhilaration I felt in those final weeks.

Air Department advised that I was to report in Wellington a day before sailing to Southampton via the Panama Canal on the New Zealand Shipping Company's passenger ship *Rangitata*. The names and addresses of any relatives or friends in Britain were requested so they could act as my guardians in that part of the world. Mum suggested I should forward details of her first cousin in Aberdeen, Mrs Mabel Rundle, as she'd corresponded with Mrs Rundle for many years and I'd once had a week's holiday on the farm of Mrs Rundle's brother, John Skinner, at North Taieri near Dunedin, New Zealand.

'You call her Cousin Mabel,' I said. 'Should I call her Mrs Rundle when I meet her?'

Mum replied, 'Just call her Cousin Mabel.'

Unfortunately a major dispute on New Zealand waterfronts was developing and, to prevent being caught by a strike, the shipping company announced that the *Rangitata* would be sailing on 17 February, a week earlier than scheduled. This put me under more pressure to be ready in time. Dad gave me a Kodak Brownie folding camera, but I didn't have the opportunity to practise with it before leaving. My model aeroplanes were a problem – I needed to get rid of them and clear out my workshop. I made an arrangement with Provan Brother's hardware store to sell them for me, as I'd bought quite a lot of model aeroplane supplies from the two brothers over the years. Various friends called to say farewell. Lyndall said goodbye from Otago University in Dunedin. Paul Barnes and Flt. Lt. Pickard saw me off at Timaru railway station. Though Margaret Hornsey had already said goodbye, I'd hoped she would also be there. When the train stopped at Temuka, Dad greeted me. Similarly, at Ashburton where Beverley was nursing, she said hello. The train arrived at Lyttleton after dark and I embarked on the ferry *Hinemoa* for the journey across Cook Strait to the North Island.

Sleep eluded me – I was too excited for that. In the early hours of the morning when I was on deck to see the ferry enter Wellington harbour I ran into Ron Chippindale, one of the Cranwell candidates I'd met at the selections. I remembered him and another candidate, Mayn Hawkins, as they were from Rangiora and had sunburnt faces and unruly hair. Ron told me he'd also been selected for Cranwell.

On landing, Ron and I went to the RNZAF Movements Unit and waited around before being taken to RNZAF Station Shelly Bay. There we met Flt. Lt. Lin Armstrong, whom we recognised as being one of the selection team and who'd written advising us of our acceptance for Cranwell. He asked us, 'Have you been attested?'

We looked at him blankly.

'You know, sworn into the Service,' he said.

We shook our heads, so he took out a Bible and had us take the oath and complete the necessary forms. Though I was sworn in first, I was given the service number of 74211, whereas Ron was given 74210. We became Aircraftmen Class 2 and were immediately remustered to the rank of Cadet Pilot.

Flt. Lt. Armstrong explained that this procedure was necessary to regularise our status and make us subject to the Air Force Act. Our service was for eight years on the Active List followed by four years on the Reserve, but this would be automatically cancelled when we received permanent commissions on graduating from Cranwell. We were also told that on becoming Flying Officers, we'd be given one year's seniority in the Air Force List, and on becoming Flight Lieutenants, we'd get another year's seniority. This didn't seem to equate with the fact that we wouldn't be commissioned for almost three years, but that sort of detail escaped us at the time.

Ron and I had many questions to ask. 'Where is Cranwell and how do we get there?' Flt. Lt. Armstrong told us that we'd be met on arrival at Southampton and given instructions as to what to do. He said that Ron and I would be the first members of the RNZAF to go to Cranwell, but other New Zealanders there were in the RAF. He advised us that Jim Brown, whom we'd seen in the selections at Wellington, had won an RAF cadetship to Cranwell and, along with fourteen RNZAF aircraft apprentices being sent to RAF schools in Britain, would be travelling with us on the *Rangitata*. An engineering officer, Plt. Off. Pete Lumley, MBE, would be in charge of us. He'd just been commissioned from the ranks and was going on a two year exchange with the RAF. Ron asked how we'd be paid. Flt. Lt. Armstrong

Figure 3. Hancock Family (except for Lyndall) at the wharves, Wellington, New Zealand, February 1951: L-R: Dad, Author, Heather, Mum and Beverley.

said that was still being sorted out, but he arranged for us to see the Accounting Officer and have a talk about finances and other things.

Flt. Lt. Armstrong also told us that John Gordon and Hal Payne, who'd also been in the selections we'd attended at Wellington, would be the first members of the RNZAF to go to the Royal Australian Air Force College, Point Cook. I remembered Hal Payne because he'd tried to dominate all the discussions and earned some antagonism from the other candidates.

Next morning, Mum, Dad, Beverley and Heather arrived by ferry and had breakfast with me. An RNZAF car took me to the Movements Unit where Ron was waiting patiently. We were then issued with passports and other documents, taken to the *Rangitata* and shown to a Tourist Class four berth cabin. There we met Jim Brown and Graham Eves, an engine apprentice. Graham, like all the RNZAF apprentices, was in uniform, having received it in previous RNZAF service, whereas Ron, Jim and I hadn't been issued with any service equipment. There was a mad scramble for bunks – Ron and Jim ended up in the top ones. We went up on deck again as the ship was due to sail at noon. Mum, Dad, Beverley and Heather came on board to have a look around and say goodbye. I was glad they'd made the effort to come all the way to Wellington and see me off, but sad that Lyndall wasn't able to be there (Fig. 3). Delays in loading meant we had a lot of standing around until the ship eventually sailed at 4 p.m. Final photographs were taken, coloured streamers were thrown from the deck to the wharf below, and shouted farewells were made. People spontaneously began singing that nostalgic song:

'Now is the hour when we must say goodbye;
Soon you'll be sailing far across the sea.
While you're away, oh please remember me;
When you return you'll find me waiting here.'

The ship's horn wailed mournfully as the *Rangitata* sailed away and I, like everyone else, leaned over the rail straining to keep the people on the wharf in view for as long as possible.

I was tired and had a slight headache. Mum had been close to tears when we parted and I wondered as the ship left Wellington harbour how she and the family would be feeling as they made their way home without me on the ferry that night. I was full of excitement heading off into the unknown, but the thought crossed my mind that my eighteen years and my background little prepared me for what lay in front of me.

CHAPTER 2

Into the Unknown

'YOU LOOK AFTER ME, and I'll look after you.'

The Liverpudlian steward stood in the entrance to the cabin, dressed in a starched, white, high-necked jacket and black trousers. He had dark, greasy hair and a dirty towel hung from a pocket of his trousers. He'd introduced himself as Mr Darling and then poured chilled water from the jug he was carrying into glasses held in a rack on the dressing table. Ron, Jim, Graham and I stared at him.

'You look after me, and I'll look after you,' he repeated.

We were too inexperienced to make a suitable reply. The emphasis of his statement seemed to be misplaced – wasn't he supposed to be serving us? Perhaps he meant that if we tipped him at the start of the voyage, he'd make our bunks, clean the cabin and generally look after us. I'd heard that passengers sometimes tipped the steward, barman and any other of the crew they came in contact with at the start of a voyage and also at the end. Tipping was almost unheard of in New Zealand. Anyway, why should we pay extra for what someone was being paid to do? We certainly didn't have spare money to waste on tips. We didn't move and Mr Darling left.

The four of us resumed fooling about in the cabin, getting to know each other. Ron Chippindale was the son of a schoolteacher who'd been a Squadron Leader engineer during World War II and had received an MBE for being in charge of RNZAF Technical Training Schools. Jim Brown's parents had come from Scotland, his father being a doctor at Seacliff Mental Hospital north of Dunedin. After much cajoling we managed to get Jim to admit that he was keen on a nurse called Llanis. He was shorter than Ron and me and had difficulty with his r's so that his surname sounded like 'Bwown'. Graham Eves was obviously feeling he was the stranger in our midst, being separated from his fellow apprentices, so didn't say much. He was from Waipara in North Canterbury and had been in the RNZAF for about a year.

I think the others had trouble knowing what to call me – my first name being rather a mouthful. Ron and Jim took delight in distorting my surname. This was something I had to get used to. Jim was the oldest of us and became known for the time being as 'Senior'. I was next oldest and was called 'Intermediate', whereas Ron, being only seventeen, became 'Junior Senior'. Graham was 'Junior'.

We were all pretty tired and after dinner turned in early. During the night, we crossed the International Date Line and so had two Saturdays, 17 February.

On our second Saturday, two Marconigrams arrived wishing me *bon voyage* – one from the Hornsey family and the other from Uncle Jack and Aunt Aileen Skinner. Ron, Jim and I rushed to the log trailing over the stern to see how far we'd travelled. We were 250 nautical miles away from Wellington. All the passengers assembled for boat drill and were shown how to put on life jackets and get to lifeboats. Then the crew had their boat drill and practised lowering a lifeboat. They did this each week throughout the voyage.

Plt. Off. Lumley had a First Class cabin so we didn't see much of him. He had all the RNZAF apprentices and Ron, Jim and me assemble on deck at 9.15 each morning for a roll call and to hear if we had any complaints. We all thought the parades were a bit of a laugh. Occasionally he would visit us in our cabins to ensure that we were keeping them shipshape. Mr Darling and a stewardess called Miss Bowie saw to that. Occasionally we saw Plt. Off. Lumley at evening functions resplendent in tropical mess kit – white, cutaway jacket and black bow tie – his black eyebrows and pencil moustache helping to give him quite a 'Clark Gable' debonair appearance. We called him 'Popeye'. He seemed a decent sort of chap.

Figure 4. Ron Chippindale, Zoë Sinton and Author on board the passenger ship *Rangitata, en route* to Britain, February 1951.

Not surprisingly, Graham Eves tended to mix with his fellow apprentices rather than Ron, Jim and me. He'd come into the cabin late at night and we soon found that he'd been seeing a girl called Zoë Sinton from Cambridge, New Zealand. She was aged sixteen, had won a ballet scholarship to Sadler's Wells and was travelling to London with her mother to take up the scholarship. Zoë looked the part – hair swept up to a small bun at the back of her head, slim and graceful with long, well-developed legs. Ron, Jim and I immediately got to know Zoë, asked her about the ring on the third finger of her left hand (it wasn't an engagement ring), and got involved with her in the deck games. As Jim said, 'We've gotta cultivate some friends.' (Fig. 4)

Ron, Jim and I threw ourselves into games of deck quoits, peg and bucket quoits, table tennis, shovelboard and deck golf. We paid NZ 5s and put our names down on a list for the games competition. In an early game of table tennis, Ron took a mighty swipe, missed the ball and lost his bat overboard. After such exertion we usually sunbathed on deck, read or slept. Dad, being a chemist, had made up a special suntan lotion to protect my fair skin, but I foolishly got sunburnt before using liberal quantities of the lotion.

Unfortunately, passengers were unable to choose whom they sat next to in the dining room. When some passengers were shuffled around to lighten the load of a waiter who wasn't coping, Ron, Jim and I almost fought to get a spare seat beside Zoë. I won. Apart from Zoë to talk to, there were two Englishmen at the table who were returning from a holiday in New Zealand. One of them, being from Lincoln, was able to tell me quite a lot about Cranwell. He said that Lincoln was about fourteen miles (as the crow flies) north of Cranwell, Newark-on-Trent was about thirteen miles to the west, Grantham was some eleven miles to the south-west and the nearest town, Sleaford, was about five miles to the south-east. The village of Cranwell was between Sleaford and RAF Cranwell. Our discussions were interrupted when the head waiter informed me that my seat was reserved for one of the ship's officers and I had to move to another table – much to the amusement of Ron and Jim.

We were all issued with a Passenger List that gave, in addition to the names of all the passengers, the names of the ship's officers, a brief history of the New Zealand Shipping Company and its fleet, and information on Pitcairn Island, the Panama Canal and Curaçao – places we were due to see on the voyage.

Ron, Jim and I were disappointed that the Passenger List recorded us as being just Cadets instead of Cadet Pilots, and Jim as being in the RNZAF instead of the RAF. The apprentices were shown as Aircraft Apprentices and not by their trades. The List was actually very handy as it helped me get to know the names of the apprentices. I discovered that two of them, Allan Carter and Keith Smith, were going to No. 6 Radio School located at RAF

Cranwell. The other apprentices were going to No. 1 Technical Training School at RAF Halton.

The List confirmed that an old friend of Mum's, Mr T.T. Ritchie, was one of the 115 passengers in First Class. As a travel agent, he was escorting a large group of people on a tour of Britain and Europe. I had several talks with him and found him to be a most helpful and interesting person. He gave me a copy of his itinerary and a map of England, and invited me to meet up with him later if I was able. Regrettably, our paths never crossed again.

Amongst the 304 passengers in Tourist Class was a chap going to the Irish table tennis championships who, with about 90 hours flying on Tiger and Fox Moths, planned to join the RAF. Another passenger was Tom Dollery, Captain of the Warwickshire Cricket Team, who'd been coaching cricket at Wellington. He and his family occupied the cabin opposite the one I was in.

I also ran into six speedway riders who were going to Britain to gain experience in the stiff competition there. The youngest, Ronnie Moore, became New Zealand's first World Speedway Champion. The speedway riders were a rough and noisy lot and seemed to have numerous parties at which they sang unprintable songs. They often had fights amongst themselves and careered around the decks almost bowling over people who got in their way. We heard that complaints had been made to the ship's officers about their behaviour. Ron, Jim and I kept away from them.

Two days out from Wellington, the calm sea became rough. The ship rolled, pitched and vibrated. I soon became seasick and had to retreat to the cabin and wait for my stomach to settle down. Ron, Jim and Graham didn't appear to be affected. Up to that time, I'd thought I was going to be a good sailor and had already got my sea legs.

Every few days, dances were held on the ship. They were quite exciting, especially when the ship was rolling and pitching in heavy weather. The dancers would suddenly move over to one side and then to the other amid squeals from the women. Trying to dance the way Miss Dorothy Thwaites had taught me was exceedingly difficult. At other times when the sea was calm, a big moon reflected on the shimmering sea and the band played 'Goodnight Irene, goodnight Irene, I'll see you in my dreams', the scene was very romantic. An attractive young passenger who happened to be called Irene was a most popular person on such occasions.

As the weather grew warmer, the ship's officers changed into tropical uniforms and the standard of dress at the dances deteriorated. Plt. Off. Lumley had initially insisted that the RNZAF group and Jim wore ties to dinner and social occasions, so we were greatly relieved when open necked shirts and sports clothes were permitted. A siesta period from 2-4 p.m. commenced. Ron, Jim and I needed the rest after engaging in strenuous deck games. I took the opportunity to teach myself how to operate the slide rule I'd bought before leaving home.

Each day, I read the radio news posted on one of the notice-boards. The New Zealand waterfront dispute had developed into a strike that was to last five months and be the costliest in New Zealand's industrial history. Somehow, I felt very remote from it all on board ship in the tropics.

The hot and cold freshwater showers on board both felt tepid. With no air conditioning on the ship – only ventilators, fans and air scoops at open portholes – the one porthole to the cabin I was in seemed inadequate. One hot night after the four of us were in our bunks and drifting off to sleep, a girl came into the cabin and started undressing in the half light from the curtain at the doorway. She was down to her underwear when something must have alerted her to the fact that she was in the wrong cabin. With a muffled scream, she grabbed her clothes and fled before we were able to recognise her face.

Another night, we stayed up till almost midnight to see the *Rangitiki*, a sister ship of the *Rangitata*, pass close by in the opposite direction. Both ships turned on their lights and flashed messages to each other. Ron, Jim and I watched as we stood in the warm air, clad only in shorts, leaning over the high stern and talking to one of our 'cultivations', the ship's surgeon, Dr N.E. Winstone, MRCS, MB. The doctor deciphered some of the messages and, in between times, told us fascinating stories about dead bodies at sea, someone who disappeared overboard and another person who nearly did go overboard.

Before I left home, almost everyone had asked me to write and tell them how I got on. Family friends had given me a Trip Book, so I began making daily entries in it until I reached Cranwell. I wrote a series of travel articles for my old school magazine, *The Timaruvian*, thinking that edited versions might be published. Later I found that the articles were published in full. 'Dogs' Kemshed also wanted me to write about life as a Flight Cadet, but at Cranwell I was soon to find I didn't have the time to do so. There were also letters to write to my family, friends and relations. Writing home each week or so became a habit that I've continued to this day.

Eight days out from Wellington, the *Rangitata* heaved to off Bounty Bay, Pitcairn Island. I was on deck early that morning to see three open longboats being sailed out to the ship. Through binoculars, I looked at the boats and the two miles long and one mile wide volcanic island. Jagged peaks rising 1,000 feet or so above sea level had poles on top which I assumed were radio aerials. The roofs of the only settlement, Adamstown, could be seen scattered amongst the bush including the large residence of the local governor. There was virtually no beach or landing place, so sailing out to passing ships depended very much on the weather. A brigantine lay off the island.

About fifty islanders, including some women, were in the boats. As descendants of the mutineers from HMS *Bounty* and Tahitians who'd colonised the island in 1789, they looked Polynesian. Sweating heavily in the humid air, most of them climbed up the rope ladders to the deck carrying flax baskets laden with goods to be bartered. The islanders wouldn't sell the goods as the day was a Saturday and, being strict Seventh Day Adventists, they weren't allowed to sell things on what was their Sabbath. We were asked to give them what we thought their goods were worth. Bartering with the islanders who remained in the boats was difficult and meant a lot of shouting and hauling on ropes as money and goods exchanged hands.

The islanders took on mail and supplies and departed mid morning singing several farewell songs in harmony. I watched them sail towards Pitcairn as the *Rangitata* slowly got under way again, feeling that I'd just had a unique experience.

We were now well into the tropics, travelling an average of 384 nautical miles per day, and shipboard life followed a sort of routine that was interesting and enjoyable. The sea became glassy, the air balmy. Now I knew what the doldrums must be like! I watched shoals of small flying fish dart in and out of the sea, and dolphins accompanying the ship. From time to time an albatross appeared out of nowhere and hovered effortlessly in the air around the ship before disappearing again. Ron, Jim and I lazed about sunbathing on deck or rested on our bunks eating fresh Pitcairn bananas. The bananas tasted different from the imported ones we were used to at home.

On deck each morning and afternoon, stewards would hand out free slabs of ice-cream and we always tried to be around at that time. There were glorious sunsets. How I wished that cameras had coloured films so that I could capture the beauty of the sea and the sky! One evening, I watched a tropical storm on the horizon and jagged flashes of lightning, yet no sound reached me other than the continual engine noise coming from the aft funnel of the ship. Some people started sleeping on deck at nights, but sleeping in deck chairs didn't appeal to Ron, Jim, Graham and me.

At 8.30 on a Sunday morning, there was an announcement that the ship had crossed the Equator. I'd heard about crossing the Equator ceremonies in which 'Neptune' ducked people who hadn't before crossed the Equator, and had looked forward to the fun. Instead, there was an early communion and later Divine Service in the A Deck Lounge. I didn't go to the communion as I'd heard that it wasn't intended for non-Anglicans. Graham said he was a fellow Presbyterian and came with me to the Divine Service. We were impressed by the very sincere way that Captain G. Kinnell, OBE, conducted the Church of England service. There was no sermon, but four hymns, one Bible reading, a venite, numerous read prayers and 'God Save the King'. The A Deck Lounge was crowded with passengers and I wondered how many of them normally went to church at home. The ship was so steady in the calm conditions that I had to look at the sea through the lounge windows to see that we were moving.

Ron and Jim weren't exactly atheists, but they questioned me as to why I believed in God and went to church. I had difficulty in answering them as I'd never been asked such things before. They also wanted to know why I didn't smoke or drink alcohol. I said I'd tried smoking and found it a disgusting habit. Also, I'd been brought up in an alcohol free home and felt that I was better without it. I didn't say that I'd signed a pledge of abstinence. To me, smoking and drinking alcohol were acquired habits that the world really didn't need.

There were chores to do like washing, ironing and mending. The four of us had been told that the ship's laundry took about eight days to return clothes so, for most of the voyage, we did our own washing and ironing. We used the small cakes of soap provided, but were constantly running out of them and had to ask the stewards for more. There were ironing rooms but, surprisingly, no drying rooms on board. The sewing kit Mum had bought me came in very useful to mend things and make new shorts fit properly. I wanted to use clothing from my trunk in the hold and, though access to the hold was very restricted, I was able to get what I wanted. I discovered my new trunk had been badly damaged and assumed that the Wellington wharfies, angry the *Rangitata* was sailing early to beat the wharf strike, had bashed it around on loading.

Every day there was some form of organised entertainment such as dances, movies, community singing, quiz shows, housie housie (tombola) and horse racing. A concert put on by the passengers comprised singing, piano playing, skits, crude jokes and a 'ballet' performed by the apprentices. The latter dressed up in twine skirts, leis etc. and did something more akin to a Hawaiian show than a ballet.

Housie and race meetings, being forms of gambling, weren't things that I really got involved in. I sometimes went along to them and watched. Jim wasn't interested in housie, but entered the competition for guessing the mileage sailed each day. Ron, Jim and Graham won a few shillings in these things – probably much less than they'd 'invested'.

I found the dances much more fun. The ladies had some amazing dresses with them, especially on the occasional formal night. Sometimes passengers could request dances. Whatever the dance, I got very hot and had to get out periodically into the fresh breeze on deck and drink a lot of ice-cold soft drink while watching the stars overhead and the fluorescence of the water below.

The initial rounds of the deck games competition were by now in full swing. Ron, Jim and I practised together for hours and had mixed success playing in the singles and doubles events. We'd cool off afterwards by having a dip in the canvas swimming pool that'd been constructed on the fore deck.

Though the pool was hardly big enough to swim in and the water was very salty, a dip was refreshing and quite exciting, especially when the ship rolled and water sloshed up and sometimes over the sides of the pool.

As the *Rangitata* passed the rocky island of Malpelo, the sea turned from blue to green. We were approaching land.

Eighteen days after leaving Wellington, we arrived at the Panama Canal. The four of us were up by 5 a.m. to watch the sun rise like a fiery ball out of the sea, and view the lights of Balboa and Panama City, and the many navigational beacons. Numerous launches came alongside and soon mail was available and I was reading a letter from Lyndall. The *Rangitata* proceeded slowly towards the Miraflores Locks while an American commented over the ship's loud speaker system on the sights.

The *Rangitata* was attached by wire cables to the electric mules waiting at the end of the locks. On entering the first of two sets of parallel locks, huge gates closed slowly behind the *Rangitata*, safety chains by the bow and stern were hung across the canal and water surged up all around. Curiously shaped emergency gates lay alongside each lock, ready to be swung into place when needed. American soldiers armed with machine guns patrolled up and down the lock. I saw my first negroes, jeeps and armoured cars. The electric mules ground their way up the steep slope to a control tower, easily pulling the *Rangitata* into the second lock, and then released the ship in Miraflores Lake, 58 feet above the Pacific Ocean.

A mile and a half across the lake were the Pedro Miguel Locks where the *Rangitata* was lifted another 27 feet. The nine miles of the famed Gaillard Cut that followed was a disappointment. Gold Hill at 660 feet above sea level didn't seem very high and, with valleys along the Cut, I had difficulty in seeing the area as being part of a mountain chain. The black rocks at the sides of the Cut looked solid enough and not prone to slips, but I knew that slips did occur and the Cut represented a great engineering feat. A large bronze plaque commemorated this. Some blasting of the hillside was going on at one point.

The *Rangitata* glided past the pleasant looking Chagres River, Gamboa and two of the largest floating cranes in the world, then at Darien entered Gatun Lake, where for the next twenty-five miles it was able to proceed at full speed. The Lake didn't look as large as it really was because numerous islands blocked the view. We passed close by a number of other ships.

When we reached Gatun, the *Rangitata* had to anchor for about two and a half hours to allow ships to come through one set of locks from the Caribbean Sea, the other parallel set of locks being closed for repairs. Eventually, the *Rangitata* entered the triple series of Gatun Locks to be lowered 85 feet to the level of the Caribbean, and proceeded to a berth at Cristobel. Passage through the canal had taken about eleven hours.

Plt. Off. Lumley briefed the RNZAF group and Jim on going ashore. Ron, Jim and I were met by Captain Greenwood, an American from the airbase at the Caribbean end of the canal, who said he'd been detailed to look after us. He escorted us in the failing light along badly lit streets towards the YMCA.

We saw many things new to us – large flash American cars, quaint horse drawn buggies, colourful old buses, frameless spectacles, strange palm trees and wonderfully coloured mosaic pavements along narrow side streets. Few shops were open. We bought one or two souvenirs. Jim got a bit carried away in buying a garish tie with a nude girl painted on it. Coloured children pestered us to buy chewing gum. Some slightly intoxicated American sailors stopped to ask us where we were from. All they knew about 'Noo Zilind' was that it was 'someplace near Australia'. Two impressive looking military policemen moved the sailors on. We passed a cabaret lit with neon signs advertising a strip show. Later we heard that one of the stewardesses from the *Rangitata* had gone there, got a bit drunk and then done an impromptu strip-tease on the stage.

The YMCA was full of American sailors, passengers from the *Rangitata* and locals. We found that people like us who weren't in uniform were unable to buy anything there unless they did so through one of the servicemen or women. Ron, Jim and I did the rounds of the jukebox, the soft drink and hamburger bars, the ice-cold water fountain and the shop selling everything from sweets to jewellery, before playing some snooker and table tennis. The place was quite spacious and even had an auditorium, a money changing bureau and a writing area.

When Captain Greenwood guided us back to the ship, he gave me the address of one of his buddies at an American base in England – just in case I had the opportunity to call on him.

The next morning, I was woken at 4.30 by the *Rangitata*'s engines starting up. As land gradually disappeared we sailed into increasingly rough seas. During lunch, the ship suddenly rolled more than usual. Green water flowed past the portholes on one side of the dining room and poured though one that happened to be open, drenching some passengers. People screamed, crockery crashed onto the floor and stewards hurried to reassure us as they tidied up.

In spite of the weather, Ron, Jim, Zoë and I continued to play numerous deck games during the two days the *Rangitata* took to reach Curaçao. On one occasion during a sudden, warm tropical downpour, we were playing deck golf and learning to hit the puck so that it slid in a curve along the wet, rolling and pitching deck to the desired mark, when Ron got rather frustrated. Looking up into the pouring rain he shook his fists at the heavens and shouted irreverently, 'Send it down Hewie,' before hitting the puck so hard that it flew over the ship's rail. We rushed to the side and watched the puck disappear into the seething waves below.

The deck games competition resumed. We found that the apprentices and the speedway chaps had all bought water pistols and cap guns at Cristobel, so for several days they engaged in their own form of games, much to the dismay of other passengers.

Plt. Off. Lumley briefed the RNZAF group and Jim on what would happen at Curaçao when the *Rangitata* stopped to refuel at five o'clock the next morning. We were up early to watch the ship berth at an oil jetty in Caracas Bay. After Customs officials had made a very casual inspection of our passports, Ron, Jim and I got into a big American taxi and were driven six miles to Willemstad, the capital, along the right side of a narrow, bumpy road. We were used to driving on the left side of roads and found this new experience rather alarming at first.

Willemstad occupied both banks of St Anna Bay and was joined by a pontoon bridge. We watched as the pontoon opened to let a Swedish ship enter the inner harbour of Shottgat, then wandered along the picturesque streets looking at the quaint seventeenth century Dutch architecture inter-spersed by modern, taller buildings. We stopped to buy Coca-Cola and were intrigued when given an hourglass-shaped glass in the upper half of which an ice filled card cone was inserted. The Coke was then poured in and we drank it through a straw.

Shopping for something characteristic of Curaçao was frustrating in that most of the shops had mainly American goods in combinations that seemed odd to us, such as cameras and clothing. Prices were exorbitant so we wandered back to the inner harbour and bought fruit from a floating fruit and vegetable market. A little disappointed, we caught a taxi back to the *Rangitata* before it sailed at noon.

Some Dutch passengers had come aboard at Curaçao, but language problems tended to keep them apart from the other passengers.

As we headed for England, we passed a number of other ships, the island of St Croix and large patches of seaweed. The weather was reasonably good, but the nights started to get colder. Shipboard life settled back into a routine again. In the deck games a large crowd watched the New Zealand cricketer, J.H. Parks, beat me after a long struggle in a semi-final of the quoits singles. Miss Ann Douglas and I won the final of the shovelboard doubles.

A heavy sea was running the day of the fancy dress dance. Many of the passengers displayed great ingenuity with their costumes, so deciding the prize winners was a difficult task. The dance was quite an event, and doing the Eightsome Reel with the ship rolling heavily was definitely hazardous. After the dance was over, more fights developed amongst the speedway riders.

When the movie *The Miniver Story* was screened, Jim sat beside Zoë and complained later that 'he'd never sat beside a sheila before and felt so cold.' The weather was definitely getting worse.

We went up forward and watched waves breaking over the bow of the *Rangitata* sending spray high above the bridge. Windows had been shuttered, portholes closed and air scoops removed. Wind howled around the deserted decks. The ship creaked and groaned as it pitched and rolled. To my embarrassment, I was sick again. The storm lasted three days though heavy seas ran for much longer.

The RNZAF group and Jim were given the opportunity to tour the *Rangitata* and we leaped at the chance, though being below deck in the rough weather of the mid Atlantic and in the noise and heat of the engine room wasn't at all pleasant. The *Rangitata* at 17,000 tons wasn't a large ship, but one could still get lost in the corridors below deck. I was glad to climb up to the bridge and be shown the radio gear in the dummy forward funnel.

As the weather cleared, the final deck competitions, dances, race meetings, housie and other activities were held. A fancy dress party occupied the children. The winners of the deck competitions each received NZ 12s at a prize-giving ceremony. The Azores passed to starboard. The ship's railings felt sticky from salt spray. Canvas awnings over decks and covers along railings were removed. Passengers began to stock up on duty-free cigarettes and liquor from the canteen. Landing cards were issued and instructions were given to return baggage to the hold and withdraw any deposits of money from the Purser. Ron, Jim, Graham and I agreed on a combined tip for our stewards. Plt. Off. Lumley briefed the RNZAF group and Jim on arrival procedure at Southampton. We now couldn't wait to get ashore. Somehow, the pleasure had gone out of the voyage.

Ron, Jim, Zoë and I played our last deck games. Zoë asked us to sign her autograph book. Mrs Sinton told me she would be only a few months in Britain, then surprised me by giving me her London address and telephone number should I want to contact her or Zoë. I felt honoured that she trusted me with her sixteen-year-old daughter after she'd returned home. Final farewells were said at a grand *Diner d'Adieu*. Afterwards, Ron, Jim and I had much hilarity in a pillow fight and expelling a drunken steward who came into our cabin and made a nuisance of himself.

The *Rangitata* passed Portland Bill early in the morning, thirty-two days after leaving Wellington. Passengers froze on deck watching the land slip by and the pilot coming aboard from a small steamer. We sailed close to the Isle of Wight and looked with considerable interest at an aircraft factory, flying boats taking off and landing, and an aircraft carrier. I saw my first lightship and double-decker bus. We passed numerous houses, people going about their affairs, a mansion occupied by the largest military hospital in the world, strangely shaped ferries and many other vessels.

The *Rangitata* went slowly up Southampton Water to its berth, close by the *Queen Mary* at the big new ocean terminus. I gulped down an early lunch, had my landing card and passport checked, and waited impatiently with the other RNZAF members and Jim to disembark. I'd arrived in England at last!

Waiting

'WELCOME TO BRITAIN. I'm Squadron Leader Furlong, and this is Flight Lieutenant Free. We're from RNZAF Headquarters, London, and are here to accompany you to London where you'll be briefed before going on leave and later reporting to Halton or Cranwell.'

Such was the introduction to our next venture into the unknown. The two officers, dressed in best blue uniform and greatcoats, had come aboard the *Rangitata* and soon made all the RNZAF apprentices and Ron Chippindale, Jim Brown and me feel at ease while we waited on deck in the cool air to disembark. As we were amongst the last of the passengers to go through Customs, we were processed together with very little checking and hurried onto a train just before it departed at 3 p.m. Some of the apprentices exclaimed that they could have brought in many more cheap cigarettes if only they'd known there'd be little in the way of a Customs check. My damaged trunk was sent on direct to Cranwell.

Sqn. Ldr. M.B. Furlong, OBE, and Flt. Lt. R.V. Free, MC, wisely left us to enjoy the two hour train ride to London. There was so much to see! The green, streamlined engine, appropriately named 'Squadron', drew gaily painted red, green and yellow carriages – so different from the sturdy, black engines and dirty red carriages to be seen in New Zealand.

The train went through undulating country waterlogged in places from recent rain, past drab houses with thousands of chimney pots, and several airfields. I tried to identify the large aircraft flying around Farnborough. On nearby roads, there were three-wheeled trucks, car transporters and other strange vehicles. As we drew into Waterloo Station, I had glimpses of the muddy Thames and tugs, barges and long, low steamers. Parliament looked just as I expected it to be, except for some scaffolding around the tower containing Big Ben.

As we were driven to our hotels, we passed the Festival of Britain site and could see in the distance the impressive dome of St Paul's Cathedral. Ron, Jim and I were put in the same room at the Alambra Private Hotel in Russell Square, where most of the group stayed. The remainder of the group were in another bed and breakfast hotel nearby. After a rather poor dinner at a restaurant, we all made our way to the Strand area to look at the sights. We passed New Zealand House, the Air Ministry and Mills Brothers – makers of one of my model aeroplane engines. A cool mist drove us into the Tivoli

Theatre to see the movie, *King Solomon's Mines*, our first experience of a continuous movie programme. On returning to our hotel, Ron, Jim and I spent a miserable night as there weren't enough blankets on our beds.

After breakfast next morning, the group was taken to RNZAF Headquarters,

Figure 5. NEW ZEALAND GROUP WITH NZ HIGH COMMISSIONER, LONDON
MARCH 1951

Back Row

L-R: Apprentices R.E. (Dick) Thomas; Sam N. West. Cadet Pilots Rutherford M. Hancock; Ron Chippindale; Jim C. Brown.

Third Row

L-R: Apprentices C. Keith Smith★; Clive A. Shaw; Dave I. Lamason★; Tom E. Enright★; J. Graham Pratt★; A. Laurie Lawless★; Jack M. McLean★.

Second Row

L-R: Apprentices R.C. (Roly) Oliver; D. Allan Carter★; Harley R. Holland; D. Graham Eves; W.H. (Shorty) Howell★.

Front Row

L-R: Plt. Off. P.H. Lumley, MBE; Air Cdre. C.E. Kay, CB, CBE, DFC (Air Officer Commanding RNZAF Headquarters, London); Rt. Hon. W.J. Jordan, PC, JP, Hon. LLD (NZ High Commissioner, London); Flt. Lt. R.V. Free, MC (Movements Officer, RNZAF Headquarters, London).

★ Apprentices who were later commissioned.

London, at Halifax House, 51 Strand, to be briefed by Sqn. Ldr. Furlong on
how New Zealanders were expected to behave in Britain, writing home, and
our immediate future. Ron, Jim and I were told we had forty-two days to
wait before reporting at Cranwell. Arrangements had been made for me to
stay with my relations in Aberdeen. The group was then welcomed by the
Air Officer Commanding the Headquarters, Air Cdre. C.E. Kay, CBE, DFC.
He was a short, stocky man of few words, and somehow seemed ill at ease.

I was glad when he and Flt. Lt. Free took Plt. Off. Lumley and the rest
of us to meet the New Zealand High Commissioner, The Rt. Hon. W.J.
Jordan, PC, JP, Hon. LLD at New Zealand House. Bill Jordan had become
High Commissioner in 1936 and was well known for his enormous affability
and compassion for the thousands of New Zealand servicemen and women
who'd been in Britain during World War II. He'd been reappointed by
successive Governments and, when I met him, was just about to retire. He
offered us sweets to eat and said (as later reported in New Zealand newspapers):

'I have welcomed boys like you in this office for the last fifteen years, and
have seen many of them become distinguished New Zealanders. I do not doubt
that some of you, in future, will be put in that category, and that your generation will be as prominent in the years ahead as your predecessors have been.'

A photograph was taken of us all – the only group one taken of the
RNZAF members and Jim Brown who'd travelled together on the *Rangitata*
(Fig. 5).

As a result of that meeting, Mr Jordan sent the following letter to my
parents (and no doubt similar letters to the parents of the other boys):

Dear Mr and Mrs Hancock,

I had the great pleasure of meeting your son Rutherford last week
when the whole draft of fifteen apprentices called at the Office. [Actually
there had been fourteen apprentices, three cadet pilots and three officers
present – Author.] It was a great pleasure to meet them. They are a fine
lot of lads. Your son was very well and was looking forward to his
training here and eventually returning to the Dominion. We shall take
a close interest in them all and if there is anything we can do to assist
them, you may be sure it will not be left undone.

My own son was an apprentice in the Air Force and eventually rose
to the rank of squadron leader. My wife and I were in New Zealand
and were at times anxious about him, as I am sure you are about your
son. I trust, however, that you will not be unduly concerned, but rest
assured that we shall be in close touch with the lads and shall do anything
we can for their welfare and comfort.

With good wishes,

Yours sincerely,

W.J. Jordan

I think this letter and one subsequently sent to Dad by Sqn. Ldr. Furlong did much to alleviate any fears my parents may have had about my welfare while overseas. In his long letter, Sqn. Ldr. Furlong said in part:

Dear Mr Hancock,

. . . I was particularly pleased to have a number of passengers come to me voluntarily, and say how exceptionally well behaved the boys had been during the voyage. It was evident in all respects, without exception, they had been a credit both to their homes and to New Zealand.

. . . Cranwell College was unable to take your son and Ronald Chippindale until the next course is due to commence, but we were able in both instances to contact the nominated guardians, in Rutherford's case, Mrs Rundle, who advised that she would be pleased to arrange accommodation, and would assume responsibility until Rutherford was required to report to Cranwell. This was felt to be an excellent arrangement, in that it will provide Rutherford with an excellent opportunity, not only for seeing quite a lot of the United Kingdom, but also will allow him to settle down gradually and without any difficulty, to life generally over here.

. . . you can be assured that this Headquarters generally, and myself in particular, will take an exceptionally keen interest in his welfare. I have had a long talk with all the apprentices and the cadet pilots, and have endeavoured to pass on to them a good deal of sound 'fatherly' advice, based on my own fairly wide service and overseas experience . . . I hope to be making regular visits to Cranwell, which will give me the opportunity of getting to know these boys better, and helping them in any problems that may arise. I would like you and Mrs Hancock to be assured that if there is anything at all you would like me to do, I will be most happy to assist in any way possible. Please do not hesitate to write to me any time. I feel that all these lads are being given wonderful opportunities, and for their sakes as well as for the RNZAF, I am most anxious to ensure that they take full advantage of them.

. . . You will be interested to know that on my visits to Cranwell I was particularly impressed with the high calibre of the RAF officers staffing the College. It was most evident that all the staff has been carefully chosen, not only for outstanding personal qualities, but also for obvious ability and enthusiasm for providing efficient training and for moulding the characters of boys of this age along sound lines . . .

Yours faithfully,

(M. B. FURLONG)

Squadron Leader

for AIR OFFICER COMMANDING

Jim was taken away for briefing by the RAF while Ron and I were given travel warrants, some food ration coupons and other documentation. When we had lunch at a nearby Fortes restaurant we enjoyed having real cubes of sugar – something that hadn't been seen in New Zealand since before World War II. Back at Halifax House, Ron and I discovered we were expected to go on a bus that afternoon with Sqn. Ldr. Furlong and the apprentices to RAF Halton. This meant that I didn't have time to book or perhaps catch the train to Aberdeen that evening. Apparently some of the apprentices didn't have guardians or friends in Britain, so the decision had been made that they would all stay at Halton and fill in the time before their training started by going on guided tours of famous places in London, such as Parliament and the de Havilland aircraft factory. Their itinerary looked most interesting.

On our way out of London, we stared at Nelson's Column, the pigeons and the National Gallery in Trafalgar Square, mounted guards with red capes, brass helmets and drawn swords in Whitehall, the white topped blackened stonework of Westminster Abbey, Chelsea embankment, Charing Cross railway station, Olympia, White City Stadium and DC3s and 4s on the tarmac at Northolt aerodrome.

Halton, once a Rothschild home, was about forty-eight miles from London and had a small airfield. The bleak accommodation blocks housed some three thousand people. Huge workshops dominated the scene. A cold wind whined about the place so farewells to the apprentices were brief.

Our bus went on a short distance to RAF Henlow, a small non-flying station, where Sqn. Ldr. Furlong wanted to be dropped. Ron and I were then taken back to London via Dunstable where we passed the London Gliding Club rooms and a large white lion carved into a hillside. Over Hatfield, a Comet jet airliner was circling the aerodrome and the huge de Havilland factory where, we were told, there were about six thousand employees. Gipsies were camped in picturesque waggons nearby.

What a day it'd been! We'd travelled on narrow roads winding between high hedgerows and on three or four lane highways. We'd seen canals, river-boats, old inns, thatched roof houses, radio and meteorological stations, London at night and so many other things that were new to us.

The bus driver dropped me off at King's Cross railway station minutes before 'The Aberdonian' was due to leave at 7 p.m. I said a hasty goodbye to Ron (who later went on leave to Prestatyn), exchanged a travel warrant for a ticket and found a seat on the train. There wasn't time to get a sleeper, so I spent much of the next twelve hours trying to sleep sitting up. Rain was falling at Aberdeen when I arrived rather travel weary, at 7 a.m.

I felt I could hardly turn up at the Rundles' place at that hour of the morning, so I filled in time by having breakfast, looking at shops along Union Street and watching people step out of streamlined trams as the 'granite' city slowly came to life.

A taxi took me to the Stoneywood area near the aerodrome at Dyce on the outskirts of Aberdeen. As the driver turned into Market Street, a large lady walking towards us along the pavement stopped suddenly and waved. The driver went on and dropped me at 9 Ruthriehill Road, a two-storeyed semi-detached house. I rang the doorbell. A well-built middle-aged lady with wispy white hair and wearing an apron opened the door. I introduced myself. She spoke softly and excitedly in what seemed to me to be broad Scots – something about Mabel.

Just then, the large lady I'd seen in Market Street came running up the path, her coat flying, holding her arms out. 'Rutherford, Rutherford,' she called, rolling her r's. 'I thought it was you. How wonderful you were able to come. We'd had a telegram from your Air Force Headquarters in London and been expecting you earlier off the train. I'd decided you weren't coming this forenoon and was going to the shops. I daresay you're hungry. Come away inside and tell us about your travels and how your mother is.'

The words came tumbling out as she, breathless, embraced me and ushered me into her living room. I concluded that she was Mabel Rundle, my mother's cousin, and the other lady was Miss Lella Skinner, her older sister. Cousin Lella had her own house but hadn't been well, so was staying with the Rundles for a while. I assured her, as Cousin Mabel put her shopping bag down and took off her hat and coat, that I'd had breakfast.

The two ladies sat on the edge of their seats looking at me expectantly. Cousin Mabel plied me with questions which I tried to answer as best as I could, while Cousin Lella held her hands in her lap, smiled, nodded her head and periodically said, 'Och aye.' I'd difficulty in understanding what they were saying at times because of their strong accents and colloquialisms, but they seemed to have no problems with my accent. They were overwhelming in their kindness.

Cousin Mabel was aged forty-nine and had thin hair starting to go grey, but the physical description I'd been given of her quite overlooked the 'heart of gold' that she so well displayed. She was to become my second mother and, in her long life, has held a very special place of affection in my heart.

The Rundles' eldest son, Leslie, came downstairs from his bedroom where he'd been studying, and I was introduced to him before he left for Aberdeen University. He was a second year science student, a Second Lieutenant in the Territorial Army, slim, of medium height, good-looking with rather longish hair, had a slightly formal manner and stuttered at times. I felt fortunate to like him from the start. I was so weary that I was taken to a spare bed in Leslie's bedroom and allowed to sleep into the afternoon.

Figure 6. Rundle Family (except for Alice) at Aberdeen, Scotland, April 1951: L-R: Francis and Leslie Rundle, Lella Skinner, Mabel and Frank Rundle.

That evening, I met the rest of the family (Fig. 6).

Mr Francis (or Frank) Rundle, a joiner at the Stoneywood paper mill, was slightly built, had darkish hair but a small gingery moustache, wore spectacles (his left eye being slightly skewed), and spoke quietly and a little huskily – having had an ulcer in his throat and tuberculosis some ten years earlier. He appeared to me to be a very gentlemanly, considerate and thoughtful person. Cousin Mabel said that he'd slowed down a lot since having TB. I found that he was quite an artist. Two of his pencil drawings of dogs adorned the living-room walls. He later copied a picture of Barra Castle for me, as one of my distant relations had once lived there.

Alice Rundle was my age and about to start a domestic science course. She wore make-up, spoke quickly in a strong Scots accent and seemed to be worried about her weight.

Francis Rundle was still at primary school and had short pants with socks pulled up as far as they would go. He was slim with gingery hair and freckles, and didn't say too much. I found he spoke indistinctly in a broad accent.

I showed the family the photos I'd brought from New Zealand. We talked non-stop until bedtime. Cousin Mabel made sure I was warm that night by giving me a stoneware hot-water bottle. Only then did I find that Francis normally occupied the bed, and that he'd been moved to a settee in the living room. Poor Francis!

In the weeks that followed, Leslie took me in hand and conducted me around Aberdeen University, including the impressive Mitchell Hall at Marischal College and King's College in Old Aberdeen. He showed me his old school, two very good model aeroplane shops, his Territorial Army Officers' Mess and arranged for me to borrow some aircraft recognition magazines. We walked to Dyce so I could meet two of his university friends, medical students George Webster and Jimmy Donald. As we returned that evening I was thrilled to see the Northern Lights for the first time. Somehow that tune, 'The Northern Lights of old Aberdeen, are home, sweet home to me . . .,' seemed very real.

On several occasions, Leslie and George took me to dances at the University Students' Union. For an entry fee of 2s. per head, the dances were the cheapest available. I found George Webster to be a lot of fun. We also went to see the well known actress Jean Kent in the play *Froufrou*.

Leslie borrowed a car and drove me to Elgin. Cousin Lella also came with us to see a friend in Huntly. At Elgin, Leslie introduced me to his girlfriend Moira Mackenzie, an arts student at Aberdeen University. I was shown Weston House (where my grandfather James Skinner once had a school), and the ruins of Elgin Cathedral. There was little time to see more before leaving and picking up Cousin Lella on our way back to Aberdeen. Falling snow seemed to enhance the beautiful Scottish countryside and glimpses of the ruined Castles of Huntly, Harthill and Dunnideer, and the monument commemorating the Battle of Harlaw, made me think that I must later return to explore such places.

I helped Francis with model aeroplanes he was building – a 34 inch wing-span glider North Wind and a 16 inch wing-span Tempest. He needed a lot of help with the glider, so I bought some model supplies and rebuilt it for him. I also bought model aeroplane kits requested by friends back home.

Francis took me to the aerodrome at Dyce to watch a Meteor 8 jet do touch-and-go landings. We got permission to inspect it on the tarmac. I warmed my hands on a hot tailpipe, breathed kerosene fumes and peered at the belly tank and other features of the aircraft. Paint on the leading edges of the wings had been worn away, and I was surprised at the lack of flush riveting elsewhere. The pilot took-off to do aerobatics for a Territorial Army group that was present. What an awe inspiring aircraft it was! My attention was diverted, however, when a clipped-winged Spitfire buzzed the airfield and landed, joining several other Territorial Air Force Spitfires outside a hangar. This famous aircraft was really worth seeing. I walked slowly around the Spitfires, had a look in a cockpit and inspected the engine of one that had the cowlings removed. Everything was very compact inside. The aircraft was so beautifully proportioned. I wished I could fly one.

On several other occasions, Mr Rundle, Francis and I walked to the aerodrome boundary to see the ATC flying Kirby Kite two-seater gliders, but cold and more snow falls forced us to return to the warmth of the living-room fire. I became used to seeing gliders, Harvards and Spitfires (including the rare sight of a formation of eight Spitfires) flying around Dyce.

Snow had fallen thickly so Francis and I had snow fights and walked through the bare woods beside the River Don, full of the nests of noisy crows, to see steeplejacks doing repairs on smoke stacks at the Stoneywood paper mill, the largest mill of its kind in Britain.

One evening, Mr Rundle showed me the new offices he'd just built at the mill and conducted me around the paper making operations. I found everything fascinating and departed rather tired – glad to escape the noise, smells and occasional wet floors of the mill. I later watched Mr Rundle feed the bees in the hives in his backyard.

Cousin Mabel very kindly took me up Deeside to Banchory where she did some shopping. I was shown the stately granite Victorian homes, Crathes Castle, the narrow part of the River Dee that Rob Roy is supposed to have jumped over, his coloured statue nearby, and the picturesque Brig of Feugh.

Cousin Mabel said nothing about the rationing of certain foods in Britain and I didn't think to ask, as wartime rationing had already ceased in New Zealand. She somehow managed to feed me out of the family ration books supplemented by the few coupons I'd been given in London. Perhaps she felt she was repaying a debt as my parents had regularly sent food parcels to the Rundles during World War II. She introduced me to Scottish food – something for which I have a great affection.

Cousin Lella was a dear who kept pushing jam and the like towards me at meal times, and who drank tea holding a little finger straight out, but she was a bit dithery, murmured away largely to herself and was teased unmercifully by Alice, who had to share her bed with her. Cousin Lella arranged for me to meet an old friend, Miss Souter, who'd been to Australia and America. Miss Souter was a most interesting person and later invited me back so that I could show her the photos I'd taken on the voyage to Britain.

When Alice and I went to see the film *The Wooden Horse*, I was intrigued to see a man playing an organ as it came up from the floor during the intervals. Then Alice and Francis took me swimming. I'd never been in an indoor pool before, let alone swum in such cold weather. Unfortunately, I dived into the tepid water with my watch on and was most annoyed to find my 'waterproof' watch had filled with water. Alice and Francis, however, wouldn't come indoor ice skating with me so I went alone on a number of occasions to Donald's Ice Rink. (I'd learnt to skate years before on an outdoor rink during holidays at Lake Tekapo, New Zealand.) At Donald's I was disappointed to find that I'd lost much of my skating ability, and ill-fitting hired boots with blunt edges didn't help. Later, when Alice did come skating with me, she quite enjoyed herself.

Cousin Mabel arranged for Alice and me to stay four days at Clune Farm, near Cullen, in Banffshire. The farm was owned by her cousins – unmarried brother and sister, Jim and Mary Currie. They greeted us warmly. Jim was lean and wiry whereas Mary was short, dumpy, and wore spectacles. I soon found them to be hard workers and stalwarts of the local church. I liked them immensely. A brother, George Currie, was Vice-Chancellor of Victoria University in Wellington, New Zealand.

Alice and I occupied ourselves watching farm activities, doing some ploughing, trying to shoot rabbits, visiting Cullen to do messages, seeing Cullen House, helping Jim distribute forms for the 8 April census and, in freezing conditions, collecting turnips from another farm. As a result of the latter, I developed a nasty cold.

We returned to Aberdeen for Alice's confirmation as a member of the Church of Scotland. Mr Rundle, being an elder of the church, got me a communion card. I'd feared that I'd be questioned on my knowledge of the catechism before being allowed to participate in the communion, but that didn't happen. On Sundays, Mr Rundle always wore a bowler hat to church.

At the Bucksburn church I was introduced to a Mr and Mrs Morgan whose son Allan was studying for the ministry at Knox College in Dunedin, New Zealand. I later met other members of the Morgan family – there seemed to be about fifty of them! I was soon involved in a coffee evening, church stalls, dances and the Youth Fellowship, and really made to feel part of the community.

Another friend of the Rundles, Mrs Cunningham, whose Flying Officer son Ian had graduated from Cranwell in No. 48 Entry, lent me five Cranwell *Journals*, and a copy of *The Royal Air Force Review* which described what life was like at the Royal Air Force College. I was fascinated to read:

On arrival at Cranwell . . . a cadet spends two terms – based on the ordinary school term – in the Junior Flight, living in barrack blocks under exactly the same conditions as ordinary serving airmen. This enables him to become conversant right from the start with the life and routine of those in the ranks and provides a personal background for the problems which he will be called on to face later when he is commissioned. During these two terms, the cadets receive their initiation into the ways and routine of the Service and sample their first taste of discipline and drill. With the arrival of the third term, they are transferred to the College proper, and take their places as fully fledged officer cadets of the Senior Flight.

The College itself is run on the lines of an officers' mess. Each cadet has his own private bedroom-cum-study in one of the residential wings of the building where he is waited on by a civilian batman who cleans his buttons and shoes, and performs other light duties 'by arrangement'. Meals are taken in the dining room with officers of the directing and instructional staff, and here again the cadet is waited on by civilian servants . . .

The cadet's day starts at 0700 hours followed by a parade half an hour later. At eight o'clock there is a meteorological briefing and, when this is over, the lectures and flying instruction and other forms of training begin. There is a break in the middle of the morning when cadets return to the mess for coffee, and then studies are resumed until lunch-time. Afternoons are usually devoted to ground combat training, tutorial periods and further lectures which continue until six o'clock.

The syllabus provides for training in general service subjects such as Air Force law and administration, drill, armed combat, physical training and air-sea rescue. Other subjects covered include mathematics, aerodynamics, aero engineering, and of course flying. During their training, cadets attend short courses in workshops where they obtain practical experience designed to familiarise them with the problems confronting the technical tradesman in the Air Force.

At the end of the term, the cadets are granted leave and, for those who do not wish to spend all of it in their homes, visits and tours to Air Force units in overseas commands and to other places of interest abroad are organised. The College offers a variety of almost every kind of sport and recreation; it has its own riding school and hunt club, a rowing club, dramatic and debating society, and its own Society run on similar lines to those existing in the universities for the promotion of social and other recreational activities.

Once every year, cadets attend camp which is organised and run entirely by themselves under the supervision of an officer.

The Cranwell cadet . . . is distinguished by a white band worn on his cap and white gorget patches on the lapels of his tunic. For the first two terms, he wears the airman's cap badge, but on transferring to the Senior Flight, the badge is changed for that of a warrant officer's type. Cadets are treated with the same respect as that shown to officers and, in accordance with tradition, are addressed as 'Sir' by the NCO instructors and other non-commissioned ranks with whom they come in contact . . .

The College has its own private bank which is provided for the exclusive use of cadets, and their pay is credited each month to their accounts at the bank, which has its own specially printed cheque-book . . .

The information in the Cranwell *Journals* and *The Royal Air Force Review* greatly added to my knowledge of what was in store for me. I rather fancied myself being called 'Sir', having a batman, and trying new sports and activities. My only regret was that there was no ice skating at Cranwell.

In my last days at Aberdeen, I wrote numerous letters, visited the Art Gallery and Museum and toured the famous Rowett Institute, one of six animal research stations in Britain.

I felt I'd got to know the Rundle family very well and teased Alice about a new hair style she'd adopted. Occasionally we went for long evening walks with her latest boyfriend and other friends. We usually ended up buying fish and chips on our way back to Stoneywood. I kept out of a verbal exchange Alice had with Leslie one day – Alice had quite a sharp tongue.

I left Aberdeen reluctantly, having a real regard for my relations there who'd looked after me so well, and feeling that Aberdeen, being known to my Scottish grandfather, was my second home.

I'd been invited to stay six days with a Dr and Mrs Stewart Wickenden at Peebles. Mum had met the Wickendens' son, Eric, at a meeting of the Timaru branch of the Overseas League, and been told that his parents were thinking of emigrating to New Zealand. As Eric was a very poor letter writer, his parents had invited me to tell them all about New Zealand.

I went to Overseas League House in Edinburgh to meet the Wickendens (as Mum had got me membership of the League). They immediately began questioning me about New Zealand while we walked through Princes Street Gardens and drove to Peebles. The Wickendens told me they'd just moved from Edinburgh to Peebles to avoid being bombed as they feared a nuclear war with Russia was imminent, but regretted buying their new home as Dr Wickenden, a medical doctor, had just been offered a position at Papakura Military Camp near Auckland, New Zealand, and they'd decided to emigrate.

Each day, Dr Wickenden drove to his Edinburgh surgery and, in the evenings, asked me more about New Zealand – what were the price of new and second-hand cars, should he take his car with him, what were salaries like, and so on. I had difficulty answering some of the questions and suggested that he write to New Zealand House in London to get specific information.

Then he would tell me about what happened in surgery that day and when he was a student. 'Did you know that dead bodies kept in a tank of formalin would lose all their hair?' he said. 'When dissecting bodies,' he continued, 'I'd have to say, "I'll have a boy today," and someone would fish one out for me.' Mrs Wickenden saw that I was starting to look a bit green and shushed her husband, but he was irrepressible and had a fund of stories. He was a cheerfully gloomy person.

I occupied myself by visiting the partially ruined Neidpath Castle near Peebles and going with Dr Wickenden to see a patient at Earlston. We had a very pleasant drive beside the River Tweed, past old mills, Melrose Abbey, and ruins of Border towers. He also took me to Edinburgh to see the sights.

At Edinburgh Castle I was immediately taken in hand by guides and amused by their little jokes – 'Those gates are quite modern being only two hundred years old,' and, 'After being in the Crown Room, come away leaving the crown there.' The castle oozed with history, and I wandered around trying to take everything in. There was the sound of bagpipes, the 1 o'clock cannon and many strange accents. From the battlements, Edinburgh stretched in a dark mass below me as far as the Forth Bridge before disappearing into smoke and haze. A Westland Wyvern naval fighter and a de Havilland Chipmunk trainer few overhead.

Holyrood Palace also helped bring history to life for me. Then I walked up the Royal Mile looking at its ancient inns, closes, John Knox's house and other quaint buildings. I tried to move quietly over the creaking floors of the Huntly House Museum and recognised, in the street outside, the Canongate Tolbooth clock, a picture of which was on a calender I had back home. In the impressive St Giles Cathedral there was the Thistle Chapel and the memorial to Sir William Smith, founder of the Boys' Brigade. I made a brief visit to the Zoo, but I was soon back in central Edinburgh exploring the observatory and tower on Carlton Hill, the National Museum of Antiquities, the National Portrait Gallery and the Anglican Cathedral.

I had afternoon tea one day with Miss Winifred Wrench, sister of Sir Evelyn Wrench, founder of the Overseas League. Mum had arranged the meeting as she'd a high regard for Miss Wrench after commenting on a regular column Miss Wrench wrote in the Overseas League magazine and then corresponding with her for many years. Miss Wrench was a dear old lady who wore old fashioned clothes and lived by herself in a jumble of memorabilia. She was a most interesting person to talk to and I was sorry when I eventually had to leave.

I'd run out of travellers cheques and had to go to the Bank of New Zealand in London to draw on the funds my parents had deposited there. Dr Wickenden very kindly arranged accommodation for me at the Victoria League in London.

Hot and tired after the eight hour train journey to London, I was given a temporary bed on a couch in the games room of the Victoria League's Excelsior House. The place was rather disorganised and full of people from the Dominions.

The Bank of New Zealand in Queen Victoria Street was shut when I called because of the ANZAC Day commemoration, so I had to return later to be instructed on how to fill out my first cheque-book and withdraw some money. When I went to see Sqn. Ldr. Furlong at Halifax House, I found that RNZAF Headquarters had moved to Adelphi Building in John Adam

Street. The Squadron Leader and I had a good chat before he gave me a first class travel warrant to get me to Cranwell on 2 May.

I then set about seeing what I could of London.

When I stopped at St Paul's Cathedral, I was surprised to see hordes of tourists milling around the inside of the huge nave and buying souvenirs while a communion service was in progress. Around the Cathedral lay the remains of buildings that had been bombed during World War II. Westminster Abbey was also highly commercialised and crowded with tourists, but all the same was most impressive with its stained glass, statues, monuments and plaques. I admired the simplicity of the Unknown Warrior's Grave and the beautiful RAF Chapel, found the plaque to Lord Rutherford of Nelson (the New Zealander who'd split the atom), and noticed that the Stone of Scone was missing from King Edward's Chair. In Westminster Hall, I recognised the politician, Aneurin Bevan.

I felt that Madame Tussaud's waxworks was well worth visiting as everything seemed so real, even the lady sitting in the foyer who breathed as she slept, having dropped a paper she'd been reading. Visitors often picked up the paper for her, thinking she was alive!

In Fleet Street, I suddenly recognised Richard Henshaw standing outside the Law Courts. He was startled to see me as he wasn't aware that I'd won a Cranwell cadetship. We'd known each other at Timaru Boys' High School though he was a year younger than me. He'd been training at Southampton for the Merchant Navy and had come to London on leave. We had lunch together, exchanged news and kept remarking on the coincidence of our meeting.

The magnificent British Museum and British Library were so huge that my feet soon got tired walking around the displays, but I saw the New Zealand section of artefacts (crammed into several large showcases), the Elgin marbles and Rosetta Stone, the Magna Carta, a whole room of illuminated Bibles, the logbook of Scott of the Antarctic, a collection of Turner's watercolours and many more priceless things. Being interested in art, I went to the National Gallery and admired the numerous paintings from all over Europe.

Tower Bridge was being repaired and had a door open at the base of the south tower so I couldn't resist climbing to the overhead bridge when nobody was looking and admiring what could be seen of London through the haze. At the Tower of London I got into a group of tourists being shown the sights by a Beefeater. Unfortunately, alterations were being made in Wakefield Tower so we didn't see the Crown Jewels, and we missed the Chapel of St Peter ad Vincula as it was being used for a wedding. There were so many historic and interesting things to see at the Tower that I wished I'd more time. On leaving, I took a ferry to Westminster.

I went to the Adelphi Theatre to see *Take it from Us*, a great show starring

Jimmy Edwards, Dick Bentley and Joy Nicholls. In walking the streets of London, I admired the work of pavement artists and was trapped into having my photo taken by a pavement photographer, who produced a sepia print of me within minutes. I thought it strange that some small parks were fenced off, being used only by those people who subscribed to them. At Buckingham Palace I saw the changing of the Guard and, on Queen Victoria's statue, the lion given by New Zealand.

Back at the Victoria League, I was moved into a room with an Australian, Ray Simmons, the son of an Anglican vicar. We decided on Sunday to attend a different church from what we were used to and ended up going to the Roman Catholic Westminster Cathedral. The inside of the huge church looked as if it'd been bombed and plaster had fallen off the walls leaving blackened brickwork and some unattractive white marble reliefs. There was no stained glass in the windows – the most colourful things in the gloomy place being the scarlet robes of the officiating Cardinal.

I went on to Northolt Airport and took a tour around the perimeter track to see the many aircraft there – Vikings, Dakotas, a Skymaster, a Superfortress, a Dominie and a Beechcraft. From the spectator enclosure, I recognised an air hostess who'd been in the news because of a bomb scare on an airliner, and a female pilot from a King's Cup Air Race.

In Holloway Road I met Henry J. Nicholls, the well-known model aeroplane enthusiast, from whose shop I'd imported my Phantom and Banshee kits. He arranged for me to get the *Aeromodeller* magazine while I was in Britain. When I travelled to East Ham to call on David Weedon, a person known to my family, I saw my first television programme. I also met Miss Moore, the daughter of a lady who'd billeted my Uncle Jack Skinner during World War I while he was recovering from being a prisoner of war. She came up to London from Eynsford especially to meet me. She was a very pleasant, elderly lady who'd been used to having home help before World War II, but was in much reduced circumstances at the time of our meeting. I also ran into Mrs Sinton and Zoë at New Zealand House and caught up with their news over lunch.

My long period of waiting rapidly came to an end. I felt almost grateful to the New Zealand wharfies whose actions had resulted in me having an unexpected amount of time in which to become familiar with so many things in Britain. Now I was anxious to get on with the flying and officer training I'd come for. I departed King's Cross station for Sleaford, changing trains at Grantham. I left my heavy luggage with the Sleaford stationmaster, then noticed several young men on the platform, some in airmen's uniform, probably wondering as I was what to do next. We soon realised we were all going to Cranwell, so hired taxis and were driven to the Cranwell Guardroom.

CHAPTER 4

Get Fell In

'PAY ATTENTION. I'm Flight Sergeant Harvey, NCO in charge of Junior Entries. Make sure you have all your luggage with you as the driver will now take you to your billet and you'll be allocated to squadrons. Any questions?'

The RAF Regiment NCO stood on the step of the RAF bus into which we new Cadets had moved outside the Cranwell Guardroom. He was lantern-jawed with a weather-beaten look, smartly dressed in blue battledress uniform, and spoke with a strong Irish accent.

Nobody had any questions, so the bus driver took us westward along the public road known as Camp Road (sometimes called Cranwell Road, now Cranwell Avenue) that went through the middle of Cranwell. I craned my neck looking for the magnificent building with the tower that I'd seen in the pre-War Cranwell brochure at the Timaru ATC (Figs. 7 and 9). When it came into sight on my right through a high wrought iron fence, I was disappointed the bus continued on past the imposing main entrance gates (Fig. 10), turned left by lines of dark wooden huts and stopped outside a two storeyed red brick barrack block (Fig. 8). F/S Harvey led us into the foyer of the block and called out names and squadrons from a clipboard he carried. I was in A Squadron, on the ground floor to the right of the foyer.

I carried my suitcases into the barrack, tried to walk quietly on the bare wooden floor and looked for a bed. All the bed areas on my left were occupied by Cadets who stared at us new arrivals, particularly our feet. I headed for an empty bed to the right in the middle of the barrack.

'Is one of you a New Zealander?' enquired a Cadet from across the barrack.

'Yes, I am,' I replied.

The Cadet came over and said, 'Hi, I'm Colin Loveday. I'm also a Kiwi. Grab that bed opposite mine. We Kiwis need to stick together. Chiefee said you were coming. I've been told to look after you. When you come into the barrack next time, get some floor pads from the box near the door.' I looked down at his feet and saw he was standing on squares of old grey blanket. Now I knew. The Cadets on the other side of the barrack were concerned lest we newcomers would destroy the highly polished surface of the floor. They shuffled everywhere on floor pads.

Colin was of medium build and good looking, with fair, swept-back hair. He sat on my bed and talked as he spit and polished his boots. I learned that

Figure 7. College main building (now known as College Hall) and parade ground, 1951.)

Figure 8. Block 77, Junior Entries, 1951.

we were in Block 77, my entry was No. 60 Entry, he was in 59 Entry, had been in Junior Entries three months, was aged twenty-one, came from Stratford, had been the junior tennis champion of the North Island of New Zealand, had joined the RAF before being selected for Cranwell and was usually called 'Kiwi'.

'There're three other New Zealanders in the RAF here,' he said, 'Ron Parfitt, Ian Powell and Jack Henderson. Ron's from Westport and in 55 Entry, A Squadron, Ian's from Wanganui and in 57 Entry, C Squadron, and Jack's from New Plymouth and in 59 Entry, B Squadron. You'll meet them shortly,' he added.

The beds on either side of mine were taken by Michael Heaney and Gordon Grierson, whom I later found to be the shortest and the tallest Cadets respectively in 60 Entry. Michael had curly hair, was very self-assured, said 'Yar' instead of 'Yes' in a very upper class English accent and had been to Marlborough College. Gordon, on the other hand, seemed just the opposite, being tall and weedy with a small head, straight black hair and a rather diffident speaking manner.

I went to look for Ron Chippindale and Jim Brown. They'd both been allocated to B Squadron on the ground floor opposite A Squadron. Jim was there, but he didn't know when Ron would arrive (he arrived a day late). Jack Henderson had been told to look after them both. I was introduced to

Figure 9. A Squadron wing of College main building, 1951.

Figure 10. RAF College main gates, 1951.

Jack, a sturdy individual who I thought swore and smoked a lot. I went upstairs and looked in on C Squadron and the remaining members of each squadron. With only twenty-one beds in my barrack room and twenty-eight Cadets in A Squadron 59 and 60 Entries, seven of the Squadron had to be accommodated upstairs.

F/S Harvey came into the barrack and distributed letters. I'd twenty-four of them! I looked for some from Margaret Hornsey, but there wasn't one. She was a year younger than me and in her final year at school, so probably had other things on her mind. (Much later when I did get some letters from her, she said she'd written to me using a Cranfield address!) I tried to overcome my disappointment – other more immediate things occupied my attention.

59A instructed 60A on what they expected of us in the barrack. Then food ration books, cutlery (known as irons), pyjamas and the 60 Entry Early Training Programme were issued (Appendix III). I read that my training began the next day. After dinner, beds were made down and, till lights out at 2230 hours, 60A watched 59A working on their equipment.

I was exhausted, having had such an eventful day, but slept poorly. The bed sheets and pillow slip were made of a coarse material and felt a little sticky (even though they were changed each fortnight). The cylindrical pillow was filled with something hard that gave me sore ears until I got used to it. There weren't enough blankets to keep out the cold coming in through the open windows. The barrack had hot water-pipes along the walls, but the heating wasn't on and all the windows had to be open a certain amount at night. I wasn't used to sleeping in a room with other people, but eventually drifted off into uneasy slumber.

An alarm clock went off at 0600 hours. The Leading Cadet of 59A ordered 60A out of bed and into the ablutions. Dozily, we queued up in the ablution area that projected from the rear of the barrack block.

59A were hard on our heels. They were well ahead in making up bed packs and getting their bed spaces into inspection order. Four blankets and two sheets had to be carefully folded and stacked on each mattress, with strips of wood inserted so that the squared bed pack presented a flat appearance from the front. A folded fifth blanket surrounded the pack.

When making down a bed, the four folded blankets were partially unfolded and carefully laid in a certain pattern on the top sheet before being held in place by the fully opened fifth blanket tucked in under the mattress on three sides. To sleep in a bed made this way took some practice without it all falling apart. When turning over, one had to remember to carefully lift the top sheet and blankets with an arm, turn one's body, then lower the bedding again. Each morning, little folding of the blankets was required to prepare them for the bed pack. Colin Loveday gave me wooden strips saved from a previous Cadet to use in my bed pack and clothing display.

In the metal wardrobe beside each bed certain articles of clothing had to be displayed in a particular order. Making up the display was very time consuming, so Cadets usually left it untouched, except occasionally to relocate the bits of wood and have a clean piece of clothing showing.

60 Entry had the task of cleaning the ablutions (or bogs, as they were commonly known) before following 59 Entry to breakfast at the nearby Junior Mess. The food was passable. There were no second helpings, and not much time to eat more anyway. I soon found that Cadets relied on their chocolate ration and snacks from the NAAFI to keep from being hungry. At 0715 hours, 59 Entry was marched off to do drill on the square in front of the Junior Mess. Blocks 77 and 78 were to the west of the square while to the east were Blocks 79 and 80. All the blocks were of similar construction, but the last three were occupied by airmen. 60 Entry then began its eleven day Early Training Programme.

Several members of 60 Entry with prior service experience had brought with them some articles of uniform. Their kit had to be brought up to standard, whereas the rest of us had to be issued with a complete set of new equipment. The Clothing Store was in East Camp, some distance from Block 77, so we were glad of the assistance of an RAF bus to transport us and all our equipment. We were soon dressed as airmen in blue battledress uniform (No. 4 Dress) except for coloured lanyards on our right shoulders (red for A Squadron, yellow for B Squadron, blue for C Squadron and green for D Squadron – the Equipment and Secretarial Squadron at RAF Digby), and a one and a half inch wide white band around the base of our field service caps. This band had to be kept immaculate, but we soon discovered that the material shrank dramatically when washed (Fig. 11).

We were all measured for officer pattern uniforms (No. 3 Dress) by representatives from Burberrys Limited. The two members of the Royal Pakistan Air Force in the Entry were told to remove the Pakistan shoulder patches from their existing uniforms. Flying clothing, parachutes and rifles were issued separately. All the clothing had to be marked in indelible ink with our rank, name and number.

Then we were lined up for vaccinations and had sore arms for days. When a Cadet mentioned he could barely lift his arm, F/S Harvey said, 'You've got to keep it moving,' and swung one of his own arms in a circle above his head. The Cadet thought the Flight Sergeant had gone mad! Those members who'd not been previously attested were sworn in. Individual and Entry photographs were taken. Later, when I saw the 60 Entry photo taken on the College steps (Fig. 12) and tried to fit names to the faces, I realised that one Cadet was missing – Mike Elliott didn't join the Entry until about a month after the term started.

We were given talks on medical matters, ground combat training, security and the study curriculum. I then realised that most of the two years eight months I was to be at the College would be on academic work and I'd do only about 300 hours of flying.

F/S Harvey took 60 Entry on a conducted tour of Cranwell (Figs. 13–17). He pointed to the Station Sick Quarters across the road from Block 77 before we travelled south by bus to the flight lines of the south airfield. Lined up on the tarmac were Ansons, Prentices, Harvards, a Meteor 7 and a Balliol. We were told that the south airfield was one of the largest grass airfields in Britain and had been used by the RAF's Long Range Flight for many record breaking flights. A short tar–sealed strip had been constructed for the maiden flight of the Gloster Whittle E28/39, the first British jet aircraft.

We were then driven eastwards past the link trainer and workshops building to the gymnasium and adjacent indoor swimming pool. I was interested to learn that the gymnasium had also been used as the Church of England church until a former airship hangar had been dedicated in 1921 as the Church of St Michael and All Angels (though it was usually called the Hangar Church). We didn't go further into East Camp as it comprised various training schools that weren't part of the College. A number of the original Royal Naval Air

Figure 11. Ron Chippindale (60B), Jim Brown (60B) and Author dressed in airmen pattern 'best blue' uniform outside Block 77, Junior Entries, Cranwell 1951.

Service buildings dating from 1915 were indicated to us. We were told that the College was only a small part of RAF Cranwell, the population of which was about 3,000 people – well below the 7,000 or so who lived there during World War II.

Going northwards, F/S Harvey pointed out the officers' mess (called York House) and St Andrew's Church (usually called the Other Denominations Church, but today known as the Church of Scotland and Free Churches Church). We passed The Lodge where the Commandant lived, drove through a small wood named The Plantation and passed the Roman Catholic St Peter's Church, the Science and Weapons Block lecture rooms, the College Museum, the Hangar Church and the Flight Cadets' Garage, before arriving at the eastern end of the main College building. The eastern end of the north airfield could be seen, intersected by a road called Lighter-than-Air Road which went to a rifle range and what was known as 'the married patch'. This was an officers' area of some sixty married quarters, built on the site of three former airship and balloon hangars, the largest of which had housed the rigid airship C13 in 1917.

The main College building (now called College Hall) was what I really

---

Opposite: Figure 12. NO. 60 ENTRY, ROYAL AIR FORCE COLLEGE, CRANWELL MAY 1951

Back Row
L-R: Cadets M.J. (Mike) Goodall; Alan G. Bedford-Roberts; Ramsay McN. Brown; J.T.C. (Tiny) Lewis; C.C. (Chris) Woods; John E. Maitland; Alan J. McLelland-Brown; T.J. (Tom) Greenhill-Hooper; Gordon S. Grierson.

Fourth Row
L-R: Cadets J.D. (Johnny) Langley; M.M. (Mike) Marsh; L.A. (Laurie) Jones; R. (Dickie) Hoare; Ron Chippindale; D.C. (Dave) Purse; E. (Ted) Reynolds; R.L. (Bob) Cartwright; P.J. (Pete) Anstee.

Third Row
L-R: Cadets R.M. (Hank) Hancock; B.K. (Dick) Hinton; A.C. (Andy) Whitson; Julian M.B. Bowes; C.C. (Chris) Taylor; R.I. (Ron) Chedgey; Duncan Allison; M.C. (Mal) Dines; E.H. (Ted) Moors.

Second Row
L-R: Cadets W.E. (Wally) Close; J. Alun Morgan; P. (Pete) McKechnie; J.M. (Bulldog) Drummond; Cecil E.V. Da Silva; R.G. (Reg) Bailey; A.S.J. (Tony) Whit-wam; John B. Gratton; R.A. (Ron) Edwards.

Front Row
L-R: Cadets I.A. (Joe) Qureshi; M.H. (Hammy) Khan; John R. McEntegart; W.R. (Wally) Martin; M.R.H. (Spike) Heaney; J.C. (Jim) Brown; Colin P. Field; Nigel R. MacNichol; T.S.B. (Sam) Boyce.

Absent: Cadet M.A.C. (Mike) Elliott.

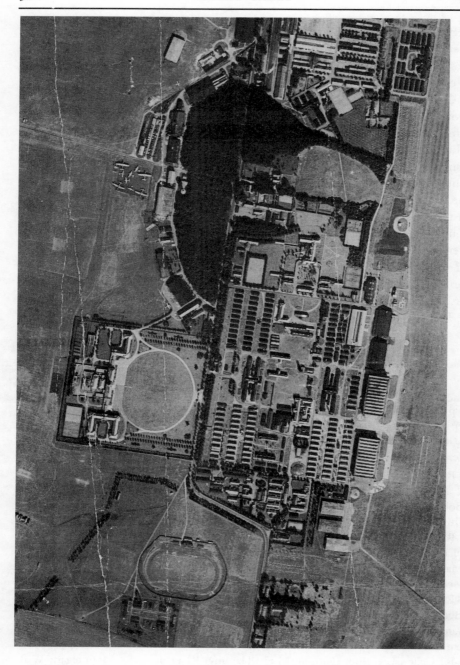

Figure 13.
ROYAL AIR
FORCE
CRANWELL
1949

wanted to see. The central rectangular block faced south and had three bent arms forming quadrangles in the British university tradition. A and B Squadrons were accommodated in the two western arms and C Squadron in the south-eastern arm. Squash courts and vegetable gardens were situated in the area of the missing north-eastern arm. The exterior of the College was finished in a neo-Georgian baroque style in red brick with white stone embellishments and columns. Above the entrances of each arm was an RAF emblem and, set in the green slate roof, a small brown ornamental tower. Above the central block an impressive white tower rose to 140 feet, topped by a green dome and a revolving light whose flashes (twenty times per minute) could be seen at night from a distance of about twenty miles.

We entered the south-eastern arm and, in hobnailed boots, tried to walk quietly without sliding on the green marbled floor of the long main corridor. Photographs of previous entries lined the walls. In the main entrance hall of the College, we admired the large portraits of Marshal of the Royal Air Force The Viscount Trenchard of Wolfeton, GCB, GCVO, DSO, DCL, LLD, who as the first Chief of the Air Staff had proposed in 1919 the establishment of a cadet college, and Air Vice Marshal Sir Charles Longcroft, KCB, CMG, DSO, AFC, who became the first Commandant of the College in 1920. Between the portraits was a descriptive marble panel and a small ornamental table supported by a gilt eagle.

We read on the panel:

The Royal Air Force College is built on a site which was used by the Admiralty in the Great War for an aeroplane and airship station. The Arms of the College commemorate both the name of HMS *Daedalus* as the station was then called and the Arms of the family de Cranewell who in the fifteenth century held the land from the Knights Templars of Brewer. The College was opened in February 1920 and for some years the staff and students were housed in temporary buildings which lay 200 yards to the south of this point. This building, the foundation stone of which was laid on 26 April 1929, was first occupied in September 1933. James Grey West, OBE, Architect.

The imposing, rotund, frock-coated figure of Mr Albert Clay, MM, the civilian Head Porter, stood in the entrance hall on a beautiful carpet square. He told us that only officers and senior year Flight Cadets were allowed to cross the hall. In the gallery above (known as the hall of fame) could be seen portraits of RAF winners of the Victoria Cross.

Behind the entrance hall was the main lecture hall and stage. A corridor going around it contained on the northern side two large moveable notice-boards. We were shown the College dining hall opposite the notice-boards. This impressive room was two stories high, had a musician's gallery at the eastern end and a stand at the other on which was the RAF Eagle and the Colour presented by His Majesty King George VI in 1948. Below the high windows, large paintings decorated the walls. Three rows of dining tables that could seat up to about 290 people, extended the length of the room. The Head Steward, Mr E. Curt, BEM, hovered near the servery doors on the northern side of the hall.

We looked in the Fancy Goods Store, several ante-rooms, the billiard room and various other rooms before walking upstairs to the library. This looked like any other library except for the predominance of aeronautical books and memorabilia such as the thesis on 'Future Developments in Aircraft Design', the first practical consideration of jet propulsion, written by Air Cdre. Sir Frank Whittle, KCB, CB, when a Flight Cadet at the College from 1926 to 1928; Alcock and Brown's logbook and a medal presented to them after they'd made the first non-stop flight across the Atlantic in 1919; a piece of wood from the first aircraft of the Wright brothers to fly; a photo of Gp. Capt. Sir Douglas Bader, DSO, DFC, who was a Flight Cadet at the College from 1928 to 1930; and the spoiled proof-copy of the *Seven Pillars of Wisdom* written by Colonel T. E. Lawrence (Lawrence of Arabia) who as AC2 Shaw was based at RAF Cranwell from 1925 to 1926. The library was obviously a fascinating place.

From the library, we looked down on the orange coloured surface of the parade ground and circular driveways (known as the Orange) going to the

Figure 14. Western (A and B Squadron) entrance to College main building, 1951.

main entrance gates, the rows of cherry trees just coming into flower, and the daffodils around the trees and in flower beds.

On returning to the ground floor, we walked to the western end of the building to meet our bus. F/S Harvey then took us further to the west past a field in which red poppies were growing wild (where Whittle Hall now stands) to see a sports stadium and the dark wooden buildings of a former radar site called A Site. We were told the buildings were used as lecture rooms. To the north, on the western end of the north airfield, could be seen playing fields and a sports pavilion, while nearer the College were four tennis courts. Our tour ended, we were driven back to Block 77.

Over the next few days we had individual interviews with our Squadron Commanders, the appropriate Station Padre, and the Director of Studies together with the Senior Tutor Humanistics and the Senior Tutor Aeronautical Science and Engineering (usually referred to as the 'Senior Tutor Science').

Tests were conducted to place us in one of three sections for Humanistics and Science. I started in Section 2 for Humanistics and, not surprisingly, Section 3 for Science. Jim Brown was in Section 2 for both Humanistics and Science, whereas Ron Chippindale was in Section 2 for Science and Section 3 for Humanistics.

F/S Harvey began drilling us on the square. When some Cadets were slow in getting on parade, F/S Harvey barked, 'Them that's keen get fell in early.' He began by calling the roll. When he called 'Martin,' Wally Martin (having previously been in the RAF) replied confidently, 'Flight.'

F/S Harvey marched briskly up to Wally, crashed to a halt and, towering over the much shorter Wally, bellowed, 'The rank is Flight Sergeant. Kindly use that in future Mr Martin, Sir!'

'Yes, Flight Sergeant,' said Wally meekly.

'Louder!' bellowed our Flight Sergeant.

'Yes, Flight Sergeant!' Wally shouted.

Some other Cadets also got special attention from F/S Harvey. He called Malcolm Dines, 'Dins' and Ted Reynolds, 'Raynolds'. When he came to the little Pakistani, Joe Qureshi, and pronounced his name 'Kereeshi', Joe objected politely by saying, 'Excuse me Flight Sergeant, my name is Qureshi, not Kereeshi.'

'Just answer when your name is called, Kereeshi!' bellowed our Flight Sergeant.

'Yes, Flight Sergeant,' Joe replied.

Nobody else tried questioning our Irish drill instructor on his pronunciation of names. As a result, 60 Entry tended to adopt the pronunciations and, for the rest of the course, Dines was known as 'Dins', Reynolds as 'Raynolds' and Qureshi as 'Kereeshi'.

Then came the inspection. F/S Harvey moved slowly along each row of

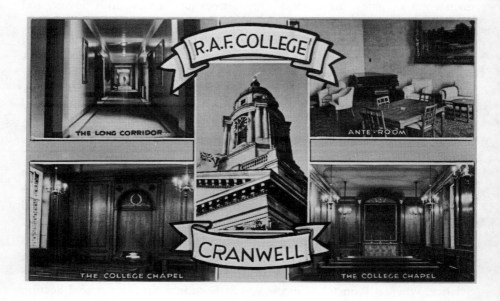

Figures 15-17. Above and opposite page: Postcard views of Cranwell 1950.

THE DINING HALL — R.A.F. COLLEGE — THE QUEEN'S COLOUR — DESCRIPTIVE PANEL — CRANWELL — THE DINING HALL

Cadets examining us minutely. When he came to the back of Ted Moors he said menacingly, 'Am I hurting you?'

'No, Flight Sergeant,' said Ted.

'Well I ought to be,' bellowed the Flight Sergeant. 'I'm standing on your hair! Haircut!'

The rest of us were killing ourselves with laughter, but we dared not let it show. Most of us hadn't heard this old joke before. Ted and the rest of the Entry duly made an appointment with the College barber and, for the remainder of our time at Cranwell, had our hair trimmed every week or two. There was a standard charge of 3s. per month no matter how many haircuts one had. Mr Creasy, the College barber, had oily hair, a rather ingratiating manner and was known, needless to say, as 'Mr Greasy'.

The drill itself was most energetic. Initially we marched at 180 paces a minute, lifted our knees with toes pointed down when turning, halting etc., and practised several special salutes. The shorter Cadets sometimes had difficulty in marching in time with the rest of us. We all discovered new muscles. Later the pace was slowed down to 120 paces a minute and we were encouraged to swagger a little.

Flt. Lt. J.C. Woods, the Adjutant of Junior Entries, regularly inspected 60 Entry on parade and in the barracks. He had a nasty habit of appearing at 0615 hours to see if anyone was still in bed. One Cadet who was and who sleepily told the Adjutant to 'go to hell,' was really given a 'rocket'. Whoever saw the Adjutant first called out, 'Room, atten . . . shun!' One Cadet tried fooling another squadron one day by putting his head around the barrack door and shouting, 'Room . . .,' stopped short when he saw F/S Harvey in the barrack, then trailed off into, ' . . . a ten shilling note has been found.'

For the first two Sundays, F/S Harvey marched 60 Entry to the College to see the weekly compulsory church parade, attend church and later watch the remainder of the College march past the Commandant, Air Cdre. L.F. Sinclair, GC, CB, CBE, DSO. Our drill had a long way to go to reach the very high standard of the Flight Cadets.

Colin Loveday taught me how to bull my equipment. The toes and heels of the Army pattern and Air Force boots had to have a mirror like finish, achieved by ironing on a thick layer of polish, then spit and polishing with small amounts of polish for what seemed like hours. I soon got to know the different characteristics of Nugget and Kiwi brands of polish.

Wearing boots was new to many of us and, as a result, several Cadets lost skin off their heels and ankles. F/S Harvey advised us to soak our boots overnight in water, then go for a three-mile run in the boots to break them in! Nobody was prepared to do that and then try and get the boots up to inspection standard.

Web equipment such as belts and bayonet frogs had to be carefully blancoed so that there was no caking of the finish. We learned to put size in the blanco to prevent it from cracking. The ninety or more brass fittings on our kit were brightly polished, even inside buckles, with Silva-glit or Dura-glit. This was very difficult to do without ruining the blancoed surface. Most of the webbing was blue, but some was white for ceremonial purposes. We went to extraordinary lengths to get new brass hat badges looking smooth, but without removing details of the badge. The wooden surfaces of our rifles had to be scraped and darkened with nugget to get an even colour and then spit and polished. Some Cadets removed wood here and there to allow the wooden parts to move and make more noise when hit during drill, e.g. when presenting arms. The rifles had to be meticulously cleaned inside and out.

Bulling became a daily chore. If our equipment wasn't up to scratch or we were deemed to have done something wrong, we'd be put on extra drill or, worse still, restrictions (usually known as jankers). This was a time wasting exercise that put Cadets under considerable pressure by confining them to barracks (except for their normal duties) and giving additional duties like Under Officer's parade for flag raising at 0640 hours, fire picket parade for flag lowering at 1630 hours, extra drill at 1900 hours and a roll call and kit inspection at 2100 hours. There was so little time to do anything else that most Cadets soon resolved to avoid jankers as much as possible. Only the bolshie ones, like Gordon Grierson, began to accumulate fourteen days of jankers for reasonably serious offences and twenty-eight days for major offences.

Some relief was achieved in those early days through organised games during allocated periods and on Wednesday and Saturday afternoons. I surprised myself by coming fifth in a wet cross-country run. Michael Heaney introduced me to squash rackets and, as this seemed a progression from the game of fives I'd played since being in Form 1, I purchased the necessary clothing and equipment. Swimming in the tiled, twenty-five yard indoor pool was initially a bit awkward for me as I had to wear a pair of shorts in the water (my swimming trunks being in the heavy luggage I'd left at the Sleaford railway station). We were herded onto the high diving board and told to do a backward somersault into the tepid water. One of the Cadets didn't come up afterwards. We got him out just in time and found that he couldn't swim! Such frantic activity ended by us having to dry ourselves and dress in double-quick time before marching off to something else. Detachable starched collars, collar studs, buttoned jackets and fly buttons were definitely not designed for quick dressing when one was in a hurry, still sweating and not properly dry.

Cadets could only leave Cranwell after duty on Saturdays and Sundays so, at the earliest opportunity, I caught a bus into Sleaford to retrieve my heavy luggage from the railway station. A Flight Cadet on the bus told me that a New Zealander was buried in the Cranwell village churchyard (Probationary Flight Sub-Lieutenant A.K. Greenwell, a trainee pilot in 1916 and the third person to die in an aircraft accident at RNAS Cranwell). On returning to Cranwell, I placed my luggage in Hut 203, the hut having metal lockers for sporting and other equipment that couldn't be kept in Block 77. I found that other Cadets who travelled to Sleaford usually went to dance and drink. On a number of occasions, they'd return to the barrack after lights out, obviously the worse for wear from alcohol, and wake everyone up.

An occasion for some relaxation was a 'Get to know 60 Entry' function. This was held in Hut 198, one of the larger huts near Block 77. I was able to chat informally with my newly appointed Squadron Commander, Sqn. Ldr. P.E.H. Thomas, AFC, and the A Squadron Cadet Wing Officer, Flt. Lt. A.W. Griffiths, and get to know Cadets from B and C Squadrons. Introductions often went along the lines of:

'Hello, my name's X . . ., what's yours?'

'Hi, I'm Rutherford Hancock.'

'Nice to meet you, Russell.'

'It's Rutherford, not Russell.'

'Sorry. That's unusual. Is Rutherford Hancock a hyphenated name?'

'No.'

'Is Rutherford a family name or are you named after the chap who split the atom?'

'It was the Christian name of a friend of my mother.'

'Oh. Have you got any other names?'

'My second Christian name is Moncrieff.'

'Kor! What were you called at school?'

'Hancock by the masters, or Rutherford.'

'Have you got a nickname?'

'Not really.'

At that point, the conversation usually went on to other things and my slightly bemused colleagues would avoid calling me anything. I was rather at a loss to suggest a nickname as some nicknames that I could think of weren't very complimentary (particularly when the origin of Hancock was from an Old English joke about a *henn* ['hen'] and a *hann* ['cock']). This problem wasn't resolved for some months. Bob Cartwright of 60A thought I sounded like a Yank, so a combination of Yank and Hancock resulted in him calling me Hank. Though I didn't encourage it the nickname stuck. (Throughout my Service and business careers, I've been known as Hank. In my private life I'm called Rutherford.)

60 Entry, with forty-six members, was one of the largest at Cranwell. Ten members had previously been in the British Armed Services – Duncan Allison, Johnny Langley and Mike Marsh at No. 1 Technical Training School, RAF Halton; Pete Anstee, Nigel MacNicol, Wally Martin, 'Tiny' Lewis and Alan Bedford-Roberts at other RAF training schools; and Dave Purse at HMS *Conway*. Ted Moors had been commissioned in the RAF a year earlier. The rest of us, apart from the Pakistani members, were direct entrants from school.

The Pakistanis, Hammy Khan and Joe Qureshi, were short, dark skinned and, at that stage, hard to understand. Hammy had apparently been to the RPAF College, and Joe said he'd a degree in economics. Cecil Da Silva, the first member of the Royal Ceylon Air Force to attend the College, also had some problems with his English. He had a big smile and the body of a swimmer – enormous shoulders that tapered to his feet. Someone unkindly referred to these Cadets as 'Black Wogs'.

Ron, Jim and I with our suntans, were referred to as 'Colonials' or 'White Wogs'. We tried to put the Pommy Cadets right about that! Someone asked, 'I suppose you play rugger?' We replied, 'Of course,' as rugby was New Zealand's national game. Some of the questions and comments addressed to me, however, seemed to be designed to make me feel inferior:

'Was New Zealand founded by convicts?'

'No, Australia was.'

'When did Europeans colonise New Zealand?'

'About 150 years ago.'

'Kor, you haven't any history to talk about, then. How many aircraft and squadrons does the RNZAF have?'

'Some Mosquitos, Mustangs, Catalinas, Sunderlands, Devons, Harvards and a few light planes I think – I don't really know the number of aircraft and squadrons, since I only joined the RNZAF the day before leaving New Zealand.'

'What, no jets?'

'There was a Meteor, a gift of the RAF, but it ran out of spares and wasn't continued.'

'Sounds like the RNZAF wouldn't even be the equivalent of an RAF Command.'

I came to the conclusion that the English-born Cadets were European orientated and knew little about places like the Dominion of New Zealand, whereas New Zealanders, having grown up in the British tradition, knew a lot about Britain. I was impressed all the same by the schools that some of the Cadets had come from – Christ's Hospital, Wellington, Marlborough and so on – the names and traditions of which were well known in New Zealand. I also felt at a slight disadvantage when I compared myself with those Cadets whose fathers were in the Armed Services and who'd lived in exotic places. Michael Heaney's father was a retired Brigadier who'd served in the Indian Army, Sam Boyce's a Group Captain, Alan McLelland-Brown's a former Squadron Leader and Laurie Jones's and Malcolm Dine's were Majors.

My nineteenth birthday came six days after arriving at Cranwell. Mum had sent me a fruit cake, soldered into an old cake tin. I broke open the tin with my bayonet and drew blood in the process. Undeterred, I used the bayonet to cut up the cake and gave slices to other Cadets in the barrack. The whole cake disappeared in minutes. Michael Heaney then admitted that his nineteenth birthday had been the day before. Later, I was to notice that 59A celebrated the birthdays of its members by lifting the birthday boy by his hands and legs and then bumping him onto the floor the appropriate number of times.

At the foot of each bed was a wooden locker. Like the rest of our kit, it was inspected regularly, so clothing in it had to be kept tidy. An orange card on the lid included the individual photo of the Cadet together with the Cadet's rank, name, number, entry, squadron and religion. We'd been asked on arrival to state our religion. Most of the Cadets said they were Church of England. This reminded me of one of the Goon Shows on the radio where Major Bloodnok asked Neddy Seagoon, 'Religion?' Neddy replied, 'Ahaaaaa,' as if he was being strangled. Major Bloodnok acknowledged by saying, 'C of E!' Four Cadets said they were Roman Catholics and several, like myself, said something else and were classified as 'ODs' (Other Denominations). Ron Chippindale said he was C of E and Jim Brown decided he was a Presbyterian.

One day, 59 Entry grabbed a member of 60 Entry who'd been reported by an RAF Regiment Sergeant as having long hair. This was 'Bolshevism' in their eyes, so they stripped the poor chap, put stripes of nugget all over him, dipped him in a cold bath, carried him into the barrack and paraded him as 'an example'. I think that 60 Entry was suitably impressed, but that didn't stop us from giving 59 Entry some cheek now and then when we thought we could get away with it.

On another occasion, 59 Entry insisted that all of 60 Entry put on an impromptu evening performance in the NAAFI. Ron, Jim and I decided to perform the haka made famous by the New Zealand rugby union team, the All Blacks: 'Ka mate! Ka mate! Ka Ora! Ka Ora! . . .' We shouted, gesticulated, stamped our feet and probably convinced everyone that we were a bunch of likeable savages as, much to our relief, we got a thumbs-up from 59 Entry. Some other members of 60 Entry weren't so lucky and were penalised.

Twice a week there were domestic evenings in the barrack, and as many semi-domestic evenings as were deemed necessary by the duty Leading Cadet of 59 Entry to maintain high standards of cleanliness. Domestic evenings involved shifting beds and lockers to one side of the barrack, sweeping the floor, spreading floor polish by flicking it from a tin with a stick, then shuffling up and down on our floor pads to polish the floor. These were great occasions to link arms and sing songs (often bawdy), most of which I'd never heard before. 59 Entry sang a song to the tune 'Old King Cole' that ended, 'There's none so fair as can compare with the boys of 59 Entry', but 60 Entry soon changed the wording to include only the boys of 60 Entry. An unprintable song (to the tune of 'The Red Flag') describing what would happen to all those who ordered us around, began, 'When Chiefee's dead, we'll raise a cheer, we'll sell the Block and buy some beer,' and finished with the words, 'A batman now can clean my brass, I am a Flight Cadet at last.' That was something we all felt couldn't come soon enough as we carefully carried the beds and lockers over to the other side and polished the rest of the floor.

Meantime, there was dusting to do, the foyer to be scrubbed, mats shaken out, and the ablutions to be cleaned. The water at Cranwell was very hard and when mixed with soap left a disgusting scum in the hand basins, baths and showers. A brass strainer in the urinals had to be taken out, washed, dried and polished. Sometimes a few Cadets would parade this on the end of a mop as the centrepiece of a mock ceremonial parade along the barrack. When all the jobs had been completed, 59 Entry would inspect the barrack before one of the Senior Entry or an Officer carried out a further inspection.

Semi-domestic evenings weren't so time consuming. Beds and lockers weren't usually moved, but 59 Entry might decide near lights out that the barrack had to be brought up to standard, and we all had to lend a hand. Nobody liked domestic and semi-domestic evenings! I wondered – if this was supposed to be the life of an ordinary airman, why did airmen join the RAF? One day, a Flight Cadet laying down the law to us said, 'It's necessary in this place to take to wine or women, or it'll get you down.' I thought differently.

Members of 60 Entry were issued with cheque-books by the College bank so that wages could be drawn by cheque. Ron and I had a problem, as authority for payment to us hadn't arrived from RNZAF Headquarters in London. We were given permission to draw up to £5 from the bank pending arrival of the authority. We were a bit peeved when we found out that the Pakistani Cadets were being paid £1 10s. per day, whereas we were paid 11s. 8d. per day and could only draw 7s. per day, the same as the RAF Cadet's rate of pay. The Pakistanis, however, had no guarantee as we did of a permanent commission on graduation. Mess bills were automatically taken from our wages each week, including a 2s. 6d. compulsory saving, a library fee and a contribution to the RAF Benevolent Fund. Unfortunately, there were always additional expenses to reduce further our meagre wages. Nothing was charged, however, for sending clothes to a laundry each Tuesday.

I wrote to Sqn. Ldr. Furlong in London to try and resolve the pay problem. I'd used up my £5 advance, cashed a Bank of New Zealand cheque and shown Sqn. Ldr. Furlong's reply to the Adjutant before the pay authorisation was found in East Camp, almost two months after I'd arrived at the College!

60 Entry was also issued with the College Calendar for the Summer Term. This was a most useful little booklet as it listed arrangements for each day, e.g. parades of various types, sporting fixtures, College drill and sporting competitions, visits to the College, guest nights, examinations, the reviewing officer for the end of term graduation parade and leave dates. I was thrilled to read that Her Royal Highness The Princess Elizabeth, Duchess of Edinburgh, was to be the next reviewing officer on her first visit to Cranwell. The booklet also contained useful information such as telephone numbers, an outline for one's personal weekly timetable, and provisional dates for future terms. In regard to the latter, I was intrigued to see that there was no Winter Term, the terms being:

Summer Term: 1 May – 1 August
Autumn Term: 11 September – 14 December
Spring Term: 8 January – 9 April.

I carried the Calendar everywhere and made a lot of use of it.

On completion of the Early Training Programme, 60 Entry began a regular Weekly Programme of Instruction (Appendix IV).

Each day began with drill. Cecil Da Silva was often in trouble for being late on parade. He'd still have kit all over his bed at parade time and once, when F/S Harvey called the roll and Da Silva wasn't present, a wag replied, 'He's still polishing da silva.' F/S Harvey hounded us unmercifully under the watchful eyes of at least three officers. Flt. Lt. Hudson of the RAF Regiment would stand with his arms back and slightly out from his sides, his chin forward under a hat well down on his head and, in a sinister voice, say to some poor unfortunate, 'Cadet, get that cap on straight.' Jim was given extra drill for looking down when he'd made an about turn, and the Adjutant told Ron to try harder. I wondered when my turn would come! I was soon 'mentioned in despatches', i.e. my name was put into the daily orders on the Block 77 notice-board as having an untidy foot locker.

A rumour spread that F/S Harvey had been a Warrant Officer, but had accepted a demotion so as to become the NCO in charge of Junior Entries. He was a Member of the British Empire and well respected by Cadets, even if we didn't relish his early morning drill. His commands were adopted as catch phrases by Cadets. Everything became 'like geezed lightning' after he'd told us when saluting to, 'Cut your hand away to your side like geezed lightning.' Another command that tickled our fancies was, 'When I say lean your rifles against that wall, then lean your rifles against that wall; right, lean your rifles against that wall.'

Twice a week we went to the workshops. These looked most interesting places with two Meteors, a Vampire, a Spitfire, a Hurricane and several Miles Kestrels and Masters in various stages of disassembly. Each aircraft had had an accident and could be used for practising riveting etc. Initially, however, 60 Entry had to acquire basic metal and wood working skills by making rather useless lamp shades and stands out of metal and wood. This was no problem for the ex-apprentices and those like me who'd done such things before, but it was frustrating not being able to work on the aircraft in the main part of the workshops. Later in the term we began working on Gipsy Minor and Rolls-Royce Merlin engines.

We started flying in lumbering Anson 21 aircraft to get air experience, local area familiarisation, and learn map reading and log keeping. With all our flying gear over our normal clothing, we sweated on the ground, but appreciated the extra clothing in the draughty Anson when airborne. One clumsy Cadet pulled the rip-cord of his chest parachute when struggling to get it and his navigation equipment into the aircraft.

On my first flight, I made sure of getting in first to sit beside the pilot, Fg. Off. W.D.C. Pratt, and so got a marvellous view of Sleaford and Grantham, the long straight of the old Roman road Ermine Street, and the Cranwell satellite airfields of Barkston Heath and Spitalgate. The English countryside seemed to be a maze of roads, railways, villages, trees and small fields that usually disappeared into the murk towards the horizon. The other four Cadets on board sat in positions behind me, each with a work table and basic instruments, but their view out of the side windows was limited by the low wing of the aircraft. On two subsequent flights when seated at one of these rather claustrophobic positions, I was airsick when the Anson flew through turbulent air. I had to clean up the mess afterwards and get used to the rubbery smell of an oxygen mask and other smells peculiar to aircraft. The

Anson wasn't easy to land, and often there'd be several bounces before the aircraft was safely on the ground.

A lot of lecture room time was utilised in learning to operate the slide rules with which we'd been issued. The practice I'd had on board ship came in useful. Wg. Cdr. W.F. Beckwith, OBE, the Senior Tutor Aeronautical Science and Engineering, became my private tutor in Mathematics and was of great help to me. English and Geography were subjects that I could readily relate to, but I had to do a lot of work in Meteorology, Electricity, Navigation and Aeroscience, though in the last my model aeroplane experience came in handy.

Ground Combat Training was rather a bore as we had to put on web equipment over our battledress, or get into battle order. The latter comprised carrying a rifle and wearing a steel helmet covered with green netting, denim overalls, a camouflage leather sleeveless jacket, anklets, and a small back pack containing a full water flask, mess tin, spare boot laces and socks, rain cape, and web equipment including ammunition pouches in which there were ten drill rounds. Then we would stand around learning field craft and how to defend an airfield, or lie on grass that was often wet and strip, assemble, load and unload our rifles. Some visiting Press Correspondents and civilians from the Air Ministry watched us one day doing manoeuvres and charging with rifles and fixed bayonets near the airfield control tower. Afterwards, F/S Harvey told us to 'get our skids on' to bring our equipment up again to inspection standard in case the visitors called at our barrack. From time to time we were taken to the rifle range to practise target shooting.

When we weren't doing GCT, our Squadron Commanders or the Adjutant of Junior Entries lectured us and showed us films. We were told the history of RAF Cranwell from the time it was originally established as a Royal Naval Air Service training station, how the College Arms had been developed from those of the de Cranewell family discovered in the village church in the seventeenth century, that the College was for all British subjects (including those from the Dominions), and the College motto 'Superna Petimus' was roughly translated as 'We seek things that are above'. The history was supplemented by a film and I was interested to see former Cadets doing things that I'd been experiencing. Other films included *Presentation of the King's Colour*, ones on field craft on which we were questioned afterwards, and popular films such as *Dangerous Journey*.

These Squadron Commander periods also included lectures on customs of the Service, leadership, discipline, *esprit de corps*, self-respect, significance of a commission, Air Force law and administration, and many other things that 'officers and gentlemen' should know.

We were given all sorts of miscellaneous information such as: cars and motor bikes were permitted from the fourth term onwards, but bicycles weren't allowed at the College until we became Senior Entry. Also, we'd be in a compulsory boxing tournament before the end of the term. This filled me with dread. I wondered how the RAF could reconcile boxing with the risk of possible eye injuries and concussion. Cadets didn't wear protective headgear and mouth guards. The purpose, apparently, was to see if we had any guts, fighting spirit, moral fibre or some such. Finally, we had to write a thesis before graduating. If a language like Russian had been taken in one's spare time, then half of the thesis was expected to be in that language.

I thought I was reasonably fit, but found the physical training hard going. Our instructors, the tall, wiry W/O Smith, MBE, and the well muscled Sgts. Free and Bendelow, seemed to believe that where there was no pain, there was no gain. They had us doing press-ups and the like until somebody collapsed. Then they would have us hold our positions until the unfortunate Cadet was able to resume the exercise. Sweating profusely, we'd be rushed into the swimming pool next door where we'd do backward flips off the high and low boards, practise for our RAF swimming proficiency certificates and receive instruction in life saving, before dressing quickly and marching off, still sweating heavily.

I was a section (or set) leader from time to time and had to lead by example and hurry the other Cadets along. Set leader's responsibilities included marching his set between lectures, giving the order 'Eyes Right (or Left)' and saluting every officer we passed. (Many a NCO driving past was startled by a salute when mistaken for an officer!) We also had to report to lecturers Cadets who were absent. When not in sets, Cadets still had to form up in groups and march everywhere, one of the Cadets taking on the job of being the group leader. Straggling wasn't permitted.

All these activities made us hungry and thirsty, so when the NAAFI van came to certain parts of West Camp mid-morning and mid-afternoon with tea, 'fly pies', raspberry slices and the like, we usually bought some refreshments. I wasn't used to drinking tea, let alone strong tasting, orange coloured tea that looked as if it'd been made from the NAAFI girls' orange coloured make-up, but I drank it because it was wet and I was thirsty.

I decided to take up gliding as a major sport that term, and helped move the gliders out of their hangar onto the south airfield, prepare them for flight, retrieve those that had landed, and generally make myself useful. There was little else I could do at first as one of the Sedburgh T21B two seater trainers had been pranged and other Entries had priority in getting the available flights. The other gliders were single seater Kirby Cadet 2, Slingsby Prefect and Grunau Baby gliders, and a two seater Kranich sailplane. The gliders were winched up to about 800 or 1,000 feet and were able to do aerobatics and other manoeuvres before completing a circuit and landing. Unfortunately, gliding took all afternoon and night was usually falling before the gliders were returned to their hangar. I soon learned to dress warmly when gliding.

Two months after arriving at the College, I had my first flight in a T21B glider with Flt. Lt. A.A. Pearce. He showed me how to do turns, stalls and other manoeuvres before letting me go solo after six flights and 21 minutes total gliding time. I was solo in a Cadet 2 for just two minutes. How quiet glider flying was! What freedom there seemed to be! I landed safely having done everything correctly, feeling a great sense of elation. Other flights followed and I qualified for the A and B Gliding Certificates issued by the Royal Aero Club.

I was getting used to Prentices and Harvards flying overhead most days and nights, but I was always on the look-out for aircraft I'd never seen before. One day, a Wellington bomber landed then took off again – an aircraft I thought was obsolete. Other aircraft I saw flying overhead were Devon communications aircraft and Lincoln, Lancastrian, Washington and Canberra bombers.

The stone wall around the south airfield had holes and patches in it, apparently where aircraft had crashed through. Reg Bailey proudly showed some of us in 60A a newspaper photo of himself beside an aero club light plane after he'd made a successful forced landing in it in deteriorating weather. Then I heard that Pete Anstee of 60C had been in a Valetta crash in Denmark in which the pilot had been killed. The rumour circulated that 30 per cent of Cranwell graduates who went on to jet aircraft lost their lives. This was hard to believe, but it was the start of a conditioning process that affected us all.

I discovered that Jack Henderson, like me, played the bagpipes. He'd worked his passage by ship from New Zealand to Britain and had had quite a tough time. This continued at Cranwell where he took ill, then, in a general fight in B Squadron barrack, Jim Brown's bayonet was accidentally stuck in Jack's knee. Colin Loveday told me that he'd done some 50 hours of Tiger Moth flying in New Zealand before doing twelve months of training at an FTS on the Isle of Man. He'd a dry skin condition and wasn't allowed to go swimming. Though the other New Zealanders at the College (Parfitt and Powell) had called to see me, I'd few opportunities to get to know them.

Every fortnight, the OD padre's hour was held at 1800 hours in the Adjutant's office at Block 77. Jim Brown told me that he enjoyed having a good argument with the OD padre, the Rev. J.M. Milne, MA, BD, as the padre knew what he was talking about and didn't say 'because it says so in the Bible'. The room was stuffy and invariably we Cadets were tired and could hardly keep our eyes open. On Sundays, the Rev. Milne would preach his sermons with his head down most of the time while standing to one side of a lectern. What he was actually doing was reading his notes on the lectern out of the corners of his eyes. Jim and I were occasionally able to meet up with the New Zealand apprentices Allan Carter and Keith Smith at church and exchange information on what had been happening since we were last able to talk together. Talking to erks (as they were called in the RAF) was rather frowned upon, much to my surprise, so our conversations were usually brief.

Each month, Flt. Lt. Woods and F/S Harvey met with 59 and 60 Entries to hear complaints about messing and other Junior Entries matters. Fresh fruit was scarce at the Junior Mess. Jam was provided infrequently, so Cadets were allowed to buy their own and keep it in a cupboard at the Mess. There was usually plenty of margarine at breakfast time when Cadets had little time to eat it, but only a cubic inch of butter for each person at other meals. When I told Mum that wartime food rationing still existed in Britain, she sent me parcels of all sorts of goodies – so much food in fact that I sent some to the Rundles and the Wickendens.

The monthly conference was also used by the Adjutant to convey information. He told us that the College was being reorganised because accommodation had become so acute. The main College building would house the top three Entries. Other Flight Cadets would be in Daedalus House on the western edge of Cranwell (known as 'Dead Loss' House), and in Blocks 78, 79 and 80 – after they'd been converted into individual rooms and batmen's accommodation. New entries would move into the nearby airmen's hut lines until Block 77 could also be converted. The NAAFI would become the Junior Mess and the hut lines between Block 77 and Camp Road would be replaced by lawn. He also told us that the College halls and passages were about to be repainted (white ceilings and stippled olive green walls), and there'd be no mid-term break, but Cadets who lived in the area could go home for the weekend and those who remained at Cranwell wouldn't have to go to church.

Work began for the 60 Entry inter-squadron drill competition. F/S Harvey would drill us each morning for forty minutes at a stretch with no stand at ease or stand easy. Each row was given a turn at being the front row, and consequently was given closer attention. We had to take off our belts so that the cleanliness of the webbing and brasses could be inspected, and lift up our boots so that the polished instep and the condition of the sixteen hobnails and heel plate could be noted. Squadrons were 'volunteered' for extra drill in the evenings. A metronome was used to help our timing. Rifles had to be lowered to the ground noiselessly, but struck hard with the hands in other manoeuvres. Dropping a rifle to the ground usually meant a ruined finish to one's boots. Rifle bolts had to be uplifted from the Orderly Room each time we used rifles.

F/S Harvey swore at us and threatened to chase us around the parade ground or leave the square if our drill didn't improve. We wished he would!

Instead, Cadets who'd offended him had to run around the edge of the square with their rifles at the high port. The feeling was that if someone hadn't been clagged for a while, then the Adjutant and Flight Sergeant would make sure they found something wrong. I was clagged for having a loose rifle sling and dirty brass. 60 Entry received a compliment, however, from our RAF Regiment instructor in GCT, F/S Nicholas, who said ours was the best Entry on drill that he'd seen in Junior Entries.

Kit inspections became more frequent. The warmer weather meant that bulling often became an outdoor activity – sometimes while watching cricket on the grass in the centre of the Orange. A joke went the rounds – a bull fighter was heard to say when a huge bull came rushing at him, 'I haven't seen so much bull since I was in the Air Force.' We were issued with ceremonial hats with shiny peaks and the usual white bands around the base of the hats. We had to wear these hats for several days to get used to them, instead of the normal field service caps. F/S Harvey told me to shave up to the top of my ears as sideboards weren't permitted. All Cadets had perfected tying a half Windsor tie without looking in the full length mirror at the barrack door, but we had to get used to brushing each other down before going on parade. Some Cadets would damp their ties and trousers before placing them in a blanket and sleeping on them. I found this to be a most effective way of pressing, provided I didn't toss about too much at night.

60 Entry was taken to watch the Assistant Commandant's ceremonial parade at the College parade ground. The parade was most impressive with about three hundred Flight Cadets parading in officer pattern uniforms with rifles, white belts, bayonet frogs and rifle slings, accompanied by the RAF band located at the College. The inspection took ages while Gp. Capt. W.H. Kyle, CBE, DSO, DFC, ADC, and party, preceded by two orderlies, slow marched along each row. Roman Catholics and Jews were ordered to fall out. (I wasn't aware of any Jews at the College. Muslims and the like were quite overlooked!) The Roman Catholics and Jews came to attention, took one pace backward and stood at ease. One of the padres then read prayers. Presumably the Roman Catholics and Jews didn't listen! They were fallen in again, and the squadrons marched past in quick and slow time, before advancing in review order. There was a general salute, and the squadrons marched off. The parade took about one and a half hours. I thought it a pity that so few people saw such a spectacle.

Then there was the King's Birthday ceremonial. 60 Entry watched the King's Colour being marched on parade, the officers and their clinking medals, and the Union Jack being raised and saluted. We all gave the King three cheers, following a carefully practised drill. Standing in the cool air left us stiff and cold so, when the parade was over, we were told to run on the spot and bang our hands on our knees to warm up. The afternoon was free, but we had to keep out of the barrack as we were expected to play or watch sport such as the athletics tournament at the stadium between the Royal Air Force College Cranwell, the Royal Military Academy Sandhurst and the Royal Naval College Greenwich. Our sporting activities each Wednesday, Saturday and Sunday afternoon had to be recorded on the Block 77 notice-board.

Private study was almost impossible in the barrack, so Hut 198 was used for that purpose and also for ironing. There were some easy chairs in the hut and quite often Cadets could be seen sitting fast asleep instead of studying. The pressure on Cadets was such that most of us had great difficulty in keeping awake during lectures, even though the subjects being taught were of great interest. Some desks in the lecture rooms had carved into them the outlines of girls, aircraft and lists such as, '2 years 1 month to graduation', '58 days to go to Easter', or '4 days to grad, wacko Joan, what'll we do'! The sudden whoosh of a jet aircraft overhead helped keep us awake and had us all looking out of the windows.

Cadets began to fall sick. Colin Loveday went into Station Sick Quarters with glandular fever, developed complications and was away a month and a half, returning just before the end of term. Jim Brown got a boil in his ear, had trouble with his eyes and just about fainted on parade. He was put into Sick Quarters. At one stage about six of 59A and 60A ended up in Sick Quarters or were on light duties.

I caught a cold and struggled for several days with swollen glands before reporting sick. The College Medical Officer, Sqn. Ldr. R.E. Woolley, GM, said my temperature was high and immediately put me in dock – the first time I'd been in hospital since being born. I slept for much of the six days I was there, except when woken by the nursing sister for the doctor's rounds, and by an orderly to have medicine and food. I rapidly lost my suntan. During my stay, I was surprised to see a Flight Cadet ask two orderlies to buy some beer for him and be given it.

One good thing to come from being sick was that I missed the 60 Entry inter-squadron drill competition and the final preparations beforehand. I heard that B Squadron won, with A Squadron second and C Squadron third. Sam Boyce of 60A fainted on parade because of too tight a hat. A Squadron won the inspection. I came out of Sick Quarters, annoyingly weak, and a day later was violently sick, having picked up a bug from other sick Cadets or food poisoning.

I was immediately into the 60 Entry Drill Qualification Parade. This was held in a hangar because of rain. The hangar was noisy and the floor slippery. Wg. Cdr. J.D. Blois, RAF Regiment and ex-Guardsman, was the chief judge. His inspection was far less rigorous than I'd expected. He tried to put a finger down between my back and belt to check how tight the latter was. I wondered what would've happened if I'd expanded my stomach and trapped his finger! He said our turnout was the best he'd seen for some time. F/S Harvey was attending his father's funeral in Ireland, so F/S Nicholas took us for the thirty minutes of drill. We were kept on our toes by slightly different commands such as, 'Flight will turn to the left in threes, about turn.' We'd worked up a good sweat by the time we were told that all but eight Cadets and one still in Sick Quarters had passed. I breathed a sigh of relief, not having to be retested.

60 Entry was now considered to be good enough to join the rest of the College in preparations for the Ferris Trophy inter-squadron drill competition and in the march-pasts after church. Following one church parade, we came back to the barrack to find some of our kit strewn over our beds. Someone had been poking around to see what was not up to scratch. We got the message and did a little extra bulling. Another preparation for the Ferris was the issue of officer pattern shoes and gloves, and a first fitting of our officer pattern uniforms.

59A began waging a campaign against members of 60A alleged to be bolshie. They started on Gordon Grierson, claiming he kept others awake at night. He'd been on jankers so much that he often hadn't finished his bulling by lights out and had to get up early next morning to do so. With hats on back to front, 59A formed a guard of honour and dunked Gordon in a cold bath. He didn't struggle, although those who did always got a bigger cheer afterwards. Three other members of 60A were stripped naked and forced to run around the outside of Block 77. This was too much for 60A, so someone tipped a fire bucket of water over Pete Redman, the boxing champion of 59 Entry. Luckily, a general war was prevented by a Flight Cadet who happened to be passing.

Venturing into other squadrons was sometimes hazardous. Michael Heaney went into C Squadron, but was set upon, lost his tweeds out of the window and had to recover them and his underpants from almost inaccessible places. As a result, the ringleader from 60C, Ramsay Brown, was lured into the ground floor ablutions, stripped and dunked in a bath. This was considered to be all good fun.

During a cold period that summer, we New Zealanders had to be careful and not say too much about the weather, like, 'Oh, to be in New Zealand, now that winter's there.' Ron made one such remark and ended up being painted with blanco. We also had to keep away from New Zealand collo-quialisms such as, 'it's a fair cow' (it's a jolly nuisance), 'joker' (fellow), 'sand-shoes' (plimsolls) and 'don't be wet' (don't be stupid).

I was transferred from cleaning the ablutions each morning to cleaning the Junior Mess. This involved waiting until most Cadets had finished breakfast, then hurriedly cleaning the tables, seats and floor and (being a member of A Squadron), turning a bust of Goering in the Mess to face the wall, as members of B Squadron used to turn it around again. In addition, Gordon Grierson and I had a fortnight of cleaning out the orderly room each evening.

Then the dreaded first term boxing was upon us. I'd got in two lots of practice beforehand instead of watching inter-squadron cricket, but I wasn't at all confident of performing well in front of the Commandant, officers, and the rest of the College who'd be screaming for blood. All Cadets were weighed and given cursory examinations of hands, teeth and mouths. Hammy and Joe claimed that as Muslims, they were fasting and couldn't box, but they were considered to be skiving, having been seen eating when most Cadets weren't around. On arriving at the gym at 1730 hours, I found the programme had me listed as a welterweight fighting Alan McLelland-Brown of 60A, the eighteenth of twenty-two contests. We'd been told that pairing was according to weight, height and ability. Nine of 60 Entry weren't listed in the tournament, but seven of 59 Entry had been included. I sat in a daze watching the slaughter − some contestants were evenly matched, but other fights were very lop-sided. Ron lost to Ramsay Brown, but Jim beat Tony Whitwam.

Someone called my name. My second, Sgt. Free, tied a red sash around my waist. I climbed into the flood-lit ring hardly aware of the sea of faces beyond, touched gloves with McLelland-Brown, waited for the bell, then attacked him with all my might. He hit me on the jaw. I saw stars, blinked, and with renewed fury, hit back. The referee, Flt. Lt. J.C. Woods, stepped in front of me. I tried to brush him aside, then saw that McLelland-Brown was flat on his back! I couldn't believe it! I'd actually knocked him down! He got to his feet and we resumed boxing. He staggered and almost fell trying to avoid me in a corner. The bell rang. I felt sick, gasping for breath. Sgt. Free loosened my sash and told me that, as a southpaw, I should move to my right, let McLelland-Brown lead with his right then hit him with my left. The second round seemed to last for ages before the bell finally rang. Gasping, McLelland-Brown and I touched gloves again. The referee collected the judge's decisions and declared me the winner! I was thankful I'd survived, hoping I'd shown the moral fibre required. The only trophy presented was to the gamest loser, Ron Edwards of 60B, who was completely outclassed by Pete Redman of 59A.

Next day, I was all aches and pains from the boxing, but some of the other Cadets were in much worse shape. Some further inoculations didn't help. Then F/S Harvey gave me a bollocking because he didn't know where I was (I'd been gliding, but my name hadn't been on the gliding detail). He wanted to give me a new magazine for my rifle. My Squadron Commander had got new magazines from the manufacturer to give A Squadron an advantage in the Ferris inter-squadron drill competition. We were back into drill with a vengeance and hours were spent bulling our equipment. The Squadron stood at attention for forty-five minutes while Sqn. Ldr. Thomas minutely inspected about two-thirds of the rifles. He told me I'd polished my rifle bolt too much! We practised endlessly, slow marching in open order – not an easy thing to do with about thirty persons in each of the three rows. 60 Entry began doing rifle drill wearing leather gloves.

Our officer pattern uniforms were delivered by Burberrys just before the Ferris. The tunics had patch pockets at the front below the waist and a single vent at the rear, whereas those of 59 Entry and Flight Cadets had no such pockets and two vents. A patch of blue barathea could be hooked onto the left shoulder to protect the uniform when carrying a rifle at the slope. Small white patches (known as gorgets) with a piece of cord down the centre in our squadron colours were sewn onto the lapels. The hats had the distinctive white band around them. Sqn. Ldr. Thomas inspected us in our new uniforms and, noting that my jacket was too loose at the waist and required tucks at the side to stop it crinkling under my white webbing belt, said, 'I hope you fill out soon, Hancock.'

When the day of the Ferris competition arrived, 60A went to the west end of the College via the Orange to protect our boots from damage on a rougher, more direct route. We waited for our Squadron Commander, arms out from our sides away from our webbing, holding our rifle muzzles so as not to spoil the spit and polished wooden panels. Sqn. Ldr. Thomas again inspected us for forty-five minutes while D Squadron (the Equipment and Secretarial Cadets from RAF Digby) were on parade. Even fingernails and handkerchiefs were inspected. Two batmen accompanied the Squadron Leader to give a final polish to our boots and brush our uniforms when told to do so.

We were reminded of the names, decorations and units of the visiting judges of the competition as we might be asked them during the parade. For the inspection, there'd be Major W.J. Evetts, MC, Royal Scots Fusiliers, and Company Sergeant Major W.J. Amour, Grenadier Guards. For the drill there'd be Major V.F. Erskine Crum, CIE, MC, Royal Scots Guards, and Regimental Sergeant Major J.C. Lord, MC, Grenadier Guards. We were also expected to know the names and decorations of College officers and the make and serial number of our rifles!

We marched on parade and I noted out of the corners of my eyes the red sashes, swords, leather belts, tartan trews, riding breeches and leggings of the Army team. Another long inspection followed. Fortunately, I wasn't asked any awkward questions, but the cold weather took its toll. I got cramp and pins and needles in my right hand gripping my rifle. In the drill, a Cadet dropped his bayonet. Another didn't secure his bayonet properly and, on sloping arms, it went flying over someone's head. A rifle magazine fell out. We knew that points were being rapidly lost and tried to do better in the march pasts. One of the visitors checked us with a pace stick.

At last it was all over. We were told that the order of Squadrons was, C, D, A and B, and the general standard of turnout was so high that no individual commendations would be given as on previous occasions. I heard that Jim had fainted on sloping arms, knocked himself about a bit and only came to after being carried into the College. That would have affected B Squadron's result. A Flight Cadet had even less luck when he fainted, as he hit his head and became dangerously ill, his life being saved by an emergency airlift to an Oxfordshire hospital.

But there was no respite. 59 Entry began end of term examinations while 60 Entry had some tests. I struggled with Aeroscience problems such as: 'A fighter aircraft weighing 8,000 pounds is fitted with four cannons each of which fires 600 rounds per minute with a muzzle velocity of 3,000 feet per second. If each round weighs a quarter of a pound and if all the recoil is taken by the aircraft, what is the loss in speed that the aircraft would experience in a five second burst of fire?'

For several weeks, 59 and 60 Entries had extra physical training in the evenings. As a result, I was one of the Cadets chosen to be part of the A Squadron team for the Knocker Cup inter-squadron gymnastics competition. Knocker practice replaced early morning drill, but having this as well as the usual PT later in the day made things rather strenuous for us. Under grey skies, the Knocker Competition went reasonably well on the parade ground, with the College band merrily playing 'Hi ho, hi ho, it's off to work we go . . .' A Squadron made few errors in the horse and mat exercises and won the Cup. Junior Entries then put on a PT display, to which the Commandant responded in his classy accent, 'A jolly good show, chaps.'

Resurfacing of the Orange parade ground in preparation for the end of term graduation meant that, for a time, parades were held elsewhere. One such parade was the ceremonial held in Hangar 30. The parade was shambolic. The inclusion of D Squadron in the restricted space, the noise of wind and rain, and echos causing difficulties in hearing commands, were factors in this. Reg Bailey dropped his rifle (he got three days jankers for that), some watches and bayonet scabbards were dropped, and a Flight Cadet managed to cut himself above his right eye with his bayonet when unfixing bayonets.

The Adjutant and F/S Harvey decided to give us a full kit inspection. This involved piling all our kit onto our beds, then pulling out the right things when called and showing our service number on the articles. I couldn't find a collar, and Flight Sergeant marked me as being 'deficient' in this. Sam Boyce had decided that the drawers, cellular, with which we'd been issued were so awful that he'd used his for spit and polishing work. When F/S

Harvey saw them covered in nugget, he ordered Sam to buy some more. I never wore my drawers, cellular, and eventually threw them away.

F/S Harvey also decided to have a tidy up and, without my permission, threw out a box of New Zealand magazines I'd been keeping in Hut 203. He'd already grumbled, 'You New Zealanders need a special bag for all the mail you get,' and had threatened in daily orders that, on a lot of matters, 'strong disciplinary action will be taken . . .' so I couldn't complain too much.

He knew that 59 Entry, having finished their exams, were planning a booze-up in Sleaford and an end of term rag, so he warned them, 'Don't throw people out of the front windows of the Block as I've got flowers planted along there – only out the back please.' Perhaps he had a sense of humour after all!

60 Entry changed into PT gear and aircrew sweaters in preparation for the coming scuffle. Lockers were closed and some of the new beds we'd been issued with were tied to the water-pipes on the walls. When a great noise began upstairs, 60A tried to find out what was going on, but some of 59 Entry were blocking the foyer and stairs. 60A got out of the windows (not thinking of the Flight Sergeant's flowers), came in the front and back doors of the Block and tried forcing a path upstairs. Someone above upset fire buckets and water flowed down into the foyer and barrack rooms. Cadets from both Entries were thrown out of the Block and a truce was called.

As the damage was being assessed, another scuffle began and every bed of 60A was overturned from the door up to my bed. A Cadet from 60C was held down in the fray and had some sort of fit. When this was realised, a medical orderly was called and the Cadet was taken off to Station Sick Quarters for overnight observation. Some Flight Cadets going night flying came into the Block and told everyone to 'wrap up, de-digitate and tidy up'. So the fire buckets were refilled, the stairs and floors dried, the barrack floor polished and everyone returned to normal.

Next morning, we heard that one of the Flight Cadets who'd stopped the fray had successfully force-landed a Harvard wheels up on a road during night flying. I heard nothing more about the accident, but seeing Harvards flying around with only one wheel down was not uncommon.

Also, the 59 Entry Duty Cadet was on the mat (as he should've kept order the night before and hadn't put in a report about the fit), together with the Leading Cadets from 60A and C (as the fit had occurred in A Squadron, and the Cadet was from C Squadron). The Adjutant told everyone off and both Entries were confined to barracks the following day – a Sunday. This seemed a lenient punishment. 59 Entry breathed a sigh of relief as their booze-up in Slush (Sleaford) was that Saturday night.

Many of 59A were worse for wear after their end of term function, but not Pete Organ. He was a ponderous chap who kept to himself and didn't get too involved in such things. He was a devout member of the Church of England, who actually played the organ, and who came in for some teasing because he knelt to pray and cross himself before getting into bed each night. I had to admire him for that.

The weather became warmer and we were allowed to wear Short Sleeve Order, which meant no battledress top, sleeves rolled up and no braces. Our trousers were held up by our airmen pattern best blue uniform belts which were tightened sufficiently and then turned inside out so that the brass buckles didn't show.

GCT was often held out of doors. We'd lie on the grass trying to concentrate on the stripping and assembly of a Sten machine carbine, while overhead, invisible aircraft weaved long white contrails all over the blue sky. F/S Nicholas (who we called Chiefee Nic) got exasperated with us one day when teaching us the correct order of stripping a Sten gun.

'What do you do next?' he asked. No one answered.

'What do you do before you shave each day?' he queried.

Wally Martin answered with a deadpan face, 'Make sure the water is hot, Flight Sergeant.'

'No, no, no,' Chiefee said. 'You take off your collar! Now, remove the collar of the Sten.'

We complied.

Firing a Sten at man-shaped targets was much more fun. This included single, repetition and automatic fire from the shoulder, and from the waist as we moved towards the targets. On one sultry day at the range, rain began to pour down. We finished the firing detail and got into the bus to return to the barrack, bemoaning the fact that our denims were soaking and the blanco on our webbing was ruined.

The GCT instructors like Flt. Lt. Hudson were very systematic in their lectures. A blackboard would have the instructor's name on it, plus the group being lectured and the subject. Sometimes irrelevant questions would be asked to wake us up. There'd be frequent recapitulations (a favourite word of the instructors), and finally the blackboard would be turned over to reveal a summary of the lecture. When giving commands, the instructor would usually look at his watch, then say slowly in a menacing way, 'When I say move . . .'

Ron, Jim and I had news that we could try flying in RAF and other service aircraft back to New Zealand during the coming leave period. We thought it was worth having a go (and I saw it as a good way to see Margaret Hornsey again), so we got the necessary permission and endured more inoculations, only to be told that all such passages east of Malta had been cancelled because the RAF was standing by in case British personnel had to be airlifted out of Persia.

One night after lights out, a rotten egg was thrown through an open window and smashed onto the foot locker of Malcolm Dines. The windows were instantly closed. Flight Cadets from the College and Daedalus House were thought to be attacking. For some time there'd been talk that 59 Entry wasn't tough enough with 60 Entry, so an attack by Flight Cadets after their last guest night of the term wasn't entirely unexpected. Chiefee Harvey and a Corporal Smith of the RAF Regiment who'd been sleeping upstairs, came around in their pyjamas and told everyone to get back into bed. A clod came through a partly closed window. We all got up again and peered out of the windows. Chiefee returned and said he didn't want any nonsense. After he'd left, there was a great crashing of dustbin lids from the foyer. Flight Cadets had got in through the ablution windows and were trying to force open the A Squadron door. Fortunately they didn't succeed as Reg Bailey had put his bed and a pile of foot lockers against the door.

The Flight Cadets then called out suggesting we join them in an attack on the annual Combined Cadet Forces camp – some eighty white bell tents, housing about five hundred cadets, erected on grass beside the stadium. We Cadets dressed and rushed outside. Just as the Senior Entry were briefing us on the attack, Chiefee Harvey appeared with a torch. Everyone ran for cover. Some Cadets went to attack the tents, whereas the rest of us were rounded up by Chiefee and kept in the barrack. I could hear thunderflashes going off and gradually the rest of the Cadets trickled back to the barrack. The College officers had anticipated an attack on the tents and were waiting in their cars. They'd switched on their car lights and caught many of the attackers. There were a few fights and some amazing escapes as security dogs were brought into the fray. Michael Heaney returned to the barrack through a window and lay fully clothed in bed, breathing heavily, having been chased by a dog, while Chiefee did another round of the barrack. Some Cadets went up drainpipes to get in upstairs windows. Sam Boyce was caught tiptoeing through the darkened foyer. Chiefee switched on the light and asked him where he'd been. Bob Cartwright and Julian Bowes returned through another window, but Chiefee came around again and wanted to know how they'd got in. There wasn't much sleep that night!

Next morning, the Adjutant had on the mat everyone whose name had been taken, but there was little that he could do about the previous night because the end-of-term graduation was imminent.

The College had been building up towards the graduation by having the Commandant's ceremonial parade (described afterwards as a 'wizard show'), a wet weather rehearsal in Hangar 30, and a graduation dress rehearsal. In the latter, Wg. Cdr. F.F. Fulton, OBE, TD, MA, Senior Tutor Humanistics, stood in for the reviewing officer, Princess Elizabeth. The band was fooled by the Wing Commander being in a different car than expected, so had to play the Royal fanfare twice. 60 Entry was given extra drill and had to prepare certain pieces of equipment for inspection each day prior to the graduation parade. A flagstaff on the Orange was removed and the Union Jack and the RAF ensign were flown from poles erected on the 'Admiral's Walk' part way up the College tower. A saluting platform and movie camera positions were set up on the Orange. Photos were taken of Squadrons, prize winners and sports teams. 59 Entry moved their kit to either the refurbished Block 78 or Daedalus House.

The graduation of Nos. 53 GD(P) and 4 E & S Entries came at last. The weather was glorious. As we waited to go on parade, a Flight Cadet looked at rifles leaning against a wall, pointed at one and said, 'Whose is that rifle?'

'Mine,' I said.

He promptly moved his rifle away from mine saying, 'You must be a finger boy having a rifle that good!'

I didn't think mine was all that good − rather, his could have done with some more bulling.

Princess Elizabeth looked delightful in her summery outfit as she arrived to a fanfare and Royal Salute, but I dared not look at her during her inspection. Her perfume carried in the air as she passed close in front of me. There was a slight booboo when the Officer Commanding the Cadet Wing, Wg. Cdr. M.D. Lyne, AFC, called the parade to 'attention' when we were already in that position. After the usual march pasts, advance in review order and another Royal Salute, the Princess made her address, congratulated us on our 'smartness and steadiness', and presented the Sword of Honour, King's Medal and Medal of Honour. The King's Colour was then slow marched into the College followed by the Senior Entry.

As soon as we were off parade, Ron, Jim and I looked for Air Cdre. Kay in the crowd on the Orange as we'd been told he'd come up from London. We failed to see him amongst the representatives of foreign armed forces, so went to have a look at the visiting aircraft on the south airfield. Later, we caught up with Air Cdre. and Mrs Kay on the Orange while the Senior Entry chatted with Princess Elizabeth and watched a flying display by three Vampires from No. 72 Squadron. The Princess was then farewelled. What an experience I'd had!

Three chartered buses waited outside Block 77, luggage having already been loaded. Somewhat light headed, I joined the other members of Junior Entries and left for Grantham railway station on six weeks leave, including a parachuting course at RAF Abingdon.

CHAPTER 5

Green on: Go

'NUMBER FOUR. Red on: stand at the door.' Sgt. A.W. Card shouted at me from beside the opening in the canvas wall of the gondola swinging below the gas filled balloon. I shuffled down the sloping floor towards the opening, followed closely by the last Cadet of the stick. I hung onto the tubular frame of the gondola and braced myself in the opening looking straight ahead, trying not to think about the 800 feet of nothing below me.

Wasn't one's whole life supposed to flash before the eyes at such a moment? I was in my sixth day of parachute training and had built up some confidence in my equipment and ability, but still, accidents do happen. Just before ascending in the gondola, I'd seen an Army parachutist break an ankle on landing heavily and be carted away in a blood wagon. Two other Cadets and Julian Bowes ahead of me had jumped and landed successfully. I could do the same, but . . .

Sgt. Card would have none of such day dreaming and startled me with, 'Did you know that the last New Zealander on a course was killed when he jumped?' He was full of such jokes – many of them unprintable. As an experienced despatcher, he prided himself with never having anyone balk at jumping. I knew his technique was to shout 'Go!' in the person's ear and simultaneously give a hearty clap on the back. The person was out in space before he could say 'Jack Robinson'. Nobody was ever pushed! A refusal to jump would have meant being sent away in disgrace and never being allowed on a parachute course again. He looked to see that Julian was clear of the dropping zone.

'Green on: go!' he shouted. I needed no clap on the back, but taking my life in my hands, jumped into space. I was very much aware of falling sheer for some three seconds. I could feel the static line attached to the gondola breaking the ties to my back parachute and the canopy began developing away from me. There was no noticeable shock of opening. Thank God I didn't have to use my chest parachute!

The Controller on the ground began talking to me through a loudspeaker. I started doing the flight drills such as making an all round observation, wriggling out of my seat straps so as to move more freely, and getting into a good parachuting posture. The ground came up increasingly fast. I pulled down on the front lift webs as ordered and, just before hitting the ground, was told to ease up on one of the lift webs. Judging wind drift, height above ground and moment of impact wasn't easy. I swung into the ground, did a parachute roll and skidded a little, knocking my rubber ring helmet partly over my eyes. I scrambled to my feet and ran around the parachute to deflate it before folding the parachute and reporting to the Controller.

I was elated! What was there to be nervous about? I would've gone up again and jumped a dozen more times. I'd survived my first jump!

Tea at 1630 hours interrupted events. I was so hungry! Before dinner at 1930 hours, I watched Ron Chippindale and Jim Brown make successful jumps, though hard landings. Later, the jumps by our course were reviewed. I had had a good exit and flight, but a not so good landing, having eased up on the wrong lift web. Comments on other chaps in the course included things like not keeping legs together and forgetting to turn the parachute release just prior to landing.

Ron, Jim and I had volunteered for the week long aircrew parachute course at No. 1 Parachute Training School, RAF Abingdon, because it seemed a fun thing to do during our leave, and some day in an emergency we might have to abandon an aircraft by parachute. (Fig. 18) We'd signed indemnity forms before leaving Cranwell and arrived at Abingdon railway station with masses of equipment that we'd been told would be needed on the course. We found out later that much of the equipment such as flying boots wasn't required. Some Cadets already on the station platform had made telephone calls to RAF Abingdon for transport (one call being put through to the Commanding Officer!). Three hours later, an RAF vehicle took us the two and a half miles to a very 1930s barrack block.

There was an enormous fireplace and chimney in the middle of each barrack. The floors were rough and dirty, and the ablutions old fashioned. Hospital style beds, nice sheets and two normal pillows seemed quite luxurious compared with Junior Entries at Cranwell. Upstairs, having finished their course, Sandhurst cadets were about to leave.

The parachute course was popular with Cranwell Cadets and Flight Cadets. We were treated as officers with airmen making our beds, and were served most meals in our own mess. Having four meals a day was new to me. During the course, we had to run everywhere in boots and this helped raise our level of fitness. Some of the College officers also participated, including the Junior Entries Adjutant, Flt. Lt. J.C. Woods.

We began with a tour of the station, introductory lectures and films, interspersed with practical work in the hangars – the fitting of back parachute harness, swinging in the harness from a high stand and exit drill from a door. Then we learned the parachute roll and practised this endlessly holding onto

suspended elastic straps before progressing to other apparatus. We jumped
from a platform at hangar roof height, our harness connected to a wire from
a winch and plywood fan. Air resistance to the fan helped break our fall. We
untangled rigging lines while suspended above the floor, ran up ramps to
practise left and right parachute rolls, and jumped off ladders from varying
heights while holding onto a long cable suspended some distance away.

The various techniques of collapsing parachutes were rehearsed outdoors.
Afterwards, the parachutes had to be carefully folded. Then we climbed a
lattice steel tower to a platform seventy-five feet above the ground. The
swaying of the tower when someone descended from it and the chilling air
hardly inspired our confidence. We were attached to a cable from an arm
above and to another cable held by people on the ground. On stepping out
into space, we were briefly suspended to practise the flight drills before
beginning our descent. When the brake to the cable above was released, the
people on the ground ran like mad pulling on the second cable, so providing

Figure 18. Author, Jim Brown and Ron Chippindale ready for parachuting at Abingdon,
August 1951.

the effect of wind drift to our landings. Flt. Lt. Woods, being rather hefty, bounced well on landing in the dirt. His fellow officers shouted encouragement – 'Good on you Timber,' and 'Well done Chippy.' Another of the officers with us crossed himself before he stepped off the tower. Somehow, we were glad to move onto other things.

Almost every day there was the opportunity to watch trainees parachuting from the huge, dark green, rather derelict looking tethered balloons. Hastings transport aircraft flew more advanced trainees to a dropping zone, often returning at dusk to land along a flare path. We couldn't wait to do our two jumps from a Hastings. When our turn came, there was the fitting of parachutes, jokes such as, 'If it doesn't work, bring it back,' waiting in the 'sweat box' or Crew Ready Room, practising in the aircraft getting into crash positions, and more waiting while an unserviceable radio was fixed. Airborne at last below rain cloud, the Hastings did a very tight circuit and landed. Only then did most of us realise that an engine had failed on take-off.

We went back to more films on parachuting and new apparatus in the hangar. One exercise was to jump up to a swinging frame and then release our grip and do a parachute roll on the mats below. The mats were like enlarged doormats and rather hard and rough until one got used to them. A development of this exercise was to be suspended in a harness below a frame which was then swung and lowered suddenly, so causing us to do a parachute roll on landing. Then there was aircraft drill in old fuselages, and going down a slide, the lower end of which was about five feet above the mats. Sgt. Card said this would help us if we had to jump from an eight foot wall to get into our girlfriend's place!

Unexpectedly, we had a free afternoon while the station was inspected by the Commanding Officer in preparation for the visit of Air Marshal Sir Aubrey B. Ellwood, KCB, DSC, Air Officer Commanding-in-Chief Transport Command. Airmen began painting everything that didn't move. I took the opportunity to photograph aircraft new to me – the Buckmaster, Bristol Freighter, Sea Fury trainer and Mosquito – until stopped by a Flight Lieutenant. Apparently, I should have declared my camera on arrival at the station! I was told to get permission from the air traffic controllers before taking photos on the tarmac, so I went to the control tower. Permission was declined, but the comment was made that if I did take photos, 'Don't get caught!' I had a close look at the many different types of aircraft and was allowed into a VIP version of the Vickers Viking.

Deteriorating weather and the C-in-C's visit extended the course into a second week. There was nothing much to do except repeat exercises and watch more training films.

Ron, Jim and I made the most of our two weekends and other free time by making several trips into the nearby town of Abingdon, and to Oxford

Figure 19. Author and Ron Chippindale boating on the Thames at Oxford, August 1951.

some seven miles away. Jim had forgotten to bring civilian clothes, so I lent him a suit and Ron lent a shirt and tie. In Oxford, we wandered along narrow footpaths gazing at the 'dreaming spires' and quadrangles of the University colleges and other ancient buildings as far as the Oxford University Press, before having a look in the Ashmolean Museum of Arts and Archaeology. Then, hiring a boat, we took turns to row slowly along the Thames and Cherwell Rivers, chasing swans, admiring the brightly painted barges used by the University boat crews, Magdalen College Tower and a swimming area, until stopped by a weir (Fig. 19). On some evenings we went to see films and the *Folies Bergère,* a saucy show the like of which couldn't be seen in New Zealand. Sometimes, bus timetables didn't coincide with our trips to and from RAF Abingdon, so we walked for miles along the narrow country roads singing every New Zealand song we could remember, sometimes at night using aircraft flying at the station to give us a sense of direction.

On other evenings, we filled in time by going to the station cinema, reading, playing two-up or cards, and being generally rowdy, tipping over as many beds as we could. Ron started smoking a skull-shaped pipe he'd bought in Wales. Cadets who went drinking and to dances in nearby towns would come into the barrack late at night and create merry hell. They put a fire bucket and a chair up the station flag pole, and lowered a pennant to half mast. Lights out was when the last person wanted to sleep.

To try and get in our scheduled parachute jumps, we were detailed for dawn or evening jumps, only to be told that there was too much wind, or there was a risk of static electricity for balloon jumps, or the cloud base was too low for an aircraft drop. We were given the task of polishing the rough floor of the barrack, making bed packs and attending the dress rehearsal parade for the C-in-C's visit. The C-in-C eventually inspected us in the barrack and later looked in on us as we did some more fan jumps in the hangar.

There was little more for us to do afterwards except to hand in our parachuting equipment, listen to the farewell address of the Commanding Officer, receive badges from the Irvin Company whose parachutes we'd used, and depart in the rain, rather disappointed that we'd been unable to complete our second balloon jump and two aircraft jumps. The RNZAF, however, later awarded Ron and me Parachutist Badges without Wings.

I'd been invited to stay four days with an old school friend at Bristol. Alan Wilkie had left Waimataitai School for Britain years earlier, but we'd kept in touch. He was just as I remembered him – tall, gawkish, with a mop of frizzy red hair, freckles and a beaked nose. He was studying to enter Bristol University and become a surveyor. Much to my surprise, I found he was about to attend a young Communists' rally in Berlin (though he claimed he wasn't a Communist), and we'd have only a day together. There being limited space in the Wilkies' apartment, I was accommodated for the first night in a nearby boarding house.

The next day, Alan took me out to lunch and, after discussing old times, talked about drama, the arts, and famous places that he'd been to in Britain and Europe. He then hired a chauffeur to take us on a whirlwind drive around Bristol. We saw St Mary Radcliffe Church, Colston School, the Theatre Royal, a leaning church tower, Wine Street, The Nails outside the Corn Exchange, Wesley Chapel, the Red Lodge, Ladies Mile, the centre of Quakerism, Landoger Trow Inn, Bristol Cathedral and the Clifton Suspension Bridge. We stopped and explored many of these places.

Alan then left on his sponsored trip to Berlin carrying only a kit-bag for his personal effects, food, Communist posters and a Union Jack. I moved my gear into his room.

He'd arranged for a friend on leave from his National Service training to look after me. Robert Grace and his family took me on a drive towards Gloucester, through Stroud and into the Cotswolds. In fading light we climbed Painswick Beacon then drove along a narrow, winding road that had high banks and hedgerows on each side. The road reminded me of an *Esquire* quotation:

> British roads gleefully detour to avoid cutting the edge of a garden, make
> a right-angle turn to spare a tree, climb steeply to show you the view,
> and then twist and turn just for the hell of it.

Suddenly, a car appeared coming in the opposite direction and there was no room to pass. Robert immediately stopped his car, but the other car kept going until it crashed into Robert's bumper. Luckily, not much damage was done and we were soon laughing in relief, but the other driver's double chins trembled for some time from the shock.

Mrs Wilkie pampered me, as apparently she did Alan, and I soon ran out of comments such as, 'Really, you are too good,' and 'Thank you, no.' After attending the Sunday service at the nearby Christ Church, I was taken to Bristol Museum and Art Gallery and shown amongst other things the first Bristol Aeroplane Company engine and the well-known painting of 'The Wedding of William Penn'. Though light rain was falling and we didn't have coats, Mrs Wilkie took me by bus to visit Bath Abbey. The Abbey tower was surrounded in scaffolding to enable eroded stonework to be replaced and blackened surfaces to be cleaned. Some windows were boarded up or were showing signs of bomb damage from World War II. Mrs Wilkie moved very slowly, so we ended up rather damp by the time we got back to Bristol. I regretted leaving Bath and not being able to see the famous Roman baths that were adjacent to the Abbey.

I could see from the Wilkies' apartment the Clifton Suspension Bridge and a hill with an Observation Tower, so Mrs Wilkie took me to see the Tower and the camera obscura in a darkened room at the top. I was intrigued to be able to observe much of Bristol in pastel colours by looking down into a horizontal concave mirror and moving a rod through 360 degrees connected to lenses in the roof. Mrs Wilkie and I also went to other fascinating places in Bristol, enjoyed lunch in town and saw *The Lavender Hill Mob* at a cinema. We came out of the latter to a cloud burst and, being again without coats, got soaked. Even the pockets of my suit filled with water! Before leaving Bristol, I wanted to see the enormous Brabazon aeroplane at Filton, but missed out as the Bristol Aeroplane Company public relations staff were away.

Back in London, I stayed with a Mrs Bartlett at 26 Kensington Park Gardens in Notting Hill. The accommodation had been arranged by the Dominion Fellowship Trust, another organisation with whom Mum had put me in touch. Mrs Bartlett greeted me with a 'Hello love, just call me Jean.' I felt rather uncomfortable as I hadn't experienced this form of greeting in New Zealand, no stranger had called me 'love' before and it was not the done thing in those days to call an older person by their Christian name on first meeting them. I was soon made to feel at home, introduced to the other guests (including Pam Dyer whom I'd met on the *Rangitata*), and invited to have supper with several young people in the room of one of them.

I teamed up with a fellow New Zealander, Michael Foster. He had a BSc from Canterbury University in Christchurch and, having just arrived in London, was looking for a job. We went to see places such as Kensington

Gardens, the Albert Memorial, the Albert Hall and Windsor Castle. Michael arranged for two nurses he'd met on the ship to Britain to accompany us to Windsor – Mary Richardson and Joan Hart of Christchurch, New Zealand. Joan knew my sister Beverley. We caught a bus at Hyde Park Corner and made a slow journey to Windsor, seeing on the way the Firestone and Gillette factories, extensions to London Airport (Heathrow), Slough and Eton.

Windsor Castle was marvellous – St George's Chapel, the Round Tower, the view from the battlements, the luxurious ornate State Apartments, the Waterloo Chamber, Queen Mary's Doll's House, the weapons in the Guard Room, and so on – it was just as I'd expected. Before leaving the Castle, we climbed the Curfew Tower to watch an ancient clock strike the hour. After strolling along the grassy banks of the Thames to look at the variety of boats and wandering through parts of Old Windsor, we reluctantly returned to London through Staines, passing the huge BOAC and BEA Headquarters, and the Battersea Power Station and Fun Fair.

I was soon off to see the Fun Fair. The place looked a bit garish in daylight, but I walked around the numerous stalls and side shows enjoying the hurly-burly and the shouts of the stall holders, 'Here's your ticket, handsome,' and, 'Everyone gets a prize.' I sat in the cockpit of one of Sir Malcolm Campbell's Blue Bird cars (in which he broke the world's land speed record) and went on the big dipper and the centrifuge machine (where centrifugal force held people to the wall when the floor was lowered). I also had a profile of my head drawn in a few minutes by an artist and found that my weight was 10 stone 12 pounds when I tried some penny-in-the-slot machines. There wasn't time to see the Zoo and other things at Battersea Park.

A major attraction in London at that time was the South Bank Festival. I queued with hundreds of other people to get in, buy a guide book and follow the suggested routes so as not to miss anything. The exhibitions inside and outside the pavilions were amazing – particularly the aeronautics section of the Transport Pavilion, where the famous Supermarine S6B, the DH88 Comet, and the Sky and Olympia sailplanes hung from the ceiling. The section also included a Whittle jet engine that had stripped compressor blades as a result of some malfunction, full-sized working contra-rotating propellers from the Brabazon aeroplane, and various flying model aeroplanes. Elsewhere, there were demonstrations of glass making, use of a forge, making weather maps and other fascinating things, as well as the Dome of Discovery, the Festival Hall and numerous static displays. Everything seemed so modern and exciting. I eventually had to leave and rest my feet.

I periodically did this in London by going to Leicester Square cinemas and seeing the films *No Highway*, *Lorna Doone* and *Alice in Wonderland* (which included a short on Princess Elizabeth at the recent Cranwell graduation). I also bought the book, *The Big Show* by Pierre Clostermann, DFC, and read it avidly.

After that, I was into museums. First there was the Victoria and Albert Museum which, though an absorbing place, was an absolute rabbit warren inside. I felt that its Festival Exhibition of Books was well worth seeing and more interesting than its displays from the Great Exhibition of 1851. The Geological Museum impressed me with its carefully laid out showcases and dioramas. Next door, the Science Museum was crammed full of beautifully made models of railways, ships, industrial plants and machines of all sorts, many of them working. I could only manage a quick look as I really wanted to visit the nearby Aeronautical Section which was overflowing with models, some eighty aero engines, replicas of historical aircraft and real aircraft such as the Gloster Whittle E28/39 experimental jet aircraft, the Vickers Vimy bomber (the first aeroplane to fly non-stop across the Atlantic Ocean) and Amy Johnson's Puss Moth 'Janson' (in which she made so many record breaking flights). There was so much to see! I had to drag myself away.

I went to New Zealand House and read old copies of the *Timaru Herald* newspaper, called on Sqn. Ldr. Furlong at RNZAF Headquarters, listened to a concert of the Royal Marines Band on the steps of St Paul's Cathedral, and tried without success to collect mail from the Air Ministry. (Mum had written saying she would send mail there, when in fact she meant RNZAF Head-quarters.)

I was invited to afternoon tea at the Dominions Fellowship Trust, Flat A, 23 Cadogan Gardens, Sloane Square. Two ladies aged fifty plus greeted me warmly. Miss Macdonald of the Isles, CBE, co-founder of the Trust and Chairperson of the Committee of Management, was small and well built, with thin white hair and a beaked nose. Mrs Fry, MBE, a Committee member, was slim, had spectacles and fine wrinkles on her face. Other staff of the Trust hovered around. I suddenly realised that of the six overseas people invited to the afternoon tea, I was the only male present!

Being in uniform, I was asked where I was based. When I said the Royal Air Force College Cranwell, the ladies immediately wanted to know what Princess Elizabeth had been wearing at the graduation parade, as the occasion had been reported in the newspapers. They appeared horrified when I was unable to tell them in detail! (The College *Journal* later reported the Princess wore 'a pale-blue, flowered silk dress, with white accessories'.)

During the afternoon tea, Miss Macdonald of the Isles chatted to one of the guests in French then asked us all to sign the visitors' book before leaving. Mrs Fry offered us tickets to a Wagner concert and Miss Macdonald of the Isles gave me a newspaper cutting of the graduation parade. Both she and Mrs Fry asked me to call at any time and treat their place as my home. I was most impressed by their kindness and the voluntary work they were doing for people from overseas. Later on, I found out that Miss Macdonald of the Isles had contacted Sqn. Ldr. Furlong for a testimonial before I'd been invited to the afternoon tea.

Before leaving London, I walked up Whitehall, watched the changing of the guard at Horse Guards, then continued on across the parade ground to St James's Park. I enjoyed sitting in the Park and watching the many different people passing by, while trying to ignore the continuous noise of London.

For 12s 6d, I booked a third class sleeper to Aberdeen on 'The Aberdonian', pulled by the famous steam engine 'The Flying Scotsman'. Bunks that let down from the walls of the sleeper contained a pillow, a blanket and no sheets. The technique was to partially undress, wind the blanket around oneself, climb into the bunk and try and sleep. This left my feet out of the blanket, but somehow I managed to pass a more restful night than when I first went to Aberdeen.

I was glad to see the Rundles again, though Cousin Lella was away at Cullen. They wanted to hear all my news and see the photographs I'd taken. Leslie and I walked to Dyce to play tennis and to inspect work on the new runway at the airport. Some houses had been demolished to make way for the extensions. Then I assisted Mr Rundle in cutting a privet hedge and Cousin Mabel took me to the Fifty-Shilling Tailors to help me buy a suit. I got one made for £12 10s; obviously fifty shillings no longer applied! The Morgan family invited me to a musical evening. I went shopping for Scottish jewellery and tartan to send home as presents, but soon found that I couldn't afford many of the things I liked. Letter writing again took a lot of my time though it was not my favourite occupation. So many friends had said, 'Drop me a line when you're settled.'

The world-famous Braemar Royal Highland Gathering was being held, so Cousin Mabel and I took a bus up Royal Deeside to see the games. A driver directed us to our bus, one of fifty-one going to Braemar, with, 'Just go as far as you can see, then turn left!' The fifty-nine mile drive was very pleasant, and I strained to see the castles of Drum, Crathes, Balmoral and Braemar, as well as Crathie Church, Mar Lodge, Invercauld House and other places of interest. Upper Deeside was especially picturesque with its rushing waters, silver painted suspension foot bridges and highland cattle on small pastures amongst the wooded hills.

Braemar was packed with some 35,000 people. Cousin Mabel and I managed to get a seat in the small arena, but found it quite difficult in the crush of people to see the games without having to stand. A big thrill was to see the strong man, George Clark of Grange, toss a 21 foot caber weighing over two hundredweight that'd never been tossed before, and then break the record for throwing a 56 lb. weight over a bar with one hand. I also watched, fascinated, kilted competitors throwing a 28 lb. stone, an iron ball and a wooden handled hammer, as well as the pipe band competitions, highland dancing, catch-as-catch-can wrestling and sprinting and jumping events.

Every so often on the loudspeakers were announcements such as, 'Mrs William Smith of Surfers Paradise, Australia, would like to meet Mr and Mrs Douglas Brown of Abadan, Persia, at 3 p.m. in the overseas visitors' tent.' I wondered if there were people at the games that I knew.

Late in the afternoon, King George VI, Queen Elizabeth, The Duke of Edinburgh, Princess Andrew of Greece (the Duke's mother), Princess Margaret, and the Duke and Duchess of Kent arrived, preceded by a parade of the massed pipe bands including the Australian Highland Pipe Band. The King looked ill and didn't walk around the arena as he'd done the previous year, but the ever gracious Queen waved and smiled happily to everyone. I took a photo of the Queen when her car passed within feet of me.

As the games came to a close, the huge crowd surged towards the exits. Cousin Mabel and I had a quick look in some of the Braemar souvenir shops, and at roadside stalls manned by gypsies selling white heather and trinkets, and telling fortunes. After the broiling heat of the day, we were glad to get in our bus again and return in the cool of the evening to Aberdeen, the sound of bagpipes still ringing in our ears.

My leave was over. I caught the train for Grantham and was interested to see on my way south a shipwreck on the Scottish coast and an aircraft carrier in the Firth of Forth. Arriving late evening at Grantham, I didn't feel like waiting for the chartered bus, so returned with some other chaps in taxis to Cranwell.

CHAPTER 6

Well I Never Did

AT THE COMMENCEMENT OF THE AUTUMN TERM, 60 Entry became the senior of the two entries in Junior Entries. We arrived back from leave a day before 61 Entry was due to report.

The Junior Entries Adjutant, Flt. Lt. J.C. Woods, took the opportunity to brief 60 Entry on its responsibilities and other matters. He would interview each Cadet twice during the term and there would be a two day mid-term break. One of our RAF Regiment instructors, Cpl. Smith, had been replaced by a Cpl. Loon (soon to be promoted to Sergeant). There would be 312 Cadets and Flight Cadets at the College, the first time that the roll had exceeded 300. Most of 59 Entry had been accommodated in the former barrack Block 78, which had been refurbished as individual rooms. As fifty-four Cadets would be in 61 Entry, ten of 60 Entry and ten of 61 Entry would be accommodated in two of the old huts nearby, rather than in our barrack Block 77, which would be converted into individual rooms the following term. The 60A Cadets to move into the hut lines would be Nigel MacNicol, Laurie Jones and Johnny Langley. Wally Martin of 60A would move from upstairs to downstairs in Block 77. The Adjutant finished with his favourite phrase, 'Bear these points in mind.'

The old wooden huts between Blocks 77 and 80 and Camp Road were being demolished by bulldozers, and adjacent underground air raid shelters were soon filled with rubble. One day, 60 Entry was pressed into helping load five trucks with rubble and unloading them at the end of Airship Road in the married quarters area. Eventually, the acres of wood and rubble were replaced by acres of grass and large beds of roses parallel to Camp Road.

I was glad I didn't have to shift out of Block 77. All I and other remaining members of 60 Entry had to do was to move across our barracks into the beds formerly occupied by 59 Entry, leaving our beds for 61 Entry. Needless to say, 60A made sure that they had the best of the available blankets!

60A had planned all sorts of degradations for 61A when they arrived, but we had a domestic evening instead as the floor was in a shocking condition and kit had to be cleaned. I was told to look after a chap by the name of Cooper (he was chopped ten months later because of ear problems). We took some pleasure in ordering the new Cadets around, having them polish the floor of our bed spaces, and savouring a few extra minutes in bed each morning while members of 61A were in the ablutions.

To help overcome congestion in the ablutions, 61A was ordered out of bed at 0530 hours.

61 Entry was given a sort of initiation at the NAAFI one evening. 60 Entry sat at the counter end of the room while 61 were at the other end. Each member of 61 Entry had to give an impromptu performance by singing or reciting individually or in groups. The cruder the performance the more likely the members were to be allowed to buy refreshments at the counter. One Cadet named Letchford got a great cheer – he must have been a lecher! When another, an Old Harrovian, gave his name as England, there was spontaneous singing of, 'There'll always be an England . . .' When Cadets failed to please, they were jeered, had refuse thrown at them and were forced to perform again.

On another occasion a Cadet in 61 Entry who'd held a National Service Commission was considered to be bolshie and was duly stripped, nuggeted and paraded through the barracks before being dunked in a cold bath.

In such ways, 60 Entry began exerting its authority. We had a lot to learn!

On the first domestic night in the barracks, I found myself in charge of three of 61 Entry cleaning out the downstairs ablutions. We slaved away for over an hour and, when Flt. Lt. Woods looked under the bath during his inspection, I suddenly realised we hadn't cleaned there. Luckily the Adjutant didn't see anything on which to comment. Later in the term, I was moved onto the easier jobs of cleaning up the rubbish bin area and, in the A Squadron barrack, to polishing the communal table and bench seats, dusting the radio, and tidying up the broom cupboard and floor pad box. That was not to last, however, as I finished up back cleaning the ablutions.

After such exertion, both Entries tried to relax sitting on our beds bulling, attempting to study or doing other things while we listened to Radio Luxemburg. 60A had inherited a radio from 59A and everyone was familiar with the top twenty tunes of the time – ones like Nat 'King' Cole's 'They tried to tell us we're too young', Mario Lanza's 'Be my love', and others like 'I'll be loving you' and 'These foolish things'. We had a good laugh when Radio Luxemburg broadcast a request from 'the two most junior entries of the Royal Air Force College, Cranwell. To Chiefee, the Flight Sergeant in charge,' the first words to the tune being, 'You are the one . . .' The Adjutant tried to find out who had placed the request, but no one was talking.

Each member of 60A also had his own ways of relaxing. Reg Bailey occasionally played an accordion in the barrack and Sam Boyce played the piano in the NAAFI. Sam and John McEntegart, two of the shortest people in the Entry, would put on other and more dubious forms of entertainment in the barrack. Michael Heaney told a long and complicated tale about a creature called a Rary, the crunch line of which was, 'It's a long way to tip a Rary!' Ted Reynolds, the oldest member of 60 Entry, regaled us with stories about his girlfriends. I preferred to read *Enemy Coast Ahead* by Wg. Cdr. Guy Gibson, VC, DSO, DFC.

One privilege 60 Entry had in being the senior entry of Junior Entries, was to be able to attend the first sitting at the Ad Astra Cinema in East Camp on Wednesday nights – if we had the time. All Cadets could go to the cinema on Saturday and Sunday nights. As a result, I saw some excellent films such as *The Clouded Yellow* and *The Galloping Major*.

The College Calendar, new timetables and study sections were issued for the Autumn Term. Though some name changes were made in the latter, the names of Pete Anstee, Mike Goodall, John Gratton, Michael Heaney, Dickie Hoare and Nigel MacNicol were the only ones in Section 1 for both Humanistics and Science subjects. They became known as the gen men. 60 Entry had another subject to study – Thermodynamics. There was still constant pressure to keep awake in lectures and to prepare for the occasional test.

We were soon into many other new things.

Bren guns became the focus in GCT. After firing Brens at the range, I was temporarily a little deaf in my left ear. (The wearing of ear defenders was unheard of in those days.) Then instruction turned to an officers' weapon, the Enfield .38 pistol. We tried twirling the pistols on our fingers like gun fighters in western movies, but our instructors soon showed us the most efficient way to draw and fire the weapon. Using a crude sand model of the Cranwell area, we were introduced to field tactics.

Ditching procedures occupied our initial swimming periods. This involved dressing in denim overalls and Mae West life-jackets, then doing forward somersaults off the top diving board into the pool and swimming to the far end. Then we learned about pilots' dinghies. Ron Chippindale was under the canopy of one when it was deliberately tipped over in the pool and he had to find his way out.

In the workshops, I helped take the nose-wheel off an experimental Vampire aircraft that'd been overstressed when the undercarriage had been lowered at too high a speed. Then I did practical engineering work relating to the undercarriage, flaps, dive brakes, flying controls and rigging of a Meteor 7 (the fuselage was found to be bowed aft of the wings). On other aircraft, I learned about pneumatic systems, brakes and the like. Later, I helped strip and reassemble a Derwent jet engine, ending up with some small pieces left over! I was more successful with another jet engine that'd been on fire.

Before flying training resumed, 60 Entry members were each issued with an Omega aircrew watch. I was glad to have the watch with its large face, sweep second hand and leather strap, as my own watch had become unreliable and expensive to repair. We began cross-country flights in the Anson 21s estimating wind drift, practising mental dead reckoning using the one-in-sixty rule and estimating times of arrival. On the first of these flights I was again air sick, just as we were about to land. I heard that eight other Cadets had also been air sick. The weather was so windy that flying had to be cancelled for a week. Luckily I was not one of the five Cadets in an Anson that made a heavy landing. One of the main wheels collapsed sending the aircraft into a ground loop. Nobody was injured. I hated Ansons!

I became aware that a Battle of Britain 'at home' day was to be held at Cranwell when Prentice aircraft began practising formation flying with pieces of cord joining their wing-tips. Unfortunately a flying instructor, Flt. Lt. A.F. Bell-Williamson, practising slow rolls at low altitude in a Harvard, crashed on the south airfield and was killed. His wife saw the accident. I had to remind myself that, statistically, flying was safer than driving a car.

Rain caused the Battle of Britain day flying display to be delayed a few hours, but the weather slowly cleared for aircraft formation flying, height judging competitions, aerobatics to spectator's orders, balloon bursting, glider demonstrations, dive bombing attacks on the south airfield by Prentices equipped with whistles and painted as Stukas, defending Harvards, troop manoeuvres, Army gun firing, mock forts being blown up and many other events. When a Meteor 7 flew low at high speed in front of the spectators, a flash of condensation occurred around it because of dampness in the air. Then a Washington bomber made a touch-and-go landing and a Vampire put on a spectacular aerobatic show. On the tarmac, the static display included Spitfire, Balliol, Vampire and Wellington aircraft. One of the hangars became a recruiting centre and NAAFI restaurant. Altogether, I thought the 'at home' was most entertaining.

On Battle of Britain Sunday special prayers for the ailing King George VI were made at a combined service in the Hangar Church.

After the service, a three engined Junkers 52 circled Cranwell and landed. Cadets and officers from L'École de l'Air, Salon, in Provence, France, had arrived for a week long visit to the College. Being in Junior Entries, I was not involved in entertaining the visitors, but the strangely dressed cadets and officers inspected Block 77 and were highly visible on other occasions.

One such occasion was the inter-squadron boxing competition which everyone in Junior Entries had to attend. Boxing was something I didn't enjoy watching, particularly when I saw people I knew like Malcolm Dines of 60A being pulverised in the ring. C Squadron won the competition.

Another occasion was the first ceremonial parade of term that showed how rusty we'd become in our drill. The French officers took part in the inspection of the Cadet Wing. On some mornings there was fog so thick that half of the parade ground was invisible and some drill commands came out of the fog.

I began playing rugby after borrowing gear from the College sports store. Later, I bought my own rugby boots, white jersey, College non-representative jersey (which I still have today – though a little paint-spotted!) and College socks. I had to get used to some positions in rugby being called different names to what they were called in New Zealand. For example, Half Back became Scrum Half or Inside Half, First Five Eight became Stand Off Half or Fly Half, Wing became Wing Three Quarter and Line Umpire became Touch Judge. I usually played as a Second Five Eight or Centre. In an early game I managed to score a try and was selected for the 60 Entry team that beat 61 Entry at rugby.

I had a dilemma, as rugby clashed with gliding unless I did gliding on a Sunday afternoon. Gliding wasn't classified as a major sport that term so I made few flights, but did some signalling with an Aldis lamp and a Very pistol to facilitate the gliding. With rugby as my major sport, squash also became a lesser priority.

Someone talked me into doing more cross-country running, but after running some six miles non-stop, I was completely creased and suffered sore muscles for days. Apparently I was the third from 60 Entry to reach the finish line, but to me cross-country running wasn't much fun.

Members of 60 Entry were supposed to stand to attention and call members of 59 Entry 'Sir' since they'd become Flight Cadets, but fellow New Zealander Colin Loveday didn't seem to mind when I called him Colin. I went to see him at Block 78 and envied his two-windowed sunny corner room, desk with bookcase above, reading lamp, desk and easy chairs, normal shaped pillows on his bed, two mats on the polished wooden floor, wardrobe, wall coat hooks and cupboards.

He genned me up on the initiation of new Flight Cadets after their first guest night at the College. The new Flight Cadets were judged on individual or group acts performed on stage. On a previous occasion a Flight Cadet had won acclamation when he took ages arranging a large sheet of glass before driving a golf ball through it without shattering the glass. Invariably, most new Flight Cadets failed to win approval and were penalised. The Senior Entry had been known to have stood around the large carpet square in the main entrance hall, forced some nude Flight Cadets under the dusty carpet, thrown clothing after them (less one set of clothing) and ordered them to dress before emerging from under the carpet. Other penalties had been to make new Flight Cadets run nude around the Orange or cycle nude the six miles to RAF Digby, illuminated by the headlights of Flight Cadets' cars. A new Flight Cadet was once tied into a large metal hoop and rolled around while fire hoses were played on him. He ended up unconscious. Colin was understandably anxious about what would befall him on his first guest night.

His fears were well founded as he was in a group of Flight Cadets that staged a scene in a barber's shop. They lathered up one of their number in a chair and made such a mess of the Flight Cadet that he got the approval of the College, but the rest of the group was penalised. Penalties included

Flight Cadets racing from one end of the College to the other pushing a tin of polish with their noses, and having to drink a glass of a strong liqueur. The Hall Porter objected to the number of naked Flight Cadets on the Orange. Jack Henderson played his bagpipes and won approval, apparently making more noise than the rest of the College! Dick Witty of 59A, performing on stilts some six feet above the stage, also impressed his fellow Flight Cadets.

One day, we New Zealanders at the College were unexpectedly lined up for publicity photographs for use back home. Ron Parfitt, Ian Powell, Colin Loveday, Jack Henderson, Jim Brown, Ron Chippindale and myself were photographed in the middle of the Orange with the College in the background (Fig. 20), informally standing on the steps leading into the main entrance of the College, and then in smaller groups having lunch, playing rugby, working on a Meteor in workshops, inspecting a glider and sitting in a classroom. Understandably, other members of the College were curious as to what the photographs were for, so we said they were for our fan clubs!

Jim Brown came into the A Squadron barrack to see me one evening. I was eating bananas, as there wasn't much fruit in our diet. He asked for a banana so I gave him one, but he threw the skin into an open foot locker. That was like declaring war! A Squadron wouldn't tolerate such behaviour from someone in B Squadron, so the skin was thrown back and soon both Squadrons were tussling with each other. The hefty Ron Edwards of 60B tried to drag me into the B Squadron barrack. A Squadron rescued me and B Squadron retreated into their barrack, turned the lights off and barricaded the door. I've never seen a door with glass in the upper half bend so much! B Squadron escaped through their barrack windows and entered through the ablution windows to again attack A Squadron. Ron Chippindale managed to get into the A Squadron barrack and tip over my bed. He was caught and his tweeds were removed. The skirmish spread outside and eventually died out. I felt that some Cadets blamed me for starting it all when Jim had been the culprit.

A similar incident occurred one evening a few days later when C Squadron set up a bucket of water against the A Squadron door. I was shaving in the ablutions and avoided C Squadron by diving out of a window and clambering in through an A Squadron window. A state of siege went on until lights out. Unfortunately, the officer pattern uniform of Pete Lewis of 61A was ripped in this skirmish.

60 Entry's first GCT night exercise was held in Bristol Wood near the rifle range on the northern side of the north airfield. We blacked our faces and wore denim overalls, cap comforters, camouflage netting and gloves. Our GCT officer, Flt. Lt. Hudson (sometimes known by the cartoon character name of 'Dick Barton'), conducted the briefing. A Squadron and half of B Squadron were defending the woods against the rest of 60 Entry who were

Figure 20. NEW ZEALANDERS AT RAF COLLEGE SEPTEMBER 1951

Back Row
L-R: Flight Cadets J.M. (Jack) Henderson, RAF-59 Entry; Ian M. Powell, RAF-57
Entry; E. Colin Loveday, RAF-59 Entry; Ron Parfitt, RAF-55 Entry.
Front Row
L-R: Cadets J.C. (Jim) Brown, RAF; Ron Chippindale, RNZAF; R.M. (Hank)
Hancock, RNZAF - all No. 60 Entry.

supposed to be paratroopers who'd landed near Leadenham. There were three sections of the defenders. I was second in command of No. 2 Section and in charge of a Bren gun. Our personal weapons were Sten guns. The night was dark. Night flying was going on and the revolving light on the College tower lit up the woods eerily. Occasionally a Very light was fired and a thunderflash would go off – probably to keep us alert.

While on patrol I sensed that someone was just ahead. The password 'Harvey' was exchanged and the unknown person turned out to be Jim Brown – one of the defenders. We whispered together for some time, but there was no sign of the 'enemy'. Then Johnny Langley of 60A was caught by the 'enemy'. His shouts of 'Harvey' brought six to eight of the 'enemy' out of the woods in front of my Bren. I had pleasure in 'shooting' them all, but a hand-to-hand fight ensued. Eventually, the defenders were declared the winners and we were all counted, handed in our weapons, had a very welcome supper and returned to our barracks by midnight. Unfortunately, we still had to get up at the usual time next morning.

At the next OD padre's hour, Padre Milne confided that prior to the GCT night exercise, Flt. Lt. Hudson had asked him if he could borrow a Scout Handbook! Padre Milne had assumed that the Handbook was required to give Flt. Lt. Hudson some clues for the exercise, and thought this a huge joke!

There were early morning periods of PT which, at that time of the year, were just when the sun was coming up. W/O Smith had us doing press-ups with our feet hooked over the second wall bar. Then we had to walk our feet up the wall bars until we were in a handstand. When he ordered us to continue bending our arms, quite a number of us fell on our noses, but had to resume the handstand position. Eventually, we were allowed to walk our feet down the wall bars and continue with normal press-ups. I'd been told that when Cadets left Junior Entries, they'd be as fit as they would ever be. I quite agreed!

Some of the early morning PT was outdoors in low temperatures on wet grass amongst ground fog. We weren't at all impressed! On one occasion W/O Smith said, 'Your feet never see the light of day' (which was quite true at that time of the year). 'Take your shoes and socks off!' He then told us to run barefoot through a layer of fog that covered the grass by about a foot. Our tracks in the fog were quite plain to see – a really strange phenomenon.

As the Knocker Cup inter-squadron competition approached, I had to attend three lots of PT a day – two Knocker practices and the normal 60 Entry PT. Furthermore, Sgt. Bendelow tried to kill us by putting us through the most rigorous exercises, leaving us creased for the rest of the day. The Knocker competition went well, but A Squadron could only manage second equal.

The College boxing team had been practising Charles Atlas dynamic tension exercises and one member from 60A, Nigel MacNicol, even slept without a pillow at night to strengthen his neck! When the College boxed the rest of Cranwell at the East Camp gymnasium, I noticed that all members of Junior Entries were present, but only twelve Flight Cadets were amongst the spectators. The College won by a few points. There was a similar result when the College boxed No. 3 Initial Training School. When 61 Entry had their boxing, I was pressed into being a whip and found myself trying to give encouragement, advice such as, 'Bash him on the chops, Pete,' and congratulations or commiserations afterwards as appropriate.

For twenty-four hours from midday, I was rostered as the Junior Entries Duty Cadet. The duties included checking Cadet's passes in and out of camp, locking and unlocking the Junior Mess and the huts we used, and turning off lights in the foyer and ablutions of Block 77 at lights out. Fortunately, I didn't have to quell any riots!

Another rostered duty was that of Leading Cadet. For a week, I had to make sure that A Squadron was woken each morning on time, compile parade states, march the Squadron to and from the parade ground, check that the barrack was left tidy before we went to lectures (e.g. windows open the required amount), run domestic and semi-domestic evenings, answer everyone's questions, turn the lights out on time and so on. Leading Cadets were recognised by a white lanyard on the left shoulder instead of the squadron lanyard on the right shoulder.

As luck would have it, I was the A Squadron Leading Cadet when Chiefee Harvey decided to go on the war-path. He started by giving me a bollocking because I'd dismissed my set at the wrong place, and had kept him waiting. Then he harangued the Leading Cadets and anyone he caught scrubbing and blancoing their webbing in the ablutions, as this was prohibited for hygienic reasons. Though we had a small hut in which webbing could be blancoed, there was no light in the hut so Cadets often scrubbed and blancoed at night in Block 77. Then at lights out, Reg Bailey found his bed apple-pied. He accused Wally Martin and tipped his bed over. Thereupon, all of the 60A beds were tipped over. 60A realised that 61A were laughing at this, so we tipped their beds over. There was so much noise that I thought Chiefee would come in, but he must have been away somewhere. Most of 60A slept on the floor that night. Chiefee came in at 0600 hours next morning, surveyed the wreckage, looked at his watch, but didn't say anything.

More bed tipping occurred that night before Cadets from upstairs rushed in and upset the remaining beds. Chiefee Harvey and Sgt. Loon arrived and told us all to settle down and reassemble our beds. I had to make out a written report on the incident by 0700 hours the next day. 60 Entry and particularly the Leading Cadets were then told off, and all Cadets from upstairs, having been caught out of their barracks after lights out, were given a formal kit inspection. I was glad when my week of being a Leading Cadet was over!

I thought there would be some warfare between 59 and 60 Entries, being in adjoining Blocks, but there was nothing apart from someone firing a Very light at Block 77 one night. 60 Entry retaliated by firing a few rockets at Block 78.

A friend of my sister Beverley wanted to visit me one Saturday afternoon. Though I was scheduled to play rugby and do cross-country running, I managed to get out of the latter, changed into officer pattern uniform and rushed to the Post Office opposite the main gates of the College where Joan Woodgate was waiting for me. Like Beverley, Joan was a nurse. I was surprised to find she had a girlfriend with her. They were both on a biking tour of Britain. I discovered that Joan had been at the Braemar Gathering I'd attended. If only I'd known at the time! I escorted the girls around West Camp and had just twenty minutes to recover before Lilian Sanson from Nottingham arrived. She was a pen friend of my sister Heather. I was loath to do the same tour of Cranwell, but I escorted Lilian and then found that a car wasn't coming for her until after 1700 hours. This meant we had to fill in time on Camp Road as there was nowhere I could take her. She invited me to stay at her place during the coming mid-term break. Later, when I mentioned this to Michael Heaney, he said with great authority, 'The women in Nottingham are pretty good.' As a result I was swamped by requests from my fellow Cadets to get them names, addresses and telephone numbers of Nottingham girls!

There was bad news from home. Dad had had a mild heart attack. He was aged sixty-three and had been overdoing things. After working long hours in his business, he kept a large fruit and vegetable garden, mowed extensive lawns and often got involved in community activities like tree planting. There was nothing I could do except write and urge him to take things a bit easier and plan his retirement. He took the first steps toward selling his business.

When Flt. Lt. Woods interviewed me for the first time, he said that if I kept on as I'd been doing, I'd be OK. This was a great relief to me, as fear of being chopped from the College was ever in the back of my mind. I kept hearing of Flight Cadets 'getting the chop'. The Adjutant then went on to ask me awkward questions such as, 'What is discipline?' and 'What would I do if I was put in charge of fifty raw recruits?'

Later, the woman at the Public Service Institute confided to me that Chiefee Harvey thought highly of the New Zealand Cadets! If this was true, it was indeed high praise!

Chiefee Harvey caught a member of 60A in bed one Saturday afternoon when we were all supposed to be out playing sports. 'Dear oh, dear oh, dear,' he said in his Irish brogue, 'on a Saturday afternoon – a Cranwell Cadet –

well I never did . . .!' These words of the Flight Sergeant, along with many of his quaint pronunciations such as 'preesay' (for precis) and 'asyouwarr' (for as you were) were mimicked by us all.

One night as a change from giving members of 61 Entry the cold bath treatment, the bed of one of their number was hung out of an upstairs window using a sheet tied to a heating pipe. Later, some of 60A removed the bed and hid it in the roof above the ablutions, forcing the 61 Entry chap to bed down for the night on the table in his barrack. The following day, Alan Bedford-Roberts of 60C decided to get some much needed sleep on the bed in the roof instead of playing sport. He was used to taking risks, being well known for gambling on race horses. (He told us that he made a lot of money out of betting, but I for one didn't believe him.)

I was getting to know the characteristics of other members of my Entry. For example in 60A, Ted Reynolds and Wally Martin seemed to be at the bottom of every prank. Wally did very little work, yet gave the impression of being a genned-up sort of person. Malcolm Dines and Sam Boyce were also into pranks. Sam could be quite sarcastic at times. Laurie Jones kept to himself and wasn't easy to get to know. Some others had more brawn than brains. For a reason that now escapes me, we began calling Michael Heaney, Spike.

We also got to know the characteristics of some lecturers. A new lecturer in Aeroscience, Plt. Off. A.H. Craven, was known for his corny jokes and his statement that, 'No one was chopped after the first examinations.' We'd news for him! He was rather verbose and talked for a full quarter of an hour one day after an airman came into the lecture room and told Plt. Off. Craven that his married quarter was on fire! Flt. Lt. K.B. Woods, our Electricity lecturer, was called 'Thermocoople' because of his pronunciation of thermo-couple. The civilian meteorologist became known as 'Teeny Weeny Little Water Droplets' after using those words when demonstrating the formation of cloud in a special box.

A break in our routine came when 60 Entry made a day visit to Annesley and Newstead Collieries, located between Nottingham and Mansfield. This had nothing to do with our studies, but was part of a long-standing arrangement whereby miners from the collieries had an outing at Cranwell each term and the opportunity to make short flights. The bus I was in went to Annesley. After a snack, we stripped off in a large, warm locker room, put on appropriate clothing, miner's helmets and lamps, joked about having a last look at our spit and polished boots, then squashed into a two-storeyed cage and dropped some 2,000 feet down a vertical shaft in about a minute. My ears popped and I remembered a cartoon on the wall of the College hairdresser that showed two miners and one saying, 'Oh, I went down 2,000 feet and stooged around a bit.'

After being searched for matches, we began to 'stooge around a bit'. Our guide took us along sizable corridors where the roof was supported by iron hoops, bricks, beams or a combination of these. Some corridors were very old with whitewashed walls and reinforcing where beams had broken. Small trucks, controlled by a cable and laden with coal, passed us constantly on one of two railway tracks. Occasionally there was a thud and pressure in our ears from dynamiting. We were soon crawling along narrow tunnels trying to protect our hands, knees and boots from sharp rocks. The noise increased as we came upon miners, stripped to the waist, using a cutting machine to excavate a two and a half foot thick seam of coal. The coal was taken away on conveyer belts to the trucks in the main corridors. I think we were all glad to hop onto a conveyor belt and have a bumpy ride over rollers and through sacking screens to somewhere quieter, cooler, cleaner and less claustrophobic. Blackened miners with white rings around their eyes peered at us as we made our way to the surface.

Back in the warm locker room, we showered and changed before proceeding to the cafeteria for a hot meal. An inspection of the pit head machinery and power-house followed – huge engines, drums, coal-fed furnaces, noisy turbines, generators and a control room containing dozens of meters and switches. Our guide gave us his views on the nationalisation of the coal industry before conducting us through the area where coal was cleaned and sorted. We left Annesley and its big slag heaps, rather tired, but glad to have had a stimulating experience in a world not often seen. I heard later that all the Cadets in the bus that'd gone to Newstead Colliery were confined to camp the next weekend as somebody had pinched a miner's helmet and a mining notice.

The weather became colder, fog sometimes continuing all day. We were given permission to wear woollen gloves when marching between lectures. The paraffin heaters in the A Site lecture rooms were barely adequate. In wet weather, groundsheets used as capes gave us little warmth or protection when outdoors. Greatcoats were used for church and other parades. Luckily the barrack room heating was turned on earlier than expected. I bought a blue, fleecy lined track suit, and a made-to-measure officer pattern raincoat.

Flt. Lt. Woods briefed 60 Entry on a survival camp in Derbyshire at the end of term. Wg. Cdr. Lyne would command it and Flt. Lt. Hudson would be the Adjutant. We would be a mobile fighting force moving field equipment from place to place. Attendance at the camp would be on a voluntary basis, but Flt. Lt. Woods made it quite clear that everyone was expected to be there. Camping in the middle of winter didn't seem to be something to look forward to!

We were given an extensive list of equipment to take to the camp – two vests (thick wool or flannel), two pairs of underpants (long), four wool or flannel shirts, four thick wool jerseys, eight pairs of wool socks (long, sea boot style if possible) and so on. I had to ask the Rundles if I could borrow a pack or rucksack and other equipment I lacked.

The mid-term break came at last. I made a tedious bus journey to Nottingham, arriving in the dark at the Sansons' house. The Sanson family was very good to me. Lilian took me shopping and to a cinema, accompanied me to St Andrew's Presbyterian Church (though she was C of E), then for a stroll by the river and a visit to Nottingham Castle. She clung to my arm and I got the strong impression that she was keen about me, but I didn't feel that way about her. Though I was asked to come again, I was somehow glad to catch a bus back to Cranwell.

I was very tired and almost asleep by lights out when I was rudely awakened by a firecracker going off in the barrack as Spike Heaney and some other Cadets returned from their mid-term break. Chiefee Harvey came in, but nobody admitted to knowing about the firecracker. This was repeated soon afterwards when Spike let off another firecracker. Fortunately, he didn't have any more so we all drifted off to sleep.

The reorganisation of Cranwell continued apace. Our locker Hut 203 was condemned, so we shifted the lockers to Hut 140. When our study Hut 198 was moved to RAF Coningsby, we were given another place in which to study near the Junior Mess. The Mess had been moved into a larger room, and the former Mess became a reading room. Only the Post Office (a relic of the Royal Naval Air Service at Cranwell, run by the original Postmaster, Mr J.W. Robinson) and the Sergeants' Mess (another RNAS relic and the original College Mess) remained on the edges of the new lawn area.

I kept seeing new aircraft in the skies over Cranwell – a Valiant jet bomber, Sabre jet fighters, a Fairchild Packet transport and an experimental Lancastrian bomber that'd been fitted with Ghost jet engines.

Drill continued as usual. In some cold weather parades we were allowed to wear woollen instead of leather gloves. On one occasion, this caused me a problem as I dropped my rifle when sloping arms – wool giving little grip on the stock of a highly polished rifle. Chiefee Harvey clagged me by giving me the standard three days of extra drill. On wet days, if the order cancelling drill arrived late and we were already on parade, we got soaked and rifles, webbing and other equipment had to be immediately restored to pristine condition.

The Ferris inter-squadron drill competition was upon us again. Rigorous preparation for it culminated in 60 Entry being taken by bus from Block 77 to the College so as not to damage our highly polished boots. We carried our white belts in our hands, fitted them before a final inspection and then marched on parade. One of the visiting judges, Captain D.A. Beckett, DSO, of the Parachute Regiment, asked me, 'Who is the visiting Company Sergeant

Major?' I knew it was Company Sergeant Major L.J. Cullen of the Grenadier Guards, but I just froze and said, 'Don't know, Sir.' The A Squadron Under Officer Phil Jevons, accompanying the inspecting officer, gave me a dirty look as he passed by me. Someone else was asked, 'What is the latest prototype aircraft!' Hammy Khan of 60C was the only Cadet in Junior Entries to be commended during the inspection. This was surprising as he wasn't known for his turnout (though he had a trim figure), and had previously been given over twenty formal kit layouts to improve his standard. In the drill, a bayonet scabbard fell out of its frog and two hats came off. As a result, A Squadron was only placed third overall.

At rugby, I travelled with the College third fifteen to play King's School at Grantham. On another day, I played for the third fifteen against Wisbech second fifteen in rain and a freezing thirty knot wind. The College won both games handsomely.

When not playing rugby, I watched B beat A Squadron in the final of the inter-squadron rugby, and the College first fifteen beat the RAF first fifteen. Playing for the RAF were Sqn. Ldr. R.G.H. Weighill, DFC, the B Squadron Commander, and Plt. Off. H.A. Merriman, who'd been the A Squadron Under Officer the previous term. I suppose old scores were settled in the scrum as the College won easily.

The College also beat the RMA Sandhurst at soccer, fencing, rugby and boxing. The latter was put on in some style – with a printed programme, a band playing and the officers, many of Air rank, in colourful mess dress and ribbons. The winner of the contest was in doubt until Johnny Langley of 60A knocked out his opponent in the last match. I always seemed to end up rather hoarse after such occasions!

As the end of term approached, exam fever overtook us. There was little time for serious swotting. To do well, one really had to be genned up prior to Junior Entries. Extra classes were held for those who felt they needed them, and most of 60 Entry attended.

After completing the majority of the exams, I almost fainted during the normal Sunday church service and had to report sick. My temperature was up again so I was put in dock for the next six days and given penicillin and a purple gargle, followed by two days of light duties. As a result, I missed the Law and Administration exam, another session as Duty Cadet, a ceremonial parade and the chance to get my light machine gun (Bren) qualification. Spike Heaney brought my mail to help me pass the time. Chiefee Harvey said my sickness was caused by the barrack windows being closed at night – true perhaps, but he would have had quite a job getting us out of bed in the mornings if the windows had been left open in the freezing temperatures.

I heard that Alan Bedford-Roberts of 60C had been interviewed by the

Adjutant over giving ridiculous answers to exam questions. Obviously, Alan was trying to get the chop. I felt I'd not done well in the exams so wasn't surprised when Ron and I got the same mark in Humanistics and I had a lower mark than he did in Science. Jim Brown did better than both of us.

Word got around that Alan Bedford-Roberts had in fact been given the chop, along with Bob Cartwright of 60A, Cecil Da Silva of 60B and Chris Woods of 60C.

With only days to go before leaving Junior Entries, 60 Entry relaxed a bit and indulged in some more schoolboy pranks. B Squadron was attacked by everyone else and beds, wardrobes and foot lockers were overturned. Two panes of glass were accidentally broken.

In 60A, Sam Boyce and Wally Martin contrived to have Gordon Grierson lead an attack on the other Squadrons which resulted in Gordon losing his tweeds. While Gordon was away, they put a lock on his foot locker, screwed down the lid and put it upside down on top of his wardrobe. They also unhooked the springs of his bed and supported the bedding with string. Gordon returned to the barrack, saw the foot locker and looked around suspiciously to see what other mischief had been done. Spike Heaney couldn't wait for the string to be discovered, so did a B36D bomber landing on Gordon's bed, ending up on the floor, much to everyone's amusement (with the exception of Gordon)!

Other 'bedtime with Grierson' activities occurred while Gordon was at the ablutions, such as making up his bed pack after he'd made down his bed for the night. He returned and looked at his bed pack, scratched his head and looked again, not believing his eyes. On another occasion, Gordon's bed was suspended below the barrack ceiling, supported by a rope that went through open windows to heating pipes upstairs. Unfortunately, Chiefee Harvey caught us doing this and made us take the bed down.

One pitch black night after lights out, Ted Reynolds tipped over my bed. In the scuffle that followed, I slipped, fell heavily to the floor and was completely winded. No one could see properly and we daren't put the lights on, so there was no more skylarking that night.

61 Entry came in for more 'bath nights'. Ron Chippindale got wet when 61 Entry retaliated. He threw a bucket of water at some Cadets up the stairs and just missed wetting Chiefee Harvey who'd come in to break up the fun. Later, A Squadron threw a firecracker into B Squadron's barrack. Then a firecracker came in through an A Squadron window and burned the polished floor by my foot locker. B Squadron's windows mysteriously got blancoed that night.

The wet weather rehearsal for the graduation parade, held in Hangar 30, was again a shambles as orders were difficult to hear. When the Commandant's ceremonial parade was held in frosty conditions, everyone just about seized up. Unlined leather gloves were no protection from cold rifle butts. The Commandant made us do the march pasts again.

Not being a Flight Cadet, I wasn't able to attend the senior entry's valedictory presentation of 'Ali Burberry and the Forty Gieves'. With a title like that, named after two well-known outfitters, the show was no doubt a success.

60 Entry's last PT period for the term comprised inter-squadron swimming races and water-polo. There was a great cheer of relief when it was all over.

An end of Junior Entries party was held. Usually such things occurred at the Bristol Arms in Sleaford, but time was limited so 60 Entry had a big meal and booze-up at the NAAFI. The place was specially decorated and we even had table cloths and serviettes, but the usual slow service! Chiefee Harvey was up with the play on such occasions, caught people singing unprintable songs outside his room and forestalled an attack by 59 Entry on Block 77.

In preparation for being Flight Cadets, 60 Entry began replacing the airmen badges on field service caps and ceremonial hats with officer and Warrant Officer pattern badges respectively. The new badges were gilt finished so required no polishing. There was red velvet behind the crown of the Warrant Officer badge. We removed the eagle patches from the shoulders of our battledress and best blue uniforms, and attached the distinctive Cranwell gorgets onto our lapels with snap fasteners. (The left gorget was removed for rifle drill.)

Photographs of Squadrons, sports teams and prize winners were taken. Members of 60 Entry were individually weighed and measured for the second time at the College. (This procedure was to occur each term.) Some equipment was handed in and other equipment, such as specially issued sleeping bags and windcheaters, was assembled for transporting direct to the survival camp. We were also issued with white shirts, wing collars and bow ties. Then we began moving our equipment and personal possessions into a storeroom or to Blocks 78 or 79, the transfer being hampered by rain showers. (Block 78 was to house 60A and C, whereas the newly refurbished Block 79 on the eastern side of the Junior Entries parade ground was to accommodate 60B.) I had my final session as Duty Cadet.

Since leaving home, I'd been worried about spending more than I was earning so was greatly heartened when Dad wrote to me saying, 'I think you have been very thrifty with your outgoings and I do not want you to stint yourself as I feel you are not the type to spend lavishly on unessentials and can be trusted to spend wisely.'

Then Sqn. Ldr. Furlong wrote to Ron and me advising us that we'd been paid 4s. per day 'danger money' during our parachuting course, and that our basic rate of pay had increased after six months service from 11s 8d to 13s 2d per day, though we could still only draw 7s per day – the same as our RAF colleagues. The difference would continue to accumulate for us and could only be used 'for special occasions' on the permission of the Air Officer Commanding, RNZAF Headquarters, London. When pilot training began next term we'd receive flying pay of 3s per day.

In his letter, Sqn. Ldr. Furlong referred to Mum by saying that he'd got '. . . a particularly nice letter from your mother . . . and a food parcel . . . a gesture which I greatly appreciated.' I was somewhat embarrassed about the food parcel, as it could be seen as currying favour, but as the season of goodwill was approaching, Ron and I decided to send the good Squadron Leader one of the College Christmas cards.

No. 54 GD(P) Entry received their Wings from the Air Officer Commanding-in-Chief, Flying Training Command, Air Marshal Sir Hugh S.P. Walmsley, KCIE, CB, CBE, MC, DFC, whose son Mike was in 57 Entry. The ceremony was held in the gymnasium. That night, an eleven degree frost made everything white on graduation day. The graduation parade of Nos. 54 GD(P) and 5 E & S Entries was reviewed by the General Officer Commanding-in-Chief, Eastern Command, Lieutenant-General Sir Gerald Templer, KBE, CB, CMG, DSO, who cut a dashing figure in an almost ankle length brown greatcoat, long curved sword and spurs. The parade went well as far as I was concerned though my hat, pulled well down to keep the low sun out of my eyes, was killing me.

Afterwards, Spike and I had a look at the visiting aircraft on the south airfield and saw General Templer off, before changing into mufti to go on three weeks leave – only to find our bus had left without us! I was lucky to get a ride to Grantham with Reg Bailey and his parents in their small car. I was so cramped with my luggage that I could barely stand up when we arrived at the railway station. The Baileys very kindly invited me to stay sometime at their place in Liverpool.

I had a long wait for 'The Aberdonian', but managed to get a sleeper and have a good night's rest – glad that I'd survived Junior Entries and unworried about what was still to come, now that I was a Flight Cadet.

Aberdeen was in the grip of an icy spell, but that didn't deter me from enjoying life with the Rundles. Alice enlisted my help to decorate the church for Christmas and be an usher for plays put on by the Antler Youth Club. Her latest boyfriend came to dinner several times. I stacked firewood with Mr Rundle and listened to bands and carollers singing in the streets. I bought a model aeroplane kit of a Grumman Panther powered by a Jetex 50 chemical jet motor and, after assembling the model, flew it in a snow covered field. New Chipmunk training aircraft of the University Air Squadron passed overhead. I also bought boots and trousers for the survival camp and waterproofed them. The Rundles made me play my bagpipe chanter for my supper.

Leslie Rundle borrowed a Student's Union card for me so we could both go to the capping of medical students at Aberdeen University. I became John W. Beveridge! The ceremony in Mitchell Hall at Marischal College was most impressive with the massive organ playing, the enormous stained glass window filling most of the end of the Hall, the ornate beamed roof, the carved wooden wall panels with large oil paintings above, the wine red curtains halfway along the Hall drawn back for the occasion, and the picturesque and colourful gowns of the academic staff and ninety graduands as they processed slowly on the parquet floor while everyone sang 'Gaudeamus Igitur'. Though most of the speaking was in Latin, which was unfamiliar to me, that didn't detract from the occasion – the first of several cappings I've attended.

Leslie's friend George Webster came with us to the end of year dances at the Students' Union. Though the start times were 8 p.m., there was little dancing until much later. Foxtrots and quicksteps gave way to the Gay Gordons, the Dashing White Sergeant and the Eightsome Reel. By 1 o'clock we were dripping with sweat, having had a marvellous time.

Christmas services, carol singing and the exchange of presents all came and went too quickly. When Leslie went to Elgin to see his girlfriend, Moira, his friends went out of their way to look after me. George Webster took me to the cinema. Jimmy Donald and Michael Morgan (who'd been an airman at Cranwell and was about to be commissioned) came with me to see the pantomime *Sleeping Beauty*. Jimmy took me to a model engineers' exhibition, invited me home to dinner, then showed me through the medical school at the University, regaling me with humorous experiences. During an autopsy, a doctor had said to Jimmy, 'Hang onto that leg.' Jimmy had asked, 'What for?' The doctor had replied, 'I'm going to saw it off!'

Distant relations of mine lived at Oldmeldrum, so I visited them briefly. Mrs Annie Killoh (whose husband's family had once lived at Barra Castle) and Mrs Elizabella Alexander were sisters and lived together at Springbank, a two storeyed stone house in Old Station Road. They were elderly ladies with indifferent health, and dressed in black. The interior of their house was straight out of Victorian times and still had gas lighting. Over afternoon tea, I let them see my photo albums and they showed me family photos including one on the wall of my Uncle Jack Skinner in his World War I uniform. He'd first visited them when recuperating from wounds received at Gallipoli. They even had Uncle's old khaki 'lemon squeezer' hat on the sideboard! I discovered that Mrs Killoh pronounced her name as 'Kee-low' whereas in New Zealand the pronunciation was 'Kill-oh'. They were dear old ladies and, with tears in their eyes, pressed into my hands when I left a tie that'd probably belonged to the late Mr Killoh. I promised to visit them again.

I had a quiet Hogmanay as the next day I had to leave for the 60 Entry survival camp near RAF Harper Hill, Buxton, Derbyshire. A sleeper for part of the way helped ease the long train journey. I changed trains overnight at Glasgow and Manchester, and then took a bus via Miller's Dale to Buxton, arriving in time for breakfast. Another bus took me to No. 28 Maintenance Unit, RAF Harpur Hill.

CHAPTER 7

The Grandest Fun on Earth

WE STARED, not believing what we'd just been told. Flt. Lt. J.H. Lewis rubbed his hands, stamped his feet in the four inches of snow, smiled at us enthusiastically and expanded on why winter camping was 'the grandest fun on earth'. Thirty-four members of 60 Entry (including Ron Chippindale, Jim Brown and me) stood shivering around him viewing the bleak, snow covered hillside known as Axe Edge where we were to live for the next week. The big strong Flight Lieutenant was one of the Flight Commanders in Flying Wing, but he'd also been a member of a John Biscoe polar expedition. I think most of us had difficulty sharing his enthusiasm.

The day before when I'd arrived in snowy conditions at RAF Harpur Hill, the highest station in the RAF, someone had told me that snow wasn't considered to be snow there until it was three feet deep, and the seasons in that part of Derbyshire were nine months winter and three months bad weather!

I was the first from the College to arrive. The bus had dropped me by the airmen's barracks and married quarters, some distance from the main part of the camp, which was basically an explosives depot. The NAAFI manageress gave me a free cup of tea and arranged for a truck to carry me up the hill to the main gate. Though I was in mufti, the RAF Police at the gate saluted me and escorted me to the Adjutant's office. I was taken to the officers' mess where I changed into battledress and read newspapers beside a roaring fire until Wg. Cdr. Lyne and party arrived from Cranwell. The Wing Commander treated me to a Pepsi-Cola before other members of 60 Entry arrived. We unloaded the Cranwell trucks. I was then part of an advance party that set up a Headquarters tent that afternoon in a desolate area at Axe Edge some five miles away. This was freezing work.

Back at Harpur Hill, we Flight Cadets had a cold and uncomfortable night sleeping on the concrete floor of a canteen that smelled strongly of new paint. Some Flight Cadets had been detailed to prepare breakfast, but our appetites soon disappeared when the porridge tasted of petrol! We packed our issued equipment – windcheaters and trousers (both proved not to be waterproof), mittens, sleeping bags, blankets, palliasses, extra groundsheets, binoculars, compasses, map cases, water sterilizing pills, and so on. Trucks took us out to Axe Edge.

My section, F Section, gradually froze as we were the last away. There were five of us – Malcolm Dines (designated as leader), Julian Bowes, Gordon Grierson and myself of 60A, and big Tiny Lewis of 60B. Tiny, having been a chef in London hotels for two years, became our cook. Flt. Lt. R.H. Merrifield, Personal Assistant to the Commandant, was in charge of Sections E and F and said he would sleep in our tent for the first three nights before moving to E Section.

Our truck took us past the Headquarters tent and the other sections before stopping. We chose an exposed camp site near a small stream rather than sheltering in a boggy valley. The sections were out of sight of each other so giving a sense of isolation. We pitched our tent in the snow, had a late lunch and spent the rest of the day settling in. That evening we walked miles to the Cat and Fiddle, the highest licensed public house in England. The landlord told us such horrifying stories about people getting lost on the moors and never being seen again that we kept to the roads as we returned to camp in the dark.

The next morning, F Section had a brisk fifteen minute walk to the Headquarters tent to watch a mountain rescue demonstration by a team from Harpur Hill. We tried stretcher-bearing over some hilly ground and found it more difficult than we'd thought. Tiny and I returned to our tent to prepare lunch. Later we moved our outdoor 'kitchen' because of a change in wind direction. Another two inches of snow began to fall and the wind increased to some 25 knots as we began a ten mile cross-country hike down a valley to Goyts Bridge and then along a former railway track. We sheltered in an old tunnel for a snack from our survival rations, but at the Buxton-Manchester road we split up – some Flight Cadets heading for a pub in Buxton, while the remainder returned to camp.

When I entered our tent a large, overweight Squadron Leader was standing shivering in the gloom beside a paraffin heater, looking absolutely miserable, a blanket around his shoulders. I discovered that this was our new Senior GCT Officer and a graduate of the RMA Sandhurst. He'd returned forty-five minutes earlier from another hike, having got a pain in his side, and had blacked over the glass of a pressure lamp when he'd tried to get it going. Though we Flight Cadets were dripping wet, we first had to light the pressure lamps, get the Squadron Leader into dry clothes, make him comfortable, and then attempt to dry our clothes. The Squadron Leader said he'd stay with us for two days, but stayed for the reminder of the camp. He took four aspirins before going to bed, yet snored loudly. He also rolled in his sleep down the slight slope in the tent, landing on top of me. There wasn't much I could do about it.

Our activities began to revolve around the Squadron Leader as he did little for himself. We discovered that his last posting was in the Mediterranean so we understood how the cold was affecting him, but he wasn't fit and kept making comments like, 'I do hope you have something hot for tea,' and, when he was snug in his sleeping bag, 'I really think you should have the lights out soon, Dines.' He wasn't our favourite officer!

We woke to find that a thaw had set in and the floor of the tent had become a quagmire. The tent had to be reorganised, the 'kitchen' shifted yet again and further attempts were made to dry our clothes. I walked to the Headquarters tent to get some more survival rations. My windcheater bulged with all I stowed inside it.

The camp was formed into flights for a ten mile cross-country speed march. No. 3 Flight (E and F Sections) decided to run downhill and at other times walk and run alternatively. The Flights were in competition with each other and set off at fifteen minute intervals. The first three miles was in mist across open moorland so we had to use compasses, but the remainder was along tracks in very rough and hilly country. I became so exhausted that when I came upon a stream, I gulped down the brackish water, thinking it was like nectar. Unfortunately, No. 3 Flight missed a turning point by three hundred yards and Julian and Tiny couldn't keep up with the rest of us. The Flight finished third in two hours forty-five minutes. That night more rations arrived and, for those who wanted it, a rum ration.

My feet were so hot and sweaty that I washed them in freezing water before going to bed. The other chaps stared at me in amazement, but I knew that I needed to look after my feet if I was to survive other long hikes.

In the morning, we Flight Cadets in F Section didn't remove our pyjamas, but just put on more layers of clothes to try and keep out the cold. As the day was a Sunday, we were told to shave (a very painful experience outdoors using freezing water) and were then marched to various churches at Buxton. This was the only occasion I've worn pyjamas in church! The Methodist congregation stared at our dirty boots and unkempt appearance, but we were given a warm welcome all the same.

The thaw caused more quagmires around the F Section tent so we became drainage engineers, redirecting the water away from the tent and forming a dam to make the drawing of water easier from the stream. The 'kitchen' was moved once more. Then we were taken to the newly built NAAFI at Harpur Hill for a singsong, an impromptu concert and supper. F Section put on a spoof about the ways people smoke cigarettes, while another Section sang (adapting the song, 'Oh thank you so much . . .') about the line (Wg. Cdr. Lyne) they'd like to shoot, men of ample girth (our Senior GCT Officer), the overlarge ration bag called a windproof smock, and so on. We had a lot of laughs.

Wg. Cdr. Lyne inspected us all next morning before we boarded trucks and were taken to Hayfield. We met up with the mountain rescue team again and commenced a three hour traverse to the Snake Inn via Kinder Scout (the 2,088 foot highest peak in the Pennine chain). The team set off at a cracking pace. Though they carried warm clothing, they were lightly clad. We reached the rocky peak without too much bother, but didn't stay there long in the cold wind and misty conditions (Fig. 21). The descent was through patches of heather, sticky black mud and running water. We had a close view of the famed Kinder Downfall – a large waterfall whose waters were being blown uphill by the strong winds. Then we came upon the remains of a Liberator bomber that'd crashed during World War II. The crash had left a sizeable hole in the ground. At the Snake Inn, F Section treated the officers to a meal while waiting for the stragglers to arrive. On returning to camp, some of us took the offer of transport into Buxton to go to the cinema and then made the long walk back to camp in the dark.

On our final morning rain was falling. We were allowed to sleep in before breaking camp in miserable conditions, packing most of our equipment into trucks, and having a meal in the Headquarters tent before striking that and departing for an unknown destination. We were crammed into the closed-off backs of trucks, sitting on wet equipment with an officer whose task was to ensure that we didn't peek out and see where we were going. We tried to keep our spirits up by singing. Darkness fell and after some three hours of travel, we were allowed to disembark and each section, using maps, worked out where we were. F Section found we were in the little village of Dunham-on-Trent, some thirty miles from Cranwell.

We were told that in the next fifteen hours we had to walk back to Cranwell by any route we chose. No rides were permitted and there was a checkpoint near the airfield at Swinderby. Each section was in competition with each other and left at five minute intervals, F Section again being the last to leave at 2145 hours. We decided to run for ten minutes then walk for ten minutes, and have a rest for five minutes every hour. We started cheerfully enough and soon caught up the other sections, but after ten miles talk diminished until we just ran, walked or limped in silence. We were lightly loaded compared with members of other sections who carried packs. All we carried were tea and sandwiches and Type C iron rations (sardine-like tins containing boiled sweets, fruit bar, sweet biscuits, oatmeal munch and chewing gum).

I think all the sections took the same route to the check point, but after that F Section lost contact with the others. We decided to cross the airfield at Swinderby to save time and risked interfering with the night flying that was in progress. Then we went cross-country for a while to make a more direct route. When the five-minute rest periods came, we just collapsed panting wherever we were – in a ploughed field or the middle of a road. Luckily there wasn't much traffic about. Our feet were killing us, but we continued with our strict schedule of running and walking. The weather was good with the moon shining brightly in a starry sky. After passing through Wellingore we topped a rise and saw the flashing light from the College

Figure 21. On top of Kinder Scout, highest peak in the Pennine chain, England, January 1952: L-R: Ron Edwards (60B), Author (60A), John Gratton (60B) and John Maitland (60B).

tower. What a welcome sight! We soon reached Ermine Street and arrived at Block 78 by 0530 hours. Chiefee Harvey was there to check us in. He told us that we were the first complete section to finish. As a result, we felt the pain was all worthwhile.

I was exhausted and could barely walk upstairs to my new room. I slept for forty-five minutes until woken by the cold. My body felt as if it had seized up, but I forced myself to the Junior Mess for breakfast. A rum ration in warm milk was available. I again slept until lunch time. There was much to be done − carefully shaving, having two baths before feeling clean, getting my things from store, organising my room and so on − before having my first meal as a Flight Cadet in the magnificent dining hall in the main College building.

The survival camp was the first of its type to be held by the College and it received some publicity in the national Press. Nigel MacNicol, Johnny Langley and Laurie Jones of 60A wrote an article entitled 'Sixty Survives' for the College *Journal*, complete with maps and photos. The Assistant Commandant, Gp. Capt. Kyle, congratulated all those who were at the camp for the fine show they'd put on and how they'd entered into the spirit of the thing. He even declared that we could have a long weekend in which to recover! We could think of easier ways in which to get a long weekend! There were things about the camp that could have been improved and no doubt corrections were made and much more demanding camps were subsequently held elsewhere in Britain and overseas. A newly arrived member of No. 62 Entry was heard to say, 'Why are so many Flight Cadets limping?' He'd soon learn!

Having done something that I'd previously not thought I was capable of, I would have walked fifty miles non-stop if required. I may not have done such a thing by choice, but I had a new perspective and, over the years, have been a supporter of Outward Bound courses and the like for the young and not so young. Perhaps I now share some of the enthusiasm of Flt. Lt. Lewis for 'the grandest fun on earth'?

CHAPTER 8

I Have Control, Sir

'WHAT'S UNDER YOUR KILT?' I looked down from the stage of the main lecture hall at the sea of flushed and excited faces, but couldn't identify who'd shouted at me.

I'd just finished playing the bagpipes at 60 Entry's initiation as Flight Cadets, after our first guest night at the College.

Jack Henderson had lent me his bagpipes and I'd had a brief practice on them in my room the previous day – much to the curiosity of 60A. Then, as we'd come from the guest night, F/C Peter Kennett of 56A had offered me the use of his highland outfit. He'd heard that I was about to play Jack's bagpipes and said he'd played the pipes at RAF Halton. I'd gratefully accepted, changed hastily, gone out to the back of the College to tune the bagpipes and on returning found that I'd be the last of 60 Entry to perform. Nobody wanted to be last as the Senior Entry was sure to clag those at the end of the programme!

I'd anxiously waited while Ron Chippindale and Jim Brown performed an energetic haka and got a 'thumbs-up'. Ex-cook Tiny Lewis had won applause as he'd attempted to kill a live hen (he eventually succeeded). Some of 60 Entry, wearing masks and with their PT clothing on back-to-front, had done arms backward bend and other strange looking exercises. The Flight Cadet audience kept throwing toilet rolls onto the stage and the Senior Entry members controlling the stage curtains kept throwing them back.

When my turn came I said as required, 'Good evening gentlemen, my name is Flight Cadet Hancock,' but there were howls of protest – I'd forgotten to finish with, 'Sir!' My borrowed bagpipes failed to start first time and there was a terrible squeal. The reeds in the pipes were very open so making the bag hard to keep inflated. I was determined not to panic and tried again. I hadn't played the pipes for over a year so the medley of a slow air, a march, a strathspey and a reel reflected my lack of practice. I ended rather out of breath.

'More, more . . .' The Flight Cadets began stamping their feet. Somewhat surprised, I played another selection of tunes.

'Come on, lift your kilt. Let's see what you've got.' The cries became more strident.

At that moment, the Senior Entry threw one of their members onto the stage – a Scotsman. Then New Zealander Ron Parfitt, the A Squadron Senior

Under Officer, was thrown onto the stage. Ron took control of the proceedings and shouted for a 'thumbs-up' or a 'thumbs-down' on my performance. I was awarded a 'thumbs-up' and in the general pandemonium, thankfully
left the stage. The Flight Cadets never did find out if I was wearing anything
under my kilt!

Those members of my Entry who weren't so lucky had to pay penalties
such as running around the Orange to the squash courts, forming a pyramid
and being drenched by fire hoses. They got off lightly.

That first guest night was memorable for other reasons. All Flight Cadets
wore officer pattern uniform with the standard issue white shirts, starched
winged collars and bow ties. I'd never worn a bow tie before, let alone a
'single ended' tie, i.e. one with the bow enlargement at one end. 'Double
ended' and ready-made bow ties were frowned upon and there were severe
penalties if Flight Cadets were caught wearing one. The collar studs and
highly starched collars were most uncomfortable. I wasn't the only person to
get assistance in dressing that night!

60 Entry assembled in the assigned ante-room before moving into the
dining hall at 1930 hours. We stood behind chairs allocated to us in the
eastern half of the three long rows of Squadron tables, C Squadron as the
Sovereign's Squadron being on the centre row. The Senior Entry came in
at the western end of the tables, followed by a number of officers who
positioned themselves amongst the Senior Entry. The President for the meal
banged a gavel twice. A padre said grace in Latin. We all sat down.

The varnished wooden tables were lit by table lamps – the only other lights
being those illuminating the King's Colour and the huge National Gallery
portraits on the walls of King Charles I and other notables. The College cups
and trophies were spread along the tables replacing the usual pot plants. The
College band played in the gallery at the eastern end. Male waiters dressed
in tails, bow ties and medal ribbons served us with soup, a fish entrée, main
course and dessert. The RAF-marked plates and cutlery were then cleared
from the tables leaving only small glasses. Port decanters were passed down
from the head of the tables, everyone using their left hands. I was surprised
how many Flight Cadets, like myself, passed on the port and had their glasses
filled with water by a hovering waiter. There were two more bangs of the
gavel and we all stood and toasted King George VI.

As coffee was served and cigars and liqueurs could be bought by signing
a chit, we began to relax a little. Cigarette lighters shaped like Toc H
lamps were placed on the tables. Wg. Cdr. Lyne was farewelled and, in his
reply speech, specifically mentioned the sterling qualities of No. 60 Entry
on the survival camp and asked that the College not be too hard on us in
our initiation after dinner. Perhaps that was why those who were penalised
got off so lightly! After some ninety minutes we rose from dinner and

proceeded across the corridor to the main lecture hall for the initiation of No. 60 Entry.

Snow fell soon after the start of the Spring Term. I tried to make my new room as warm and comfortable as possible. The room was upstairs on the north-eastern side of Block 78, the two windows overlooking the Junior Entries' parade ground. Green curtains framed the windows, the lower parts of which were opaque. There were similar furnishings to what I'd seen in Colin Loveday's room. A strong smell of paint came from the cream walls and grey door. No pictures were allowed on the walls so I pinned Margaret Hornsey's photo to the inside of cupboard doors above my desk. I went to see Ron and Jim's rooms in Block 79. Ron's was like mine, but Jim's was a corner room. They had the same problem as I had in keeping warm. The wall radiators were inadequate and, as portable heaters were forbidden, the solution seemed to be to pull the curtains, block up the two small ventilators in the walls, invite one's friends in for a smoke and put towels along the bottom of the door.

My status having changed from that of an airman to that of an officer, I shared a batman with several other Flight Cadets. Mr Clarricoats woke me when he brought a cup of tea into my room, introduced himself as my batman and advised me that I should pay him 10s per month in cash for cleaning the room, making my bed, polishing my shoes and pressing my uniforms, or 12s per month if I also wanted him to clean sports clothing. He said the military laundry was on Mondays and the civilian laundry on Wednesdays. He also did limited sewing if requested! Having a batman was a great help, but I still had to spit and polish my footwear and keep my rifle and web equipment up to scratch for parades and when the Assistant Commandant or the like inspected our rooms.

Those of 60 Entry who'd been on the survival camp had to help sort out things used on the camp. We folded the dried tents and blankets, packed away other equipment and ended up throwing around toilet rolls and flour bags that'd got wet on the last day of the camp. Later on we each had to pay 5s to cover the cost of things that hadn't been returned from the camp. I was aware a rolling pin had gone up in smoke!

Ron and Jim went away for the long weekend we'd been promised by Gp. Capt. Kyle, but I stayed at Cranwell and made my first visit to Lincoln accompanied by Alan McLelland-Brown and Bob Cartwright. I was intrigued by the twisting narrow streets, the ancient buildings and the hilltop Cathedral towering above the rest of the city. Tired from sightseeing, we had a meal and went to a cinema.

I was surprised to see Bob Cartwright and Cecil Da Silva still in 60 Entry after hearing at the end of the previous term that they'd been chopped. Apparently they were to be given flying tests before a final decision was made. Bob survived his flying test, but Cecil was suspended after his and left Cranwell to have private tuition in London for a year and then return to the College. (Much later I heard that Cecil had had a marvellous time in London, failed all his exams and been sent back to Ceylon!) John Tucker was relegated from 59A and became part of 60A.

There were some big changes in our programme of instruction. Electricity, GCT, Geography, Meteorology and Workshops were replaced by Aerodynamics, Airmanship, History, Radio, Aircraft Structures and War Studies. PT was reduced to just one period a week, replacing drill on Wednesday mornings. In Humanistic subjects, Ron Chippindale went up from Section 3 to Section 2, whereas Jim Brown went down from Section 2 to Section 3. The gen men in Section 1 for both Humanistics and Science were Julian Bowes, Mike Goodall, Spike Heaney, Laurie Jones, Johnny Langley, John Maitland, Mike Marsh, Nigel MacNicol and Alun Morgan.

I found the new subjects fascinating, though often difficult. Aerodynamics began with the effect of various shaped objects passing through air, this being demonstrated in a small apparatus using water and sawdust, with the results being projected on a wall screen. Aircraft Structures was largely a mathematical subject about stresses and strains, resilience, Young's Modulus and the like. I began to understand things such as why the geodetic frame of the Wellington bomber was so strong and why the Sydney Harbour Bridge was shaped like a coat-hanger. War Studies had a close correlation with History and we soon knew by heart the Principles of War and the Principles of Administration.

60A was allocated to No. 2 Squadron of Flying Wing. The Commanding Officer, Sqn. Ldr. J.B. Coward, was tall and lean, and had a flaxen handlebar moustache and an artificial leg. Stories circulated as to how he'd lost his leg. Ten of 60 Entry, including me, were placed in D Flight under Flt. Lt. D.sW. Bedford. Fg. Off. H.McC. Vincent became my flying instructor. The latter was aged about twenty-seven and seemed to be a likeable chap though Colin Loveday told me they didn't get on because he'd once proved Fg. Off. Vincent wrong on some matter.

Fg. Off. Vincent also had Alan McLelland-Brown as a pupil and together we were shown the cockpit layout of the Prentice, given talks on the theory of flight and told to learn the masses of pre-flight checks, flight checks and vital actions. There were thirteen pre-starting checks, six starting checks, seventeen checks while the engine warmed up, three checks when preparing to taxi, six checks before running up the engine, nine checks before take-off, five checks after take-off, eleven checks before stalling, spinning and aerobatics, twelve checks in the event of fire, five checks for joining the circuit, six checks when downwind in the circuit, six checks when overshooting, four checks after landing, six checks when running down the engine – and that wasn't all!

After much hard work we learned the checks – using mnemonics where appropriate, e.g. for take-off:

T   – Trim : one degree tail heavy, rudder neutral.

T   – Throttle : friction nut fingertip tight.

M   – Mixture : automatic, carburettor air cold and filtered.

P   – Pitch : fully fine.

F   – Fuel : port tank.

F   – Flaps : up, indicator up.

G   – Gyro : synchronise compass and uncage.

H   – Hood : closed, harness secure.

I   – Instruments : final checks.

We were also given a blindfold cockpit check – having to touch and name the nineteen or so instruments, and also the numerous controls, switches, lights etc. The Prentice had a Morse key and downward identification light for use in an emergency should the radio fail, so we had to learn the Morse Code.

The all metal Prentice T Mk 1 (Fig. 22) had been designed during World War II when there was a limited time in which to teach a large number of people to fly. The theory was that by adding a third seat just behind the seats

Figure 22. Percival Prentice T MK 1 at Cranwell, April 1952.

of the instructor and first pupil, the second pupil could watch and listen to what was going on, thus saving the instructor from a lot of repetition. I thought the Prentice rather ungainly with its large cockpit, tilted up wing-tips and fixed undercarriage. A Gipsy Queen 32 engine gave it a cruising speed of 95 knots.

My initial flight was as first pupil and began with the effect of controls, but lasted only twenty minutes. Much to my embarrassment, I was airsick. Fg. Off. Vincent wasn't too worried and said that the oily smell of hot air from the engine and outside air turbulence had probably affected me. The same thing happened a few flights later when, as second pupil, I was sitting in the third seat and had to watch Alan practise stalling then descend to circle Cranwell in bumpy conditions while a Meteor 7 landed. I was told to get airsickness pills from the Station Sick Quarters. The pills worked wonders as I had no problems when later stalling and spinning a Prentice. In time, I found that I didn't need the pills.

Fg. Off. Vincent took Alan and me to the nearby RAF airfields of Barkston Heath and Spitalgate to practise our take-offs and landings. Doing cockpit checks in the air was quite different from practising them on the ground, as the aircraft had to be flown, a good look-out maintained and radio calls made. Fg. Off. Vincent told me I was a menace and would shout at me (though he usually apologised afterwards) when my head went into the cockpit, or when at Cranwell I strayed off the grass take-off and landing area for Prentices. (Prentices went left of the runway controller's caravan; Harvards went right of the caravan.) Sometimes he would leave Alan or me on the ground at Barkston Heath while he concentrated on sorting out one of us. We had to return unexpectedly from Barkston one day when oil from the propeller hub covered the windscreen.

Wally Martin, who'd flown Prentices before, was given a flight check and immediately allowed to go solo. Other members of the Flight were progressively sent solo. I started being concerned as to when I'd be good enough to do this.

My turn came after I'd completed six hours of dual instruction. Fg. Off. Vincent gave me a check circuit and after landing said, 'You have control,' and got out of the Prentice. 'I have control, Sir,' I replied and, full of confidence, took off, completed a circuit of the airfield and made an almost three point landing. When Fg. Off. Vincent climbed into the cockpit again, he'd his flying helmet on so I wasn't able to see if he'd any grey hairs as a result of my first solo. 'Congratulations,' he shouted above the engine noise, 'the circuit was better than the first one.' I wondered how he was able to tell that from the ground. Overjoyed that this first hurdle had been passed, I sent telegrams to Mum and Cousin Mabel saying, 'Solo 15 minutes at Spitalgate – Rutherford.'

In the next few days Alan and the remainder of the Flight went solo. Jim Brown told me he'd also gone solo, but Ron Chippindale didn't have his solo flight until some time later.

A New Zealand Group Captain visiting the College met Ron and Jim, but I was flying at the time and couldn't find him later.

Snow began to fall once more and flying was cancelled. D Flight was given tasks like bringing flying logbooks up to date, reading the Flight Order Book again, having aircraft recognition tests and cleaning the Flight. We thought that our days of polishing floors were over so we didn't take kindly to a chore that became a monthly routine. I was rostered as the D Flight Duty Cadet and had to make out a parade state of the Flight Cadets present or absent, get the meteorological forecast and brief the Flight, as well as organise the sweeping and polishing of the linoleum, cleaning of the blackboards, emptying of the ashtrays and waste paper buckets etc.

Then we were sent to the link trainer section at the western end of the workshops building to learn instrument flying. The link trainers were supposed to be state-of-the-art equipment that simulated flight, but I found them sluggish or over sensitive at times and not easy to trim. They gave me the impression that I was balancing on a pinnacle and would fall off unless I operated the controls correctly. For the remainder of my time at Cranwell, the NCO pilot instructors helped me to fly relying on instruments instead of my senses, and master various instrument landing systems.

Another bad weather task was compass swinging. This involved someone in the cockpit turning the aircraft through 360 degrees on the ground with the engine running and calibrating the compass. Another person some distance to the rear of the aircraft took sightings with a landing compass along the centre line of the aircraft and signalled the results to the person in the cockpit. Sam Boyce was unfortunate to burst a tyre of a Prentice when compass swinging. I helped swing the compass of one of the new de Havilland Chipmunk training aircraft.

There was great excitement when the first Chipmunk was allocated to D Flight. We rushed to inspect it and generally agreed it was a 'peach'. Our instructors began flying the Chipmunk and said it would replace the Prentice next term. The rumour went around that 60 Entry would have to come back ten days early in the next leave period to convert onto Chipmunks.

The A Squadron Commander, Sqn. Ldr. Thomas, interviewed each of 60A. He read to me extracts from reports made by persons with whom I'd been in contact. Some comments were complimentary, some not so complimentary, some true, some half truths. I was left in no doubt where I needed to improve. Altogether, I found it a chastening experience.

Sqn. Ldr. Thomas then spoke to all of 60A on service matters such as officer uniforms and what civilian clothing would be required at the College.

Mufti could be worn on Wednesday, Saturday and Sunday afternoons. Flight Cadets could now travel in mufti instead of uniform (as had been required in Junior Entries). Airmen pattern shoes could be worn instead of boots, except for drill and GCT. We were given details of the British Parcels Insurance Company scheme that was offered exclusively to the College for the insurance of service and personal clothing and equipment. We were also told that small purchases from the Fancy Goods Store at the College could be made by signing a chit, payment being through the monthly mess bill. The prompt payment of mess bills using College cheques was impressed upon us.

One of the standard charges in our mess bills was a payment of £2 per month towards the Cadets' Activities Organisation. Sqn. Ldr. Thomas explained that the charge helped pay for the many CAO activities we could participate in during leave periods, such as pot-holing, mountaineering, gliding, canoeing, sailing and numerous private venture outdoor pursuits. The intention of the CAO was not only to provide recreation and entertainment, but also to give experience in planning the operations and carrying them out, and to encourage a spirit of adventure, personal enterprise, endurance and the building of character. Other leave activities such as parachuting, air navigation exercises and Service visits weren't directly sponsored by the CAO, but they were an important part of the Cranwell training.

We were also encouraged to participate in activities of the College Society such as aero-modelling, angling, archery, beagling, chess, dancing (Scottish and ballroom), debating, dramatics, engineering, field shooting, fine arts, jazz, male voice choir, music, natural history, philately, photography, printing, radio and riding. Then there were sports like athletics, boxing, cricket, cross-country running, fencing, hockey, rowing, rugby, shooting, squash, soccer and tennis. There was so much that I wanted to try, but didn't have the time for!

Ron Parfitt and other members of the Senior Entry also spoke to 60A on things they thought were getting a bit slack, including respect for the Senior Entry and the need to call Flight Cadets in 58 Entry and above, 'Sir'. They briefed us on the protocol required for meals.

We were to assemble in our ante-room at 0705 hours for a roll call before breakfast. Only the centre door into the dining hall was to be used – the other doors being reserved for officers and the Senior Entry. There was self service at breakfast, lunch, tea and high tea. (We weren't told, however, that the Senior Entry could crash meal queues!) Tea comprising bread, buns, butter, jam and tea, was at 1630 hours. High tea on Wednesdays and Saturdays was a combination of tea and dinner. There was another roll call ten minutes before dinner commenced at 2000 hours and, on guest nights, at 1930 hours. Guest nights were held twice a month. Best blue uniform was required for dinner and officer pattern uniform for guest nights. We weren't to talk or sit down at dinner and guest nights until the Senior Entry and officers were seated. Also, we weren't to smoke at dinner and guest nights until the President for the meal gave permission, and the Senior Entry and officers had to leave the dining hall before we could leave.

We soon got into the routine of the College. There were at least three notice-boards that we had to look at almost daily. The Fancy Goods Store selling beer, cider, cigarettes, chocolate and the like became a popular place to visit. Rationing and the College rules restricted what could be purchased. A television set in the room was also an attraction. The billiard room was not so popular, but I played enough billiards and snooker to get a general idea of each game. Our ante-room with its large leather covered chairs and settees, fireplace and numerous magazines and newspapers was a great place in which to relax. I became an avid reader of magazines and newspapers.

Ron Parfitt claimed I'd beaten him in one of the compulsory cross-country runs we'd previously done for the Chimay Cup, the inter-squadron games competition, so insisted that I get into training for the A Squadron team in spite of me still having blisters on my feet from the survival camp. I duly went on A Squadron cross-country runs in the snow, kept coming third and ended up creased as before. When the inter-squadron cross-country race was held, the hopes of A Squadron foundered in the treacherous mud along Ermine Street.

The first ceremonial parade of term was held in a freezing wind and, as expected, was a shambles. Ron Parfitt got tough with A Squadron and I, along with about half of 60 Entry, was given two days of Under Officer's parades for having a dirty rifle barrel and two days jankers for not carrying my Form 1250 Identification Card. Some other members of the College expressed their sentiments about the Senior Entry one night by making huge, uncomplimentary words in the snow on the Orange.

Then I was given two days of jankers, along with Spike Heaney and several others of 60A, because we hadn't locked some lockable drawers in our rooms and hadn't left our windows open while we were at drill. The extra drill at 1900 hours couldn't be held outdoors in the dark, so we were made to 'sweat for it' under the lights of the former hangar that'd become the Flight Cadets' Garage.

At one of the compulsory church parades, Ron Parfitt told me to be the Other Denominations marker. This involved marching the length of the parade ground with the other markers, so that the ODs could form up on me. Then at church, someone told me to take up the offering. The place was packed and the congregation had to sing two more verses of a hymn until all the money had been collected. A new electric organ was dedicated.

Afterwards, a communion service got me out of the usual march past the Commandant.

I was rostered with another Flight Cadet for fire picket duty. This meant we had to wake everyone in Block 78 by 0630 hours, check the fire equipment in the Block and remain in uniform all day.

I read that there'd been heavy snow falls in Derbyshire and was glad that I wasn't still on a survival camp. Doing drill in snow was bad enough. At one rehearsal for a ceremonial parade, slushy snow wet not only our boots, but our trousers, rifles and gloves. On some other parades, freezing snow stuck under our boots making standing and marching rather uncomfortable.

News that King George VI had died put us all into mourning. Black ties were worn, flags were flown at half mast and the King's Colour was draped with black material. Memorial services were held and everyone at Cranwell had to attend. Trying to squeeze some three thousand people into the churches was quite a job. There was standing room only. I think we were all touched by the circumstances in which the young Princess Elizabeth, who'd visited us so recently, returned from overseas as Queen Elizabeth II.

Fg. Off. Vincent was one of the Cranwell group to attend the King's funeral, so Flt. Lt. F.A. ('Bud') Abbott took me on my third and last supervised solo flight. Then Flt. Lt. Bedford flew me around the local area before I did my first solo navigation flight to Digby, Boston and Grantham. Thick smoke and haze in the Grantham area prevented me from actually seeing the town so, as instructed by Flt. Lt. Bedford should something like this happen, I called the Cranwell control tower:

'Rickshaw 403 calling Poor Girl, request practice homing, over.'

'Rickshaw 403 this is Poor Girl, transmit, over.'

'Poor Girl, this is Rickshaw 403. My course is 260 degrees, height 2,000 feet, speed 95 knots, over.'

'Rickshaw 403 this is Poor Girl, steer 030 degrees, out.'

I turned onto the heading and soon entered the Cranwell circuit. The Cranwell tower, however, had asked me to transmit twice more, but there was so much crackling on the frequency that I'd missed the calls. As I taxied back to dispersal, the air traffic controller asked me why I hadn't replied to his calls. I could almost see him glaring down at me from the tower!

Flying in bad visibility soon became routine. When downwind in the Cranwell circuit and barely able to see the landing area, let alone the horizon, I was glad of those hours in the link trainers practising instrument flying.

I felt a little smug one day when authorised to do solo circuits at Spitalgate in a gusty wind of 30 to 35 knots that was partly across the runway, and Alan McLelland-Brown wasn't allowed solo in such conditions. I must admit, however, that I was glad finally to land safely after that flight.

Fg. Off. Vincent took me east of Sleaford to demonstrate practice forced landings in the forced landing area. He concentrated so much on telling me what to do that, when he came to climb away again, he had to bank steeply to fly between trees at the end of the field. This was hair raising stuff, but nothing like the flying we did next in the low flying area. I knew that any flying below 2,000 feet away from the circuit was considered to be low flying. We were flying 200 feet above ground level when I was told to go down to 100 feet. Fg. Off. Vincent then took control and went down to thirty feet. He had to climb to go over haystacks and flocks of birds! Seeing a church steeple higher than we were as we banked steeply around it was quite an exhilarating experience.

On another occasion Fg. Off. Vincent told me to hold the Prentice in a spin until the attitude of the aircraft flattened in the spin. The attitude didn't flatten and the Prentice continued in a steep and tight spiral. I was then instructed to recover. The Prentice came out of the spin very quickly and flicked over into a spin in the opposite direction. Fg. Off. Vincent then took control and recovered, pulling many times the force of gravity as we came out of the dive. He mopped his brow and said it was one of the most vicious spins he'd ever been in. We'd lost 3,500 feet of height in it.

As we taxied into dispersal, Fg. Off. Vincent said he wanted me to go and try some more spins myself. I demurred as I wasn't keen to spin what I thought was a rogue aircraft. He didn't insist I get airborne again and admitted, in the crew room, that the spin had been quite scary. One thing this experience taught me was that aircraft of the same type can sometimes have quite different flying characteristics.

Various officers lectured 60 Entry in early evening sessions on Airmanship. We were given good common sense instructions about flying, such as 'thou shalt not go right in a left hand circuit', and worthwhile information on other matters like aviation medicine.

60 Entry had been told that on becoming Flight Cadets we were to call on the Commandant, Air Cdre. Sinclair, and sign his visitors' book. The Commandant was a remote figure whom we saw only at certain ceremonial parades, guest nights and church parades. Most of us put off paying our respects until reminded. I went with two other chaps after high tea one Wednesday. Wearing suits and felt hats, we knocked on the door of The Lodge and were surprised when 'Sinc' himself, carrying a child, opened the door. He said the staff were off duty and asked us if we'd come to sign the visitors' book. We went into an inner porch and signed the book, wished the Commandant a good evening and left with alacrity.

I was involved as usual in the Knocker Cup gymnastics competition. One practice ended in disaster for Nigel MacNicol of 60A when he broke his ankle doing a backward somersault off the broad box. A Squadron triumphed, however, in spite of losing him. As one of the gen men and having flown Prentices before, Nigel was assured of not being relegated to 61 Entry.

Rugby and squash also occupied my time. Though a Flight Cadet, I still had to record what sport I did each Wednesday and Saturday afternoon, but there was no check on Sunday sport as had been required in Junior Entries.

I took up ballroom dancing lessons during the winter months to consolidate what I'd learned at Miss Dorothy Thwaite's Dancing Academy. A man from Sleaford held the lessons in the main lecture hall, but didn't provide any women as partners! Having to take my turn at being a female partner was confusing to say the least.

At guest nights, the College entertained a succession of VIPs such as the Air Officer Commanding-in-Chief, Fighter Command, Air Marshal Sir Basil Embry, KBE, CB, DSO, DFC, AFC. Headmasters from prominent schools were often present and, depending on who was there, the College band sometimes had to play more than one national anthem when the time came for making toasts. On several occasions, only about half of 60 Entry could be seated in the dining hall because of the number of guests and Flight Cadets. Those Flight Cadets who missed out were given high tea beforehand. After dinner there was usually a lecture by one of the guests. For example, a meteorologist from London gave an illustrated address on the theory of standing waves; a Dr Pye described his voyage in a small boat across the Atlantic; and the famous test pilot John Derry spoke about high speed flight.

On Saturday mornings, I was a little annoyed (but also a little satisfied) to be woken by Chiefee Harvey drilling 62 Entry on the parade ground outside. I smiled to myself when I remembered that once when in mufti in the main College corridor, Cadets from 62 Entry had mistaken me for an officer and given me a snappy 'eyes right'. I attended the first term boxing of 62 Entry, but didn't get any enjoyment from it.

'Thermocoople' became my tutor. Flt. Lt. K.B. Woods was also tutor to Bulldog Drummond, Mike Goodall and John Gratton as well as being the lecturer in Radio. We all went to see him and arranged times for our weekly tutorial. Flt. Lt. Woods was clued up, but he had us in fits of laughter when he likened the radiation of a radio beam to that of an electric light bulb – 'except that an electric light bulb didn't radiate, but if it did the beam would be like it!' On another occasion he couldn't make an equation work, so he said 'if we put a V^2 in, that will make it right – you won't understand it now, but you will later!'

D Flight was equipped with Chipmunks earlier than expected. 59 Entry began to be converted onto them. Spike Heaney was one of the first in 60 Entry to go solo in a Chipmunk, but managed to tip the aircraft on its nose when taxiing for take-off. I saw the fire engines and blood wagon rush out onto the airfield and was greatly relieved when Spike returned none the worse for wear. There was little damage to the Chipmunk.

After some frenzied swotting, I sat tests in various subjects then went on the mid-term break.

Reg Bailey offered me a ride in a car to Newark. Then a bus took me to Nottingham and I booked into the Black Boy Hotel. I made no attempt to contact the Sansons as I just wanted to do my own thing for a while.

I wanted to see a game of ice hockey so found the Ice Stadium and watched the Nottingham Panthers narrowly beat the Wembley Lions. The hooters, rattles and shouting of the audience competed with the playing of an organ. The speed of the teams and rough-and-tumble on the ice was quite something to see.

Then there was shopping to do and a dance to attend. The floor of the Palais was beautifully sprung. Tables were placed around the edge of the dance area and in the balcony above. I soon got overheated from dancing, so watched a 'Teddy Boy' energetically swinging his partner between his legs and over his shoulders as they rock 'n' rolled. The couple were dressed in the height of fashion for the time and made me feel, in my blue, double-breasted suit, rather 'square'.

I ran into some of the Senior Entry and members of 59 Entry who'd come to the dance in 'Jezebel', their ex-London taxi. We got talking and, to my surprise, a Flight Cadet Sergeant invited me to stay at his home in London should I ever be stuck for somewhere to go!

On returning to Cranwell, two invitations were awaiting me. Miss Macdonald of the Isles of the Dominions Fellowship Trust (she signed herself as Celia Macdonald of Sleat) invited me to a reception at Drapers' Hall, London, at which Her Majesty Queen Elizabeth The Queen Mother would be present. I felt that there was no way in which I could go on a Tuesday afternoon so reluctantly declined the invitation. The other invitation, also from Miss Macdonald of Sleat, was for tea with the New Zealand High Commissioner. This too was declined.

A letter from Cousin Mabel advised me that a fortnight earlier Fg. Off. Ian Cunningham had been killed in a flying accident in Egypt. He was to have been married the following month. Though I'd never met this Old Cranwellian, I felt sad for his family and friends in Aberdeen and grateful for having been lent his copies of the Cranwell *Journal*.

Water-pistols came into fashion amongst 60 Entry and were even used surreptitiously in the lecture rooms. At one lecture, several Flight Cadets made up excuses to leave the room temporarily so as to reload their water-pistols! In Block 78, water-pistol fights led to bed tipping and several of us lost our tweeds.

I wasn't the only one to be teased about my accent. Ted Reynolds, who was from Portsmouth, came in for a lot of mimicking. Amongst the generally good-natured name-calling, I was incorrectly called a 'bush Baptist' and the Pakistanis were 'those queer men'.

Ted Reynolds and Colin Loveday expressed interest in joining the RNZAF, but I suggested to them that the RAF would probably be reluctant to let them go after investing so much in them.

The reorganisation of the College continued. Junior Entries moved out of Block 77 into huts called the South Brick Lines near the Junior Mess. 60C moved out of Block 78 into the new single-room accommodation of Block 80. Thus, Flight Cadets who weren't accommodated in the main College building were spread over Blocks 78 (A Squadron), 79 (B Squadron) and 80 (C Squadron). Later, when Block 77 had been converted into single-room accommodation, it was used to house the remaining Flight Cadets from the three Squadrons. The former NAAFI building was refurbished as the Junior Mess.

Ron and Jim went solo on Chipmunks before I'd had my first flight in one. I'd flown 13 hours on Prentices before D Flight got its quota of Chipmunks and Fg. Off. Vincent took me up to do the basic exercises and circuits at Barkston Heath. The rate of climb was terrific – much more than a Prentice and even a Harvard. The controls were very sensitive so more accuracy was required to fly the aircraft well.

The Canadian designed de Havilland Chipmunk T Mk 10 (Fig. 23) had a smaller wing-span than the Prentice and the distinctive de Havilland look about it. Of all-metal construction apart from fabric covered rudder, elevators, ailerons and flaps aft of the hinge line, the Chipmunk had a fixed undercarriage and a Gipsy Major 8 engine giving it a cruising speed of 90 knots. A cartridge

Figure 23. de Havilland Chipmunk T Mk 10 at Cranwell, April 1952.

was used to start the engine instead of a battery cart. Two cockpits were provided with identical controls, the forward one being for the pupil and the rear one for the instructor. The instrumentation was simple compared with a Prentice, there being only six flying instruments, two engine instruments, a compass and various levers and switches in each cockpit.

After 3 hours 10 minutes dual instruction, I was authorised to go solo. As with the Prentice, I had to sign a certificate stating that I understood the fuel, oil, pneumatic and hydraulic systems, the radio, electrical and ignition systems, the starting and running down procedures, the cockpit drill, the action in the event of fire in the air and on the ground, the procedure for abandoning aircraft, and the action in the event of engine failure on take-off.

There was a little bit of drama when I was on the final approach to land. The air traffic controller in the airfield caravan fired red Very lights to warn me off while an Anson and then a Prentice taxied across my landing path. This meant going around again twice and extended my first solo to 30 minutes.

There were other dramas to come. On another day, special instructions were broadcast to all Cranwell aircraft because a hunt had got onto the south airfield and there were horses and dogs everywhere. Then Tony Armstrong of 59B crashed a Prentice in the low flying area. Apparently he was practising forced landings, went below the minimum height of 50 feet, touched the ground, lost his undercarriage, tried to climb away, but lost height under full power and forced landed. Tony was unscathed, but his Prentice was rather a mess.

I was the second detail on a Chipmunk flight with Fg. Off. Vincent. He taxied into dispersal, dropped his first pupil without stopping the engine and, as I strapped myself in, taxied out for take-off. At altitude, I was practising steep turns in clear air between magnificent cumulus clouds when Fg. Off. Vincent throttled back the engine and told me to do a forced landing without power. I made a hash of it so he then demonstrated a perfect forced landing. We climbed to do some instrument flying and I put up amber screens around my cockpit and wore goggles with blue lenses, the effect of these colours being to black out everything except the instrument panel.

A few minutes later the engine spluttered and Fg. Off. Vincent took over control. I removed the instrument flying gear and looked at the fuel gauges on the wings. There was still fuel in the tanks. Fg. Off. Vincent headed for RAF Digby and broadcast a Mayday call, giving our height as 1,500 feet and location about two miles north of Ruskington. The engine cut out at about 1,200 feet so a forced landing was inevitable. Fg. Off. Vincent chose quite a good looking field in a bad selection of fields – the others all seemed to be square and ploughed. Telephone wires caused him to come in higher than desired. There was a light crosswind. He side-slipped to lose height, but overshot the field and headed for the ploughed field beyond, the furrows of which were pointing in our direction. He completed the forced landing checks and shouted to me to tighten my straps again and get my head down. We touched tail first, but the Chipmunk tipped onto its nose, hesitated, then fell on its back.

Upside down, we struggled to get out of the Chipmunk. Fg. Off. Vincent told me to release my parachute harness, but not the seat straps. I couldn't open the sliding hood because it was resting on the ploughed field, so I pushed out the emergency exit panel on the port side. I still couldn't get out as the port wing was touching the ground. Fg. Off. Vincent bashed his way through the rear part of the hood as at that point it was off the ground. He began scraping the earth away with his hands so as to give me space to get out. Some locals who'd seen the crash walked at an infuriatingly slow pace towards us. Fg. Off. Vincent got them to lift the port wing and, after some four or five minutes upside down, I released my straps, fell on my head and eased myself out of the Chipmunk.

Various aircraft circled above us and a Prentice did a low fly past to see if Fg. Off. Vincent and I were all right. We waved energetically. One of the locals went to ring Cranwell, but we felt sure that the circling aircraft would have got help on the way. We stayed with the Chipmunk and surveyed its bent propeller, crushed canopy and damaged fin and rudder. I was starting to get cold when a blood wagon and two fire engines arrived. Fg. Off. Vincent and I slung our parachutes over our shoulders and, carrying our leather helmets, entered the blood wagon, watched by a lot of curious people. Back at Cranwell, a doctor asked me to touch my toes, enquired if my back felt all right and looked at my eyes before passing me as fit. I was deluged with questions by other Flight Cadets in the crew room, but gave just a brief description of what'd happened.

I was niggled by Flight Cadets who called me 'Prangcock,' or said, 'Oh, there's the chap who pranged a Chipmunk,' when I hadn't done the forced landing. There was much speculation as to what had caused the engine to cut out. The freezing level had been very low that day and Fg. Off. Vincent had put hot air onto the carburetter to prevent icing. Nevertheless, icing could have occurred. I was very much aware that I had the dubious distinction of being in the first crash of a Royal Air Force College Chipmunk.

The next day Flt. Lt. J. Lindsay Bayley, who'd taken over D Flight on the promotion of Flt. Lt. Bedford to Squadron Leader, took me up for a flight. Fg. Off. Vincent had been grounded pending a court of inquiry into the accident. Flt. Lt. Bayley had fearsome looking whiskers, but was a very mild mannered officer. After I'd done some upper air exercises, he asked me to fly over the crash site. We could see two trailers leaving the field with parts of the Chipmunk. On our way back to Cranwell, Flt. Lt. Bayley asked how many hours I'd flown in Prentices and Chipmunks. When I said about 22, he replied he'd call it my 25 hour test and that I was making good progress. No doubt Fg. Off. Vincent was pleased when he heard this news. I was relieved to have got off so lightly as I wasn't given the expected oral test after the flying test.

Flt. Lt. 'Bud' Abbott took me up for more instrument flying and my first aerobatics in a Chipmunk. I started to feel airsick again and had to put my head out into the slip-stream to feel better. Then the fair haired Flt. Lt. R.B. Sillars became my regular flying instructor. He was a very pleasant person.

Fg. Off. Vincent and I were summoned to the College Headquarters building for the court of inquiry into the crash. He'd already told me that the engine failure had been through lack of fuel – the fuel gauges had been over reading. He admitted that he should've got the Chipmunk refuelled before our flight as it hadn't been refuelled since the morning of the accident. He hoped to get away with a reprimand. The Chipmunk had Category 4 damage, i.e. repairable by the makers. The court of two Flight Lieutenants and a Flying Officer heard Fg. Off. Vincent's testimony first. After three hours of waiting, I was ushered before the court and asked in Fg. Off. Vincent's presence to run through the flight as I remembered it. Then everything had to be taken down in longhand. I heard nothing about the results of the inquiry, but several months later Fg. Off. Vincent was posted away from Cranwell.

There was other bad news. Jim Brown went into Station Sick Quarters with influenza. Wally Martin of 60A was sent to RAF Hospital Nocton Hall with ear problems and, after a decompression test, was allowed to return to the College. Dave Purse of 60C was chopped because of airsickness and transferred to No. 12 Entry at RAF Digby as an Equipment Branch Cadet. Ian Powell of 57C was also chopped, so his departure left only five New Zealanders at the College. Fg. Off. Vincent had told me he was amazed how many Flight Cadets were worried about being chopped. I thought we had just cause to be worried!

Sqn. Ldr. Furlong sent news that two more members of the RNZAF would be coming to the College – Geoff Wallingford, son of the Air Member for Personnel, and Guy McLeod. They would join No. 63 Entry. Ron and I decided to write to them and give them the low-down on Cranwell.

Before the end of term, Sqn. Ldr. Furlong made a two day visit to the College. Ron and I had tea with him each day in the guest room adjoining the billiard room. I gave him a conducted tour of Cranwell including my room. He made no mention of the progress Ron and I were making, but no doubt he had been well briefed on that!

The weather began to improve though there were still occasional snow storms, so I resumed gliding with the hope I'd be selected for a gliding camp at RAF Scharfoldendorf in West Germany during the coming leave.

One of my glider flights at Cranwell was a disaster. I'd just taken-off in a Cadet 2 and was climbing steeply, pulled by the winch, when I suddenly noticed my airspeed falling off. I immediately pushed the nose of the glider down to gain airspeed, but had insufficient height in which to do so. After a quick flare-out, I landed heavily and went through the plywood seat taking skin off my lower spine. The wings sagged and one of the supports buckled. On leaving the glider, I tried to work out what'd happened.

The Officer in charge of Gliding concluded that the Flight Cadet using the Aldis lamp to signal the winch driver had been too close to my take-off path so that the glider had interrupted the signals seen by the winch driver. Dashes were signalled to take up the slack in the towing cable, then a continuous signal for full power to tow up the glider, but the winch driver having seen dashes following the continuous signal had stopped winding in the cable.

There was no court of inquiry that I was aware of, but the Senior Flight Cadet on gliding that day told me to report to his room in the College at 1900 hours. When I presented myself, he casually turned in his chair to face me, looked me up and down and acted as if he didn't know why I was there. He left me standing to attention and eventually said he didn't want me bending aircraft and, as the crash hadn't been my fault, I was still on the list to go to Scharfoldendorf. I left greatly relieved, but still very sore at the base of my spine.

I didn't tell Mum or Cousin Mabel about this second accident as I felt they'd still be upset over the Chipmunk crash. Cousin Mabel later wrote saying she'd dreamt that I'd had two accidents, not one. I didn't enlighten her as she'd probably contact Mum about it.

I continued gliding and made several flights in the two-seater Kranich, one of the types of glider I would experience at Scharfoldendorf.

Flt. Lt. Sillars and I went on a cross-country flight in a Chipmunk to Doncaster and back. He supervised me closely as I went through the flight planning stage, advised air traffic control and did mental dead reckoning. Everything was working out so well on the flight that he took control and quite deliberately went off track before asking me to work out a new course for Cranwell. My estimate of heading was better than his one! He then took away my map for a while and asked me where we were. Luckily I knew! As we passed RAF Swinderby, we saw skid marks and the remains of a crashed Varsity aircraft.

The weather continued changeable. Snow fell during a ceremonial parade when we weren't wearing greatcoats and a cold 35 knot wind blew many hats off. One day when flying was cancelled because of the weather, Sqn. Ldr. Coward helped occupy 60A by telling us about the post-war air forces in Belgium, France, Holland and Norway.

I decided I'd had enough of the Knocker Cup inter-squadron gymnastics so didn't compete that term.

When the Ferris inter-squadron drill competition came around, I accidentally touched my hat with my rifle when sloping arms. The hat ended up on the back of my head, but that didn't stop A Squadron from winning the arms drill section. Our march pasts, however, let us down. A Squadron came third overall.

An inter-squadron competition was held over several weeks so that Flight Cadets and Cadets could qualify for athletic standards. I easily qualified in the high jump, the long jump and the hop, step and jump, and eventually reached the standard in the 100 yards sprint. I decided to concentrate on the Western Roll in the high jump as I hadn't got above 5 feet 3 inches with the Scissors technique. I bought two pairs of track shoes and had one pair specially modified for high jumping by having two spikes inserted below each heel.

Light rain and snow marred the inter-squadron athletics, but A Squadron gained sufficient points in this and other inter-squadron competitions during the term to be named Queen's Squadron for the following term.

Malcolm Dines tried to interest me and other members of 60A who didn't have transport in buying an ex-London taxi. Some members of 60A already had motor bikes or cars. He said Reg Bailey, Sam Boyce and Julian Bowes were interested. I didn't see myself making much use of the taxi, but agreed to participate. Ted Reynolds later joined the syndicate.

I decided to visit the College Museum in an old hangar near the Hangar Church, and also the gun and turret room in the Weapons Lecture Block. The Museum was full of mainly German World War II aircraft such as a ME262 jet fighter, a Focker Wolf 109 piston engined fighter, a Heinkel 162 jet fighter, a Heinkel rocket propelled flying wing interceptor, a flying bomb and a V2 rocket. There was also a Japanese Baka suicide plane, many jet engines including a German Juma jet engine and a Whittle engine of the type that powered the first successful British jet aircraft, some piston engines and cannons. I sat in the cockpits of the aircraft and imagined flying these historic planes. In the Weapons Block, I was most impressed by the size of the bouncing bomb and the 1,000 pound bomb.

During the term, Sqn. Ldr. Thomas held a series of Squadron Commander's meetings for 60A on such things as promotion (the odds of getting to high rank were slim!), standards of dress, and marriage in the Air Force (not before age twenty-five or -six!). We'd heard a rumour that one of the Senior Entry was married, contrary to the policy of the College! He'd married after his first term at the College and been immediately chopped. Then the Commandant had apparently said, 'Jolly good show,' and allowed the Cadet to stay on at the College. Presumably the wife lived somewhere near Cranwell and saw her husband infrequently.

As the end of term approached, there was another round of tests, a briefing for the eleven Flight Cadets going to Scharfoldendorf, and photographs were taken of Squadrons, sports teams and prize winners. Ron Parfitt was awarded the Sword of Honour, the highest award at the College, and was the first New Zealander to have achieved that distinction. He was third overall in the Order of Merit. Sam Boyce found that his door key could open Reg Bailey's door so some of 60A had an end of term party in Reg's room while he was at Lincoln. Liquor was brought from Sleaford and during the party, damage was done to things in the room. Needless to say Reg was pretty brassed off about this on his return. 61 Entry celebrated becoming Flight Cadets by setting fire to the airman patches they'd taken from their uniforms, and letting off firecrackers.

The Senior Term of the Swedish Royal Air Force College made a week long visit to Cranwell, flying from Uppsala in twenty-four Mustangs with officers and supporting ground staff in a Junkers 86 and a Dakota. I heard that the Cadets carried suitcases in the wings of their Mustangs where cannons were normally housed. The Cadets all seemed to be tall and blond, wore black uniforms with gold trimmings, and were pilots before going to Uppsala. They were highly visible at the final guest night of term and the presentation of Wings to 55 GD(P) Entry by Air Marshal Sir Alick C. Stevens, KBE, CB, formerly Air Officer Commanding-in-Chief, Coastal Command. After the graduation parade of Nos. 55 GD(P) and 6 E & S Entries, reviewed by The Rt. Hon. Lord de L'Isle and Dudley, VC, Secretary of State for Air, the Swedish aircraft circled Cranwell several times in formation before beginning their long return flight to Uppsala.

I'd just enough time to photograph the visiting aircraft before they left, plus a Shackleton 1 and a Proctor. I didn't want to stay for the graduation ball that night so caught a chartered bus for Grantham and travelled by train to London. I thought I'd stay at Overseas League House, located in a cul-de-sac off St James's Street, since Mum had arranged League membership for me. About half of the accommodation seemed to be occupied by members from Britain rather than members from overseas. The big advantage of Overseas League House was its central location and modest charges.

I tried to find Jennifer Langford-Jones in the telephone directory. Jennifer was the daughter of Mum's cousin, Hugh Skinner, who'd been a medical doctor in China. She was an actress, had been performing in *A Streetcar Named Desire* and had just started in television. Her husband Robert was the manager and stage director of the farcical comedy, *The Gay Dog*, starring Wilfred Pickles, at the Piccadilly Theatre. I couldn't find the Langford-Jones's number so decided to visit them at their address in Earl's Court Road. Jennifer came to the door dressed in a white towelling robe, smoking a cigarette and with a wine glass in one hand. She wasn't the glamorous female I'd expected, being short with the sort of face that could be made-up to look like almost anyone. Her hair was tied in a pony-tail. As she was just about to have a bath, she invited me for lunch in two days time.

When I called again, Jennifer was fully made-up and very presentable. We walked to her mother's place in Redcliffe Square for lunch – Jennifer carrying a Siamese cat. Mrs Skinner was plump, even shorter than Jennifer and had given her hair a blue rinse. We had a very pleasant lunch talking about family and looking at photographs. Jennifer said her stage name was Jennifer Gray. She invited me to later see *The Gay Dog* and meet her husband Robert.

I began exploring the streets in the St James's area, stopping to look at the exclusive clubs of Boodles and Whites, guards outside St James's Palace, choir boys going into Queen's Chapel, horse guards riding down The Mall, crowds in Trafalgar Square and neon signs in Piccadilly Circus. Then I went further afield to the Imperial War Museum – a marvellous place packed full of everything conceivable about war.

Somewhat footsore, I went to the Royal Albert Hall to see Sir Malcolm Sargent conduct the Royal Choral Society and the London Symphonic Orchestra in Handel's *Messiah*. There was only space in the 'gods' so I climbed to the top gallery and admired the faded Victorian splendour of the huge auditorium. With no seats in the gallery I sat on the floor with enthusiasts who, with backs to the balustrade, were following the score in music books or just sitting with their eyes closed listening to the soloist, Isobelle Bailey. Not being able to see the performance without standing, I decided to leave – *Messiah* wasn't my sort of music anyway. The Last Night at the Proms was more my style.

When walking down a Soho Street, I saw the advertising sign of a fortune-teller. Just for a laugh, I decided to have my fortune told. On climbing the stairs I came upon two very ordinary looking middle-aged women having afternoon tea together. When they saw me, one of them said, 'I see you've got a client,' and left. I sat down opposite the other woman. She held the finger tips of my right hand and looked intensely at my palm. I told her I didn't want to know about my death and received her assurance on that. She commenced by telling me several thoughts I'd had earlier that day and that I'd soon be sending someone flowers. She said my destiny was in some foreign country and I was fond of someone in that country, but I would meet another person and, though there'd be many difficulties, we'd marry and be very happy together. She also said, amongst other things, that in later years I'd periodically experience some tension which I should try and avoid, and that I'd live to a ripe old age. I thanked her, said that I was a New Zealander and had a girlfriend in that country. She offered to go into a trance so that she could tell me more, but I felt I'd had enough for one day! I left, wondering to whom I should be sending flowers!

(Some time later, I saw an advertisement in one of the tabloid newspapers that a Mr Mir Bashir was offering a free self-analysis if sent the imprint of the palm of one's right hand. I responded and received the following:

You are endowed with good imagination and a creative turn of mind, however you have a leisurely approach to life and may tend to put things off. You obviously seem to prefer reflection to action and are liable to lose sight of the material aspect of life. Watch this tendency. There is an innate urge to travel; foreign lands in fact will always attract you and it is more than likely that you will endeavour to settle down in a place far from the native soil. Probably your destiny is associated with a country abroad.

I wondered how true these predictions would be.)

On two Sundays, I went to the packed out church of St Martin-in-the-Fields and enjoyed splendid services even though my long legs were cramped in the pews of a gallery box. Access to the box was through a low door. The magnificent architecture of the church was affected by the lack of stained glass (removed during World War II) and scaffolding where war damage was being repaired. I felt sure after one service that the Prime Minister, Winston Churchill, left the church before the rest of the congregation.

I rang Miss Macdonald of Sleat as she'd asked me to do so when next in London. She must have got the impression I was at a loose end as she immediately arranged a date for me with an American girl. Grace turned out to be a most attractive girl, dressed in a very fetching, tight black dress, pillbox hat and veil. The only problems were that she had a fiancé who was a Rhodes Scholar at Oxford, her excessive make-up reminded me of the orange coloured make-up I'd seen on NAAFI girls at Cranwell, and she'd been to all the popular shows in London. We wandered through Green Park into Hyde Park, listened to the Irish Guards Band near the Serpentine and watched the Armstrong Whitworth 56 experimental flying wing jet aircraft fly overhead. Grace told me that American friends had invited us to tea at their flat in Notting Hill Gate, so we had a very pleasant time with them before going to see a Japanese film at a cinema. I felt I was having a really international experience!

On visiting Sqn. Ldr. Furlong, I was taken to see Air Cdre. Kay to tell him about Ron Parfitt winning the Sword of Honour. Air Cdre. Kay said he'd send congratulations and get the public relations people onto getting Ron some publicity back home.

Miss Moore came up to London again to see me. She took me to the Sadler's Wells ballet *Coppélia*, and then dinner at a very nice restaurant – insisting on paying for everything though I felt she could barely afford to do so. She appeared to be having difficulty making ends meet with the rationing system still in force and said she led a very quiet life at Eynsford. I showed her my latest photos and she was interested to hear news about my family.

A Leonardo da Vinci exhibition at the Royal Academy of Arts helped to increase my interest in art. Then I went to the Westminster Theatre near the Royal Mews to see the play *Midnight Abbey* by Thomas Love Peacock, as I'd enjoyed writing an essay on the story in my school-days. I kept passing historic places like the house in which the artist Gainsborough had lived. My walks around London made me footsore so I rested by going to cinemas and seeing excellent films such as *Quo Vadis, 5 Fingers, Angels One Five* and *A Streetcar Named Desire*. I was intrigued by the buskers entertaining the cinema queues, there being no buskers in New Zealand at that time.

London was such a fascinating place! With some reluctance I made my way to RAF Hendon for my next big adventure.

CHAPTER 9

Scharfoldendorf

I ARRIVED EARLY AT THE HENDON DEPARTURE LOUNGE. Other Flight Cadets soon appeared and we waited for the three Cranwell Ansons, one being delayed because of bad visibility. There were three officers and only eight Flight Cadets on the ten day trip to RAF Scharfoldendorf – three members of the Senior Entry having to stay behind for ejection seat tests. We passed through Customs, donned parachutes and Mae Wests and took-off on the four-hour flight to RAF Bückeburg near Minden in West Germany. The Anson I was in was flown by my Flight Commander, Flt. Lt. Bayley.

Hendon was a very small airfield and our Ansons just cleared the four-storeyed buildings at the end of the runway. We climbed slowly over London to 3,000 feet before heading towards The Naze and out over the North Sea. I tried to go to sleep until the Dutch coast was crossed just north of The Hague. The coastal dykes were pitted (war damage?), but beyond them extended brilliant green fields, many ploughed fields, large red fields (tulips?), houses, canals, barges, windmills and several lakes with yachts on them. We continued into Germany over dark forests, hilly country through which the River Weser meandered and an abandoned airfield pock-marked by water filled craters before eventually landing at RAF Bückeburg.

There were several dozen RAF Meteor 8s and 9s on the well laid out airfield, together with some Ansons, British European Airways aircraft and other planes I was unable to identify. A German guard dressed in a dark green uniform, white belt and black ski-type hat guided us to where we could change our money into BAFs (British Armed Forces currency, used at military establishments in the British Zone). We had a meal at the officers' mess before leaving on the fifty-mile bus ride to Scharfoldendorf.

Near Bückeburg were several large mansions set in delightful surroundings. Signs indicated that they were the Headquarters of the British Armed Forces in West Germany. The buildings didn't look like the usual military establishments. Our German driver kept sounding his horn to clear a way along the narrow, cobbled streets of the many villages through which we passed. Apple trees coming into flower lined many of the country roads. Farmers and their families were working in the fields, the men and boys often dressed in leather shorts and plain or diamond pattern knee-high socks. Their houses reminded me of the Tudor buildings I'd seen in England. We passed under an *autobahn* and I was impressed by the no expense spared way this super highway cut through the countryside. At the sizable township of Hamelin, we crossed the Weser and saw British engineers practising bridging the river. In fading light, we drove past the little village of Scharfoldendorf and up the zigzag, white dusty road on the scarp of the ridge beyond. I could see at the top of the ridge the three-storeyed airmen's block and a glass-walled direction finding station set into the steep roof.

On arrival at the airmen's block, we Flight Cadets were taken up wide stone stairs and along corridors to two of the eight-bed dormitories. Our beds took some getting used to as the solid mattresses were in sections, the bedding barely tucked in underneath and the pillows could hardly be dented. In the ablutions we were intrigued by floor to ceiling tiling and fittings such as a trough that had adjacent wall bars – apparently for airmen being sick!

We were told that the facilities of the officers' mess were available to us so we went there for meals and to relax in the comfortable lounge of the adjoining bar. When we thanked the German waiters for their service, they also said, 'Thank you.' After a while this repetition got a bit wearing.

I heard that Scharfoldendorf had been a German gliding centre prior to World War II and many pilots of the Luftwaffe had received initial training there before moving onto powered aircraft. The airfield (if one could call it that) was a small, irregular shaped, grassy slope on top of a twelve-mile long wooded ridge. When the prevailing wind blew at 40 knots or more up the scarp slope (enough to rattle the windows in the airmen's block), gliders and sailplanes could soar along the ridge for hours at a time. When big cumulus clouds developed in the area cross-country flights could be undertaken.

After World War II, Scharfoldendorf had become an RAF Rest Centre as, in addition to gliding, there was horse riding, tramping, tennis, indoor roller skating, swimming, skiing, a children's playground, a games room, a cinema and other leisure facilities and activities. The well-kept buildings, some of chateau style, were set amongst very pleasant trees and flower beds. Flt. Lt. Osland, a few RAF NCOs and airmen and about twelve Germans ran the Centre. Several British families, ten British Army chaps and some foreigners were staying there, but they all wore civilian clothes so disguised their identity.

Near the end of World War II, there'd been two hangars at Scharfoldendorf storing gliders and sailplanes brought from all over Germany to keep them out of the hands of the advancing Russians, but one of the hangars had been burned down before the War ended. When I was at Scharfoldendorf, the remaining hangar contained some twenty German gliders and sailplanes such as the Grunau 2B, Kranich, Minimoa S-41, Meise, Mu 13, Rhönadler, Rhönbuzzard, Rhönsperber, SG 38 and Weihe. The rafters and walls held spare wings and other aircraft parts. A damaged Horten 15 flying wing glider lay in one corner. The pilot had to lie face down to operate the unique flying controls. Unfortunately the glider had proved to be unstable and crashed

– the pilot's head leaving a hole in the long perspex canopy. I lay in the glider and found the prone position quite comfortable, though frighteningly close to the ground.

Each morning, the Cranwell contingent assembled for a briefing in the gliding club rooms known as The Glide Inn.

We were told not to go ridge soaring unless certain we could get back with 500 feet of height above the airfield. There was mention of a Flight Cadet who, on a previous visit, had run out of height along the ridge and landed on top of the fifty foot high trees covering the ridge. He should have landed in a field below the ridge. His rescue and the recovery of the glider had taken some time. If we landed away, we'd be fined for the trouble we'd caused.

We were also warned not to fly into the Russian Zone some fifty miles to the east as another Flight Cadet had landed just short of the Zone and almost caused an international incident!

The weather was glorious and I was soon as sunburnt as the children at the Centre. I began by helping shift the gliders on the uneven surface of the airfield. The gliders were winched into the sky up the dip slope or along the ridge depending on the wind direction, but landings were always up the dip slope. The technique on final approach to land was greatly to increase airspeed so as to get through the down draught on the lee side of the ridge, and then round out and land going uphill. This took a lot of judgement and in my first attempts to land I badly undershot, or overshot in spite of side slipping and using air brakes.

After four flights in the two-seater Kranich, I was allowed to go solo in a Grunau. The fresh air in the open cockpit was very cooling after the heat on the ground. Also, the view along the ridge and down the scarp to Scharfoldendorf and other villages and to the township of Eschershausen was quite breathtaking.

One morning I thought I had the plague as there were red spots all over my body. Someone with medical knowledge said I probably had heat rash, but decided I'd better see the medical officer at RAF Bückeburg. A Corporal drove me in a German station wagon to Bückeburg where a young Flying Officer doctor gave me some pills and kept me in hospital for the weekend. As the only patient in the hospital I received royal treatment in one of two single-bed rooms reserved for officers. I felt fine, but had to stay in bed listening to the radio, reading magazines or looking out of the window at passing aircraft and a beautiful, blossom covered apple tree. A Polish driver with little English returned me to Scharfoldendorf in a rear-engined Opel car. We got lost in the streets of Hamelin so the journey took much longer than expected.

I hadn't missed much gliding while in hospital as some new arrivals from the local gliding club and twenty-six ATC cadets from all over Britain had been given priority with the gliders. When not flying, the cadets had drunk a lot of cheap liquor and often made themselves sick. Flt. Lt. Bayley had slipped a disc so took no further part in the flying.

When the weather was suitable, we flew all day. I progressed in the Grunau from nose launches (where the towing cable was attached to the front of the glider) to C of G launches (where the cable was attached at the glider's centre of gravity). The wind speed didn't go above 20 knots so extensive ridge soaring wasn't possible. Most of my flights were of short duration around Scharfoldendorf, but one flight of 29 minutes along the ridge gained me my Royal Aero Club C Gliding Certificate.

Some of the more experienced Flight Cadets went on cross-country flights, but got no further than twenty-two miles when they ran out of thermals and had to land in a field. Another Flight Cadet climbed to 10,000 feet under a large cumulo-nimbus cloud.

To liven things up on a day when there was no thermal or ridge soaring, we had a spot landing competition. Cpl. McKercher, the Deputy Chief Flying Instructor, won by landing within ten feet of the designated mark. I made a horrible landing in one of the many hollows scattered over the airfield.

When unable to fly, I climbed the stairs to the direction finding station to admire the view and talk to the RAF airmen there. An Old Cranwellian whom I'd met at RAF Bückeburg beat up the airfield in a Meteor and succeeded in stopping further launching of gliders until he'd disappeared into the blue sky.

On other occasions, I frequented the hangar and talked to the Germans servicing the gliders and sailplanes. They had great skills in working with wood and I learned a lot from them about glider construction and the characteristics of each aircraft. Before World War II, sailplanes like the gull-winged Minimoa were designed to fly just above stalling speed to enable them to take advantage of the slightest thermal. Since the War, sailplanes like the British Olympia sailplane (developed from the German Meise sailplane) were designed to fly at much higher speeds with a very low rate of sink so enabling them to make long cross-country flights in much windier conditions. The German craftsmen made model gliders in their spare time and sold them for a few pfennigs. The Minimoa and Grunau display models I bought, beautifully finished in laminated woods, grace my study as I write.

I took lots of photographs at Scharfoldendorf and was pleased when they all came out well and the other Flight Cadets ordered a total of eighty-four prints plus a few enlargements. Some photos were later submitted to the College *Journal*, but only an article on the trip was published.

More photographs were taken when an RAF Corporal married a WRAF Corporal in Eschershausen and had their wedding reception at RAF Scharfoldendorf. When I visited Eschershausen, I bought sweets (as they were more readily available than in Britain) and some excellent black and white photographic postcards.

On two evenings, we Flight Cadets made the uncomfortable journey in the back of a truck to Hamelin for more extensive shopping. I tried to buy an Iron Cross, but the asking price was too high. An elderly German female customer in the shop told me quietly in English that the shopkeeper was ripping me off, so I went elsewhere and bought a small, coloured wooden carving of the Pied Piper of Hamelin. Slot machines selling a variety of sweets proved very popular. We had difficulty in a restaurant making ourselves understood and resorted to sign language and pointing at things. A cinema catering for British servicemen was showing a forgettable American western film so we left and went to the Salvation Army's Pied Piper Club for a snack and the latest British newspapers. The truck got us back to Scharfoldendorf by midnight.

Our time at Scharfoldendorf rapidly came to an end. I was hoping to convert onto the Minimoa when it cracked a former and had to be disassembled. Then I was about to fly the Rhönbuzzard when a front passed over Scharfoldendorf and flying was cancelled. We had an excellent five course dinner with Flt. Lt. Osland the night before leaving. Another uncomfortable truck ride took us to RAF Bückeburg where we changed our money back into pounds sterling, proceeded through Customs and boarded our Ansons.

Just before take-off, we discovered that we were being taken to RAF Manston on the south-eastern tip of England and not Hendon. Some of us didn't have enough money left for the train fare to London! Luckily, travel warrants were issued for the train journey, but we had to pay for the warrants on returning to Cranwell.

Our flight took us over the impressive Rhine delta to Manston where American Thunderjet fighters, Goose amphibians and Packet transports were amongst the aircraft operating from the one enormous runway. I watched with awe the almost vertical climb of the Thunderjets, marked by long trails of black smoke and much noise.

An RAF bus took us to Margate where we filled in time by looking at amusement arcades on the waterfront and an abandoned World War II fort out in the English Channel, and having tea in one of the numerous restaurants. The train journey to London would have been interesting if we'd not been so tired. I was soon asleep at Overseas League House.

When I later travelled with a lot of other Flight Cadets back to Cranwell, I decided that if at all possible I must visit Scharfoldendorf again.

CHAPTER 10

A Jolly Good Show, Chaps

MALCOLM DINES RETURNED FROM LEAVE driving the ex-London taxi I had a share in. He'd christened it 'Henrietta' (Fig. 24). The syndicate members, Mal, Sam Boyce, Julian Bowes, Ted Reynolds and I, all wanted to go for a ride in it so, with Julian at the wheel, we made a hair-raising trip to Newark. The brakes weren't too good – nor was Julian's driving! The driver sat virtually in the open on top of the petrol tank, with a space to his left for luggage. A magnificent curved horn to the right of the driver made a terrible honking noise. The passengers were somewhat more comfortable on a black leather covered padded seat behind curved sliding doors. A small collapsible seat opposite the passengers faced the rear. By the time we arrived at Newark we certainly needed a cup of tea! Somehow we returned to Cranwell safely.

Other members of 60A had returned with transport – Reg Bailey with a sporting little MG car, and Sam Boyce, Ted Reynolds and Joe Qureshi with motor bikes.

The Summer Term had begun and everything looked rosy. The weather was good, the lawns were green, there were flowers on the trees and in the flower-beds.

I visited Junior Entries to meet Geoff Wallingford and Guy McLeod, the two newly arrived RNZAF members of No. 63 Entry. Ron Chippindale, Jim Brown and Colin Loveday had already been to see them. Geoff and Guy seemed likable chaps. We talked for a while before I wished them all the best and offered them assistance should they need it. I wasn't to know how well they'd do at the College!

60 Entry was excluded from 61 Entry's first guest night because of the limitation on seating in the College dining hall, and few members could be bothered to get dressed up to attend the initiations afterwards.

When the new timetables and set lists were issued, the main changes were that 60 Entry no longer had Squadron Commanders' periods, there were three half days for flying instead of four and there were more periods for private study. Some changes had been made amongst the gen men (in set one for both Humanistics and Science), but their number remained at nine. 'Thermocoople' was still my tutor.

Getting back into the routine wasn't easy. Each lecturer gave us masses of work to be done in our own time. In Aircraft Structures we started with the composition of metals, in Thermodynamics there were experiments on the

Figure 24. 'Henrietta,' the ex-London taxi at Cranwell, May 1952: L–R: Julian Bowes, Malcolm Dines, Sam Boyce and Author (All 60A).

Riccardo engine and in Radio we had aerial theory. Our drill needed close attention. Rain occurred during a church parade and we all had to sit through a service in wet uniforms. A solid PT session showed how unfit we'd become. 60A was told off by Sqn. Ldr. Thomas over the state of our rooms. There was kit to be replaced necessitating tedious visits to the Clothing Store in East Camp, form filling in triplicate, visits to the Accounts Section to pay minor sums of money and then return visits to the Clothing Store to draw the kit required. The air temperature was high and we were all glad when permitted to change into Short Sleeve Order.

The College held a Mess meeting, then the A Squadron Under Officer, Roger Streatfield, briefed 60A on what he expected of us. There was also a meeting of gliding club members. After a guest night, the well known British gliding expert, Philip Wills, gave an illustrated lecture on Advanced Soaring and then went off to Spain and became World Gliding Champion. I got into training again for the Knocker Cup inter-squadron gymnastics competition.

An artist called Pat Rooney appeared in our ante-room one day drawing caricatures of those Flight Cadets who wanted to sit for him. I sent the likeness he drew of me home to Mum and had to explain the inclusion of the nickname 'Hank' (Fig. 25).

Flt. Lt. Sillars showed me how to do a forced landing with power and then sent me solo to practise this and other procedures including my first

Figure 25. Caricature of R.M. (Hank) Hancock.

solo spin in a Chipmunk. I returned early from one flight when the engine began to run roughly. Flt. Lt. Sillars had me do a lot of instrument flying. We did various manoeuvres at altitude before beginning circuits using only the instruments. On one occasion, the humidity in the cockpit was so high that my blue goggles kept misting over and we had to abandon the exercise.

As my Flight Commander, Flt. Lt. Bayley, was still nursing a slipped disc, Flt. Lt. 'Bud' Abbott took me for my instrument flying test. I had to do an instrument take-off and circuit. Instead of landing I was instructed to overshoot and climb to 4,000 feet and do a stall. Flt. Lt. Abbott then took control, deliberately fell out of a slow roll to topple the artificial horizon and then went into steep left and right turns. He gave me control and told me to recover using the remaining instruments. That successfully completed I was allowed to remove the blue goggles and amber screens and return to Cranwell.

I felt I'd done much better instrument flying with Flt. Lt. Sillars, but Flt. Lt. Abbott seemed quite pleased, told me I'd put on quite a creditable performance and cleared me for my first lot of night flying.

A and D Flights assembled in the main briefing room at 2050 hours for the night flying briefing. I was in the first detail. Flt. Lt. Sillars and I took-off from Cranwell along a path lit by goose-necked flares and headed for RAF Barkston Heath. The sealed runway at Barkston had wartime Drem lighting that could be seen when taking-off, but not from other directions. For this first night flying session, goose-necked flares had been placed on each side of the runway to make things easier for us. The sky had become completely dark and I practised circuits by referring to the instruments and the flare-path. A more extensive radio procedure was required compared with circuits in daylight.

Using a special call-sign, I called the control tower, 'Item taxi.' Clearance to taxi was given. After doing checks at the take-off point, I called, 'Item take-off.' The tower then gave me clearance. Part of the airborne checks was the call, 'Item airborne,' and this was acknowledged. I switched off the downwards identification light under the port wing.

At 1,000 feet, I began a rate one climbing turn through ninety degrees to the left, straightened up crosswind and levelled off at 1,400 feet, commenced another rate one turn through ninety degrees to the left, then straightened up and called, 'Item downwind.' The tower again acknowledged. To allow for a slight crosswind, I had to make an adjustment to my heading so that the Chipmunk tracked parallel to the flare-path.

I did the downwind checks, switched on the light under the port wing and timed the downwind leg so as to turn onto the crosswind or base leg at the appropriate moment.

I commenced a rate one turn through ninety degrees to the left and began descending. As I made another rate one turn through ninety degrees to the left while still descending, I called, 'Item finals.' The tower cleared me to land. Theoretically, I should then be at the right height and distance from the touchdown point and in line with the runway, but I wasn't always so!

After landing and clearing the runway, I called, 'Item clear,' and did the after landing checks.

I completed three circuits with Flt. Lt. Sillars before Flt. Lt. I.K. Salter gave me my night flying solo check. I was then sent solo for a fifteen minute circuit. The night was clear and I could see for miles in all directions. The lights of Grantham seemed very close. The air was beautifully smooth, but a strong crosswind had developed near the ground causing the Chipmunk to start drifting sideways. I made an adjustment to keep on track and applied rudder at the last moment to land safely along the runway, quite pleased that all had gone so well.

The time was 0130 hours. I said good night to Flt. Lt. Sillars, but he was less than charitable, being tired and about to fly with Alan McLelland-Brown. I later heard that the crosswind became stronger, so members of the second detail weren't allowed to go solo and returned to Cranwell by 0300 hours. Back at the College I ate the light supper left out for those on night flying before bedding down in a room belonging to a member of 59A in the main College building. Some of 59 Entry had been asked to swop rooms with those of 60 Entry who were on night flying, because the Assistant Commandant was going to inspect our accommodation Blocks early in the morning. In that way, those of us on night flying after midnight were able to sleep undisturbed until 1130 hours.

Unfortunately, aircraft accidents still kept happening. Tom Greenhill-Hooper of 60B was given fourteen days jankers for taxiing a Chipmunk into another aircraft. Brian Huxley of 57A, who'd been at Scharfoldendorf with me, crashed a Harvard when practising a forced landing without power – the engine not responding after he'd opened the throttle on completion of the exercise. Then Nigel MacNicol of 60A did a tail slide in a Chipmunk, causing the hood to fly open and jam. He landed safely and found that the fuselage had buckled.

I began gliding in Cadet 2s again before converting onto the more advanced Prefect (a British development of the German Grunau). I also got some dual instruction in the Sedburg T21B two-seater trainer. The new Officer in charge of Gliding, Flt. Lt. 'Bud' Abbott, asked me to make out the gliding detail and hand it to him each week. I began having dual instruction on the winching of gliders and was surprised on one occasion when told that I'd winched the Commandant into the air.

Sports afternoons were mainly taken up by athletics. Fg. Off. F.W. Rickard, the new Officer in charge of Athletics, introduced a training programme in which everyone interested in athletics had a go at each event. Later, he asked me to be a steward at two triangular athletics matches held at the College. I kept practising the Western Roll technique in the high jump and was helped by two professional coaches who were visiting Cranwell. Unfortunately, I didn't jump well enough in trials to be selected for the College athletics team going to L'École de l'Air, Salon.

Then a member of 60A who was in the College athletics team flying to Salon, took my new track shoes without my permission, though he left a note saying he'd done so as his new track shoes weren't yet available. I was inconvenienced by this and rather put out as so many of 60A had previously borrowed things from me like blanco brushes and Dura-glit and needed to be reminded to return them. A week later when the track shoes hadn't been returned to me, I discovered they'd been lent to another Flight Cadet! When they were finally returned, I was disappointed to find that some of the spikes had come loose. I made my displeasure known, but declined an offer to replace the track shoes with a new pair.

While high jumping at the Cranwell Stadium, I saw a formation of ten Vampires fly overhead. They were an impressive sight. Later, twelve Chipmunks circled Cranwell in different formations while being photographed from another aircraft. Then a beautifully finished blue Meteor 4 appeared on the tarmac of the south airfield before being housed in the Cranwell museum. I heard that it was the one in which Gp. Capt. E.M. Donaldson had gained the world air speed record of 615.81 m.p.h. almost five years earlier.

One day when Ron Chippindale and I were playing squash (I beat him), he told me he'd met up with a girl from Andover called June Spackman and she was going to Kesteven Teachers' Training College near Grantham. I wiped the sweat off my brow and said, 'Great,' little realising that Ron was falling in love.

Flt. Lt. Hudson advised 60 Entry that some of us had been selected to represent the College in a combined escape and evasion exercise with Bomber Command in Scotland at the end of the next leave period, during which we'd travel about seventy-five miles in three days. Ron, Jim and I were amongst those chosen, but we weren't at all keen (having visions of another survival camp) – and anyway, we'd already put our names down for a Dutch barge cruise in Holland if we couldn't fly back to New Zealand. In the event, the exercise was cancelled, but some Flight Cadets went on a fortnight's survival camp in north central Norway.

Navigation exercises began to assume more importance. I had to fly Flt. Lt. Sillars via Worksop and Brigg and was thrilled to pass by RAF Scampton, which I'd read about in Paul Brickhill's book, The Dam Busters. Another flight took us to a railway crossing near Leicester and then to Ely. Later, I was sent on solo navigation flights to Peterborough and Loughborough and, in poor visibility, to Burton-on-Trent and Louth.

This led to a navigation test with Flt. Lt. 'Bud' Abbott to Hibaldstow and a pin point near Mansfield. I made some silly mistakes in flight planning which I'd never done before and, when flying the third leg, set the compass incorrectly. I was told afterwards that I was above average to exceptional on the first two legs, but spoiled things on the third leg and in the flight plan. As a result, I had to do the test again. Several other members of 60 Entry had also failed their tests. On the first leg of my second flight, Flt. Lt. Abbott began talking non-stop about Lincoln and Ely Cathedrals, asked me mental dead reckoning questions while we were in hot and bumpy conditions and then, during the second leg, told me to divert at East Retford back to Cranwell. I passed the test with an average mark. Flt. Lt. Abbott said I had to be quicker at thinking in the air.

During other solo flights, I practised various authorised exercises, and also managed to fit in some unauthorised aerobatics such as loops and rolls. Fortunately, Flt. Lt. Sillars soon gave me instruction on how to do such manoeuvres correctly and I felt some exhilaration in being able to perform a few of the aerobatics that I'd seen Sqn. Ldr. Bob McKay do in a Meteor over Timaru during my school-days.

I was wondering where to go at the mid-term break when Julian Bowes asked me to stay with him in Surrey. I was surprised at the invitation as Julian was one of the gen men, had been to the Roman Catholic school of Douai, and though we'd played tennis together, were involved with 'Henrietta' and so on, I felt that we weren't close friends. Julian seemed to me a very 'man about town' sort of person – tall, debonair, well-dressed in tweed cap and jacket, cavalry twill trousers and tightly knotted tie. He smoked a straight stemmed pipe out of the side of his mouth or held a cigarette between two straight fingers. I gratefully accepted the invitation and began making arrangements.

There were seven of us and our luggage in 'Henrietta' when we set off for London. Though one Flight Cadet got out at Grantham, our ex-London taxi was still very crowded. 'Henrietta' required a push start, and complained by losing power (through worn valve seatings) at critical times. Stops had to be made to try and rectify the problem and get petrol. The service station attendant walked around the old taxi and had to ask for the location of the petrol tank! Malcolm Dines got off the driver's seat so that the tank below could be filled. As we passed RAF Bassingbourn, I could see Canberras and Meteors lined-up on the tarmac. The brakes of our vehicle began to fade and we went through several red lights when Malcolm couldn't stop in time. The 120 mile journey took six hours!

Julian and I went to an Officers' Club near the Gloucester Road underground, but it was full. Lodgings were found nearby at Bolton House, though we had to share a room with a young National Service Army officer.

We had dinner at a Spanish restaurant that Julian knew in Soho called the Casa Pepe. Bull fight scenes decorated the walls and musicians played tango music on guitars. The menu was in Spanish, but Julian was fluent in the language and ordered for both of us. A waiter demonstrated how to drink wine from a glass container shaped rather like a watering can. He held the container a few inches from his mouth and directed the wine pouring from the spout into his mouth. Then he let the wine pour onto his forehead and trickle down his nose into his mouth. Julian, swathed in serviettes, tried drinking this way, but wasn't as skilled as the waiter. After a very pleasant meal, which cost a lot more than I was comfortable with, we wandered around Soho while Julian pointed out to me girls who were likely to be prostitutes. Rain drove us back to our lodgings.

The next day, Julian left to stay overnight with Malcolm Dines while I did some shopping. I came upon a pavement artist drawing some marvellous pictures in chalk. That evening I visited the Adelphi Theatre to see the show *London Laughs*, starring Jimmy Edwards, Tony Hancock and the incomparable Vera Lynn. What a grand show it was, complete with not one, but two real waterfalls on the stage!

Julian met me at Victoria railway station and we travelled to Horley and then by bus to The Duke's Head Inn. A short walk took us to part of an old manor house which was the home of Mrs Wood, Julian's aunt. Apparently Julian's parents had separated and he'd lived with his father until his father died. He hadn't seen his aunt for a while, hence the visit. I was introduced to Mrs Wood, her eighteen-year-old daughter Rosemary, and Julian's grand-mother – a dear old lady who, to my surprise, had lived most of her life in Wellington, New Zealand!

Rosemary was keen on horses so Julian and I found ourselves riding her horse, not worrying how sore we'd feel afterwards. I even managed to stay on the horse when it decided to jump a two foot hurdle! Mrs Wood showed us over the impressive East Grinstead hospital where she worked. Then Julian, Rosemary and I played table tennis with a girl who lived in another part of the manor house, and were soundly beaten by her. After a very enjoyable weekend, Julian and I left for London. Mrs Wood invited me to come and stay again.

Back in London, Julian and I went to Wyndhams Theatre to see the excellent play *The Love of Three Colonels* starring Peter Ustinoff and Moira Lister. An absolutely stunning girl sat down beside me. I was about to strike up conversation when her escort arrived and rather spoiled things. Julian and I later met Malcolm Dines as arranged at King's Cross railway station, but there was no 'Henrietta' – valve trouble had put the old taxi out of action. After a long wait, we caught a train and eventually returned to Cranwell.

My Squadron did surprisingly well in the Knocker gymnastics competition, winning handsomely from the other squadrons. On the same day, Junior Entries put on a display of exercises using rifles, accompanied by the College band. Then Junior Entries members demonstrated various self-defence moves.

Unfortunately my batman, Mr Clarricoats, developed tuberculosis and had to leave employment at the College. He was replaced by a cleaner from A Site.

Bob Cartwright had all of 60A amused after winning two goldfish at a Newark fair. He called one Harvey (after a well known Flight Sergeant!) and exercised them daily in a bath until they both were called to the goldfish heaven.

One weekend, I became aware that something unusual was happening at roll calls when the names of Ted Reynolds and Malcolm Dines were called. Two members of 60A were answering 'Sir' on their behalf. Apparently Ted and Mal felt that they needed a weekend off to do things like seeing their girlfriends and, as permission for this was unlikely, had involved a lot of people to cover for them. Their beds were made up to look as if they were asleep in them so as to fool the duty Senior Flight Cadet when he came on his rounds after lights out and shone his torch into their rooms. Some chaps got around the hall porter and signed Ted and Mal in from late leave, whereas others put their names down on the list as being present at church parade. We would all have been clagged if the deceptions had become known to the authorities, but nothing happened and Ted and Mal returned safely from Portsmouth after a rather wet weekend on a motor bike.

The word went around that Chris Woods who'd previously been chopped from 60C was being given a short service commission, one of 59 Entry had left the College for compassionate reasons, a Flight Cadet in 61 Entry was being chopped for lack of flying ability and another for colour blindness, and two of 63 Entry had asked for voluntary suspensions. Then Wally Martin of 60A was chopped on recurrence of his ear problems. We were to miss his cheeky retorts.

Selected commercial organisations visited the College almost every week selling uniforms, civilian clothing, shoes and the like. Representatives of firms such as Bates, Burberrys, Gieves, Moss Bros. and Poulsen and Skone would lay their wares out on the green baize of the billiard tables for several hours and await customers.

Burberrys measured 60 Entry for the RAF free issue of College blazers and caps. We were generally disappointed by the design of the single-breasted blazers. The collar contained an Air Force blue strip of cloth and the breast pockets had the College crest embroidered on them, but that wasn't too bad. What disappointed us most was that the blackish-blue cloth of the blazers attracted fluff and the seven brass buttons required polishing! No instructions were given by the College as to when we should wear the blazers, so they tended to be worn during evenings when we were allowed to wear mufti. The light blue coloured caps had the College crest embroidered above the peak and were mainly worn by cricketers.

One rainy night, Spike, Mal and I were on the second detail for night flying and travelled with ground crew in a truck to RAF Barkston Heath to await our flights. We had fun watching the first detail doing touch-and-go landings, but rain and tiredness drove us indoors to a bare room in the control tower where we tried to make ourselves comfortable on our flying suits and parachutes. Then the first detail arrived dripping wet, having been forced by rain and low cloud to cease flying. While we waited for conditions to improve, we drank some tea and ate sandwiches, but general weariness eventually caused us to put out the light and try to get some sleep. The meteorological staff must have forgotten the day was Friday the 13th! When our night flying was finally called off, the Chipmunks had to be flown back to Cranwell. I felt lucky to return by truck as those who flew to Cranwell did so under a 100 foot cloud base and couldn't see the Cranwell pundit flashing the red identification 'CP' until they were almost overhead it. The weather was so thick that one aircraft was accused by the Cranwell air traffic controller of not having its navigation lights on! On arriving back at the College for our night flying supper, we were finally able to relax and talk about our eventful night.

I was pleased when Miss Macdonald of Sleat, on behalf of The Dominions Fellowship Trust, sent me an invitation from The Lord Mayor and The Lady Mayoress of London to an 'at home' at Mansion House. I went to see Sqn. Ldr. Thomas about it, as the invitation was for 1630 hours on a Monday and I had private study from 1400 hours that day. He said I could leave after lunch on Monday, but I had to return by lights out.

I missed lunch to shave and change into a suit. Then Reg Bailey very kindly drove me in his MG to Grantham railway station. On reaching London, I used the underground to arrive at Mansion House by 1630 hours. My invitation was checked in the vestibule before I climbed a broad staircase to what appeared to be an enlarged hallway, complete with pillars, paintings, statues and chairs. Servants in old fashioned uniforms ushered me into the Egyptian Hall for a buffet tea. I looked around at the ornate barrel roof, stained glass windows, weapons on the walls, statues in alcoves and a dais at one end of the Hall.

Several hundred people were there – mainly from the Dominions and the United States of America, I was told. I began talking to a young chap with a beard and glasses and discovered his name was Keith Maslen and he was an Old Boy and had been a relieving teacher at my secondary school, the Timaru Boys' High School, before taking up a scholarship at Oxford University! I noticed Grace, the American girl I'd met, accompanied by a tall, weedy looking chap whom I assumed was her Rhodes Scholar fiancé. All the RNZAF chaps training at RAF Halton were there in uniform. Allan Carter from No. 6 Radio School at Cranwell was also present. I had a good chat with them and met some of the latest airmen from the RNZAF to go to Halton. They all seemed to be having a much easier time at Halton than Flight Cadets had at Cranwell.

The Lord Mayor and The Lady Mayoress, Sir Leslie and Lady Boyce, entered the Hall in full regalia along with some aldermen. A short speech of welcome was given by the Lord Mayor before he outlined the history of Mansion House and described what the building contained. Then Miss Macdonald of Sleat spoke in reply. I later went to thank her for getting me the invitation, but at first she didn't recognise me as she remembered me as being in uniform. When people began to leave I had a look at the other rooms open to the public, including one containing a display of gold plate, cups and ornaments, and a tiny court-room. I sat in the judge's chair of the court-room and thought that the big, jewel studded, two-handed sword above would look well in my room at Cranwell. After signing the Lord Mayor's visitors' book, I reluctantly went down the staircase and returned to King's Cross railway station.

On leaving the train at Grantham, I caught a bus for Sleaford (ignoring an instruction that Sleaford was out of bounds to Flight Cadets during term time) and found that the bus stopped at every little village on the way. I could hardly keep my eyes open – I was so tired! Luckily, I was able to catch the last bus from Sleaford to Cranwell and got back to my room half an hour after lights out, having had another memorable experience.

One afternoon, I realised that Alan McLelland-Brown of 60A was missing. The news came through that he'd crashed a Chipmunk when doing a solo practice forced landing with power. He'd been too high on his approach so had throttled the engine right back, only to find that the engine wouldn't respond when he went to open the throttle again. After landing in a corn field, he'd hit the bank of a canal, collapsed the undercarriage and ripped the port wing off. He was shaken and, on returning to Cranwell, had been taken flying by Flt. Lt. Sillars – this being the best way for Alan to get his confidence back. As a result of this accident, Alan was given a series of reprimands and became known as 'Sabre' (having swept back the wings of a Chipmunk making it look like a Sabre jet aircraft). Also, Flight Cadets were prohibited when solo from practising forced landings with power and, in forced landings without power, were not permitted to descend below 250 feet above ground level.

At one of the periodic guest nights the Assistant Commandant, Gp. Capt. Kyle, was farewelled and another Old Cranwellian, Gp. Capt. E.D. MacK. Nelson, CB, was welcomed as his replacement. Afterwards, a number of high spirited Flight Cadets pushed a car parked at the west end of the College onto the north airfield and left it in the cricket nets. Hopefully, the owner being an Old Cranwellian, would have understood the prank, but Sqn. Ldr. Thomas wasn't so pleased when he found his little green Austin car had been lifted and deposited between two trees so that he was unable to drive it away. He got members of 59B out of bed to free the car.

Another prank affected me when mud was thrown through the open window of my room and water was poured under the door. I was well aware that, being a New Zealand non-alcoholic drinker, non-smoker, non-gambler and non-swearer who'd voluntarily go to church, I didn't fit into the mould that was general at that time, and therefore was a likely target for derision and even animosity. I felt that some of my colleagues hadn't matured enough to tolerate my peculiarities as much as I tolerated theirs.

On one of the ceremonial parades, S/F/C G. McA. ('Max') Bacon, a former member of 52 Entry, was presented with his Wings and commissioned about seventeen months after he'd lost the tips of four fingers in an accident when operating a glider winch.

After the usual frantic preparation, the Ferris inter-squadron drill competition was again held. When A Squadron won in very warm conditions, Chiefee Nicholas was actually seen to smile!

'We now come onto the uninteresting part of the syllabus in discussing the construction of the Admiralty.' This was a typical introduction of Lt. Cdr. J.W. Millar, DSC, RN, before one of his War Studies lectures. He would then give a lecture that kept us spellbound and nobody noticed when he went ten minutes or more over the allotted time. We were also intrigued to hear that in his opinion we were receiving a much better education than was available at Britannia Royal Naval College, Dartmouth. Unfortunately, this excellent officer was posted soon after his series of lectures were completed. He was to be missed, not only for his racy style, but also for things such as the trays on his desk marked, 'In,' 'Out' and 'Too Bloody Difficult!'

Aircraft and cars began to arrive at the College as if a graduation was imminent, and gold braid was everywhere. The occasion was the dedication of the Memorial Chapel, known as St Michael's, in an upstairs area of the main building of the College that'd been damaged when a Whitley bomber flew into it and caught fire during a night training flight in 1942. Though the structure of the building had been repaired, the area (which had once been two lecture rooms) had remained derelict for many years until Air Cdre. Sinclair decided it should become a chapel in memory of the 477 former Flight Cadets who'd lost their lives out of a total of 1,096 who were trained at Cranwell before World War II.

The Rt. Rev. Lord Bishop of Lincoln and fifty of the senior visitors lunched with the upper entries of the College before attending a church parade (for everyone except Roman Catholics who'd already been to church that morning). Some 1,200 people squeezed into the Hangar Church for a pre-dedication service, the sermon being given by the Bishop. The official party then went in procession to the College for the dedication of the forty-seater Chapel, while the rest of the College went to a late lunch.

Three days later I was able to view the Chapel for the first time. I was most impressed by the beautifully carved oak panelling of the well appointed Chapel, particularly the crests on the many gifts from Air Forces and RAF

Commands. In the Sanctuary, the Ispahan rug presented by the Royal Pakistan Air Force was exquisite, and certainly the most magnificent I'd ever seen.

Soon afterwards, work began on the installation of a chime of six bells in the College tower, a gift of the Shell Group 'as a memorial to those Old Cranwellians who have given their lives in the service of their country and as a daily reminder of their gallantry and sacrifice.' Scaffolding surrounded the tower for the rest of term for the difficult task of lifting and installing the bells along with an elaborate mechanism to strike the hours, ring the quarter-hours in the Westminster chime, and sound 'Retreat' at the daily lowering of the ensign. Glass windows in the tower were replaced by wooden slats. Weird noises emanated from the tower for many weeks as the bells were tested.

I accompanied Colin Loveday up the tower one day to assist him in lowering the flags at retreat, and took the opportunity to inspect the installation of the bells and view other things to be seen from such a vantage point. The concrete dome of the tower echoed tremendously when inside it.

Instrument flying and night flying continued when weather permitted. While I was flying on instruments, Flt. Lt. Sillars talked me down to a landing. I found it quite strange being told to round out and then feel the Chipmunk touch the ground in a three point landing. My confidence in the instruments and my instructor increased considerably. During solo flights in daytime, I continued to practise such things as steep and maximum rate turns, loops, rolls off the top, stalls, stall turns, barrel and slow rolls, precision flying, forced landings without power, simulated engine failure after take-off, touch-and-go landings, flapless landings and landings with full flap.

I was up solo one day when Ted Reynolds, also solo in a Chipmunk, began a dogfight with me. We careered all over the sky, hoping that no one would see us. When we tired of that, Ted ranged up alongside me and did some unauthorised formation flying. Soon afterwards, Sam Boyce and I with our instructors practised formation flying and I found out how much concentration was required to fly accurately only a few feet away from another aircraft. The temptation to do some more unauthorised solo formation flying was still there, however, and Mal Dines, Spike Heaney and I did some on several occasions.

60A arrived at D Flight one day to find all the flying instructors furiously cleaning the Flight because the Commandant and various other top brass were about to make an unscheduled visit. The instructors handed things over to us and we soon had the place looking spick and span.

After coffee at one guest night, some of the Flight Cadets turned the tables through ninety degrees while still sitting at them so that there were numerous parallel rows instead of the usual three long rows. At the next guest night 60C forced Colin Field, the smallest of their members, under a table and somehow took his tweeds off. Such goings-on didn't escape the notice of the Commandant who told us all off about 'the growing disorder at guest nights'.

I think that a first class performance at the Commandant's Ceremonial parade helped restore his confidence in us and overcame the need for further ceremonials, other than a wet weather rehearsal, before graduation day.

At that time, we attended two excellent illustrated lectures – one from a Mr Proctor of Flight Refuelling Limited on flight refuelling and the other from a Professor Poole, Head of Bomber Command's Operational Research Section, on his role in that organisation. To my mind, the Professor appeared to be a genuine boffin – if his presentation and clothes were anything to go by.

To hitchhike by air back to New Zealand in the coming leave period meant that I had to be inoculated all over again. After permission had been granted for me to go, Sqn. Ldr. Thomas told me that the RAF would only be able to fly me as far as Singapore and I would have to sign a statement saying that I'd private means to pay for an air fare from New Zealand to Britain (should Service transport not be available), so as to get back to Cranwell for the start of the next term. I gave away any ideas of flying home after that.

When an athletics match with No. 3 Initial Training School and No. 6 Radio School was held, I was told to join the College team as an unofficial member in the high jump. I jumped five foot six inches using the Western Roll technique, beating the College representatives, and coming second in the competition. This assured me of an official place in the team for future competitions, the first being against the Milocarians Athletic Club comprising officers of the three Armed Services. I came second to a Royal Navy officer.

At the same time, I practised the long jump and the hop, step and jump, but at that stage was unable to better Laurie Jones of 60A who broke the College record in the hop, step and jump.

Mal Dines got 'Henrietta' going again in London and returned the ex-taxi to Cranwell. He drove Ted, Sabre and me to Welbourn to see a 'slick chick' known to live there, but Reg Bailey arrived in his MG sports car and departed with the girl! Soon afterwards the others turned the tables on Reg and went out with the girl. The engine of the ex-taxi was still giving trouble, however, restricting our recreational activities, so Sabre and I went by bus to Lincoln and had a good look around the inner city.

One Saturday night, five of 60A were away from Cranwell after lights out. The rest of us made up their beds to look as if someone was in them. Of the five, Reg Bailey was the only one caught, having been seen at a dance at Ancaster. He was in deep trouble because he was already on jankers and wasn't allowed away from Cranwell. As a result, he was given jankers for the rest of term and forbidden to use a car until he was in the Senior Entry.

I wanted to see a particular film at the Cranwell cinema that finished after the lights out time for Flight Cadets. I made up my bed to look as if I was in it and went off to the cinema. On returning to my room, I found it a complete shambles with everything overturned. Suspecting that some of 60A were the culprits, I rushed to their rooms and found that their doors were locked. There wasn't much that I could do other than make sure that 60A were aware of my displeasure. What hurt was that I'd covered for them on many occasions, yet they turned over my room, causing some damage, and left me exposed to being found out of bed by the duty Senior Flight Cadet. Luckily the duty Senior Flight Cadet hadn't looked in my room. Tidying up took over half an hour.

After one of the church parades, all Flight Cadets had to put on white belts and carry rifles so that publicity photos could be taken for *The Times* newspaper.

On conclusion of the end of term tests, Ron Chippindale told me that he'd been put on special report because of his Thermodynamics results. I heard that Gordon Grierson had also been put on special report – this often being one of the steps before someone was chopped. There was news that another member of 59 Entry had left the College.

60 Entry began to shift their things to the main College building in preparation for the new term. I was pleased to be allocated a sunny upstairs room overlooking the Orange in the A Squadron wing at the western end of the College.

As the term came to an end, there were some significant changes in personnel – the Commandant, Air Cdre. Sinclair, was to be replaced by another Old Cranwellian, Air Cdre. H. Eeles, CBE; the Officer Commanding No. 2 Squadron in Flying Wing, Sqn. Ldr. Coward, was to be replaced by Sqn. Ldr. A.C. Shirreff; the Senior Drill Instructor at the College, W/O D.J. Millis, MBE, was replaced by W/O R.A. Masters, BEM, and the A Squadron Drill Instructor, Chiefee Nicholas, was to be replaced by F/S Greenhalgh. Sqn. Ldr. Furlong wrote to say that he was about to be posted, his replacement at RNZAF Headquarters London being Sqn. Ldr. D.J. Gavin.

At the final guest night of term, the farewell and welcome speeches were followed by the Senior Entry review in which the Commandant was well taken off with his favourite expression, 'A jolly good show, chaps.' Afterwards, some Flight Cadets wired the main gates of the College shut, so making the exit of official cars from the parade ground a little more difficult. We were all warned not to go near the tents by the stadium of the annual Combined Cadet Force camp, but somehow the camp flag-pole made its way to the Orange where it flew a Jolly Roger before being hastily removed the next morning.

No. 56 GD(P) Entry received their Wings from the Vice-Chief of the Air Staff, Air Chief Marshal The Hon. Sir Ralph A. Cochrane, GBE, KCB, AFC, known as one of the finest brains in the Royal Air Force. I was particularly interested to see him and hear his address because of his relationship with the RNZAF. In 1936, Gp. Capt. Cochrane (as he was then) had been brought to New Zealand to prepare a scheme and assess the costs for the newly established RNZAF which had just been separated from Army control. His far-sighted report assured him a place in history as the architect of the RNZAF. From 1937–9, he was the first RNZAF Chief of the Air Staff.

Graduation day for Nos. 56 GD(P) and 7 E & S Entries began with rain, but the weather soon cleared. The reviewing officer was the Minister of Defence, Field Marshal The Rt. Hon. Earl Alexander of Tunis, KG, GCB, GCMG, CSI, DSO, MC, DCL, LLD. Amongst the large crowd at the graduation parade were visiting Canadian Air Cadets and their officers, and personnel from the Combined Cadet Force camp. The Senior Entry lunched with the VIPs in the dining hall while the rest of the College had an excellent buffet lunch in the billiard room. I then went to the south airfield to see aircraft new to me such as a Beaver, Gemini, Heron and Skymaster.

When I returned to the Orange, all the New Zealanders at the College met with Air Cdre. Kay and Gp. Capt. A.B. Greenaway, OBE, the Commanding Officer of RNZAF Station Wigram. Ron Parfitt was also there and publicity photographs were taken of us all as we watched an aerobatic display by four Meteor 8s. Ron told me he'd been posted to RAF Bassingbourn and would be flying Meteor 10s on photo reconnaissance. He planned to visit his family in New Zealand in six months time and said he'd call on my parents if he could.

At 1530 hours in the main entrance to the College, The Rt. Rev. Lord Bishop of Croydon dedicated the newly installed bells in the College tower and unveiled a commemorative plaque. A Squadron then marched onto the parade ground and at 1600 hours presented arms for the first lowering of the ensign while the bells sounded the 'Retreat'. Amongst the Shell Company representatives present was that famous Old Cranwellian, Gp. Capt. Douglas Bader.

That evening, the graduation ball was held. 60A had been told that everyone had to attend or get the approval of Sqn. Ldr. Thomas to stay away. This presented me with a problem as there was no particular girl (other than Margaret Hornsey in New Zealand) that I wanted to invite to the ball. I decided to go unaccompanied and found that a number of other Flight Cadets, including Ron and Jim, were in a similar situation. I still managed to do quite a lot of dancing – Pete Organ asked me to look after his girl while he went off somewhere and Sabre McLelland-Brown, who couldn't dance, lent me the girl that Ted Reynolds had got for him!

The centre of the College was transformed for the occasion. The senior year ante-room became the Senior Entry bar, the junior year ante-room was used as a lounge and the main lecture hall became a bar for everyone else. In the middle of the fron' 'all (as the hall porters called it) was a huge punch bowl. Part of the main corridor was fitted out as a lounge and everywhere were floral decorations, greenery and pot plants. The dining hall was cleared of tables for dancing. A floodlit scenic cliff face dominated the gallery end of the hall, with water cascading down from the gallery to a pool below. The swing section of the College band played popular tunes at the other end of the balloon decorated hall. Beneath the flashing lights of an illuminated mirrored globe danced Flight Cadets in interim mess dress (officer pattern uniform with white shirt, winged collars and black bow ties), officers in full mess kit with miniature medals and ladies in long ball gowns – all forming a most colourful scene.

At midnight, everybody went out onto the Orange to watch a fireworks display. The College tower was illuminated and added to the spectacle of rockets and other fireworks going off and '56 Entry' outlined in fire on a framework erected near the main gates of the College. When the ball concluded at 0200 hours, those of us who were left went outside to cool off and sat on the main entrance steps sipping beef soup from large mugs. I'd had quite a night – even without a girlfriend.

On returning to Block 78, I came upon a member of 60A loitering in the corridor and nervously smoking a cigarette.

'Hi, what's up?' I asked.

'I'm waiting for some . . .' He was interrupted by a partly clad girl putting her head around the door of his room and whispering, 'I'm ready for you now.'

My colleague made a hasty retreat to his room, while I returned to mine wondering about what I'd seen. I was too tired to think properly and was soon fast asleep.

Later that morning at too early an hour, those of us going to Grantham railway station staggered onto chartered buses and made our way to our various destinations. I went to Overseas League House in London and slept until late in the day. Refreshed, I called briefly on Sqn. Ldr. Furlong to wish him well in his new appointment.

I was on six weeks leave and began to relax. There was shopping to do and, when footsore, films such as *Ivanhoe* at the Ritz cinema and *The Sound Barrier* at the Plaza cinema. The latter film was really first class and up to date, and had me sweating and gripping my seat. Then Ron Chippindale rang and we went sightseeing together around London.

The next morning we left for Holland.

CHAPTER 11

Welkom and Auf Wiederseh'n

I HADN'T BEEN TOO KEEN to go on the week long barge cruise through the western parts of Holland and Belgium, thinking it'd be flat and uninteresting, but went mainly because fellow New Zealanders Ron Chippindale and Jim Brown were going. I was soon to be pleasantly surprised about the Low Countries. The £50 cost of the voyage and some of the other travel was subsidised by the Cadets' Activities Organisation.

At Liverpool Street railway station I met other Flight Cadets going on the trip. Apart from Ron and Jim, there was Ron Chedgey, Sabre McLelland-Brown, Tony Whitwam (all of 60 Entry), Harding of 61 Entry and Butt of 62 Entry. I chatted with some Dutch folk on the train to Harwich. After our passports had been checked, we departed by ferry for Hook of Holland. There was quite a swell on, but the weather was fine so we Flight Cadets ate and amused ourselves on deck during the five and a half hour voyage looking at the many passing ships. We were still hungry on arrival so, after passing through Customs, we bought bananas and huge slabs of chocolate from a barrow boy. When asked if he spoke English the boy replied, 'And German too!' On the electric train to Rotterdam an attractive Dutch girl sat near us and, though she claimed she could speak little English, she was obviously following and interested in our banter.

The eldest son and daughter of Captain Feyfer met us at Rotterdam and took us by tram to the little yacht harbour where the Dutch barge *Willem Barentsz* was moored. The young Feyfers paid the tram fare for us saying that if we paid we'd be overcharged. Captain Feyfer, his wife and two younger sons greeted us warmly with 'Hallo, *welkom* to Holland.' They took us below into the main cabin which, surprisingly, was equipped with a piano and writing desk in addition to several tables. The bathroom, toilet and kitchen were indicated to us as we were taken to one of the seven berth cabins. Also on board were some Dutch and Swiss people – twenty-three of us in all including six women, plus an ugly dog of uncertain pedigree called Beer.

We all crowded around the tables for a bread and butter tea with hundreds and thousands being used instead of jam. Captain Feyfer called, 'One moment please,' banged the flat of his hand on a table and there was silence. Then he banged his hand again as the signal to eat. The same occurred at the end of the meal – presumably for silent prayers. We soon got used to this procedure at each meal and the different food. Our appetites increased daily.

Captain Feyfer, who spoke five languages, divided us all into watches – bridge, deck and steward. I started off as a steward and was soon peeling potatoes, shelling peas and doing the dishes. Most of our Dutch companions could speak or understand English, having learned it at school. When we asked if they spoke English, they'd say in broken English, 'No, I can't speak English!' In talking with the Feyfers, I discovered that they were based at Terschelling and did sightseeing trips as a living, except for the eldest daughter who worked in Amsterdam.

We Flight Cadets decided to stretch our legs by walking around the deserted streets of Rotterdam before bed at 2300 hours. At that point we found there were no sheets on our bunks – just rather hairy blankets. Someone had forgotten to tell us to bring sheets, so we slept without them during the voyage!

The next morning was occupied in exploring Rotterdam and doing a little shopping. Much of the city centre had been flattened by bombing during World War II so there were only a few modern buildings standing amongst acres of waste land or rubble.

After lunch, we left on the barge and motored down river before turning into other waterways towards Brielle. I'd never seen so many ships before, let alone floating docks, shipyards, huge cranes, refineries and the like. There was a large bridge with a centre section that could be raised and smaller lifting bridges that were hinged at one end.

Brielle was a delightful little town with quaint houses, streets cobbled in a zigzag pattern, small lifting bridges with counterweights above and a huge church that was out of proportion to the size of the town. We went ashore to have a look around. The church was closed as it was under repair from bomb damage. I climbed a ladder, looked in a window and was intrigued to see that the pulpit was in the middle of the nave with pews arranged in a circle around it. In the evening, with little else to do, we visited the local cinema, which was just a large room in a hotel. One of the newsreels showed Dutch people receiving passports before emigrating to Christchurch, New Zealand. Ron, Jim and I cheered! Another newsreel showed Vampires performing at an air display, but the English sub-titles said they were Meteors! A similar mistake was made regarding Sabres.

We continued to motor along canals, through locks and past bridges that rolled back as we approached, before coming to open water at Hellevoetsluis. Captain Feyfer lowered into the water large fan-shaped boards attached to the sides of the barge, raised the three sails and switched off the diesel motor. In the light winds, we were able to swim alongside the barge in the brown, brackish water, or hang onto a rope and be dragged through the water. The sun dried us on deck and I, being on deck duty, soon became sunburnt (Fig. 26).

Figure 26. Cruising on the barge *Willem Barentsz*, Holland, August, 1952: L-R: Jim Brown (60B), Author (60A), Tony Whitwam (60B) and Ron Chippindale (60B).

On arriving at Willemstad, I headed for the nearest toilet as I'd had enough of the one on the barge – the smell in the confined quarters let alone the intricacies of the pump and valves were too much except in an emergency. The search for a toilet became the usual procedure for most of us after we'd moored at the end of each day. Little villages like Willemstad appeared to be scrupulously clean in the best Dutch tradition. Jim, Tony and I then set off to inspect the church dominating the village. The church was surrounded by a moat and appeared to have been recently repaired with old bricks. The steep sloping, slated roof culminated in a domed bell tower at one end. A young girl was showing some people through the church so we tagged along, noted the bare interior and admired the plain windows in which were set rather attractive stained glass crests. Another major feature at Willemstad was a large windmill used for making flour. I climbed it to photograph the village below.

Eating ice-cream and sweets, we returned to the barge and found that it was about to sail to Bruinisse for the night. By the time we arrived at Bruinisse harbour the tide was out and many of the ships there were lying high and dry. We walked in the twilight to the nearby village and were interested to see the local people wearing the colourful dress for the area, chatting by the front gates of their houses or walking in their clogs, hand-in-hand along the streets.

Early next morning we left on the tide for Zierikzee, arriving there about noon. Zierikzee was quite a large town, but we only had a short time to go shopping and have a meal before departing for Veere. Being on bridge duty, I took a turn at steering the barge. We stopped on the way to go swimming again. Veere was another small village with several churches. We climbed the tower of one before wandering back to the barge.

Tied up alongside the *Willem Barentsz* was another barge, full of young women from various countries! We soon overcame the language difficulty and found that they were on a similar cruise to ourselves. Those who spoke some English did so with an American accent. We had to leave for Middelburg and, with much waving of hands, promised to meet up with them when they arrived there the next day.

Middelburg was a sizeable town with a national fair being held at its centre. We had a morning to try all the sideshows, but got into trouble on some dodgem cars when we deliberately bashed into some Dutch Army chaps and other people, thinking it all great fun. Attendants jumped on the fenders of our cars, waved their arms and shouted at us. Sometime later we became aware of a large notice saying, '*Verboden te botzen*' − bumping forbidden!

We moved to the local market where just about anything was for sale. The Dutch china all seemed to be blue scenes on white backgrounds. I was fascinated to see two men dressed in red boater-type hats and traditional Dutch clothing carrying a red elongated dish-shaped pallet on which was a pyramid of huge round yellow cheeses. One man walked behind the other, each carrying the weight of the pallet by leather straps around their necks. A lot of men and women were coming and going on bicycles and light motor bikes. I noticed a Salvation Army group singing, several beggars and a number of people who appeared to be Indonesians. A man turned the handle of a magnificent barrel organ and played very tuneful music, drawing quite a crowd of listeners. We ran into the young women from the other barge and talked with them until we had to leave for the harbour.

Captain Feyfer hoped to sail to Flushing, but said a bridge there was only open at certain times and to go under it would mean having to lower the masts of the barge. This would delay us some twelve hours, so we motored back to Veere and then sailed to Wemeldinge before motoring through another canal to Hansweert − a place that was little more than a church, two shops and a hotel. Rain began to fall, but that didn't stop the two younger Feyfers from having another swim.

I filled in time reading *The White Rabbit,* about Wg. Cdr. F.F.E. Yeo-Thomas, GC, MC, and catching up on my letter writing. The Dutch remarked on me using my left hand as apparently in Holland all people were taught to be right handed!

The Dutch men on board all smoked strong smelling cigars or elaborate pipes. Some of the Flight Cadets had noticed the great variety of cigars and pipes available in the Dutch shops and competed to buy the largest, best looking and most ornate pipe they could find. We also began to compete in growing beards and moustaches as shaving was difficult on board – there being no hot water when the motor was stopped. I grew a moustache for the duration of the voyage.

After an overnight stay at Hansweert, we passed through the locks and Dutch Customs, raised the sails and headed in strong winds over choppy water for Antwerp. We were in a main waterway and began seeing numerous large ships of many nationalities. Then on the horizon appeared the high buildings and cranes of Antwerp and flames from a tall pipe of an oil refinery. We anchored briefly to pass through Belgian Customs and wondered how we could acquire one of the cute black, red and gold pill box hats of the Belgian officials. Eventually we berthed in a sheltered haven at Antwerp and a picturesque *gendarme* came on board to have us fill in some forms.

Ron, Jim, Tony and I went exploring. To my eyes, the Belgian houses didn't appear so neat and clean as those in Holland. The narrow back streets of Antwerp looked decidedly seamy with people sitting on the footpaths in front of rather uninviting shops. We held our breaths and quickly passed urinals that were open to the street. Along some streets and in two small squares there were empty stalls, coloured lights and the sound of music as if in preparation for a fair. In the better areas, the shops looked quite modern with many cafés, some extending well out onto the footpaths. Tiring of sight seeing, we had a drink at a café, played a soccer machine and, eating extremely solid ice-creams on a stick, went to a cinema.

On our final morning on board the *Willem Barentsz*, we had what Captain Feyfer called an English breakfast. We packed our things, signed the visitors' book, said farewell and went by taxi to the Central Railway Station. Ron, Jim, Tony and I set off for Brussels in a rather spacious electric train. Rain pouring down combined with hard wooden seats made the journey one we'd prefer to forget. Our connecting train to Ostende, coming from Germany, was going to be two to three hours late so we decided to go to another station where a train was leaving for Ostende in twenty minutes. We caught a taxi, but it broke down, wasting precious minutes. Another taxi took us on an exciting dash through Brussels in heavy rain, the wheels slipping on tram lines and bouncing over the cobbles. We missed the train! Eventually we boarded another wooden seated train that took us to Ostende via Gent and Brugge over flat uninteresting country.

The rain stopped and the sun came out as we explored the narrow streets of Ostende. The place was full of souvenir shops and hordes of people, many of whom spoke English. I noticed that a fashion item for the young women was a reversible elastic belt about four inches wide with a smart gold buckle.

I bought a belt that was red on one side and grey on the other for one of my sisters. Along the seafront, there was one café after another. When we stopped at the Normandie Café to have tea and cakes, the tea was served in a bag (the first I'd seen) and the elderly waitress fetched the cakes from another café! That reminded us of a cartoon we'd seen showing a chap in a café turning around to ask someone in the adjacent café to pass the salt!

Though we went to the ferry in what we thought was plenty of time, there was already a long queue to get aboard and we realised that we'd no chance of getting a cabin for the overnight voyage to Dover. The *Prince Phillippe* sailed at midnight into a stormy English Channel. Hundreds of people without cabins tried to sleep on deck or in public places below. There was no protection on deck from the wind and spray. I had a most miserable night in a wooden deck chair, my brief periods of dozing being interrupted by people rushing to the rails to be sick. The cliffs of Dover looked less than white in the cold light of dawn, but they were a welcome sight to me as, stiff and cold, I drowsily went through Customs. A woman burst into tears beside me as a Customs officer pulled undeclared liquor bottles from her husband's suitcase. I was glad to stumble onto a dirty train for London.

Overseas League House said my room wasn't ready, so I had breakfast at a Lyons Corner House, watched a television crew filming by the Eros statue, then read newspapers and washed and shaved in a communal bathroom at Overseas League House until I was given a room and could at last go to sleep.

I had several days to fill in before leaving for ten days gliding at Scharfoldendorf so I began by touring the West End of London.

One place I happened to pass was No. 10 Downing Street, the London home of the British Prime Minister. I wasn't impressed by its location in a dingy little cul-de-sac, as I expected something much more grand. The only visible security for the Prime Minister was a policeman standing by the glossy black painted door.

At St Paul's Cathedral, I joined the hundreds of people viewing the various parts of the vast church. I trudged up the three hundred or more steps to the 'Whispering Gallery', overheard what a clergyman was saying to tourists on the far side of the gallery, and peered down at the people far below on the floor of the church. On an outside gallery around the base of the dome, I was able to get a good view of London between the many statues of saints. The latter had flat backs with lightning rods going from head to feet, and concrete filling the gaps between the stones.

I went out one evening and, in another remarkable coincidence, ran into the New Zealander Ian Powell. We had dinner together while he told me that, since leaving Cranwell, he'd got out of the RAF and become a clerk handling iron and steel statistics. We walked to Hyde Park Corner, listened to the soap box orators lecturing on subjects ranging from religion to Communism, wandered into the Knightsbridge area talking all the time, then went our separate ways. I've sometimes wondered what happened to Ian since that chance meeting.

Robert Langford-Jones, Cousin Jennifer's husband, invited me to see the play *The Gay Dog* at the Piccadilly Theatre. He bought me a ticket for one of the best seats, then rushed off to do his stage manager work. Robert wore glasses, had dark swept-back hair and seemed a very likable chap. I thoroughly enjoyed the play and also the tea and cakes brought around on small trays during the intervals. Afterwards, Robert took me backstage to meet the star of the play, Wilfred Pickles, then to supper with Jennifer. I was surprised when Robert said he'd never met his father-in-law, Hugh Skinner. Jennifer showed me photos of her recent trip to Portugal and talked about a film of *The Gay Dog* she was starting that week in which she was the chatty neighbour.

When I read in a newspaper about a Mr St George, a famous shoeshine 'boy' in Piccadilly Circus who'd cleaned the shoes of and dined with princes and ambassadors and who was renowned for being able to pick where people came from, I decided to try him out. He cleaned my shoes well enough, but I was disappointed when he said I was an Australian!

After buying a pair of brown crepe-soled shoes that were in fashion at the time (commonly called 'brothel creepers') I realised I was running out of money, so I telegraphed my parents in the hope they could send me £50. When tired of walking around shops, I saw *Gone with the Wind* at the luxurious Empire Cinema, and *The Importance of being Ernest* at the New Gallery Cinema. I visited RNZAF Headquarters again and met Sqn. Ldr. Gavin for the first time. He seemed to be a very pleasant officer.

I was up early and left without breakfast to catch a train from Victoria Station to Margate. When a taxi took me to RAF Manston, a Squadron Leader looked at me with surprise and said that the Cranwell Ansons had left for Scharfoldendorf the previous day! I was dumbfounded, not knowing how I could have made such a stupid mistake. There was nothing the RAF could do for me, so the Squadron Leader suggested I try the American Base Operations in the control tower. Luckily a USAF Dakota was about to take-off for Landstuhl in the American Zone of West Germany, so I was hurried through Customs, driven out to the aircraft and had my rank, name, number and unit entered into the flight forms before climbing aboard.

An American officer and several airmen sat in bucket seats around a jet engine strapped to the floor of the Dakota. The engine was apparently to replace one that'd flamed out over Landstuhl. A dinghy, parachutes and the aircraft steps lay loose on the floor. There was no time for introductions. The Americans stared at me and what to them was my strange looking flying suit and uniform. The Dakota droned over the English Channel. I was half asleep when there was a sudden noise and rush of air – a ditching hatch had flown open when the officer had inadvertently leaned on the release lever! Fortunately the hatch was hinged and soon secured.

Landstuhl runway and dispersal areas looked as if they were made of bathroom tiles – huge square areas of concrete. We landed at 1400 hours and parked near the point of touchdown. As we disembarked, over twenty Thunderjets and a Shooting Star buzzed the airfield, peeled off, lowered their undercarriages as they slowed in the circuit, and landed about 60 feet away, their small tyres screaming and giving off smoke on touching the runway. The aircraft were brilliantly painted with chequers, stripes and other squadron insignia. A B26 bomber then landed and a Thunderjet roared past as it taxied for take-off. My ear drums vibrated with the noise.

I was driven with my American friends to Base Operations. An officer advised me that no aircraft were going to the British Zone, but the Dakota was continuing on to Neubiberg near Munich, where I might be able to get some help.

After the jet engine was offloaded, I returned to the Dakota and climbed aboard with some officers and airmen who were going on leave. During the one and a half hour flight, a Colonel and a Captain shared chocolate and nut bars with me. I was ravenous, not having eaten since dinner the previous day, and most grateful for the snack.

At Neubiberg, there were no suitable flights for me that day, so I was taken to the officers' club and left to fend for myself. An officer at the bar told me that the week had been a difficult one in which the local air defences had been tested and now that it was Friday, everyone was going to relax with some hard drinking and only visitors were allowed to wear a tie. He gave me a squash drink and a dollar for a meal before introducing me to the other officers at the bar. The Americans expressed surprise at meeting a New Zealander in such a place, then got on with their drinking. I decided to have dinner – an enormous though rather tough steak, with buns, butter and iced coffee included in the dollar price.

An American officer wearing RAF wings came up to me. He'd recognised my uniform, having been at Cranwell during World War II, and explained he'd been born in England, but was now an American citizen. He was most helpful, taking me back to Base Operations and arranging for me to fly to Wiesbaden near Frankfurt, which he said was the nearest American airfield to the British Zone. This good samaritan gave me another drink at the officers' club, then drove me in a borrowed car through a military police barrier (as a result of two Thunderjets mysteriously blowing up on the airfield) to a waiting Dakota.

Night had fallen and a spectacular electrical storm commenced as the Dakota got airborne. The pilot was a Colonel and very experienced at flying in such conditions. I sat behind him and the co-pilot with the only other passenger, a Corporal, watching the vivid flashes of lightning all around us. At times we would come out of cloud into black holes of clear air, and then fly into heavy rain and more turbulent cloud. The flight took two and a half hours because the Colonel wanted to get some practice over Wiesbaden in GCA landings. I listened to the radio patter between the Colonel and the ground controller, finding it all very interesting.

After landing, the Colonel very kindly drove the Corporal and me to the transit billets in the USAF camp at Wiesbaden. The time was well after midnight. An orderly made out a form to allow me to sleep in an airmen's dormitory, gave me blankets and sheets and showed me where to go. I opened the dormitory door and put on the light. 'Turn the bloody light off,' a voice cried. I hastily complied, having just enough time to see that the dormitory was full of two-level bunks. I felt around until I found an unoccupied bunk (an upper one), then made my bed in the dark and went to sleep. Shortly afterwards a lot of airmen came into the dormitory, switched on the light in spite of further protests and went to bed.

I was late up that morning, being very sleepy and having forgotten to reset my watch to the local time. Breakfast was over, but the kitchen staff took pity on me and gave me a free meal in the servants' area. I had no Script (United States Armed Forces currency, used in military establishments in the American Zone) and they weren't interested in the pounds sterling that I offered. I ate well, not knowing when or where I'd next get a meal.

After collecting my gear, I caught a bus that was free to the American community and made my way to the Wiesbaden railway station. USAF military police looked at me curiously, but didn't stop me. Some American airmen obviously weren't sure if my uniform was that of an officer or not and saluted me – just to be on the safe side! Wiesbaden was a big place, full of modern shops and Americans. I saw little sign of war damage. At the railway station I ran into a US Army officer who, surprisingly, was trying to fly to England! He persuaded me to return to the air base (as he called it) and see if there were any flights to the British Zone. We caught another free bus back to the airfield.

I hung around Base Operations for a while, but there were no suitable flights, so I returned to the railway station with two NCOs who were going that way in their car. (A military policeman who checked my documents got me the lift.) At last I was able to change my travellers cheques into German currency and buy a ticket to Frankfurt. The clerk in the American ticket office on the platform wrote instructions for me in German so that I could make the right connections and get to Scharfoldendorf. The train left two minutes later.

At Frankfurt, I'd just enough time to flash my instructions and buy a ticket for Kreinsen before the train left the station. For the next six hours I sat on the end of my suitcase in the corridor of the hot, crowded train, feeling most uncomfortable in my uniform. A lot of other passengers also sat in the corridor, having to move frequently as people pushed their way along the train. I was unable to speak to my fellow passengers so filled in the time by looking at the passing scenery. There were interesting castles perched on promontories above a broad river, while below, tugs pushed long narrow barges through the water. The train passed near the Wasserkuppe (a well known gliding centre) and then through Göttingen (where a famous series of aerofoils originated). When the ticket collector came, he made sure that I understood when to get off the train – otherwise I'd end up at Hamburg.

So at Kreinsen I left the train and was told at the ticket office that I should immediately board a train leaving for Vorwohle. This I did and survived thirty minutes of sitting on the edge of a hard wooden seat of an ancient train expecting to be able to buy a ticket from the ticket collector, but no official came along. The station-master at Vorwohle had been informed I'd no ticket and was frantically searching for the right ticket when I arrived on the platform. He couldn't find it so let me get on a little rail car that was just leaving for Scharfoldendorf and spoke briefly to the guard. Unfortunately, the guard wanted a full explanation from me as to what had happened, but my German was as non-existent as his English. An elderly German male passenger on the rail car, who spoke a little English, straightened things out. I then paid my fare, though I suspect that it was only from Vorwohle to Scharfoldendorf.

At last I could relax a little and enjoy the scenic thirty minute, mainly downhill, journey in the narrow gauge tram-like rail car. I arrived at Scharfoldendorf at 1900 hours and began to walk the two miles or so up the scarp to the RAF Rest Centre. A bus full of men and women from the Second Tactical Air Force Headquarters pulled up beside me and offered me a lift which I gratefully accepted. They were going gliding for the weekend.

I found that Flt. Lts. D.A. Cree and R. Edwards, DSO, were in charge of the Cranwell group at the Rest Centre. They'd assumed I'd mistaken the day of departure from Manson and asked how I'd got to Scharfoldendorf. I outlined what'd happened, expecting them to blow their tops over me arriving two days late. 'Better late than never,' one of them said, 'Jolly good show hitchhiking all that way in such a short time.' I breathed a little more easily, feeling lucky to have successfully completed an unscheduled adventure.

I was starving, so I quickly washed, changed into mufti and went to dinner at the officers' mess. The nine other Flight Cadets were surprised to see me and all wanted to hear my story. They then went off to dances in the officers' and airmen's messes, but I just wanted to have a hot shower and go to sleep. The showers, however, were out of use because of a water shortage so I had a swim in the outdoor pool – a German guard turning on the floodlights for me.

The next morning I was given a dual check in a Kranich by Air Cdre. L.R.S. Freestone, OBE, one of the weekend visitors, before making several solo flights in a Grunau.

A day of light winds saw a number of the Flight Cadets convert onto other gliders. I began flying the Rhönbuzzard and found it better to handle than a Grunau, but much harder to land because of the curved skid under the fuselage. Touching down at the wrong speed meant a bouncy landing and banging one's head on the wing projecting over the cramped cockpit.

I also converted onto the SG 38 primary trainer (Fig. 27), commonly known as 'the flying stringbag' because of its open construction fuselage and many wires going from a triangular structure above the wing through each wing to the bottom of the fuselage. The pilot sat out in the open at the front of the fuselage – a position of great vulnerability. I saw another Flight Cadet do a hammer head stall in an SG 38 (where the aircraft is almost inverted after the stall and recovery from the ensuing dive is through the vertical position) – a most frightening manoeuvre when there is just nothing in front of you, the air is screaming through the wires and open fuselage, and there is no parachute. My stalls in the SG 38 were just sufficient to get the feel of

Figure 27. Author and SG 38 glider at Scharfoldendorf, Germany, April 1952.

the glider at the stalling speed (there being no airspeed indicator or other instruments)!

On one of my Grunau flights, I felt a slight jerk at the top of the launch when I pulled the cable release (which was not unusual), then on the downward leg of the circuit I noticed an Aldis lamp flashing at me from the winch area. I looked around to see what was wrong and saw that I'd some 300 feet of cable hanging below the glider. I pulled the cable release again, but the cable still hung there. When turning onto finals and increasing my airspeed to get through the down draughts to the lee of the ridge, I could feel the cable dragging across the tops of the trees on the approach to land. Fortunately the cable didn't catch on anything and I landed safely, though a little short of the usual mark. The cable release worked perfectly on the ground. Sepp Niederstadt, the German winch operator and former commandant of Scharfoldendorf during the War years, told me that cables didn't always release when required for a variety of reasons, and he'd saved me from a sticky end by cutting the cable with an axe. I thanked him and later heard that two other Flight Cadets had had similar incidents that leave period.

When the weather changed to fog and rain, I visited Hanover in the car of a Scottish Captain with F/Cs L.A. (Chas) Boyer of 57 Entry, J.S.R. (Sammy) Salmond of 58 Entry, Flt. Lts. Cree and Edwards, and a Frenchwoman called Simone. Rain was still falling when we arrived in central Hanover, so we went to an officers' club in a mansion just outside the city and filled in time drinking, having lunch and reading magazines. The three officers paid the bill. When the rain cleared we drove back into Hanover along streets that had piles of rubble on each side – the results of 'fire storm' bombing during World War II. Chas, Sammy and I went sightseeing and browsing through some modern shops, but too soon we had to join the others and return to Scharfoldendorf. An electrical storm broke during our journey so we stopped off at a hotel for drinks and boiled sausages, mustard and bread, until the thunder, lightning and heavy rain had passed. The sausages were apparently a German delicacy, but like rubber tyres to eat. We Flight Cadets paid the bill.

Foggy and wet weather continued so Chas, Sammy and I hitchhiked to and from Eschershausen to have a look around the shops. Back at the Rest Centre, we decided to do some horse riding. The horses were most reluctant to leave the stables and go along the wooded trails of the Scharfoldendorf ridge, but when we turned to head back they broke into a gallop down a steep and slippery trail, leaving us to hang on as best as we could. On another visit to Eschershausen, we fancied pork chops so bought some and had staff at the officers' mess cook them for us. They were delicious. Then we got a ride to Hamelin to do more shopping. I bought a Sixtomat exposure meter for my camera.

As the weather improved, Sammy and I walked down a tree-lined gully in the ridge to the village of Hunzen in the valley below, a picturesque little place with winding cobbled streets, crude footpaths and compost heaps adjacent to the Tudor-style houses. I'd heard that people from such villages got typhoid occasionally and this I could understand on seeing and smelling the compost heaps. We drank lemonade at a guest house and slowly wandered back to the Rest Centre. Another walk to explore some of the rock outcrops on the ridge resulted in us finding all sorts of strange bugs and insects. I revisited the glider hangar to watch the skilled German workmen rebuilding the nose of a Grunau and, in their own time, making models of the gliders for sale to visitors.

On Sunday, Flt. Lt. Edwards decided there ought to be a church service for us Flight Cadets, so when we'd assembled in a lounge he prayed, Sammy read the Bible and we all said the Lord's Prayer, so completing a very short service!

Our evenings were spent lounging in the officers' mess listening to a three-piece orchestra, reading, seeing old movies like *Odette* and *High Treason*, and going to dances. A square dance in the airmen's mess was great fun, particularly when we borrowed someone's girlfriend and dunked a bolshie Corporal in the pool. An Army chap provided entertainment by hypnotising people. Dances at the officers' mess weren't so enjoyable as we had to cut in on the wife of a Wing Commander or the like to get a partner. The weekend crowds tended to monopolise things and certainly reduced our flying time.

One of the weekend visitors learning to fly did a short hop in a Grunau along part of the undulating airfield. I continued the launch and did a low, two minute circuit to bring the glider back to the normal starting point. An airman overshot in landing a Grunau and ended up with the glider's wing-tip stuck in a tree. When the Rhönbuzzard was being towed out of the hangar one morning, the towing hook broke away so necessitating a major repair. I never flew the glider again. A two-seater Govier glider (which I hadn't seen before) was brought into use to help cope with the weekend visitors. When its air brakes were extended for landing the glider looked rather like a Canberra bomber.

In gusty wind and low cloud conditions, I managed to ridge soar a Grunau for 39 minutes – my longest flight to date. On coming in to land, I lost my sun hat when I put my head too far out of the cockpit.

We woke one morning to find light rain falling and a strong ridge wind that rattled the windows of the airmen's block. I got airborne in a Grunau on the short launch across the ridge, gaining only about 300 feet in height. With great difficulty I ridge soared towards the highest point of the ridge, but the lift decayed with each shower of rain and I faced losing it altogether and being unable to get back to the airfield. The wind gusts caused the glider to go backwards in relationship to the ground, or into a steep turn in spite of my attempts to maintain straight and level flight. Eventually, with my airspeed indicator filled with water and stuck on 150 km/hr, I decided to return to the airfield. Arriving with only 100 feet of height, which was insufficient for a circuit, I had to fly out over the valley and land in a clover field beside a road leading to the village of Scharfoldendorf. My flight time was exactly three hours. One and a half hours later the Deputy Chief Flying Instructor, Cpl. Mac McKercher, arrived in a jeep towing a trailer. We disassembled the Grunau, loaded it on the trailer and returned to the Rest Centre. Soon afterwards, flying was cancelled because of worsening weather. I was fined 7s 6d for making a valley landing, but I had some consolation in that many Flight Cadets before me had had to do the same.

The ridge wind was there the next day, so under ragged clouds I set off again in a Grunau and soon got to an altitude of 3,060 feet below a large, black bottomed cloud. I was well out over the valley heading towards the village of Bodenworder. The vertical speed indicator showed very good lift as I entered the cloud. Unfortunately, the Grunau had no bank and slip indicator to allow cloud flying so I had to extend the air brakes and descend. The cloud was being blown over the Scharfoldendorf ridge so I wondered if I should stay under it and make a cross-country flight. As I'd not been briefed for a cross-country, I headed for another promising cloud over Eschershausen. Rapidly losing height, I had to return to the ridge and slowly regain height by ridge soaring.

Kites and buzzards soared in the rising air currents going over the ridge, but they turned in much tighter circles than I could in my Grunau, and they took advantage of much smaller areas of lift. Still, they were a good indication of where lift could be found. I also tried to position my Grunau downwind of villages in the valley so as to get into any rising warm air from them. Unfortunately, other pilots were trying to do the same and I had to be ever vigilant in order not to collide with one of the other gliders.

I tried filling in time by singing current 'pop' songs such as:

'Auf Wiederseh'n, Auf Wiederseh'n – we'll meet again Sweetheart. This lovely day has flown away – the time has come to part. We'll kiss again – like this again – don't let the tear drops start. With love that's true – I'll wait for you. Auf wiederseh'n Sweetheart.'

After some hours in the open and cramped cockpit, I became cold and wanted to relieve myself. As this was an ever present hazard for glider pilots most of us carried a paper cup or small tin in the cockpit. Trying to use the container while still flying the glider was difficult, but having done so there was the problem of its disposal. The answer was to drop the container over the side of the cockpit – preferably when another glider was about to fly beneath! I don't think any glider was hit in this manner.

Tired and cold, I landed after 5 hours and 13 minutes, knowing that I'd achieved the 5 hours duration requirement for the Royal Aero Club Silver C Badge. The barograph installed in the Grunau confirmed this, but showed that I'd just missed out on the 3,000 feet gain of height above take-off point requirement for the Silver C Badge. If only that cloud had been a bit higher! I had hopes that I could achieve the gain of height and the cross-country requirements for the Silver C in my last day at Scharfoldendorf, but that wasn't to be. Some of the other Flight Cadets also got the duration requirement and one the gain of height, but nobody was able to achieve the cross-country requirement that visit.

Air Cdre. Freestone happened to be at our end of visit function and talked to me about a trip he'd done to New Zealand. Sammy Salmond was presented with a model glider for 'the best show' that visit, and Mac McKercher was given two German beer mugs for all his assistance. Photographs were taken with Mac, his dog Scottie and the Officer Commanding Scharfoldendorf, Flt. Lt. Smith, before we were driven to RAF Bückeburg. I noticed two paddle boats on the Weser – one with the paddle wheels at the sides, the other with a large paddle wheel at the stern. We were given lunch boxes as we boarded our Ansons. I couldn't sleep as we flew to RAF Manston, so watched the passing German countryside and thought it looked like medieval strip farming. A USAF truck driver gave us a lift into Margate. We'd missed the fast train to London and had to wait ages for a slow train. While we were having a snack in a café, the waiter mistook our uniforms and asked us if we were foreigners! Eventually we reached Victoria Station and I made my way to Overseas League House.

The next day, I went to the Bank of New Zealand and was much relieved to find that my parents had forwarded money as requested. I was then able to pay the Overseas League bill and afford the luxury of a two-berth sleeper on the train to Aberdeen.

On arrival at the Rundles' place, Cousin Mabel told me that Leslie was on a course in London, Alice was in Perthshire and Cousin Lella would soon be going to stay with the Curries at Cullen. I was just in time to accompany Mr Rundle and Francis to church. We had to enter by a temporary door as the adjoining hall was being rebuilt. Later, we went to the aerodrome at Dyce to see the progress being made on the new runway.

When I heard that Leslie's friend Jimmy Donald was recovering from a hernia operation I walked to Dyce to see him and his family. Jimmy insisted on taking me to see a local variety show at the Tivoli Theatre. Unfortunately I wasn't able to follow all the jokes because of the broad Scottish accents. He later showed me over the phosphate works at Dyce, where he'd done holiday work in the laboratory. I found that Jimmy's young sister Frances was interested in dancing so I took her to the Savoy Ballroom in Aberdeen.

The top floor of the Savoy had modern dancing, the floor below a café and the floor below that old time dancing. We tried the latter, dancing the Lilac Waltz, and other favourites, but the place was full of older people so we climbed the stairs and finished the evening rock 'n' rolling amongst people more our own age.

I made another trip to Oldmeldrum to see my relations, Mrs Killoh and Mrs Alexander. The old ladies proudly showed me the roses in their garden. Mrs Killoh told me a man did the gardening for them as she suffered from a broken thigh and that was why she limped, and Mrs Alexander had a bad heart and arthritis. We exchanged news and gifts – I gave them fruit and a book on New Zealand; they gave me two ties and a very useful book about touring Scotland. They said my Scottish grandfather, the Rev. James Skinner, had the highest of reputations before he left for New Zealand and I came from 'good stock'! I was sorry when the time came for me to leave them and return to Aberdeen.

In the last days of my holiday at Aberdeen, I went skating at Donald's Ice Rink and took the Rundles to the cinema. A newsreel of the Farnborough Show featured the famous test pilot, John Derry, and his observer. They described what it was like flying faster than sound in the de Havilland DH110. On leaving the cinema, I was sad to read newspaper headlines saying that Derry and his observer had been killed that day when the DH110 had crashed into spectators at Farnborough. This seemed to be a real set-back to aviation, but I'd no doubt that ways would be found to overcome the problems associated with high speed flight.

My leave ended, I caught the train south. On approaching Newcastle I noticed a huge corrugated iron shed on which was painted in faded lettering, 'Airship Construction Co. Ltd.' – a reminder of a bygone era. Jack Henderson and the new C Squadron Under Officer, L.R. Davis, got on the train at Newcastle, so we talked together for the remainder of the journey to Cranwell.

CHAPTER 12

Make or Break

MY ARMS FELT SIX INCHES LONGER after making several trips to shift my things from Block 78 to the main College building.

Charlie Collishaw, my new batman, greeted me cordially and was soon pressing my uniforms and polishing my shoes. 'Just call me Charlie,' he said. Dressed in a white jacket and black trousers, he was rather short, a little deaf and whistled as he bustled endlessly between his room and the rooms of the Flight Cadets in his care. Having been at the College twenty years, he was one of a select group of long term College servants. I paid him 15s a month and valued his services during the remainder of my time at the College. Ron Chippindale and Jim Brown told me that their batman had been batman to the former Commandant, AVM Sinclair, when he'd been a Flight Cadet.

My new room, Room 37, had similar furnishings to my former one in Block 78 except that it had a small wash-basin in the corner to the right of the window, a mirror and cabinet above the wash-basin, a good sized bookcase, brown linoleum below the mats on the floor, and a high, white tubular, hospital-type bed, under which my boots and shoes were neatly placed in a line. I could place my feet against the wall heater under the desk by the windows, and watch what was going on at the main gates to the College – there being no frosting on the windows as in Block 78 (Fig. 28). There was a strange lock to the door. The key could only be inserted from the corridor side and had to be turned to open the door. There wasn't a door knob on the corridor side. Though the key could be removed, it was usually left in the lock so that people could enter the room. Inside the room, the lock had a knob on it that had to be turned to open the door. A locking device could be activated from inside the room.

Spike Heaney was allocated a room beside mine. Across the corridor was a box room and nearby were ablutions, smoke doors and stairs leading down to the open courtyard between the A and B Squadron wings of the College.

As I was settling in, a power failure blacked out much of the College. Dinner that night was by candlelight. Afterwards, with no light in my room, I had no choice but to go to bed.

The Autumn Term began with news that F/C M.M. Ispahani of 59C had been killed during the previous leave when hitchhiking on a RPAF Bristol Freighter to his home in East Pakistan. A rumour went the rounds that the pilot had tried looping the Freighter!

Figure 28. View from Author's room, A Squadron, College main building, 1952.

Then Tim Scroggs of 59B, the son of a Group Captain, was relegated to 60B and Ron Chedgey of 60B asked for voluntary suspension. Ron wanted to fly on a part-time basis through the RAF Volunteer Reserve and hoped to be commissioned in due course. He'd been offered a job in the timber industry. Jim Brown took over his room.

In Flying Wing, Flt. Lt. 'Bud' Abbott became C Flight Commander and Flt. Lt. Sillars the Deputy Flight Commander of D Flight. Flt. Lt. Sillars retained Sabre McLelland-Brown as a pupil, but I was transferred to Fg. Off. L.J.A. Maisonpierre. Louis (as he was known to Flight Cadets, but not to his face!), was of Dutch origins, of slight build with a Hitler-type moustache, and spoke English with an accent. I felt that I didn't have the same rapport with him as I'd had with Flt. Lt. Sillars. For example, on my first flight with Louis, he told me to climb to 1,000 feet and then turn onto 225 degrees. As I climbed he said, 'On reaching 1,000 feet, turn onto 330 degrees.' So at 1,000 feet I turned onto 330 degrees. He then wanted to know why I wasn't on 225 degrees! I believe that Sam Boyce, who was also Louis's pupil, had similar problems with him.

Ron, Jim and I remained in the same sets for lectures as we'd been the previous term. The gen men were much the same as before. Aerodynamics and Aircraft Structures were combined into Performance – in my opinion one of the most interesting subjects. Mathematics had been dropped, but we were told that we'd be tested on it in ten weeks time. Like a lot of my colleagues, I'd not answered some Radio questions we'd been told to do during the leave period, so completing them was one of my first priorities. I was then glad to start on radar during our Radio periods. In War Studies, the USAF Exchange Officer, Major William E. Charlson, began an interesting series of lectures on the United States Air Force.

There were meetings to go to – Squadron, senior Mess, model aeroplane, gliding and librarian's. At the Mess meeting, Ted Reynolds got Gordon Grierson elected (in spite of his protests) as the House Member representing Flight Cadets on the Mess Committee. Quite a number of 60 Entry (who were supposed to be 'conscientious types') were rostered by the new civilian librarian, Mr A. Bray, to be duty librarian every fortnight – for late afternoon, early evening or late evening periods. When Ron and I were rostered, we looked on the duty as an excellent way in which to have a good browse in the library and get off our Squadron Orderly Cadet rosters. The duties weren't arduous – mainly checking books in and out of the library.

Battle of Britain Day was heralded by Flt. Lts. Abbott and Cree practising the lowest level glider aerobatics I'd seen. Then three gliders were winched into the air simultaneously. A signal was fired from a Very pistol, but the signal landed outside the boundary of the south airfield in a field of stubble and started a fire. I joined the rush of people to put the fire out. Ten minutes later a fire engine arrived! The flying then resumed with Chipmunks and Harvards practising formation flying, but we Flight Cadets had to return to the Flying Wing crew rooms and clean them in preparation for the 'at home' day.

When Battle of Britain Day arrived, I assisted in handling the gliders in the display. When a cable broke towing a glider into the air, I helped in dragging the heavy cable around the perimeter of the south airfield back to a hangar while aircraft kept performing overhead. The programme was much the same as I'd seen the previous year, but none the less exciting. I saw for the first time an Athena advanced trainer, a Vampire T11 two-seater trainer, a Meteor NF11 night fighter and a Meteor 8 with a flight refuelling probe. Two Sea Fury piston engined fighters put on a spectacular dogfight with the jet aircraft. One Meteor pilot did an outside loop (flying upside down then going up into a loop). The negative G must have made his eyeballs hang out. Fly pasts included formations of nine Sabres and three Canberras. Again, a most enjoyable show.

On Battle of Britain Sunday, I forgot about the time and was late on church parade. As a result I was made the Other Denominations marker and put on Under Officer's parade for a day. The OD church had been redecorated with royal blue carpet and curtains. Some of the Senior College were sent to the Battle of Britain service at Lincoln Cathedral.

A short ceremonial parade commemorating the Battle of Britain was also held. Being early in the term, the parade wasn't of a high standard.

The first guest night of term was an unpleasant occasion for me – I don't think the jugged hare agreed with me. After dinner, members of 62 Entry were initiated into the College, the best acts being a speedway motor bike race around the Orange with flaming torches, and someone doing fire-eating. Toilet paper thrown around the stage of the main lecture hall caught fire several times. Ghastly forfeits followed. There was so much soot, paper, water, flour, treacle and other rubbish in the main lecture hall that 60 Entry was told to lend a hand in cleaning up the mess.

I was all aches and pains because of rugby trials (I didn't get into the A Squadron team), squash and early morning gymnastic practices for the Knocker Cup. I was glad when my usual fitness returned. The first term boxing and inter-squadron boxing competitions were poorly attended until the Squadron Commanders rounded up every Flight Cadet they could find in the College.

After sport one Saturday afternoon, I travelled by bus to Lincoln with some other Flight Cadets. I wanted to buy light-bulbs of a higher wattage than those in my room. (Five months later, approval was given for the Stores Section to issue 100 watt bulbs and replace the 30 and 60 watt bulbs in our rooms.) We walked around the hill on which the Cathedral stands before having drinks at the Saracen's Head and going to a dance at the Co-Op. Unfortunately, without late passes we had to be back at Cranwell by 2300 hours.

Next morning, I heard that Ted Reynolds and Gordon Grierson had gone for a motor bike ride the previous day, but the bike had broken down west of Newark and they'd had to abandon it and walk some sixteen miles back to Cranwell, arriving at 0400 hours! Ron Chippindale bought himself a motor bike.

Most of 60A were detailed to host a visit of senior apprentices from the Daimler Motor Company at Coventry. The lads were about our own ages and seemed to be a real mixture from working class homes. Though their visit coincided with an afternoon of private study, I quite enjoyed showing them around Cranwell.

Strong winds affected flying for several days. Taxiing a light aircraft such as the Chipmunk was particularly difficult. Solo flying by 60 Entry was cancelled, then all flying was cancelled. When flying resumed in bad visibility, it was with instructors only. Spike Heaney and I had 'wizard fun' formation flying through the murk with our instructors.

I continued to do gliding when I could and was authorised to operate the winches without supervision. Fuel blockages and cable breaks sometimes made winch operating a frustrating job. Fg. Off. Maisonpierre and his fiancée came to watch one day. On another occasion the new Commandant and Assistant Commandant, Air Cdre. Eeles and Gp. Capt. Nelson, stopped and talked to me while having a leisurely stroll around the south airfield (presumably to have a private conversation and see if there were any mushrooms!).

The weather continued cold and wet. Some drill was cancelled, but a ceremonial parade without greatcoats or gloves went ahead in spite of falling rain. We all ended up soaked through and frozen. The central heating in the College was still to be turned on.

The Commandant addressed a meeting of the College and said that in future the Queen's Colour wouldn't be paraded on every ceremonial because of wear and tear to the Colour, but only on important occasions such as Battle of Britain Sunday and graduations.

Ron and I were instructed by RNZAF Headquarters in London to wear New Zealand shoulder patches on our uniforms. When we showed the instructions to our Squadron Commanders, the Commandant wrote to Air Cdre. Kay saying he didn't like the idea as we wouldn't appear to be the same as other Flight Cadets. Air Cdre. Kay referred the matter to RNZAF Headquarters in Wellington and that was the last Ron and I heard of it.

During a clothing parade I was fitted for another battledress uniform and experienced once again the frustrations of having to deal with the Clothing Store and Accounts Section in East Camp. I well understood the saying, 'If it doesn't fit, you're abnormal!'

At one of the periodic guest nights one of 60A, having bought his quota of liquor, wanted to reimburse me for my quota of liquor. When I said I wasn't buying any liquor, he said I was anti-social and made other disparaging remarks about me and New Zealand. When the time came to toast the Queen, my attention was diverted and a wine bottle cork was put in the water of my glass. I removed the cork only to be accused of drinking something alcoholic! This was all rather petty, but still a problem for me as nothing I could say in my defence at that time had any effect on my colleagues. The whole thing was a lot of fun to them so I tried not to make too much of such events.

I was all ready to go on a navigation flight with Louis when he cancelled the trip. A member of the visiting Central Flying School Examining Wing wanted to check his instructing ability. As a result, Louis's instructor category was upgraded from B2 to B1. I was sent solo in a brand new and improved Chipmunk that had a slightly enlarged tail for better control during aerobatics. I headed for Boston while climbing to 12,000 feet and did aerobatics over the sea. When I was upside down, small pieces of fluff and other rubbish floated into the canopy then disappeared when I came right side up. The plane was certainly nice to handle.

When Louis and I went on a navigation flight to Ramsey and a railway crossing south-east of Leicester, he took my map away during the first leg. On returning it, he asked me where we were and I had to make corrections in heading to fly over Ramsey. During the second leg, he wanted me to get a true bearing from Cranwell and work out a diversion back to base. While flying on the diversion, I had to do a dog-leg around the American airfield of North Luffenham so as not to get in the way of the Sabres operating there. I was then required to call Cranwell and get a course to steer back to base.

Sam Boyce had warned me that Louis would go on a bit during the flight and sure enough, he did. Louis said he was going to sleep while I did the landing, but he 'woke up' when I decided to do a flapless landing without power. Admittedly my airspeed was a bit high when we touched down, but I got a real earful about bravado, being over-confident and so on! Back in the crew room, Louis calmed down and said my flying was OK, but I needed to do more work on my navigation.

Though I'd been busy during the navigation exercise flying the aircraft, making radio calls, and keeping a log and a good look-out, I was able to recognise a passing Lincoln bomber, a Vampire fighter, two Harvard trainers and a Prince communications aircraft – the last being a type I hadn't seen before.

The dismal news went around that another Old Cranwellian had been killed in a Meteor accident.

Early in a game of rugby, I was tackled with the ball. My opponent held onto the third finger of my left hand as we fell. I felt pain, but thought I'd only strained the finger. I continued playing and helped my team win the game. Though my hand swelled up, I went with six other Flight Cadets to a dance that evening at Eaton Hall Teachers' Training College near East Retford. We Flight Cadets were in competition with some Loughborough College students and a few National Service officer cadets, but managed to have quite a good time. I met a girl called Ann Maltby.

The next day there was the usual church parade. I wrote an essay on the relationship of the Principles of War to the Mesopotamia Campaign, then went to the cinema.

On Monday morning, my hand was no better so I reported sick. The doctor arranged for me to go for an X-ray that afternoon at the RAF Hospital Nocton Hall. I filled in time by having instruction on a link trainer. Rain was falling as I and other passengers travelled in the back of a covered truck to Nocton Hall. We were as wet and cold inside as it was outside. After a delay caused by a power failure, I was told the X-ray showed that torsion had caused a spiral break to my finger. (The X-ray also showed that a bone about the size and shape of a dice in my left wrist had been broken at some time in the past. All I could think of was having fallen on my left hand playing fives at Waimataitai School – a strained wrist having been diagnosed at the time!) Plaster of Paris was put on my forearm, except for my fingertips, and I was given three weeks of light duties.

This meant no flying, no drill and no Knocker Cup practice. What worried me, however, was the possibility of being relegated to 61 Entry through loss of flying hours. Writing with my left hand was very awkward, but this didn't get me out of doing a Radio test. Dressing – in fact everything I did – was difficult while my forearm was hurting and in plaster. A nose cold resulting from the cold, wet trip to Nocton Hall made things worse.

I became a spectator at rugby and soccer games and at the Knocker gymnastics competition. In the last, Julian Bowes strained a finger vaulting. I then recalled that other members of 60A had had similar problems to my own – Nigel MacNicol had broken an ankle in a previous Knocker competition, Laurie Jones had also broken a finger playing rugby and John Tucker had broken a thumb at boxing. Junior Entries put on a display of relay races while the marks for the Knocker Cup were being added up. A Squadron came last – the team was without me of course!

On one sports afternoon, I had a look through the fuselage of a Halifax bomber that'd been left near the College on the edge of the north airfield.

During flying periods, I did odd jobs at D Flight, tried to study for the coming exams or do some more link training. In one of the night flying sessions I missed, Ron Chippindale was taxiing a Chipmunk when he knocked off part of the flaps on a sodium runway marker. He was given seven days of jankers.

At a Mess meeting, the Assistant Commandant announced that the Riding Club would go out of existence unless there were more members, and more Flight Cadets were required for a proposed skiing trip to the Continent next leave period. Ron and I had already put our names down and paid £34 4s 2d each for the latter.

The College woke one morning to find rubbish bins had been emptied around the Orange and there were words in chalk on the pillars outside the main entrance. The naval officer cadets at RAF Syerston were apparently the culprits, so a few nights later 58 Entry visited Syerston (about twenty miles to the west of Cranwell), painted words on the runways and spread around key areas toilet paper on which had been printed, 'HMS Landlocked – back to the sea you penguins.'

I was told of a much earlier prank where Flight Cadets visiting the RMA Sandhurst decided to 'borrow' a gun weighing several tons, take it to Cranwell and tie it to the flagpole that was on the Orange at that time. They disassembled the gun, loaded it on a hired truck and were on their way back to Cranwell when they were stopped by police. Apparently one of the Flight Cadets had mentioned the escapade to the Press! He was later chopped for lack of initiative.

There was always something going on at the College to relieve high spirits. Just prior to a Thermodynamics lecture, some of us were in the process of throwing Hammy Khan out a window when our lecturer, Fg. Off. F.A. Leckie (a Scotsman) came into the room. Very tactfully he withdrew until we'd completed the job. Then we were on edge during his lecture waiting for him to push the lower blackboard up so that the upper blackboard would come down and be used. One of Hammy's shoes, left on the upper blackboard, fell off and hit Fg. Off. Leckie on the head! He wasn't hurt and joined in our laughter.

Mid-term break seemed to arrive suddenly. I travelled with other Flight Cadets to London. There were no empty seats in the train carriages, so Mal Dines, Julian Bowes and I went to the dining car, bought one lunch, divided it between us and sat eating it as slowly as possible beside a rather pretty girl.

I'd booked into Bolton House again and found myself sharing an enormous room with a Belgian chap who'd just arrived from Antwerp to study economics at London University. His English was understandable, but quaint. He would ask me if he could go to dinner, if I would excuse him while he went to the toilet and, when he didn't understand a comment or know what to say, made extensive use of a dictionary.

I felt my Belgian friend wanted to practise his English on me, so on Sunday when he wanted me to go with him to the Roman Catholic Westminster Cathedral, I went along just for the experience. On the way, we stopped at Buckingham Palace to see the changing of the guard. A Comet airliner with its undercarriage down whistled low overhead *en route* to Heathrow. After the service, we continued talking as we walked through much of the West End of London, finishing with a cruise up the Thames from Parliament to Tower Bridge and a visit to a cinema.

When I went to have a bath at Bolton House (there was no shower), I found that the large bathroom window didn't have curtains or blinds. The night was so dark outside I couldn't see what was beyond the window. There could have been rooms of another wing of the building, a brick wall or just open space. I rigged up a bath towel to act as a curtain and turned on the hot water tap of the deep sided bath. No water came out, so I turned on the tap a bit further. A distant rumbling occurred and the tap started to vibrate. Eventually, rusty looking water started to come out of the Victorian plumbing. I waited for the water to clear and go down the plug hole before filling the bath with lots of lovely hot water. Then, below an assortment of ladies underwear suspended on drying racks from a pulley on the ceiling, I had my bath.

I rang Cousin Jennifer, but she was about to leave for the Hippodrome Theatre at Eastbourne where she would be acting in *The Late Christopher Bean* and *Jane Eyre*.

When I rang Zoë Sinton and asked her out, she wanted to see the play *The Innocents* at Her Majesty's Theatre. I noted that Zoë had changed a lot, having developed at Sadler's Wells from being slim and attractive to being a rather strapping girl.

With time running out before having to return to Cranwell, I did some more window-shopping and general sightseeing. Rather footsore, I went to the Odeon cinema and saw the film *Limelight*. While queueing to get in, I noticed the well-known actor Jack Hawkins and his wife leaving the cinema.

Bad weather continued to affect flying at Cranwell. At D Flight, I learned some more of the Morse Code and was given the task of marking certain things on wall maps and drawing flags of a new system of aerodrome control. Louis Maisonpierre pessimistically said I'd missed so much flying that I might have to go down an Entry, but my Flight Commander, Flt. Lt. Bayley, reassured me that I should be able to make up 10 hours of flying during study periods and sports afternoons following the Intermediate Examinations and before my Basic Handling (flying) Test.

The examinations were on everyone's mind. We were to be tested in eleven subjects and every spare minute was occupied in swotting.

I wasted much of a day going to the RAF Hospital Nocton Hall to have my finger X-rayed again before the plaster was removed. The doctor gave me another fortnight of light duties. So many people had caught colds as a result of going to the hospital in the back of a truck that a bus had been laid on. This resulted in queues of people waiting to be treated and the bus not returning to Cranwell until late afternoon. I was given lunch at the officers' mess. Unable to swot, I had to fill in time reading newspapers and magazines.

Letters from Margaret Hornsey became fewer in number and then ceased completely. She'd never been a good letter writer. Though I wrote to her regularly, I was forced to come to the conclusion that she wasn't as keen on me as I was on her. I asked Mum to enquire of Margaret's parents as to what had happened. The reply wasn't favourable so, bitterly disappointed, I tore up her photos and letters and threw them away. I felt some consolation when I remembered that the fortune-teller had said I'd meet another person and we'd be very happy together.

One light in all this gloom was that I missed the Ferris inter-squadron drill competition. Other members of 60A borrowed my white belt, bayonet and gloves for the occasion, but A Squadron still came last, thus losing the final chance to be Sovereign's Squadron next term. I took some photos of my colleagues on parade.

A strong rumour went around that the Duke of Edinburgh would be coming to Cranwell for basic flying training. I could imagine air traffic control clearing the circuit when he was about to take-off or land – just as they did for the College Meteor. We were later to hear that he would do his training at RAF White Waltham, Headquarters of Home Command.

At another guest night, John Tucker kept 60A amused while coffee was served by blowing large soap bubbles with smoke in them. We also learned how to make strange noises by wetting a finger and rubbing it around the edge of a wine glass. Some irresponsible Flight Cadets even set fire to the liqueur in their wine glasses and caused the glass to melt. Afterwards, we all attended an illustrated lecture on the Outward Bound Trust by a Director of the Trust, Lieutenant Colonel P.D. Maud, MBE.

On Guy Fawkes night, a fireworks display was held at Cranwell. This was the culmination of a craze for fireworks in 60A. There were so many burn marks on the linoleum in our rooms that fireworks were banned from the College.

One evening, 60 Entry gathered in the Junior Ante-room to hear two distinguished ministers who were part of a Mission to the Royal Air Force. A question and answer session was held before we crowded into the College Chapel for a short service.

The whole College (except Roman Catholics) later went to the Hangar Church for a service, taken by the Bishop of Croydon, that was broadcast on national radio. In the march past afterwards, we wore greatcoats for the first time that term, the weather having turned quite cold.

Jim Brown's flying instructor thought he should try for his 'White Ticket' in instrument flying, though this wasn't a requirement until the last term at the College. Jim wasn't keen to do so and wasn't surprised when he failed the test.

Then the depressing news came through that a member of the Senior Entry had been relegated to 58 Entry and three of 58 Entry had been chopped – one voluntarily, one because of airsickness, and one for being caught for the second time doing unauthorised formation flying. Another member of 58 Entry was relegated to 59 Entry for unauthorised formation flying.

Hammy Khan of 60C got himself lost above cloud and, with little fuel remaining, had to declare an emergency. He was able to get help from RAF Waddington, a master airfield about ten miles north of Cranwell, and land safely. Mal Dines of 60A also had a 'dicey do' when he noticed his oil pressure was zero just after taking-off during night flying. He continued his circuit and landed without further incident.

On a guest night late in the term, the guest speaker, Air Cdre. A.V. Harvey, MP, gave a most interesting talk on the history and procedure of Parliament. He took a sip from a water filled carafe and grimaced – someone had put salt in the water! During a break before questions were asked, the official party left the main lecture hall. The new Cadet Wing Adjutant, Flt. Lt. A.T. Talbot-Williams, MA, then returned to test the water and fell down the stairs as he left the stage with the carafe. Laughter erupted and, during the confusion, some of 60A decided to have some more fun and pulled my tweeds off.

When the official party returned, I had to sit there trouserless trying to look as if nothing had happened!

Thick fog enveloped the College for several days. I had the task of raising and lowering the flags on the College tower, but they could hardly be seen from the ground. A ceremonial parade went ahead as if there was no fog. Then the days became frosty and caused the B Squadron Flight Sergeant to lose his footing during a parade.

60 Entry had a week of sitting in the main lecture hall for the Intermediate Examinations. Most of the papers were three hours in length. This really seemed to be make or break time. A number of my colleagues said they hadn't been able to sleep at night so, when the last paper was finished, there were cheers of relief. Many of 60 Entry went off to pubs to celebrate.

The examination results were drip fed to us over the next few weeks. In Humanistics, I was average in the Entry and came ahead of Jim and Ron, but in Science Jim was above average followed by Ron and me. Spike Heaney topped the Entry in order of merit.

With the exams over, we started studying jet engines in Thermodynamics. Major Charlson lectured us in War Studies on Russia – our first confidential lecture in which we were not allowed to take notes. At other times we were shown a most interesting film called *Rocket Flight*, and films on jungle survival, the effects of G, the theory of flight and rubber dinghies.

The Cranwell siren began wailing – there was a fire at the Dental Section in Station Sick Quarters.

The weather was so frosty that a Cranwell–Sandhurst soccer match was cancelled because of 'hard ground'. In one of the whitest frosts I'd seen, my shoes were sticking to the ground.

While still on light duties, I was watching a rugby match when Laurie Jones of 60A was knocked unconscious in front of me. We spectators covered him with our coats to keep him warm until he'd recovered enough to leave the field.

When I resumed full duties again, I flew at every opportunity including private study periods and sports afternoons. I'd forgotten some things and Louis harangued me about them for a while. He'd little sense of humour so I was careful not to make joking remarks in case they were taken the wrong way. Louis's other pupil, Sam Boyce, coped with this by saying (with his tongue in his cheek), 'I think you're a wizard bloke, Sir,' or 'I couldn't agree more, Sir.'

Louis and I went on another cross-country flight, this time to St Neots and RAF Feltwell.

Night flying was cancelled one night because of fog. The next night I flew on a late detail and didn't get to bed until 0200 hours.

When I was rostered at gliding for winching duties, I was quite pleased as winching appeared to be warmer than flying in an open cockpit. Even so, I froze. Sabre McLelland-Brown of 60A made a heavy landing in a Grunau and broke the skid.

The whole College had to attend the finals of the RAF Boxing Championships held that year at Cranwell. I heard that a number of contestants had been 'press ganged' into competing as there weren't enough volunteers! Three bouts were of some interest as Flight Cadets or Old Cranwellians were in them.

I began playing squash again, trying to strengthen my backhand. Though Spike Heaney could still beat me, he was prepared to give me a game whenever we could find the time.

One Saturday evening, Mal Dines and I travelled by bus to Newark, had a meal and then went to a dance at the Corn Exchange. Snow was falling as we returned to Cranwell.

Every Flight Cadet had to write a thesis before graduating from the College. We could choose the subject, but it had to be something that would be of use later on. A long list of Humanistic and Science subjects were suggested and there was the possibility of an oral examination being given on the subject once the thesis had been completed. Members of 60 Entry had until the end of term to decide their subjects. I thought I'd write on delta winged aircraft as they appeared to be at the forefront of aviation development. Aircraft like the Avro Vulcan bomber and experimental 707B had already flown and others would soon follow. Ron said he was considering writing on soil erosion in New Zealand. I felt he ought to have chosen an aviation subject.

Occasionally, items would appear on the main notice boards that would have us in fits of laughter. For example, a photo from the *Tatler* showed our former Senior GCT Officer dining at the Dorchester Hotel, but someone had written below the photo the words, 'Local chop makes good!' (I later heard that the officer had married a Countess and retired from the RAF.) Another example was amendment instructions to a manual – placed there no doubt by a frustrated Flight Cadet – which read, 'On page X, paragraph Y, line Z, put ",", instead of ".".'! A cartoon appropriate to the Cranwell weather at that time showed a chap covered in bandages in a hospital bed. A visitor by the bed was saying, 'Wish I had the money to go skiing.' When suggestions were requested for music for a mid-term dance, advantage was taken of Jim Brown's difficulty with his r's, one request being, 'Jim Bwown's body lies a-mouldewing in his gwave,' – signed, 'three hopeful Flight Cadets!'

All Cadets and Flight Cadets were issued with the latest *List of Graduates of the Royal Air Force College Cranwell*. This publication was most interesting as it included details of all graduates since the College began (listed in alphabetical order and by entry), the names of Flight Cadets killed during flying training at the College, College squadrons that'd been King's or

Sovereign's Squadron, the number of awards and decorations to ex-Cranwell Cadets, post-World War II sports results, ex-Cadets who were commissioned other than through the College, and the names of past Commandants and Assistant Commandants of the College.

I browsed through the List and read details of renowned graduates such as Air Chief Marshal The Earl of Bandon, GBE, CB, CVO, DSO, MID, commonly known as 'The Abandoned Earl'!

I was interested to see that I was the fourth Hancock to have been at the College. C.G. Hancock had graduated in the first entry (the February 1920 [Naval] Entry), R.C. Hancock had been in the September 1920 Entry but left the College and was later commissioned, and G.N. Hancock had graduated in the September 1931 Entry. I wondered if I was related to any of them.

Changes were still occurring at Cranwell. Clean-up work continued in West Camp south of Camp Road, but in East Camp No. 6 Radio School was disbanded and its pupils were moved to No. 1 Radio School at RAF Locking. I was thus unable to meet up with Allan Carter and Keith Smith again until we'd all returned to New Zealand.

I was asleep one night when something awoke me. A noise seemed to be coming from the windows. 'Let me in, Hank, I'm falling' – I recognised Ted Reynold's voice. Very drowsy from a deep sleep, I got up in the dark and opened one of the windows. Ted was standing precariously on the narrow ledge below the windows and clinging to my partially opened windows. He was in imminent danger of falling a storey onto the chrysanthemum stakes in the garden below. I thought that only Ted or Gordon Grierson would be crazy enough to go clambering around the outside of the College at night. I let him in, not knowing that Mal Dines was also outside moving from the next door window of Mike Kelly (61A) to mine. Ted pushed past me to unlock my door and let in other members of 60A. They proceeded to wreck my room. Infuriated, I fought with them and in the process grabbed my bayonet. Somebody shouted, 'He's got a bayonet.' The light was put on, I was sat upon and disarmed. Their task done, my colleagues left. In tidying up I found that my reading lamp had been broken. I took a long time to get to sleep again that night. I was aware that I wasn't the only Flight Cadet on which such pranks were played. What I didn't know was that 60A would never again try a prank like that on me.

The Lincolnshire weather was certainly peculiar. On one morning when there was thick fog, a very white frost and the parade ground was dangerous to walk on, we were given warm-up drill on the frozen grass of the Orange! On another morning, we paraded without greatcoats and practised march pasts on the icy parade ground. Many Flight Cadets slipped and fell. Wet weather then caused a rehearsal for the graduation parade to be held in Hangar 30 and resulted in us being given a 'rocket' for poor drill. Who could blame us in the circumstances? We had to do another hangar rehearsal. The last ceremonial parade of term also had to be held in the hangar, this time because of snow. A Flight Cadet beside me became so cold he almost fainted and had to leave the parade.

Only limited flying was possible. D Flight filled in time by practising radio calls on a tape recorder. Our voices seemed strange when they were played back to us. A full kit inspection also occupied our time, causing us some consternation in having to find all our equipment and then lay it out in the approved manner. When I did get airborne, there was thick industrial haze up to 3,000 feet that considerably reduced visibility. At 5,000 feet over Sleaford, I could barely see the town and Cranwell was completely obscured! Flying was cancelled that afternoon.

I was sent solo on the longest navigation trip to date − to a pin point near Nottingham and then to Leconfield aerodrome (north of Kingston upon Hull). I encountered very strong winds and used more fuel than expected, so made a diversion back to base. Needless to say, Louis wasn't at all pleased when he checked my navigation and log.

Louis was able to take me on only one flight that covered all the things I'd have on my Basic Handling Test. I couldn't do anything right in his eyes. This was hardly a good lead-up to such an important test! He said to me, 'Don't be nervous about the test,' but he wished Sam good luck for his test.

My Flight Commander, Flt. Lt. Bayley, tested me on a day that was reasonably clear and calm. He followed me as I talked my way around the Chipmunk on the pre-flight inspection. The take-off direction was into the bright rays of the low sun and I could hardly see a thing ahead. This was also a problem in circuits when doing various types of landing, and in simulated forced landings. My aerobatics showed my lack of recent practice. Only in low flying did I feel I'd done well. After the flight, I was asked questions on meteorology, range and endurance, instruments, theory of flight, air traffic control and so on. Flt. Lt. Bayley said that my five weeks off flying would be taken into account in assessing my performance. I was overjoyed when I heard that I'd passed the test − even if I was only classed as average, just 7 percentage points less than above average! Louis said I ought to have done better.

On returning from the flight lines, I was shocked to hear that Reg Bailey had been chopped, Gordon Grierson had been relegated to 61 Entry and Tim Scroggs had been transferred to No. 14 Entry at RAF Digby as an Equipment Branch Cadet. This meant 60 Entry had lost, up to that time, eight out of its forty-six original members plus Tim Scroggs, who'd been relegated to 60 Entry just three months earlier. Rumour had it that two other members of 60A had been given the word by Sqn. Ldr. Thomas to de-digitate or expect suspension. Also, a member of the Senior Entry, two members of 59 Entry and two of 61 Entry had been chopped.

We could never be sure why individual Flight Cadets were chopped or relegated. (Statistics showed that 35.4 per cent of Flight Cadets left the College voluntarily, 32.3 per cent were suspended for flying reasons, 12.4 per cent because of character, 11.6 per cent through academics and 8.3 per cent for medical reasons.) Sometimes Flight Cadets were chopped and departed while the rest of us were flying or at lectures. Someone said that twenty-three people had left the College that term. No wonder there was some apprehension amongst the remaining Flight Cadets!

With a little more free time at my disposal, I rejoined the winter dancing class, helped in getting 'Henrietta' back on the road and played squash, snooker and billiards. Jim Brown just beat me in the latter games, but I was able to defeat him in squash. I was asked to represent the New Zealanders at the College on the *Journal* Committee, and readily accepted.

Early one Saturday, a large contingent of Flight Cadets set off from Cranwell in five buses for Aldershot Stadium to support College teams in various games with the RMA Sandhurst. Five miles south of St Neots, we ran into dense fog and there was no way in which we could be in time for the games. Some Flight Cadets caught a train to have the weekend in London while the rest of us returned to Cranwell. I later read that the fog in London had been the worst for years.

At last I was authorised to do solo formation flying, albeit with another Chipmunk containing an instructor and his 61 Entry pupil. Louis told me that I'd caught up on flying hours, but lacked sufficient formation flying and instrument flying. While I did more instrument flying, the rest of the Flight went on an aerial treasure hunt. This involved deciphering clues while airborne and acting on them, e.g. given the clue, 'A famous tea party', one then flew to Boston and counted the number of aircraft on the aerodrome. This seemed a lot of fun and I was sorry to have missed it.

The cold conditions caused problems with the cartridge starters on the Chipmunks and propellers often had to be hand swung. One of my flights was cancelled because of a snow storm. On another, I had to return from the take-off point as the wind was gusting to over 30 knots. Those people who did get airborne had trouble with pitot heads icing up or got lost in snow storms and had to divert to RAF Waddington.

When low cloud caused flying to be cancelled, D Flight was given a lecture on the Middle East Air Force and saw films on the Farnborough Show and the Invasion of Europe (from an Air Force point of view).

D Flight decided to have a party in the Red Lion Hotel at Caythorpe. We Flight Cadets wore our new College caps. After a good meal, some serious drinking began. Ted Reynolds said in front of the officers, 'I hope

Hank doesn't get drunk on orange squash!' I noted that one of the flying instructors, Fg. Off. J. Primrose (a Scotsman), didn't drink alcohol either. We were all very well behaved. When returning to Cranwell on a motor bike, Ted and an instructor ran into a hedge and ended up rather scratched.

Flt. Lt. Sillars invited his present and former pupils to the christening of his youngest son, David Charles, in the College Chapel and to tea afterwards. I thought this really nice of him, but had to decline the invitation to tea as Ann Maltby had written asking to see me at Newark and I was unable to contact her to postpone our meeting. I'd asked Ann to the graduation ball and she wanted to find out more about it. I wrote a letter of apology to Mrs Sillars.

I'd also asked Jennifer and Robert Langford-Jones to the graduation parade, but they declined as they would be on tour with *The Gay Dog* Company and would probably be recording the play at Leeds for radio on the day of the graduation. My old Sunday School teacher, Miss Ronaldson, was visiting Britain and asked if she could come to the graduation, so I advised her what trains to get and booked her into a local hotel.

The final guest night of term was marred a little by more comments about me not drinking alcohol, and extra saccharine tablets being placed in my coffee when I wasn't looking, making it undrinkable. Twelve officers were farewelled in the after dinner speeches. The 57 Entry review, 'Split Whittington', was the best I'd seen. This pseudo pantomime portrayed the struggles of a bright-eyed, bushy-tailed young Flight Cadet to become an Under Officer in spite of the foul schemes of the Chief Flying Instructor and others determined to foil his progress. A series of hilarious original songs, accompanied by the College band, together with excellent impersonations of College notables, brought the house down. The script and scenery were very well done. 57 Entry certainly went out in a blaze of glory, and even the officers who were impersonated must have enjoyed the show.

The snow melted as rain fell and end of term photographs had to be taken in the Junior Ante-room instead of on the steps leading to the main entrance to the College.

Air Marshal Sir Hugh S.P. Walmsley, KCB, KCIE, CBE, MC, DFC, presented Wings, individual prizes and squadron trophies in the main lecture hall to Nos. 57 GD(P) and 8 E & S Entries. His son Mike received his Wings from his father.

The weather on graduation day was fine enough except for a very strong, cold wind. A gust of 111 m.p.h. was recorded that morning – the strongest ever recorded at Cranwell and the highest in Britain that day. Miss Ronaldson sent me a telegram saying she wasn't coming to the graduation because the roads were too icy.

Needless to say, the decision was made to hold the graduation parade in

Hangar 30, this being only the second time in fifty-six graduation parades when bad weather had made this necessary. Spike and I were adjusting each other's uniforms and missed the buses taking Flight Cadets to the hangar. We sprinted to the hangar and arrived, breathless, just as the Flight Cadets were forming up in squadrons. Spike was wearing three pullovers under his uniform whereas I had one pullover and my pyjama trousers under mine. Some other Flight Cadets tried to keep warm by having their silk flying gloves under their unlined leather gloves. Greatcoats weren't permitted.

The western doors of the hangar had been closed to protect everybody from the wind, but some of the parade commands were lost because of the metallic cacophony and poor acoustics of the hangar. The Chief of the Air Staff, Marshal of the Royal Air Force Sir John C. Slessor, GCB, DSO, MC, reviewed the parade and gave his address. Just as we halted from a restricted manoeuvre, one of the Junior Entry Cadets standing to attention at one side fainted, knocking over a post supporting a rope barrier. This was rather unfortunate as photographers were everywhere recording each moment of this unusual parade.

The parade over, the guests were taken by bus to the College whilst we Flight Cadets marched there. A cold, buffet lunch was awaiting us. In spite of the weather, the ice cream didn't last long amongst a crowd of hungry Flight Cadets and guests. Ron Chippindale introduced me to his girlfriend, June Spackman. We then went outside into falling snow to give Sir John Slessor three cheers as he left to inspect Flying Wing.

After that, I lent a hand in preparing for the graduation ball to be held in the main lecture hall – the dining hall being reserved for a sit-down supper. Groups of tables in the dining hall had table lamps and candles on them. The huge globe of the world in the main corridor was dressed up to look like a Christmas pudding and placed in the main entrance hall. Coloured balloons and a moon were suspended from the gallery above. Chairs, carpets and pot plants were located outside the main lecture hall. The Fancy Goods Store, some ante-rooms and the main lecture hall were decorated with coloured streamers, balloons and special lighting. Altogether, the effect was stunning.

The Commandant and Mrs Eeles received people as they arrived. Ann Maltby and I danced foxtrots, quicksteps and waltzes until about 2300 hours when a greater variety of dances were played by the College band. Ron and June didn't dance. Jim Brown was without a partner and went to bed early. Colin Loveday again had a very elegant fashion model from Dundee as his partner. There was a self-service continuous supper. Time seemed to pass quickly and at 0300 hours, buses left to take guests to various destinations.

Later that morning, I caught a bus to Grantham only to find that I'd quite a long time to wait for a train heading north. I bought Pierre Clostermann's second book, *Flames in the Sky*, to read during my four weeks of leave. I had time between trains at Edinburgh to walk along Princes Street and admire the Christmas decorations in the shops and the huge illuminated Christmas tree near Edinburgh Castle. Arriving at Aberdeen late at night, I was glad to get to the Rundles' place and go to sleep.

CHAPTER 13

May I Have the Honour?

'MAY I HAVE THE HONOUR OF THIS DANCE?'

'Yes.'

The girl and I glided away across the crowded floor. She was an excellent dancer – light on her feet and responsive, but not responsive enough when I made the wrong movement and stood on her feet.

'Sorry about that,' I said. I seemed to be doing that all the time! She looked up at me and smiled, and with more vigour followed me into another turn as we waltzed.

She was slim and attractive with lovely blue eyes and short brown hair. Being only five foot two inches in height, she only came up to my shoulders. She was wearing a grey and white checked dress that had little bows on the shoulders.

Between manoeuvring in the crowd and trying not to step on her toes, I asked her her name. 'Betty – Betty Aitken,' she told me.

I reflected on how I'd come to meet such a lovely person.

Leslie Rundle had come home after lectures that Friday night and asked me if I'd like to come with him to the end of term dance at Mitchell Hall in Marischal College. 'Everybody goes,' he added. I wasn't too keen and had said, 'But I'm not a member of Aberdeen University.' 'No problem,' said he, and promptly arranged for me to borrow the Union card of his medical student friend, George Webster. So I'd come as George Webster. Luckily, I wasn't asked anything at the door, otherwise my accent would have given me away. 'Well, we'd better dance,' Leslie had said, 'That's what we came for.' He'd then gone off dancing with his girlfriend, Moira Mackenzie, leaving me to my own devices. I'd turned to the first girl on my right, thinking I'd work my way along the girls sitting on the seats around the hall. Somebody got in first and asked the girl to dance. I'd then asked the girl next to her – and that happened to be Betty! How lucky could I get!

The music came to an end. I escorted Betty back to her seat and sat beside her, reluctant to go away. She was with friends – Linda Cook, Morag McLeod and several others. Betty introduced me to them. I thought she sounded very English compared with the broad Scots of her friends.

I discovered that Betty was just a nickname – her real name was Elizabeth Mary – but in Aberdeen, Betty was just one of several contractions of Elizabeth. She was seven months younger than me and in her second year studying Biochemistry. I told her a little of my background and somehow got onto the subject of delta winged aircraft. This must have bored her, because she and her friends disappeared into the ladies' room for an extraordinary length of time – no doubt trying to lose me!

When they returned, Betty and I went off dancing again. In fact, we danced together all evening – an almost unheard of event. We rather lost track of time and Leslie, unable to find me, thought I must have gone home ahead of him.

Cousin Mabel and daughter Alice recorded the occasion as follows:

A sweet young lass from Aberdeen
at a 'Marischal Hop' one night was seen
by a New Zealand lad, there by defraud,
as he didn't possess a student card.
Cousin Leslie smuggled him in
even though so tall and slim.

He asked this lovely bright-eyed girl
on the floor to have a whirl,
and as the evening did go on,
head over heels he found he'd gone.
At the end of the dance no thought of time,
he took home his bonnie quine.

The last bus had already gone,
so how was he to get on home?
Not to worry, he had two feet
and set off walking up the street.

Leslie by now was home and dry,
Cousin Mabel let out a cry,
'Tis midnight and where has Rutherford gone?'
'Oh,' says Les, 'What have I done?'
'You'd better go and seek and find
the boy that you have left behind.'

Two hours later, sure enough,
although a little out of puff,
they both arrived home safe and well,

but didn't dare to ring the bell.
In the morning he was asked
as to where the hours he'd passed.
'Betty, a lovely girl I met,
made time fly past like a jet.'

When I told Leslie that I'd invited Betty to the Christmas Eve dance at
the Students' Union (though technically, I would be her guest), he said, 'I'm
sure she came third in the recent Queen of the Arts Ball contest.'

The Christmas Eve dance was one of the most enjoyable I'd ever been to.
The Union hall didn't have the magnificent stained glass, carved woodwork
and aura of Mitchell Hall, but that didn't seem to matter. I hoped Betty
enjoyed being with me as I did with her. She told me that her father had
died unexpectedly a few months earlier of a cerebral thrombosis. He'd been
a Royal clock maker and the family had spent many holidays at Balmoral
Castle while Mr Aitken overhauled the clocks. I heard that Betty had a
younger sister, Hazel, and gathered that Mrs Aitken was a semi-invalid. After
the dance, Betty and I wandered along Union Street admiring the floodlit
buildings, the coloured lights in trees and, in the suburbs, the Christmas trees
in the front windows of homes. Church bells were playing hymns. Somehow
it all seemed so romantic. Betty invited me to her place for the evening on
Christmas Day. Having again missed the last bus, I had to catch a taxi to the
Rundles' home at Stoneywood.

On Christmas Day, I got lost on my way to the Aitkens' and arrived late,
but was warmly welcomed by the family. They looked at the photo albums
I'd brought with me and wanted to know what things were like in New
Zealand and at Cranwell. I invited Betty to the next graduation and she was
all keen to go, but I didn't press her mother for instant approval. After all,
I'd just met her and no doubt she wanted to discuss arrangements with
Betty.

We had so little time together before I had to leave for a fortnight of
skiing in Austria.

Mr Rundle and Francis took me to see the completed runway at Dyce.
Vampires and Meteors were constantly landing or taking-off and we were all
getting used to the noise. Jimmy Donald invited Leslie and me to dinner at
his place at Dyce and afterwards to church to hear children singing Christmas
carols. Then Cousin Mabel had Jimmy along to dinner and they introduced
me to the card game of whist. Leslie showed me through the new science
block at the University before going off to Elgin to stay with Moira Mackenzie.
I went shopping and bought skiing gloves, a jacket, and stuff to waterproof
my old grey trousers. I also bought an Empire 'Aristocrat' portable typewriter
on which to write my thesis.

I travelled overnight to London and then to Folkestone. On arrival at the wharves, I was met by a representative of The Wayfarers Travel Agency Limited, which had arranged the skiing trip for the Cranwell group, and was ushered through Customs onto the ferry, *The Isle of Thanet*. There were seventy people in the Cranwell group – officers, Flight Cadets, Cadets, family and girlfriends. The Officer in charge of Skiing, Sqn. Ldr. Thomas, was in overall command. Ron Chippindale and I had dinner together as the ferry headed for Calais.

The French Customs put a chalk mark on our luggage and let us board the train that would take us through northern France to Basel, Baden, Zurich and Buchs in Switzerland, and then to Feldkirch and Bludenz in Austria. On the train, we had reserved apartments seating up to eight people in each. I felt lucky to have only five people in my apartment as, when night fell, we had somewhere to sleep – one on the floor, two on the seats and two in the luggage racks. I was in one of the luggage racks, but didn't get much sleep – the rack was like some form of medieval torture. When the French ticket collector came in and I put my hand down with my ticket, he looked up in amazement – presumably thinking that only Englishmen would sleep in a luggage rack!

We went through Swiss Customs at Basel while an electric engine and a dining car were attached to the train. Breakfast was a piece of cake, rolls, butter, jam and lots of coffee. Though the weather was dull and misty, I enjoyed looking at the steep mountainsides covered with fir trees and snow, the chalet-type houses and two large lakes. I regret that all five of us in the apartment took some souvenirs from the train, such as small metal plates that said in English and German, 'Don't lean out of the window,' and another in five languages, 'In case of emergency, pull the handle.' If we could, we'd have probably souvenired the rather cute hat of a railway porter!

Soon after the Austrian Customs checked our passports at Feldkirch, we arrived at Bludenz and were divided into three bus loads depending on where we would be staying at Gaschurn. For the next hour and a half we had a hair-raising ride as the buses climbed up into the Vorarlberg Mountains. Snow lay thickly on the roads, on the roofs over bridges and on the steep mountainsides. Our driver drove at a cracking pace as we went under concrete canopies where the mountainside threatened to descend upon us, tooting his horn around hairpin bends, seemingly unaware of the sheer drops at one side of the bus. I was mindful of a recent disaster in Austria in which a bus had been hit by an avalanche and three New Zealand girls had been amongst those killed.

With some relief, we arrived at Gaschurn outside the Posthotel Rössle and disembarked. The Burgomaster and the hotel manager, Herr Oscar Kessler, greeted us warmly in German and the local band, dressed in national costume, played enthusiastically. Apparently, our group was the largest from England to stay there since World War II. Sqn. Ldr. Thomas replied briefly in German. Our buses then took us to where we would be staying.

Ron and I were in a chalet known as the 'Emil Dependence', a ten minute walk away from the Posthotel Rössle where the officers and ladies were accommodated. We dropped our luggage and returned to the Posthotel for tea in the heavily curtained, wooden panelled dining room with its animal head trophies, guns, plates, beer mugs, mirrors and paintings displayed above the panelling. Then we were fitted with boots and skis. Herr Kessler seemed to be in charge of everything, so he was soon known as 'Wingco Skiing'.

Supper followed and, with such a horde of us wanting to be fed at once, the three waitresses were hard pressed to cope. One of them, a young, plump and pleasant girl called Hanni, we nicknamed, 'Honey'. Herr Kessler eventually had to lend a hand and help interpret the menu – *Fridattensuppe* (soup with what looked like cut up pikelet in it), *Kalbsragoutpastetchen* (savoury pastry with meat etc. inside), Roastbeef (we knew that one!), *Bratkartoffel* (roast potato), *Butterbohnen* (buttered beans), *Preiselbeerkompott* (sour raspberry jam) and *Starnitzel mit Schlagrahm* (cream filled trumpet). Unfortunately, the servings weren't large enough for our appetites so, there being no returns, we took lump sugar from the dining room and retreated to the bar.

I was in a single room at the Emil chalet, but Ron had to share with one of the Ceylonese Cadets. The unpainted pine construction gave a sweet aroma to the inside of the chalet. Each window had double glazing and shutters. The duvets on the beds proved adequate though the wall radiators heated by a furnace in the basement were turned off at odd times. Some facilities, however, were rather basic – a long drop toilet near our upstairs rooms (at least it was indoors!) and for washing, a china basin and jug of cold water. When we had to shave using cold water, Ron and I began growing moustaches.

Ron and I were up early to look around Gaschurn. The village was at the upper end of the Montafon Valley, about 4,000 feet above sea level. The brochures said it was a skiing and health resort, a starting place for walks, sightseeing, hunting of chamois, access to the Silvretta area and so on. At the centre of Gaschurn was the fifty-bed Hotel Rössle with its post office, sports shop, skating rink and ski hire business. High on the mountainsides below the tree line, chalets, farm buildings and wayside shrines were covered with what seemed to be large white slabs of melting ice-cream. The crisp air and magnificent alpine scenery were certainly invigorating.

We picked up our skis and crossed the valley for our first skiing lesson on the beginners' slopes. Our instructor (an Innsbruck University student) showed us how to move sideways up and down the slopes on skis, turn and then snowplough down. In spite of many falls, we were full of confidence and got on the T-bar and went up the short tow. Coming down was much more difficult! I wasn't the only one to hurtle down, vainly trying to turn, causing consternation amongst people below. A deliberate fall was often necessary so as not to go over the edge of the ski area and into trees. The instructor had to rescue me on one occasion when I ended up face down in the snow with one ski pointing uphill and the other stuck vertically in the snow.

As the skiing lessons continued, my muscles became like jelly and I was all aches and pains. Julian Bowes fractured an ankle, the New Zealander Geoff Wallingford broke a ski, somebody else broke an ankle and numerous people lost skin off their heels and noses and developed bruises.

The evenings were occupied in drinking, playing whist and gin rummy, singing songs like 'Rule Britannia' (plus some unprintable ones), talking and dancing. A dozen or so students from Wye College, London University, joined in with us. One of them, a very pretty girl, celebrated her twenty-first birthday on New Year's Eve. I managed to get a dance with her and was even given a piece of her birthday cake. Wine flowed freely and after midnight when things got rather riotous somebody let off tear gas. That certainly broke things up! The locals celebrated the New Year by skiing down the mountainsides in the dark with lanterns, and the band, illuminated by a single electric light, played outside the hotel in falling snow.

New Year's Day was like a Sunday with church services, bells ringing from time to time and shops shut. Opposite the local church was a graveyard that looked quite picturesque with snow and icicles covering the decorated gravestones. A living tree nearby was lit by white electric lights.

The local men dressed for the occasion in thick grey jackets and trousers with green trimmings on the lapels and pockets. Carved horn buckles were used instead of buttons. Women, particularly the older ones, were dressed in black velvet or plain material, and wore shawls and boots. Few vehicles were on the roads. The locals used sleighs drawn by horses with bells hanging from their harnesses.

When skiing lessons resumed, we were divided into groups depending on our progress. An old man became my instructor, but his English was so poor that an interpreter had to be used. He was incredible in that while standing on his skis, he could bend forward so that his head touched his skis, and he could ski backwards. We were soon into stem-turns, skating steps, sidestepping and so on. Eventually, I was able to go down the small tow without falling over. I was ready for the big ski tow!

'Wingco Skiing' took some of us up the big tow and guided us down the easiest route through soft snow that'd fallen overnight. Not only did we fall off the tow, but we kept falling and losing skis all the way down. We were covered in snow and rather wet by the time we got to the bottom. I took forty-five minutes to cover what my instructor could do in less than three

minutes! Undeterred, I continued to ski down from the top of the big tow
and gradually improved in skill.

I needed a hot bath to easy my aches and pains. The tiled bath in the Emil
basement had a slope at one end on which to lean. Hot water had to be
carried by bucket from a hot cistern and then cold water added to get the
right temperature. What luxury to just lie there and soak up the heat!

Sunday was the time for skiing competitions. Slalom races were in the
morning and downhills in the afternoon. This wasn't a time for beginners to
compete so I found a good vantage point and was thrilled to see the experts
dicing with death between stakes in the snow, or hurtling downhill and
becoming airborne when they hit bumps. I noticed these skiers had laces to
hold their skis on whereas beginners had a spring attachment. There were a
number of spectacular spills and two people broke their legs and some others
couldn't continue. 'Wingco Skiing' and helpers brought the injured down
on toboggans. Gold, silver and bronze medals were awarded depending on
times for each category, these being whether one was male or female, a local,
an Austrian, a Continental or somebody from outside Europe. I was later
surprised to find that anyone could buy the medals at the local souvenir shop!

We drew on Julian's plaster cast and signed our names before he and other
people left Gaschurn. So many people had broken bones, dislocated knees or
ankles, slipped cartilages and strained knees or ankles. I wondered why some
of the Pakistani and Ceylonese members of our group stayed on, as they sat
on the Hotel's sunterrace much of the time and did little skiing. They told
me they'd come for a holiday and skiing was just a sideline!

Ron and I were allocated much better rooms, this time in the Annexe to
the Posthotel Rössle. The advantages were hot and cold water, a basin and
mirror, three lights, two windows and being closer to the hotel. I also
discovered that my door key operated the door to a modern bathroom. The
disadvantage was that my reading lamp fused all the lights on my floor! Ron
fixed the fuses, but had a problem with his own reading lamp – it wouldn't
turn off.

When a platoon of French soldiers arrived at Gaschurn, I realised we were
in the French zone of Austria. Before going skiing, the soldiers did a little
drill, using their skis as if they were rifles. On grounding their skis, an NCO
came along and straightened them up!

On the twelfth day after Christmas, church bells rang periodically all day
and shops were closed. We'd finished skiing lessons, so I used up my remaining
tickets on the short tow before returning to the big ski tow. On one descent,
I suddenly came upon a large Alsatian dog which began barking and chased
me to the bottom of the hill. My descent time had never been so fast!

Dancing in the evening became less popular because of our various aches
and pains. The band, comprising an accordion, a guitar, a trumpet and drums,

played a selection of tunes at a tempo that was faster than I was used to, and in the confined space one could do little more than rhythm dance. We helped Bob Cartwright of 60A celebrate his twentieth birthday.

Some of us decided to take a day off and go by bus to the nearby town of Schruns where we were told there was better shopping than in Gaschurn. The problem was that we were all starting to run out of money, so we did a lot of sightseeing and window-shopping before making a few purchases. I bought Betty a small bottle of French perfume and a silver bracelet that had enamelled shields on it representing Austrian mountain ranges. We looked in the local Roman Catholic church and admired the high vaulted ceiling covered with religious paintings, and the remainder of the elaborate gilt-decorated interior. The church was so cold that the holy water in the foyer was frozen solid!

Snow began to fall again and skiing became almost impossible as we couldn't see where we were going. The snow was soft and dry, coming almost to our knees and to our waists in snow drifts. Skiing without seeing one's skis was quite strange, but at one place (named Hell Fire Corner) where the new snow had been swept aside exposing hard snow, I fell and slid about thirty feet on my back down a steep slope. Ron had the bad luck to fall and break a ski.

Time trials were held for the Cranwell group. I abandoned all caution and skied down from the top of the big tow as fast as I could, successfully negotiating Hell Fire Corner and a jump called Byard's Leap (named after an area near Cranwell), but falling three or four times in The Chute (a narrow area with treacherous turns between trees). A ski came off in one fall. Luckily, it didn't go downhill so I put it on again and continued down to the finish.

I thought I'd blown my chances so was most surprised to find that out of twelve competitors, I was third in six minutes twelve seconds and had won a bronze medal! If I hadn't fallen so often and lost a ski, I might have won a silver medal! The snow was too deep for gold medal times. Of the eight medal winners, two other members of 60 Entry got bronze medals – Ron Chippindale (who was sixth) and Bob Cartwright. Only two silver medals were awarded (Fig. 29). Sqn. Ldr. Thomas watched the skiing from a sledge, having injured himself a few days earlier. He congratulated us all. That evening, 'Wingco Skiing' presented the medals in the café and said he was pleased to see so many of us win medals after so little experience.

Our last day at Gaschurn was beautifully fine, with the sun glinting on the snow crystals. I went skiing carrying my camera and took some more photos, one of which was later published in the College *Journal* accompanying an article entitled, 'Uncontrolled Descent Through Snow . . .' The day was spoiled, however, by the Digby Under Officer shattering a leg and having to remain in Austria for an operation.

Figure 29. Skiing winners outside the Posthotel Rössle, Gaschurn, Austria, December 1952: Back Row L-R: Ron Chippindale (60B), Author (60A), John Dobson (62A), Bob Cartwright (60A), B.H. Jones (62B). Front Row L-R: John Hare (61B), Paul Chamberlain (59A) and I.A. Sahibzada (58C).

We returned to England the same way we'd come. During a two hour delay at Basel, we filled in time at the railway café on the Swiss side, tried all the slot machines with foreign coins and took a short walk to the nearest shops. Unfortunately, no breakfast car was attached to the train at Basel. The north of France was covered by a white frost and fog, making our journey rather uninteresting. After passing Amiens, I saw a large war cemetery and monuments. The area near there was pitted with craters, and earthworks could be seen on the hills. There were large bare sandy patches of countryside and very little second growth vegetation. Farm buildings also showed signs of the ravages of war.

At Calais, we boarded the ferry *Canterbury* and headed straight to the dining room for a good meal. Wartime fortifications were still prominent at Calais including a painted sign on one of them, 'Ridgeway go home.' Ron travelled from Folkestone to Cranwell on his motor bike, so I took his suitcase on the train with me to London and then to Cranwell.

I arrived at Cranwell with only 3s left in my pocket, having thoroughly enjoyed a marvellous holiday in Austria. This happy feeling was to be shattered by the tragic news that awaited my return.

CHAPTER 14

We Press on Regardless

'SPIKE'S BOUGHT IT!'

'What?' I said.

'Spike's killed himself on his motor bike coming back to Cranwell,' my colleague said as we continued to walk along the main corridor of the College.

'I can't believe it,' I said. 'How did it happen?'

'There was smoke over the road from a wayside fire. Spike swerved to avoid it and ran into a lorry on the other side of the road that'd stopped because of the smoke – and that was the end of Spike. Apparently there was quite a mess.'

'How awful.' I could hardly comprehend that someone I knew so well was now dead. I'd never experienced anyone dying before, other than Mum's mother – but I'd been very young at the time.

We arrived at the main entrance hall. The hall porter approached me. 'Mr Hancock, Sir, did you know that Mr Heaney had had an accident?' I nodded, still stunned by the news.

Spike had slept in the bed next to mine in Junior Entries and then in the room next to mine in the main College building. He'd taught me how to play squash and we'd got on well together. He was one of the gen men in 60 Entry and I considered him a friend. Now he was gone. I think all of 60 Entry were staggered by the news.

More bad news was to come. Two flying instructors (one of them an Old Cranwellian) had been killed when snowy weather closed in on them during mutual flying instruction. Also, Gp. Capt. R.H. Cleverly, RAF (Retired), the Secretary of the Senior Mess had died suddenly.

Nos. 60 and 64 Entries were summoned to an urgent meeting before tea that night to be given a briefing on Spike's funeral arrangements. Apparently some other members of the College were involved in Gp. Capt. Cleverly's funeral. Spike would be buried with full military honours at Wakes Colne (about seven miles north-west of Colchester) though the service wouldn't be at the Wakes Colne church, but in the nearby church at Chappel (where apparently more parking was available). We'd have to practise in the next few days, including the weekend, the special drill required for military funerals. 60A was asked to provide pallbearers. I volunteered, along with Sam Boyce, Bob Cartwright, Mal Dines, Laurie Jones and Ted Reynolds.

As a pallbearer, I didn't have to carry a rifle so was excluded from practice carrying a rifle reversed, but we all slow marched to muffled drum beats and went through various manoeuvres endlessly to reach the required standard. Spike must have been laughing his head off seeing us bulling our kit and doing drill on a sports afternoon! After the Sunday church parade, we had a full dress rehearsal for the funeral – complete with black armbands, white belts, greatcoats and officer pattern uniforms.

Early the next morning, we travelled in three buses to Chappel, passing through Cambridge and stopping at Haverhill for an hour. I think we were all tired and scruffy on arrival at the tiny Church of England church, but we smartened ourselves up as best as we could. The bearers, pallbearers and officers entered the church. I carried the wreath of RAF Cranwell and noted that the wreath from 60 Entry was a circle of white flowers with '60' in red tulips at the centre. I gazed at the thick walls, small stained glass windows and heavy beams supporting the roof. Spike's coffin lay before the altar. I seemed to be in a dream and after the service found myself outside forming up in the funeral procession.

Two padres led the procession, followed by the commander of the parade, the escort party, the firing party (which included Jim Brown), the College band, a truck pulling a trailer on which the coffin had been loaded (the bearers and pallbearers being alongside the trailer), the officers and reserves, the Heaney family and finally friends of the family. We set off slow marching to the cemetery at Wakes Colne, breaking into a quick march for a period to reduce the time taken. The burial service was brief. Vapour trails weaved all over the hazy sky. The Heaney family made their final farewells before we pallbearers went up individually to the grave, saluted and moved away, heavy in heart.

Brigadier and Mrs Heaney invited the officers and pallbearers to join them and their family for refreshments at their home in Wakes Colne, Old House Farm, while the rest of the Cranwell party had tea in the village hall. We were made very welcome in the Heaney's lovely sitting room, with its white walls, low beamed ceiling and huge open fire. I met Spike's elder brother and younger sister. Brandy and other strong drinks were brought to us. When I asked for a soft drink, I think Brigadier Heaney was a little taken aback, but he didn't say anything and eventually managed to find some orange squash in the kitchen. The Heaneys spoke as if Spike was there and I couldn't help thinking what a brave face they were putting on when they must have still been in shock. Brigadier Heaney expressed surprise on hearing us refer to his son as Spike. 'Why do you call Michael, Spike?' he asked. I don't think we could give him a clear answer. As we left, the Heaneys very generously invited us to look them up if we were ever posted to the area.

On our way back to Cranwell that evening, we sang just about every song that we knew. No doubt we were all trying to put aside in our minds the recent sad events, but vivid memories of Spike are probably still with each of us today. The College *Journal* later commented, 'Michael Heaney was a Flight Cadet of outstanding promise. He had charm of manner and independence of mind, and he excelled easily but modestly. With marked academic ability and a natural bent for many forms of sport, and the highest standards of character, he was of the material that the Service and the College could least afford to lose.'

We later heard that an RAF investigation into Spike's death had recommended that all motor cyclists should wear crash helmets.

With such a start to the term, 60A formed a '7's Club' in Flying Wing when we found that there were seven of us in E Flight — if one of us got the big chop, then the other six could be pallbearers!

E Flight was in No. 3 Squadron, led by Sqn. Ldr. K.J. Derisley, DFC. Sam Boyce and I became pupils of Flt. Lt. A.J. Thompson, but I was told that a new flying instructor was arriving and I would probably be transferred to him. When Flt. Lt. Thompson showed Sam and me around a Harvard, we asked him what certain holes were for. He said he didn't know, being new on Harvards. Sam gave him the nickname of 'Thrombo'. Flt. Lt. Thompson took me up on my first flight, but it only lasted ten minutes because of fog.

My impression of the North American Harvard T Mk 2B (Fig. 30), powered by the Pratt and Whitney Wasp engine, was that it was a great lumbering thing that cruised at 120 knots and had a huge cockpit and nose, compared

Figure 30. Author and North American Harvard T Mk 2B at Cranwell, April 1952.

with the Chipmunk. The distinctive noise from its short, direct drive propeller was much louder than other training aircraft I'd been in (the cockpit noise being about ninety-two decibels), but the Harvard flew nicely and was reasonably forgiving when mishandled. Some Harvards tended to drop a wing when stalled and this could be dangerous on landing. We knew that the Harvard was due to be replaced by the Balliol, and the rumour was that Chipmunks and Balliols would later give way to Provosts and Vampires – it was all just a matter of when.

Sam, being quite short, had difficulty reaching things in the Harvard cockpit and had to keep unlocking and locking his safety harness. I could just reach the Ki-gas primer without unlocking my harness. The primer was often stiff to operate and petrol fumes from it could be nauseating.

Before one flight, Flt. Lt. Thompson told me to give eight strokes on the primer. When I pressed the starter, the engine belched flame from the exhaust pipe on the right hand side of the fuselage and a crosswind blew the flame through the open hood into the front cockpit. I felt the heat – my leather helmet being off at that stage. My right eyebrow, eyelashes and the hair on the right side of my head were singed, leaving a noticeable colouring. I was sure that Flt. Lt. Thompson in the rear cockpit must have seen what'd happened or smelled burnt hair, but he made no comment. When I washed my hair that night the colouring of the burnt area went, but I looked a bit lopsided! The next day I got Mr Creasy to cut my hair very short. He said he thought I'd deliberately tried singeing my hair to be fashionable! I was very cautious of the Ki-gas primer after that incident.

In addition to swotting the Harvard Pilots' Notes, we were given the Meteor 7 Pilots' Notes to read in preparation for flights in the College Meteor. Johnny Langley of 60A was given an early flight in the Meteor and ended up bursting an eardrum.

We had an extra half day flying this term compared with the previous term, so it wasn't long before I'd done all the necessary exercises in the Harvard, been given a solo check by the Flight Commander, Flt. Lt. L.A. Ferguson, signed the certificate stating that I understood the Harvard systems and procedures, and been sent solo after 8 hours and 35 minutes of dual instruction. I felt I should have gone solo after 6 hours dual, but high winds during circuits at RAF Spitalgate prevented this on one day, flying near dusk thwarted me on another day, and then a solo check was required as Flt. Lt. Thompson wasn't yet authorised to send pupils solo. Laurie Jones had gone solo after 5 hours of dual instruction.

My first Harvard solo was uneventful except for a flock of birds getting airborne when I was in the final stages of the approach to land. The windshield was covered with blood stains, but no damage to the aircraft could be found after the flight. Somehow the flight didn't seem to be as important as previous first solos.

The weather was still frosty and fog or smog was common, limiting flying at times. Ten Varsity aircraft trying to get to RAF Swinderby landed at Cranwell because the visibility was too poor for them to continue. In E Flight, we Flight Cadets were rostered to give daily meteorological briefings prior to flying.

When the timetables and calendar were issued for the Spring Term, I found that Airmanship, English, Navigation, Thermodynamics and War Studies were continued, Aerodynamics had been reintroduced, but History and Performance had been replaced by Economics, Law and Administration, and Weapons. Radio had become Navigation/Radio, and PT and the Squadron Commander's period had been reintroduced. Apparently someone thought we were getting unfit so there was one period of PT a week ending as usual with a swim in the indoor pool, plus early morning PT in lieu of drill once a week.

In Humanistics subjects, Jim Brown went up to Set 2 again and Ron Chippindale went down once more to Set 3. I remained in Set 2 for Humanistics and Set 3 for Science subjects. Later, a revised set list was issued in which Jim Brown went up from Set 2 to Set 1 in Science subjects. Without Spike Heaney, the gen men were still nine in number – Julian Bowes, Mike Goodall, John Gratton, Laurie Jones, Johnny Langley, John Maitland, Mike Marsh, Nigel MacNicol and Alun Morgan.

In his first Squadron Commander's period, Sqn. Ldr. Thomas briefed us on Form 1369, the officer confidential personal report form. I was amused that one part of the form had a range of options from 'Does not drink' to 'Drinks often and unwisely'! He emphasised again that we should not get married early in our service careers. I think all of 60A smiled when we heard (not from Sqn. Ldr. Thomas) that after graduating, 57A had each sent Sqn. Ldr. Thomas a Christmas card signed, 'Plt. Off. and Mrs . . .,' and the Pakistani member of 57A had added, 'and little Ali'!

When Sqn. Ldr. Thomas first saw me after the previous leave he said disapprovingly, 'Not you, Hancock!' I wondered what he was referring to, then realised he was looking at my moustache. I assured him it was coming off. Ron Chippindale had already shaved his off.

Sqn. Ldr. Thomas gave each of 60A our Intermediate Reports. In my interview, he read out what various officers thought of me and gave me my Intermediate Exam results on a scale of one to ten. I was intrigued to hear what some people said about me when I'd had no direct contact with them, e.g. the Chief Flying Instructor and my former D Flight Squadron Commander. I'd made steady improvement in flying though handicapped by my rugby injury. I still had 10 hours of flying to make up to complete the Basic

Stage. No problems were expected on Harvards. On the academic side, I'd made good progress considering the little science I'd done before coming to Cranwell, but I needed extra tutoring in Navigation. Very complimentary things were said about my performance on the survival camp.

Overall, my mark was above average. Sqn. Ldr. Thomas said I was smart in appearance, always ready and willing, not always to the fore, but had the qualities of a good officer and should develop in the final year at the College. I was rather surprised, as I had fully expected him to tear strips off me and tell me I had to pull up my socks in just about everything.

Ron and Jim told me later that they also got quite reasonable reports, though Ron said some officers thought he felt out of place at the College. I heard from Julian Bowes that he'd been told he was over-confident, and from Sam Boyce and John Tucker that they ought to relax a bit. Sam's comment on that was, 'I don't know what Thomas thinks I do on sports afternoons!' The only sport Sam ever seemed to do was shooting, then crawling into his pit saying, 'I'm feeling so ill!'

A new drill programme was announced – we'd be drilling in Entries, rather than by Squadrons. On the first church parade of term, the Queen's Colour was paraded. Sqn. Ldr. Thomas inspected our rooms.

I was again rostered for library duty. Then I was elected as the House Member on the Senior Mess Committee. This involved attending meetings and arranging for problems to be fixed such as an unserviceable ante-room radio. When I went to stand and nominate my proposer, I was held down in my seat! Nobody wanted to be on the Mess Committee. I was also appointed Deputy to Steve King of 59A, who was Leader of the A Squadron Knocker Cup team. We had to go to a special PT session where Leaders and Deputies from each squadron were guided through the gymnastic exercises for the competition later in the term.

Mike Kelly of 61A in a room next to mine, started learning to play the banjo. His efforts weren't always appreciated when I was trying to study, but I suppose he had to put up with me doing touch-typing exercises from a handbook I'd bought. I never did get past using three or four fingers of each hand.

Flt. Lt. H.M. Dean, BSc, CEng, MRAeS, MinstP, an Aerodynamics lecturer, became my tutor and supervisor for my thesis on Delta Winged Aircraft. Tutorials were not so rigid as previously, so I virtually turned up when I wanted to. Flt. Lt. Dean just needed to know how my thesis was going and suggested other lines to pursue when I got stuck. I began doing research while duty librarian and read papers such as, 'The effect of spherical water drops on boundary layer control of a wedged-shaped aerofoil at transonic speeds.' The higher mathematics in such papers were rather daunting, but I read anything relevant I could find in the College library. Mr Bray, the librarian, was very helpful in obtaining magazines and articles not held in the library. I discovered that Dickie Hoare of 60C was doing a thesis on flying wings, so we tended to follow each other around the library.

Betty Aitken and I were corresponding weekly, so when her mother wrote allowing Betty to come to the next graduation, I was delighted. Mrs Aitken even said she thought I'd make a good host! Betty and I had some common interests – she was a churchgoer, having been brought up in the Church of Scotland, didn't drink alcohol, had tried smoking and given it up – but the chemistry, biochemistry, microbiology and statistics she was studying at university were a mystery to me. Mum began asking me all sorts of questions about Betty and even started writing to her!

On the first guest night of term, the College band played 'The Post Horn Gallop' using hunting horns. This piece of music became a College favourite, especially when one of the band used a rifle barrel fitted with a mouth piece instead of a horn! The College shouted, stamped and clapped for encore after encore. Once dinner was over, members of 63 Entry were initiated into the College. Their performances on stage were quite impressive until the Senior Entry realised that few of 63 Entry would have to do forfeits. The Senior Entry then got tough and began handing out so many penalties that the rest of the College began chanting, '58's depraved, 58's depraved . . .'

Practices for the Knocker Cup inter-squadron gymnastics began. I was put in charge of those members of A Squadron who were concentrating on the broad box exercises. One of the PT instructors told us that Knocker Cup gymnastics were as good as any seen at the school for PT instructors. In our normal PT, 60 Entry began to learn some judo.

Then 59 and 60 Entries were lined up for routine medical examinations. I had a nose cold and was spared having to blow up a column of mercury and holding my breath for as long as possible. I could still clear my ears and was allowed to continue flying.

Being in my final year at the College, I began to enjoy privileges such as walking over the carpet in the main entrance hall (I'd actually done so unseen much earlier!), not having before dinner roll-calls, using the short cut from the west end of the College to Camp Road, being able to travel during term time up to fifty miles radius of Cranwell and having late leave till 0100 hours.

A guest night was held, attended by many officers of Air rank and other important people such as His Excellency The High Commissioner for the Union of South Africa, Dr A.L. Geyer, who presented to the College on behalf of the officers of the South African Air Force, a portrait of Field Marshal J.C. Smuts, OM. The Smuts' Report of 1917 had influenced the formation of the Royal Air Force, so it was appropriate that his portrait should hang near the main entrance hall with that of Mr Winston Churchill who, as Secretary of State for War and Air, had been responsible with Air Marshal

Sir Hugh Trenchard for the initial development of the Royal Air Force. Churchill's portrait had been presented a little earlier on behalf of Rolls-Royce Ltd. by Lord Hives (whose son, the Hon. David Hives, was in 58A). Churchill's portrait seemed to be alive in that his eyes followed us as we walked past it along the main corridor, but Smut's portrait didn't have the same quality.

After dinner, some of 60A went into the College rooms of the Cadet Wing Adjutant, Flt. Lt. Talbot-Williams, and the new A Squadron Cadet Wing Officer, Flt. Lt. H.D. Hall, decorated the rooms with toilet paper and took their beds out into the middle of the Orange. Other members of 60A were caught, however, by the A and B Squadron Commanders transporting the huge figurehead representing Pegasus from the old Sergeants' Mess in West Camp south of Camp Road to the front of the College. The Mess was being demolished, having originally been the Royal Naval Air Station Ratings' Mess, then the Flight Cadets' Mess when the College was established, and in several other capacities over the thirty-seven years of its existence. The intention was to put the figurehead up the College tower on the 'Admiral's Walk'. Instead, 60A was told to return it to the old Sergeants' Mess. On our way back to the Mess, we decided to hang it between the posts of the main gates to the College. The figurehead was heavy, requiring the use of a cart and four or more people to lift it. When the Commandant left the College that night and drove around the Orange, he stopped when he saw the figurehead, then slowly drove under it.

The next morning, the figurehead had been removed before a ceremonial parade began, the first to commemorate Founders' Day (the first course having entered the College thirty-two years previously). There was a white frost, and the South African High Commissioner, 65 Entry (including a New Zealander who'd joined the RAF, Christopher Richmond of Wellington, New Zealand), and the officers who were watching were probably as cold as those of us on parade. A Flight Cadet beside me was greying out and almost fainted from the cold.

I was given several periods of supervised solos, where my instructor sat in the caravan at the take-off point and watched me do circuits and bumps. I'd been transferred to a new flying instructor, Flt. Lt. J.P.M. Reid, who'd also become the 60 Entry Airmanship instructor. John Reid had a lot of letters after his name (but usually omitted them), and had been an engineer at Rolls-Royce and a test pilot. He'd a relaxed manner, occasionally flew the College Meteor, and was obviously a man of many talents – being Officer in charge of the College Orchestra, writing in the *Journal* an article entitled 'Test Flying Experience' and becoming the Assistant Editor of *The Poacher*, a magazine for all of RAF Cranwell which unfortunately didn't survive to a second issue.

Jim Brown told me that during his supervised solos, he'd dropped a wing on landing and dented a wing-tip. He was given jankers as punishment. After his supervised solos, Ron Chippindale said he'd just got airborne again with his instructor when an oil pipe burst. Oil had covered the windscreen obscuring forward vision so Ron had opened the hood to get a better forward view and got a face full of oil. He'd forgotten to pull his goggles down! An emergency had been declared and a safe landing was made.

The Officer Commanding Flying Wing and Chief Flying Instructor, Wg. Cdr. D. Peveler, DSO, DFC, went flying with Sabre McLelland-Brown and Joe Qureshi, but didn't send them solo. Everyone else in E Flight had gone solo on the Harvard, so the chop for them seemed inevitable. Joe told me that he'd 50 hours on RPAF Harvards, and I presumed that some had been solo. He was relegated to 61 Entry, and Sabre was transferred to No. 14 Entry at RAF Digby as an Equipment Branch Cadet.

Then Johnny Langley had more trouble with his ears and had to have a nose operation to correct a boxing injury. He was relegated to 61 Entry. 60A began to feel that there wouldn't be enough of us left by the time we were Senior Entry to have one Flight Cadet Under Officer and three Flight Cadet Sergeants, as seven of our original fifteen members had gone. Ted Reynolds made up a jingle in the 'Ten Little Nigger Boys' style to explain our predicament and put it on the College notice-board. Tiny Lewis of 60B was also chopped after not going solo, so reducing the original number in 60 Entry from 46 to 33.

Snow fell and flooding in The Wash occurred. Flt. Lt. Reid and I flew low over King's Lynn to inspect the flooded areas. Back at Cranwell, a member of 59B was having dual instruction in a Harvard when he overshot on landing, put the brakes on too hard and overturned. The Flight Cadet couldn't open the sliding hood, but both he and his instructor survived, though a little shaken.

A low passing over Cranwell had a pressure of only 961 millibars – the lowest pressure ever recorded at Cranwell. We continued to do drill in two inches of new snow that had frozen slush underneath. When flying was possible, the aircraft left tracks in the snow all over the south airfield. On becoming airborne, we had to be very careful not to get lost as the usual landmarks (such as a triangular lake near Sleaford that pointed towards Cranwell) were almost unrecognisable under ice and snow. I was given dual instruction homing on a radio beam followed by a controlled descent through cloud to circuit level (known as a QGH). After PT one day, we changed into swimming trunks and were about to dive into the tepid indoor pool when we were ordered outside and told to have a snowball fight! I wondered if the College motto should have been, 'We press on regardless!'

There were a number of unofficial snowball fights on the Orange and snowballs were thrown into rooms after Flight Cadets were in bed. Some bed tipping followed and a few wardrobes were tampered with so that they were difficult to open.

Mal Dines didn't turn up at PT one day, so when W/O Smith called his name during roll call, someone answered, 'Sir.' W/O Smith then said, 'Which one is Dines? – I know his brother!' There was some confusion for a while, but after that, Mal made sure he didn't miss any more PT.

Sqn. Ldr. Thomas continued with his Squadron Commander's periods, telling us how guest nights in an RAF officers' mess differed from those at the College. The discussion drifted into etiquette at dinner parties. He then instructed us on calling etiquette when posted to an RAF station, the composition of Mess committees and the duties of committee members. A comparison was made of the College quarterly financial reports and those to be expected in an officers' mess.

The Assistant Commandant carried out an inspection of A Squadron rooms. In E Flight, our navigation and flying equipment was checked. I found that someone had stolen my three pairs of flying gloves (double silk, leather gauntlet and white kid) and my copy of an *aide-mémoire* to the Harvard Pilots' Notes – no doubt to make up his own equipment deficiencies. My locker was one of several that had no hasp on it and couldn't be locked. When I went to get new gloves from the Clothing Store, the Store was closed for stocktaking and an airman suggested I come back the following month! I argued with the airman as I'd been told that flying gloves could be renewed at any time. After quite a hassle, I was given three different forms to complete in triplicate before being issued with the gloves.

The loss of my flying gloves didn't surprise me as I'd heard that a lot of pilfering of tools went on in the Flight Cadets' Garage where some Flight Cadets spent hours of their free time renovating old cars.

'Henrietta' was considered to be roadworthy again, so trips were made in her just to get away from the College for a while. Ron and Jim bought a little Ford 10 car for £100 and were most concerned when I tried starting it and nothing happened – someone had changed the ignition leads around! The car had a folding top, but weather considerations meant that the top was invariably up rather than down. Ron sold his motor bike.

RNZAF Headquarters in London began periodically to send me daily news bulletins about New Zealand to circulate amongst other New Zealanders at the College. I'd complained about being rather cut off from current New Zealand news as there was little on New Zealand in British newspapers. The All Blacks captained by Bob Stuart, undefeated in their tour of the United Kingdom, got barely a mention. Even my family had forgotten to give me the results of a New Zealand general election!

Flt. Lt. Thompson told me one day to go and start a Harvard and wait for my instructor. Imagine my surprise to find the Chief Flying Instructor climbing into the rear cockpit and telling me to do a circuit! My heart sank, as I thought I was about to have a chop check. The weather was terrible, low cloud forcing me to do a low level circuit in bad visibility. I missed the runway on the approach to land and had to go around again. I now felt sure I'd be chopped by the 'Demon King' (as Wg. Cdr. Peveler was known). After landing, he told me my flying hadn't been too accurate, but I'd a good excuse – not having previously flown a Harvard in a low level circuit in bad visibility. When I could, I asked Flt. Lt. Thompson why Wg. Cdr. Peveler had flown with me? He replied, 'Oh, the CFI just wanted to do a weather check and your aircraft just happened to be the nearest available!'

Afterwards, I began to reflect on Wg. Cdr. Peveler's reputation for chopping people who were short and unable to reach things in the Harvard cockpit without unlocking their safety harness. He himself wasn't tall, had broad shoulders, long arms and needed several cushions to sit on when flying a Harvard! I knew that being tall and long in the upper leg could also be a disadvantage as one was likely to lose both kneecaps in an ejection from the confined cockpits of some jet aircraft.

As the bad weather continued with cloud down to 300 feet above ground level, Flt. Lt. Reid and I did some more instrument flying. We had to put one Harvard unserviceable as the engine idling speed was too fast, causing us to taxi with the brakes on. Then, during short take-offs and landings in another Harvard at RAF Barkston Heath, Flt. Lt. Reid noticed that the undercarriage hadn't fully retracted when we got airborne. He closed the throttle temporarily and the warning horn indicated the undercarriage was unlocked. He then tried lowering and raising the undercarriage several times and yawing the aircraft, but the undercarriage lever wouldn't move into the up position. With the lever in the down position, we flew past the Cranwell control tower and were told by the air traffic controller that the undercarriage appeared to be locked down. Flt. Lt. Reid then told me to lift and push the undercarriage lever fully forward into the emergency position to manually lock the undercarriage. When the throttle was closed for landing, there was no sound from the warning horn, but I must admit I was sweating a bit!

In better weather, Flt. Lt. Reid and I went on a series of wind finding exercises. We'd try flying to a destination not allowing for wind, note where we were when we should have been at the destination and mentally work out the wind speed and direction. The wind so found would then be applied to get us to the next destination. Our flights took us all over the countryside. When passing over Nottingham, Flt. Lt. Reid showed me his home, then did some unauthorised low level aerobatics on our way back to Cranwell. I was sent solo on several occasions to practise this wind finding technique.

The A Squadron Knocker team was selected by myself and four other people. Unfortunately, A Squadron came second in the competition by only

1.3 points because some of the broad box exercises had been done in the wrong order. This was quite a set-back as we were very keen to become Sovereign's Squadron for next term when the Queen's Coronation would be held.

We were advised that in the Coronation term each squadron in the Cadet Wing would have a Senior Flight Cadet Under Officer, three Flight Cadet Under Officers and no Flight Cadet Sergeants. The Senior Under Officers would be distinguished by a loop of Flying Officer braid on the lower part of their jacket sleeves in the same manner as the Under Officer's Pilot Officer braid. (These changes were later deferred until 60 Entry became the Senior Entry.)

As the weather began to improve, I started gliding again and training for athletics. The track at the Cranwell Stadium was being upgraded, so I had to keep away from it for several weeks.

I travelled with other Flight Cadets to Lincoln to do some shopping and have a look around. As we passed RAF Waddington, traffic lights stopped us while a Lincoln bomber passed about ten feet above the road as it came in to land. We finished our visit by going to see the film *Phantom of the Opera*. On another Saturday I went with friends to Boston and was able to have a close look at the church tower landmark known as the 'Boston Stump'.

After guest nights, we continued to have interesting lecturers. Lieutenant Colonel H. Llewellyn spoke about riding Foxhunter at the Olympics and someone from the Department of Labour briefed us on the political situation in Persia. I and three others from 60A attended a guest night of the Equipment and Secretarial Wing at RAF Digby, the guest speaker being Air Cdre. C.H. Lowe, CB, CBE, ADC, Director of Organisation.

In two War Studies periods, we re-enacted Operation Whitebait, an air raid on Berlin that failed during World War II. I had the part of an intelligence officer and gave the debriefing.

In near perfect weather, Flt. Lt. Reid and I went on a high level cross-country flight to Cambridge and Rugby. We flew at 10,000 feet and could see at least fifty miles in most directions. Several jet aircraft flew past us, their pilots probably surprised at seeing a Harvard so high. To lose height on our return, Flt. Lt. Reid cut the throttle, dived until our speed was 200 knots and did some aerobatics. I'd never before been so high or fast in a Harvard.

Then we did a low level navigation trip to the small town of Kibworth Harcourt (just south-east of Leicester) and a pin point a little north of Ely. We flew about 250 feet above the ground. Things certainly looked different from that height. We passed over a hunt and could see numerous cars and men with white flags forming a circle about a mile in diameter. No doubt our presence wasn't welcomed! After returning to Cranwell, we climbed and did aerobatics over Lincoln. I was then authorised to do immediately the same low level flight solo. Again, I finished with aerobatics, landing only when about to run out of petrol. E Flight was trying to beat the Cranwell record for the number of flying hours in one week. I think we broke the record in spite of not being able to fly on one half day.

I left with others of 60A in 'Henrietta' to drive to London for our mid-term break. We just managed to reach the garage at Ancaster, on the south side of Cranwell, to get a petrol feed problem fixed. The rest of the journey was uneventful if one ignored the sloppy steering, the indifferent brakes, the spark plugs needing work done on them, the lights not working and the insurance having expired! As we passed the aerodrome at Hatfield, we had a close look at a Comet jet airliner on the tarmac.

Based at Overseas League House, I walked many miles on sightseeing trips around London. I then caught an underground train back to the West End and saw the films, *Hans Christian Andersen* and *Appointment in London*. At New Zealand House there were newspapers and magazines from home to read. A policeman was holding up traffic outside St James's Palace. I rushed to see what was happening and caught a glimpse of Queen Elizabeth, the Queen Mother. When I attended a service at St Martin-in-the-Fields, the interior was still full of scaffolding with planks up near the ceiling.

At RNZAF Headquarters, Sqn. Ldr. Gavin took me to see Air Cdre. Kay as the latter had said he wanted to speak to any RNZAF members who dropped in. We discussed amongst other things what would happen to Ron and me, assuming we graduated from the College. The Air Commodore thought there was no point in us converting onto jets in Britain as the RNZAF had commenced flying Vampires in New Zealand, and we'd probably be sent home on one of the RNZAF Hastings transports that made regular flights to the United Kingdom. I was a bit disappointed as I wanted to stay longer in Britain and then go home by sea.

Neighbours in Timaru by the name of Davies had suggested I visit their relations the Thomsons in London, so I'd written to the Thomsons and been invited to their place. They picked me up from Overseas League House, took me to their home in Finchley, gave me lunch, a drive in the countryside and then tea. I enjoyed meeting them and gave them surplus ration coupons, for which they were most grateful.

(Soon afterwards, the rationing of certain foods and goods that'd been in place since World War II, ceased in Britain. Initially, this had little effect at Cranwell other than that ration coupons weren't required when things were purchased at the Fancy Goods Store. Later, a plentiful supply of sweets and other goods became available.)

As arranged, I waited at King's Cross railway station for Mal Dines to arrive in 'Henrietta'. When he didn't arrive, I caught a train to Grantham and returned to Cranwell with other Flight Cadets on a chartered bus. Mal later told me he'd forgotten about me as the other chaps had decided not to return in 'Henrietta' – no doubt thinking that other transport was much safer! I gathered Mal had spent much of the mid-term break trying to make our ex-London taxi more roadworthy!

At the next guest night, 60A was in a silly mood. Julian Bowes had left notes about a scandal all over the place – even on the Commandant's chair. The Commandant laughed when he read the note. (Laurie Jones, being involved in the scandal, later wrote a reply in verse and left copies of that around the College.) After coffee was served, Sam Boyce, disappointed that the band hadn't played 'The Post Horn Gallop', played the tune on a gramophone he'd smuggled into the dining hall and placed under our table. 60A looked expectantly up at the band in the gallery, the airman conducting the band that evening looked down with his mouth open, and the rest of the College looked in our direction and had a good laugh. Mal Dines made good use of his water pistol and there was general dart throwing – after lighting the tail of the darts.

Once dinner was over, some of us climbed up the back of the College to the roof via drain pipes and parapets and poured a fire bucket of water down the chimney of the ante-room where the Commandant just happened to be warming himself by the fireplace. I imagine he was more surprised than pleased!

Then seven of 60A drove in 'Henrietta' to RAF Spitalgate, along with other members of 60 and 61 Entries in various modes of transport, to borrow whatever could be moved. There was dense fog, so we were undetected as we walked across the airfield to the wind-sock. Somebody foolishly tore the wind-sock instead of taking it down in one piece. We then split up, and those of us in 'Henrietta' came upon the runway caravan. What a lark it would be to put it in the middle of the Orange! While going for 'Henrietta' we came upon a car (which we thought was one of ours) parked at the side of the airfield. Ted Reynolds called out to the occupants, 'What the hell are you doing here?' An irate officer and his girlfriend appeared on the back seat and told us where to go and how to get there! We later heard that others from Cranwell had come upon the car and had had much the same reaction!

A locked gate was lifted off its hinges to allow 'Henrietta' to be driven onto the airfield. Luckily we found the caravan again in the fog. With the caravan tied to 'Henrietta', we started back towards Cranwell. Two large red lights from the caravan were arranged so that they shone as rather bright tail lights. When we came to hills on the thirteen-mile journey back to the College, we got out and pushed 'Henrietta' or just ran alongside. 'Henrietta' started to run out of petrol, so a little was borrowed from a tin in the caravan. 'Henrietta' coughed and began to sound even more like a tractor than usual.

At about 0300 hours we arrived at Cranwell and left the caravan at the west end of the College to avoid the hall porter, as he'd seen us come in the main gates. The Flight Cadets' Garage was locked, so 'Henrietta' was parked elsewhere and later returned to the Garage. We climbed in unlocked downstairs windows and went to bed.

At breakfast, a road sign saying, 'Blankney and Sleaford 9 miles' could be seen in the musician's gallery of the dining hall. On coat hooks nearby there were jackets from the officers' mess at Spitalgate and hats from the naval unit at RAF Syerston. The A Squadron notice-board sported a copy of the Syerston routine orders. Apparently, 59A were responsible for the latter. Sqn. Ldr. Thomas had found out from 59A that 60 and 61 Entries were up to something, then lent 59A his car so that they could participate, as they claimed they were without transport!

Sqn. Ldr. Thomas had all of 60A on the mat. He told us unofficially that the caravan stunt was a jolly good show, but warned us that we might, along with everyone else who'd borrowed things, have to write a letter of apology to the authorities concerned and pay for any damage incurred. Nothing more was said. At first, the College officers thought the caravan was that from Cranwell. When this had been ruled out, we imagined 'Sorbo Bill' (as the rotund Cadet Wing Adjutant, Flt. Lt. Talbot-Williams, had become known) having to ring around local stations asking if they'd lost a caravan! We later had to write to the Officer Commanding RAF Spitalgate apologising for borrowing the airfield caravan.

Geoff Wallingford and Guy McLeod, in a report on the College to the RNZAF, said about such pranks, 'Providing not too much service equipment was damaged, we found that the authorities viewed these activities with favour. They know, perhaps better than anyone, the value of high morale and a good spirit.'

Rather tired from lack of sleep, I went flying with Flt. Lt. Reid. Some instrument flying and aerobatics with excessive G made me sick and I had to put my head and hands out into the slip-stream to help me feel better. Laurie Jones was also off colour and was admitted to Station Sick Quarters with German measles.

That evening, Flt. Lt. Hall sat with 60A during dinner when a new custom was introduced to bring the Senior Mess in line with a normal RAF officers' mess. After coffee had been served, the Mess President banged his gavel twice, stood up then sat down, so indicating that we were free to leave when we liked.

We didn't leave as Flt. Lt. Hall had us enthralled about the coming Coronation. He told us that officer cadets from Cranwell, Sandhurst and Dartmouth would be lining Parliament Square adjacent to Westminster Abbey where the Queen would be crowned. We'd have to stand all day, be at the 'slope' for about six hours and at the 'present' for about twenty minutes.

Even VIPs would have to be in position forty-five minutes before the Coronation began. We'd be going to Sandhurst for training prior to the Coronation and the remainder of the RAF contingent at the Coronation would be receiving their training at Cranwell.

Flt. Lt. Hall mentioned that in future, the word 'graduation' would be replaced by 'passing-out'. I preferred the use of 'graduation' though we didn't qualify for a degree, as 'passing-out' seemed to refer to what some Flight Cadets did on parade – they fainted (or passed out).

We were also told that 60 Entry and some of 61 Entry would be flown to West Germany in the last four days of the coming leave to observe manoeuvres of the British Army of the Rhine. We had the choice of going to armoured, artillery or infantry units. I was interested in seeing an armoured unit as I fancied tearing around in Centurion tanks.

Some people found their boots were missing and were rather dismayed to find them on the wrought iron spikes of the main gates, on top of a flagpole up the College tower, or on the lightning rod at the very top of the tower. To get to the latter was difficult and dangerous as the person concerned had to climb outside the tower, up the dome and past the revolving light and weather-vane. A billiard cue was probably used to reach past the light and weather-vane. I wasn't surprised when Ted Reynolds and Gordon Grierson were each given seven days of jankers for putting the boot on the lightning rod. Their punishment read, 'for courage, but contravening Station Standing Orders.'

One day my Flying Wing Squadron Commander, Sqn. Ldr. Derisley, flew with me. I was told he just wanted to fly as it was a beautiful day and I'd been chosen at random. We did aerobatics and low flying. I found him to be a first rate pilot and instructor. Luckily, I did everything right for him. On being sent solo, I continued with aerobatics until recalled because of increasing industrial haze. In fact the haze got so bad that in the circuit, radio calls had to be made at each position as in night flying.

Then Flt. Lt. E. Markwell, one of the officers I'd seen at the Court of Inquiry into the Chipmunk prang that Fg. Off. Vincent and I'd been in, flew with me on a high level cross-country flight. This time I was above stratus cloud and only saw the ground once. I navigated by obtaining radio bearings.

After doing circuits at Spitalgate one day, I returned to Cranwell via Barkston Heath to see a Chipmunk that had crashed there the previous night. A Flight Cadet on his first night solo had apparently stalled the Chipmunk on the approach to land and hit a telegraph pole. He'd survived, walked to the caravan at the end of the runway and surprised the air traffic controller by saying that he'd just pranged. The controller had heard the Flight Cadet call 'finals' on the approach to land, but hadn't noticed if the Chipmunk had landed!

A week later, I was doing circuits at Barkston Heath and saw the Harvard that Jock Brand of 59B had crashed during night flying. His engine had failed just after take-off (possibly because the fuel cock wasn't quite on) and he'd landed wheels down in a ploughed field. The fuselage, engine and wings had separated in the impact and looked quite a mess. Jock had been found unconscious. His face was badly cut and he'd a strained shoulder. Fortunately, he recovered and eventually passed out with his Entry.

E Flight continued periodically to use a tape recorder and practise radio calls. Mal Dines told me I sounded like an announcer on the BBC's Third Programme! Perhaps I was beginning to develop an English accent.

The Senior Mess held a formal dance in the main lecture hall to which girls from the Kesteven and Leicester Teachers' Training Colleges were invited. I went along and enjoyed myself. There was no alcohol and quite a reasonable supper.

An announcement was made that the new Secretary to the Senior Mess was an Old Cranwellian, Gp. Capt. F.E. Nuttall, CBE, MID, RAF (Retired). With a name like that and being considered by some Flight Cadets 'as only the Mess Sec', he was soon known as 'Group Captain F . . . all'. We heard that he'd represented Britain in the high jump at the Berlin Olympics in 1936, and would assist in coaching the College athletics team.

I'd practised high jumping for much of one sports afternoon at the partially renovated stadium, showered and changed into mufti, when I was told that Gp. Capt. Nuttall was at the stadium waiting for me! I immediately put sports clothes on again and returned to the stadium. Gp. Capt. Nuttall was tall and slim, wore a tweed sports suit and cap, and seemed to be a likable sort of chap. He told me that he used to clear six feet in the high jump using the Scissors technique, but knew little about the Western Roll and other techniques. He gave Laurie Jones and me tips on the three jumps – high, long and hop, step and jump.

The Officer in charge of Athletics, Fg. Off. Rickard, made out a training schedule for Armand Coleman of 59C and me as we were the only Flight Cadets who could clear five feet six inches in the high jump. Then Mr D.C.V. Watts, one of the Amateur Athletics Association coaches visiting Cranwell, gave me some coaching and showed slow motion films of Olympic athletes in various events. My layout over the high jump bar gradually improved.

A visit by cadets from L'École de l'Air, Salon, involved some of 60 Entry in that they were hosts and had to share their rooms with the French visitors. I wasn't so involved, but we all had a lot of fun trying to communicate and learning about the differences between our two Colleges.

A guest night held in honour of the French and some visiting public school headmasters went very well with the band playing French tunes, and speeches in broken French and English (plus a lot of sign language!). Those Flight Cadets who were hosting French cadets wore ceremonial eighteen inch daggers borrowed from their French counterparts.

Afterwards, we changed into casual clothes and 'paraded' on the parade ground. Cars and motor bikes were raced around the Orange. Even the Commandant's car was unofficially driven around the north airfield. We then tried to lift a car into the main entrance of the College, but had to give up when the owner arrived. The back wheels were lifted off the ground before the owner was allowed to drive away. The newly appointed Director of Studies, Mr Anthony Constant, MA, PhD, unused to such high spirited activities at the College, was not so lucky. His Morris Minor was lifted up the steps into the entrance hall and the large carpet was folded over it. A noisy conga line formed around the car. Officers in the gallery above seemed to enjoy the fun as much as we did. No doubt Mr Constant was relieved when his car was lifted out onto the parade ground again, none the worse for wear.

Things deteriorated after that. The leather covered furniture in an ante-room was lined up and a version of the famous Aintree horse-race was held, with Britain versus France. Then there were handstand races and feats of strength. A raid was made on B Squadron to pull out of bed those Flight Cadets who'd retired early. Jim Brown was caught, but Ron Chippindale had wisely locked his door. As I retired to bed at about midnight, I saw some Flight Cadets pushing a man-sized teddy bear into the College room of one of the officers. I wondered where the bear had come from.

The French contingent was greatly impressed with the drill in the Ferris inter-squadron drill competition. Flight Cadets who'd seen their drill at Salon a year earlier said it was shambolic — the French cadets drilled only once a week, cigarettes were stamped out as the inspecting officer arrived and 'stand easy' meant they could do just about anything except walk away!

For the first time, the Royal Marines were the judges for the Ferris. They gave the seventy or so Flight Cadets in A Squadron a very thorough thirty minute inspection before we went on parade. My bayonet and the buckles at the rear of my belt were closely examined. I also had to lift one foot so that the sole of my boot could be seen. Almost every second person had to take out the magazine spring of his rifle. No awkward questions were asked as on previous Ferris parades.

Our drill manoeuvres went very well except for a bayonet being dropped and a hat falling off, so we were overjoyed when the announcement was made that A Squadron had won. This meant that A Squadron, having won the Ferris and come second in the Knocker competition (15 and 10 points respectively), had only to win the athletics and thus the Chimay Cup for inter-squadron games (25 points) to win the Prince of Wales Trophy and become Sovereign's Squadron for Coronation term. My hands were sore and swollen for some time after the Ferris because of the effort I'd made in hitting my rifle during the drill.

We played the French in rugby and fencing, and beat them soundly. Damp, cold weather caused the cancellation of an air display for the visitors, but escorted tours were undertaken to Lincoln Cathedral and other places. After a memorable visit, the French departed in two Dakotas in instrument flying weather during a church parade.

The Assistant Commandant then gave all Flight Cadets a 'rocket' for behaviour after the last guest night – particularly the racing of cars and motor bikes around the Orange as that was strictly against College Standing Orders. One Flight Cadet was given fourteen days of jankers for driving a motor bike without a light.

Sqn. Ldr. Thomas and Flt. Lt. Hall had said that if A Squadron won the Ferris, they'd come on parade with us one day, so we were not surprised when they took their places in our ranks. The A Squadron Under Officer, Paul Gray, appointed the immaculate Sqn. Ldr. Thomas as the marker and had us in fits of suppressed laughter by telling him to smarten up! Sqn. Ldr. Thomas took it all in good part and answered, 'Sir!'

The A Squadron Drill Instructor, F/S Greenhalgh, left the College soon afterwards and was eventually replaced by F/S Legg.

Then I heard that a Flight Cadet who'd previously flown solo at night had refused to do solo night flying again. He was given two hours to leave the College. There was also news that a former member of 57 Entry, Plt. Off. G.T.R. Pitts-Tucker, had been killed when the engine of his Vampire cut during a circuit.

Flt. Lt. Reid and I signed three certificates relating to Harvard aircraft. They said that I was proficient to be captain for mutual exercises in accordance with the College syllabus, and that I was cleared for instrument flying and flight testing in accordance with College Standing Orders.

The Senior Entry was behind in its flying so the Harvards that 60 Entry E Flight were due to use were taken for bombing exercises. Ted, Mal and I were given the task of each taxiing a Harvard to the perimeter of the south airfield where the bombs were loaded, and then handing the aircraft over to the Senior Entry. Mal and Sam managed to get some dual formation flying in Chipmunks, but the rest of us filled in time trying to complete our link trainer hours for the term.

This situation occurred several times before the end of term. Mal and I were lucky to occupy ourselves by flying with D Flight instructors in a three Chipmunk formation. We were in the rear cockpits for the first time and found flying from that position rather strange. Mal made rude signs while I did formation flying on him, no doubt trying to put me off. The instructors did some formation aerobatics including inverted gliding. Mal and I then joined the others in E Flight polishing the floor and doing various odd jobs.

The weather started to get quite warm and having dual instruction in simulated instrument flying with the amber screens and blue goggles became an energy draining experience. Later, when solo, the Harvard I was spinning lost over 2,000 feet of height before reluctantly coming out of the spin. This gave me quite a fright.

Flt. Lt. Reid and I went flying one brilliant day when there were enormous cumulo-nimbus clouds overhead in which heavy clear rain ice was reported. We avoided the clouds, flying around them through deep 'canyons' of clear air. The spectacle was so great that Flt. Lt. Reid took control from me and began doing an aerobatic sequence that seemed to illustrate his love of flying. I think we were both captured by exhilaration – one of those soul-warming occasions which only pilots can appreciate that makes flying so worthwhile. We eventually came down to earth and put the Harvard unserviceable because of distorted radio transmissions, but I felt as John Gillespie Magee Jr. must have felt when he wrote:

> Oh, I have slipped the surly bonds of earth
> And danced the skies on laughter-silvered wings;
> Sunward I've climbed, and joined the tumbling mirth
> Of sun-split clouds . . . and done a hundred things
> You have not dreamed of . . . wheeled and soared and swung
> Put out my hand, and touched the face of God.

I was sorry when I heard that Queen Mary had died. The Queen's Colour was draped in black, flags were flown at half mast and everybody had to wear black ties with mufti during the period of mourning. Rumours abounded that there wouldn't be any more guest nights and dances at the College that term, and even the graduation ball might be cancelled. Fortunately, the latter didn't occur.

Flight Cadets were invited to a formal dance at Kesteven Teachers' Training College. Ron was keen to see his girlfriend and drove me there in his car. I was most impressed by the College, housed in a converted mansion and set in spacious grounds. The girls at the College all seemed to be wearing strapless gowns. I was intrigued to see a gown on one girl that'd been worn by another Kesteven girl at a Cranwell dance! I wondered who was the owner. June Spackman wanted to dance so Ron got the message that he'd better learn to dance.

Early in the term, Ron had decided to transfer from the Church of England to the Other Denominations Church, saying that he'd become undenominational. Certainly one advantage of attending the OD Church was that the ODs occasionally missed out on having to march past the Commandant on the way back to the College. The OD Church needed more members as many people had been transferred when No. 6 Radio School had been disbanded.

I attended a meeting of the Aeromodelling Club and started rebuilding my Jetex powered Panther which had been damaged in posting it from Aberdeen to Cranwell. I also commenced building from a kit an Avro 707B delta winged Jetex model.

When ACM Sir Hugh W.L. Sanders, KCB, KBE, MC, DFC, MM, Air Deputy to the Supreme Allied Commander Europe lectured the College on the Supreme Headquarters Allied Powers Europe (SHAPE), he noticed that someone had put the man-sized teddy bear behind the lectern in the main lecture hall. He joked that he'd come to tell us all sorts of secrets, but couldn't with a Russian bear present!

Good Friday was notable in several ways. A ceremonial parade was held and, for the first time, there was no inspection beforehand. This was to allow those of us who wanted to attend church, to do so before lectures and flying commenced. Once again, the Senior Entry took the E Flight Harvards so 60A had to find other things to do such as swotting for the end of term tests.

60 Entry made a short visit to RAF Langtoft (between Bourne and Peterborough), a ground controlled interception station and part of the Digby Sector in eastern England. A briefing was given on the GCI organisation before we were taken to a site two miles away where there were radar scanners and underground control rooms. Airwomen were shifting markers on a huge map table. Around them were state boards and glass fronted cabins three storeys high from which officers surveyed what was going on. In other darkened rooms nearby, plan position indicators and small plotting charts were being used for liaison purposes within the Digby Sector. Controllers were speaking with the pilots of aircraft practising interceptions. We were shown the power plant, ventilation system and teleprinter room. There was much to absorb in a short time. After a light tea we returned to Cranwell, stopping at Bourne to buy fish and chips.

For weeks the College members had been trying to beat the athletics standards in preparation for the inter-squadron athletics competition. I'd managed to pass the standards in the 100 yards, the 110 yards hurdles and the high jump, but missed being judged in the hop, step and jump because of library duty. While I was training with Laurie Jones, he stumbled on a hurdle and dislocated a knee. This was most unfortunate as he was one of the better athletes in A Squadron. As a result, I took his place in the hop, step and jump and the 4 x 110 yard relay, and also represented the Squadron in the high jump.

A tug of war was included in the competition. The heaviest Flight Cadets in A Squadron trained for this by pulling on a rope that went over a pulley suspended above the vertical shaft of an air raid shelter and tied to a half ton lump of concrete.

On the day of the competition I won the high jump, but more importantly A Squadron won the inter-squadron athletics and thus the Chimay Cup, and as winners of the Prince of Wales Trophy would be Sovereign's Squadron for Coronation term. Sqn. Ldr. Thomas could hardly contain his excitement and embraced all of the A Squadron winners. The College record was broken in the javelin throw.

On taxiing into the dispersal area one day, I saw a fire engine beside a Harvard. Mal Dines had tried starting the Harvard, but flames had engulfed the engine. He'd put out the flames by operating the Graviner system. The Fire Section, however, hadn't taken any chances and emptied several portable fire extinguishers into the engine nacelle. John Tucker also had some bad luck when he dropped a wing on landing and buckled a wing-tip. Then Colin Loveday of 59A ran a Harvard into a marker board. John and Colin were each given fourteen days of jankers.

The news that S/F/C I.A. Sahibzada of 58C had been killed in a Harvard accident shocked the College. He and S/F/C M.J. Armitage had been on a mutual cross-country flight to RAF Valley when they'd had a problem and hit a tree while attempting to land. Mick Armitage received a crushed disc, broken or strained ankles and cuts. Those of 60 Entry who'd been pallbearers at Spike's funeral were excused from Sahibzada's funeral at Cranwell Cemetery as we hadn't practised the special funeral drill, but everyone else in 60 and 64 Entries did a refresher course in the drill before attending the funeral.

Further shocks came when the final 'chop list' for the term became known. In 60 Entry alone, Bob Cartwright of 60A, Dick Hinton of 60B and Mike Elliott of 60C were suspended for flying or academic reasons. Furthermore, Armand Coleman and Dave Vickers of 59C had been relegated to 60 Entry. I also heard that a Flight Cadet Sergeant in the Senior Entry had been demoted to Senior Flight Cadet because he'd taken a weekend off without permission.

Some good news came when the promotions for the next term were promulgated. These included New Zealanders Jack Henderson of 59B becoming the Flight Cadet Under Officer of B Squadron and Colin Loveday of 59A becoming a Flight Cadet Sergeant. In addition, Colin would be given the honour of carrying the Queen's Colour.

As A Squadron would be Sovereign's Squadron next term, Sqn. Ldr. Thomas told all of 60 and 61 Entries to line up with officer pattern hats on so that he could decide who'd be the Colour Escorts and the Commandant's Orderlies. Similar height and build seemed to be the criteria. John Tucker of 60A and Brian Letchford of 61A were selected as the Colour Escorts because they were about the same height and build as Colin Loveday. Ted Reynolds and I were told we'd be the Commandant's Orderlies. Sqn. Ldr.

Figure 31. Nos. 58GD(P) and 9 E&S Entries Passing-out Parade, April 1953: A Squadron leading the parade, closing open order after passing the saluting base during the slow march past. Author (with rifle) fifth from left in front row.

Thomas said he'd thought of making us alternatives as Colour Escorts, but we were taller than Colin Loveday and, considering what we'd done for the Squadron, we should be the Commandant's Orderlies. He added that we were doing a jolly fine job and wished there were more like us in the Squadron! Little did he know what really went on around the place!

Major G.J.S. Cotton, the British Army Instructor at the College, briefed 60 Entry on the coming visit to the British Army of the Rhine. Too many of my colleagues wanted to visit an armoured unit so, to my disappointment, I was allocated to an artillery unit stationed at Hanover. Ron Chippindale was told he wouldn't be going on the visit as the CFI required him to return to Cranwell two days early for extra flying.

Ron and I were amongst a group of Flight Cadets who filled out forms and had photographs taken in applying for private pilot's licences. An examination for the licence was cancelled for some unknown reason, but several B Squadron Flight Cadets managed to arrange an examination for themselves at another time. As a result, Ron was awarded his private pilot's licence. He really didn't have the opportunity to make use of the licence, but at least he'd qualified for it.

On the last navigation flight of term, Flt. Lt. Reid and I flew to RAF South Cerney and landed there, as Flt. Lt. Reid had someone to see. Much of the navigation was by using radio bearings, but on the return leg, Flt. Lt. Reid increased our speed to make up time and caused me some navigational problems.

On the academic side, the results of the final tests were all rather depressing. To cheer ourselves up, Mal, Ted and I went in 'Henrietta' to see a film in Lincoln. On our way back to Cranwell, we called at RAF Hospital Nocton Hall and visited Laurie Jones who was recovering from a knee operation. In the bed next to him was a rather depressed Mick Armitage. We tried to brighten the chaps up a little. On resuming our journey in 'Henrietta', we began singing. Ted found that I wasn't too sure of the words of some traditional English songs, such as 'Cockles and Mussels,' 'There is a Tavern in the Town,' and 'On Ilkley Moor b'aht 'at,' so he sang the last for me.

After seeing an excellent film, *The Card*, at the Cranwell cinema, I found that my door key was missing. Sqn. Ldr. Thomas had said about pranks, 'If you can't think of anything original – don't do it.' This latest prank seemed to me to be a bit childish. Some other Flight Cadets had also found their keys missing. Eventually Mal told me to look for the key on the ledge above my door. I was then able to get into my room. One of C Squadron made a comment that to me seemed very relevant, '60A are always cutting each other's throats.'

The end of term postings included the Chief Flying Instructor, Wg. Cdr. Peveler (replaced by an Old Cranwellian, Wg. Cdr. I.N. MacDougall, DFC), and the E Flight Commander, Flt. Lt. Ferguson (replaced by Flt. Lt. A.G. Woods).

As usual, we had wet and dry weather ceremonial parades in preparation for the coming passing-out parade. Squadron and other photographs were taken before the final guest night. The Senior Entry review called 'Take Us

Figure 32. DANCING AT NOS. 58 GD(P) AND 9 E&S ENTRIES PASSING-OUT BALL
APRIL 1953
Miss E.M. (Betty) Aitken and Flight Cadet R.M. (Hank) Hancock.

From Here' (after the Jimmy Edwards/Dick Bentley radio comedy show, *Take It From Here*) was, as expected, very pointed in its characterisation of College staff and also rather rude.

The Commandant presented Wings, individual prizes and squadron trophies in the main lecture hall to members of Nos. 58 GD(P) and 9 E & S Entries in the presence of their relatives, members of the College and officers.

After supper, Ron drove me in his car to Grantham railway station to meet Betty. She greeted me shyly and seemed to be just the same wonderful person I'd met some four months earlier. I introduced her to Ron and we headed for Cranwell. The individual rooms in the refurbished Block 77 had been made available for girlfriends, so I left her there for the night.

Air Chief Marshal Sir Hugh P. Lloyd, KCB, KBE, MC, DFC, LLD, former Air Officer Commanding-in-Chief, Bomber Command, reviewed the passing-out parade in cold blustery conditions with showers imminent. The parade went well (Fig. 31). I was told later that amongst the spectators, there were two RNZAF officers, but they made no attempt to contact me when the parade was over.

As soon as possible I went looking for Betty, but couldn't find her in the crowd on the Orange. Ron found her for me and we went off to a buffet lunch and a tour of West Camp. We were in the College library when I heard Jack Henderson on the parade ground outside shout, 'On Parade'. I then remembered I should've been on the fire picket parade for the sounding of 'Retreat' and lowering of the ensign! I'd been one of the Flight Cadets specially chosen because of height and bearing to be in the fire picket and put on a good show for the visitors. Thinking I was bound to be given some jankers, I rushed to apologise to Jack as he came off parade, but he took one look at Betty, gave me a knowing wink and said nothing.

For the ball that evening, Betty wore a full length white sleeveless dress with a halter top. A bolero in the same material covered her bare shoulders. Over one of her long white gloves she wore the Austrian bracelet I'd given her. We found that the dining hall had been decorated with greenery as 'Cranwell Park' and signs such as 'Keep off the Grass'. In the centre was the 'bandstand' – a fenced off area containing the College band, around which people danced in an anti-clockwise direction. The only illumination was above the coloured streamers of the bandstand 'roof' and the paintings on the walls. One painting of an evil-looking person had been improved by an orange moustache suspended by a thread from the hooded light above!

Betty and I danced for much of the evening. Photographers seemed to be everywhere and our photograph was taken while dancing (Fig. 32). We wandered into the main lecture hall which was fitted out as a lounge with a water garden and fountain at one end, and then through the tastefully decorated main entrance hall and corridors. Bars had been set up in the ante-rooms and a good supper was in the billiard room. By 0200 hours we were rather tired, so I escorted Betty back to Block 77.

I'd survived another term and felt sure I was in love.

CHAPTER 15

Aberdeen

THE MORNING AFTER THE CRANWELL BALL, Jim Brown and I picked up Betty from Daedalus House where she'd had breakfast, and headed for Edinburgh. Jim drove his Ford 10 car and I navigated from the back seat. For some of the way Betty slept on my shoulder, so disproving Ron Chippindale's claim that 'nobody could sleep in that small car'. In cold rainy conditions, we stopped for a late lunch at Newcastle. When we reached Edinburgh, Jim dropped Betty and me and continued on his fourteen days of leave.

There was no suitable train to Aberdeen, so Betty and I found overnight accommodation at the St Andrew Hotel almost opposite Waverley railway station. That evening and the next morning we did some sightseeing around Edinburgh before catching a train to Aberdeen. I escorted Betty to her home and thanked her mother again for allowing Betty to go to the ball. Mrs Aitken was in bed and apparently unwell.

Cousin Mabel greeted me with motherly concern, 'My, you're looking thin!' She was on a diet – again. The only trouble was that Cousin Mabel seemed to forget about the diet on Sundays, birthdays, holidays . . . I settled in at the Rundles' place and caught up with their news. Cousin Lella had just returned from a wedding in Southampton and was once more feeling fine. Leslie's friend George Webster had qualified as a doctor of medicine and high winds had felled a lot of trees in the plantation near the paper mill.

Like Mum, Cousin Mabel wanted to know all about Betty so invited her for dinner. We were impressed that Betty had won a free place, one of seven available, to Aberdeen High School for Girls, been a prefect and won four bursaries to Aberdeen University. The Rundles thought her an awfully nice girl (and so did I)!

Betty was swotting for beginning of term exams so Leslie occupied my time by taking me to see the Vampires and Chipmunks operating from the aerodrome at Dyce, visiting the Donald family, going shopping and seeing the film, *The Cruel Sea*. Cousin Mabel took me to see a play, *The Lady from Edinburgh*, and I helped Mr Rundle in the garden. We saw a Meteor 7 fly overhead towing a sleeve for air-to-air gunnery practice. Leslie then began swotting for exams and preparing his Territorial Army mess accounts for auditing.

I offered to pay board while I was at the Rundles' place, but Cousin Mabel wouldn't hear of it. She said I was very welcome at any time.

I'd just got my traveller's cheques for the visit to the British Army of the Rhine when a telegram arrived saying that my visit to Germany had been cancelled. (When I later returned to Cranwell, I found that two officers and thirty-four members of 60 and 61 Entries had been flown to Germany in Varsity aircraft from RAF Swinderby. Apparently there'd been a limit placed on the number of aircraft flying near the Russian Zone and, as a result, I'd been one of the Flight Cadets to have missed out on the trip. Jim Brown had been one of the lucky ones and visited an infantry unit.)

Sqn. Ldr. Thomas had told 60A that we needed to get visiting cards made for use at the College and later as Pilot Officers. They had to have a particular format, e.g. 'Mr' was to be used instead of our rank as the convention was that only Flying Officers and above could include their rank. Accordingly, I had an Aberdeen printer engrave a copper plate with, 'Mr R.M. Hancock, RNZAF' and print fifty cards. I later put one of the cards in the card holder on my door at Cranwell.

When Betty had finished her exams, I called a little earlier than expected at her home. She expressed surprise on seeing me as she hadn't changed her dress, done her hair or put on her make-up. Without anything on her feet, she was shorter than usual and also she was wearing spectacles. I discovered she needed spectacles for seeing things in the distance. This incident made me resolve always to be exactly on time when making a social call!

Betty and I went ice skating again. The blades on my hired boots were quite blunt so I kept falling, much to my annoyance. I found more enjoyment walking with Betty by the Don River and dancing in Mitchell Hall at Aberdeen University. The dance was the start of the University's Charities Week in which money was raised for various worthy causes. We began to realise that we'd been to Aberdeen University dances before the one at which we'd met, but yet we hadn't seen each other. Perhaps our stars or something weren't quite right for such a momentous happening! A Charities Ball Queen was chosen, but I felt that the winner didn't look half as nice as Betty.

We later returned to Mitchell Hall for the Rector's Inter-university Coronation and Charities Debate which was recorded by the BBC. Mr Gilbert Harding, MA, formerly of Queen's College, Cambridge, proposed 'That the English gentleman is not outdated.' This was opposed by Sir Compton Mackenzie, OBE, BA, LLD, FRSL, formerly of Magdalen College, Oxford. Delegates from British universities also spoke. The debate was most amusing and, being held in such a magnificent place with many of the university people wearing colourful robes, was a most memorable occasion. If there was a winner of the debate, the result was lost in the applause. I was there once again under false pretences, having borrowed Leslie Rundle's Union card to get in!

Betty had no difficulty in persuading me to accompany her on some of the madcap activities of Charities Week. We needed to get dressed up to collect money from schools, but when I tried to hire a costume, the hire shop owner refused, saying that he knew what happened to costumes during Charities Week! There was no time to do anything other than go as myself (I probably looked funny enough anyway), so I climbed on a truck with weirdly dressed students – some boys dressed as girls and girls dressed as boys – and was driven to five schools near the sea that somehow thrived in air smelling of fish. The school children shrieked with delight at our antics on this unexpected visit as we rattled collection tins and wheedled coins from them and their teachers. I thought it all great fun, especially when I found I'd collected more than Betty.

The next morning, I borrowed Leslie's old laboratory coat (it barely held together because of holes from acid burns) and wore it askew over my oldest clothes. Being so dressed in Charities Week, I was given free rides on the buses. With two other students, I sold fish outside the YMCA building in Union Street, and soon got to recognise 'yellows', filleted cod, 'finnans' and kippers. Most of the housewives who ordered fish or asked questions about it did so in the broadest Scots. This had me really flummoxed. One said to me, 'You're not from around these parts, are you?' Some housewives haggled, some selected their own pieces of fish, some bought several fish because they were at bargain prices, while others wanted only 6 oz of a particular fish when the price was $1s$ $3d$ per lb – and we had no halfpennies for change!

Nevertheless, the fish stall did a roaring trade. One of the students had brought a little brazier, so we cooked and ate kippers on the main street, and gave some away to the crowds of children and adults standing around us. Leslie's friend Jimmy Donald brought in more supplies of fish from time to time and told me that our stall was doing much better than a similar one in Union Street beside the statue of King Edward VII.

I had little time to see other students playing instruments, scrubbing the street, shaking money tins – in fact doing anything to collect money for charity. Betty, dressed as a peasant woman, had been shaking her tin further along Union Street. She called at the fish stall on her way home so I sold her a lot of fish at a very special low price.

After trying to get rid of the smell of fish from my person, I accompanied Betty that afternoon to His Majesty's Theatre to see the student review, *Pick of the Pack*. There was a great deal of dancing and singing and unconnected skits that were full of humour, e.g. a 'professor' said that the University was founded for the pursuit of all that is lovely and beautiful – thereupon a screaming girl dressed in a red undergraduate gown ran across the stage hotly pursued by a similarly dressed boy. I found some of the spoken words hard to follow because of the accents.

Betty invited me to dinner at her place. Mrs Aitken regaled me with stories about Betty and her sister Hazel when they were young – much to their embarrassment.

I had to return to the Rundles' place to change my clothes before Betty and I joined in the student's torchlight procession as it left the quadrangle of Marischal College. There were a number of floats in the procession. We paraded along Union and other streets, shaking our money tins and trying to persuade the crowds of onlookers to make a donation. The children loved all the fun, but the adults seemed to be much more reserved in parting with their small change. Betty had more success than me in collecting. Somewhat hoarse from shouting, I didn't get back to the Rundles' until the early hours of the morning – feeling that my participation in Charities Week had been another unique experience. I thought I still smelled of fish!

Betty came to see me off at Aberdeen railway station. We'd had a terrific time together during my short leave and I was loath to depart, knowing that I'd not see her for another three months. We kissed – a lingering kiss.

CHAPTER 16

Coronation Term

THE COLLEGE WAS ASSEMBLED FOR A BRIEFING on the Coronation of Queen Elizabeth II. Almost all the Flight Cadets would go to the RMA Sandhurst on 29 May for training with the Army cadets before proceeding to London on 2 June for the Coronation. Cranwell cadets would line the north-west corner of Parliament Square from Parliament Street to Westminster Abbey, while Sandhurst cadets would line the Abbey side of Parliament Square and Dartmouth cadets the remaining side of the Square to Parliament Street. Thus, the Cranwell contingent would see the Coronation procession going from Parliament Street to the Abbey, but little of the procession from the Abbey around the remainder of Parliament Square to Parliament Street. We would be on parade in Parliament Square from 0830 to 1600 hours. On being released from duty at Sandhurst we could go on leave until midday, 4 June, this leave being in lieu of a mid-term break.

With the Coronation just a month away, we'd very little time to arrange accommodation in London if we wanted to join in the festivities and see the sights after the Coronation. I immediately wrote to the Overseas League, but no accommodation was available. I knew that Cousin Jennifer's flat was very small and unlikely to have a bed for me, even if she and Robert were in London at the time. Fortunately, Miss Macdonald of Sleat, of the Dominions Fellowship Trust, was able to find me a bed in a guest house at 120 Lexham Gardens.

There was a lot to do before the Coronation. Ted Reynolds and I were taken aside with the Colour Party and given special drill instruction to get us used to our new roles. Then Ted and I went to the rear of the College where we couldn't readily be seen, to be coached by a former Orderly at being Commandant's Orderlies. There were times when we'd be quick and slow marching shoulder to shoulder and other times when we'd be standing at opposite sides of the saluting base of the reviewing officer. The problem was how to get our timing right and work as one without any commands being given. The answer was to sniff when we were shoulder to shoulder and perfect our timing for when we were apart. For example, Ted would sniff twice before we did the first part of a ninety degree turn at the halt, then again sniff twice before we completed the second part of the turn. This initially caused some hilarity, but we had to assume poker faces as it would never do to be seen smiling when in front of a ceremonial parade.

As Commandant's Orderlies Ted and I didn't carry rifles, but wore aiguillettes made of rope on our right shoulders. The white blanco on the rope tended to rub off on our uniforms and the gold plated metal tips of the aiguillettes swung as we marched causing small dents on the brass buttons of our uniforms and brass buckles of our white belts.

Our first official parade as Orderlies was on the march past after the first church service of term. I had to leave the OD Church during the last hymn and miss communion to get to the Hangar Church in time to meet Ted and form up in the parade. Ted and I weren't satisfied with our performance, but it was, after all, our first time. We decided to get steel toe plates put on our officer pattern shoes so that we could make more noise in our drill. The Colour Party paraded the Queen's Colour.

On the first ceremonial parade of term, Ted and I saluted the Queen's Colour during the inspection when we slow marched along the ranks in front of it, but forgot when we slow marched to the rear of it. We felt the eyes of the Assistant Commandant from two yards behind us burning our necks. When the Assistant Commandant stopped to inspect or speak to a Flight Cadet, we had to shorten our slow marching steps so as to keep just in front of him. Sometimes a Flight Cadet in the ranks would help us as we went past by whispering without moving his lips, 'Slow down' or 'Speed up.' During prayers we stood at ease when the College was ordered to stand easy. While the College carried out the quick and slow march pasts and the advance in review order, we had to stand to attention. Being so visible on parade, we were very conscious of every mistake we made. Initially this was quite a strain, but we soon got used to it.

Ron Chippindale, Jim Brown and I went as soon as we could to meet the latest RNZAF members in Junior Entries – Geoff Hubbard and Graham Derby. Geoff, being tall and slim with a small head, looked like Gordon Grierson, but apparently was rather 'brainy'. We wished Geoff and Graham all the best in No. 66 Entry – a very small Entry of only twenty members. Later, at the first term boxing, I saw Geoff get beaten and Graham win his bout.

The usual College Calendar was replaced by a Sports Fixtures booklet that included the name of the officer in charge and secretary of each sport at the College. I thought this a pity as the College Calendar used to contain much more than just sports fixtures.

When the timetables and set lists were issued for the Summer Term, other changes were evident. Airmanship, Aerodynamics, English, Flying, Law and Administration, Navigation, Private Study, Thermodynamics, War Studies and Weapons had been retained, but Economics, Navigation/Radio, PT and the Squadron Commander's period had been dropped. Meteorology had been reintroduced. Ron, Jim and I remained in our previous sets for Humanistics and Science subjects. The gen men had gone down to eight – Julian Bowes, Mike Goodall, John Gratton, Dickie Hoare, Laurie Jones, Nigel MacNicol, John Maitland and Mike Marsh.

In E Flight of Flying Wing, 'Thrombo' (my former instructor Flt. Lt. Thompson), had been appointed Deputy Flight Commander. Nigel MacNicol and John Tucker were moved into the Flight to keep the numbers up, leaving Julian Bowes as the only member of 60A not in the Flight. We were shocked to hear that an E Flight instructor, Flt. Lt. A. Turner (formerly 49 Entry), had been killed in a Meteor accident.

The story went around that one of the Squadron Commanders in Flying Wing had baled out of a Chipmunk and landed safely. Apparently he'd put his golf bag in the rear cockpit (as he was going away for the weekend), but the bag had moved and jammed the control column. The Chipmunk crashed near a house containing a pregnant woman and the shock caused her baby to be born. I never heard what happened to the Squadron Leader.

Flt. Lt. Reid gave me a dual check before sending me solo. Flt. Lt. Markwell then checked me on doing forced landings without power so that I could do those solo. Everything went well. The weather had become hot so I sweated when simulated instrument flying recommenced and Flt. Lt. Reid and I did radio beam letdowns (QGHs) and ground controlled approaches (GCAs). I was authorised to do QGHs solo.

Then we began Pattern Fs – a timed precision flying exercise required for a White Instrument Flying Certificate:

1. Fly north straight and level at 120 kts for 2 minutes at 1,600 r.p.m. and 25 inches of boost.

2. Set 2,000 r.p.m. and 26 inches of boost within 30 seconds and commence a turn to port at 100 kts climbing 1,000 feet at 660 f.p.m. for 1½ minutes.

3. Fly east straight and level at 130 kts for 2 minutes at 1,750 r.p.m. and 26 inches of boost.

4. Set 2,000 r.p.m. and 14 inches of boost and commence a 360 degree turn to starboard at 100 kts descending 1,000 feet at 400 f.p.m. for 2½ minutes.

5. Set 25 inches of boost and fly south at 100 kts climbing 1,000 feet at 500 f.p.m. for 2 minutes.

6. Set 1,600 r.p.m. and commence a level turn to port at 120 kts for 1½ minutes.

7. Set 2,000 r.p.m. and 25 inches of boost within 30 seconds and fly west at 100 kts climbing 1,000 feet at 500 f.p.m. for 2 minutes.

8. Lower the undercarriage, set 16 inches of boost and commence a 360

degree turn to starboard at 100 kts descending 2,000 feet at 800 f.p.m. for 2½ minutes.

9. Raise the undercarriage, set 1,600 r.p.m and 25 inches of boost and resume normal straight and level flight heading north.

Flying this and other patterns on instruments, often in hot and bumpy conditions, required quite a lot of effort. After practising endlessly, I was eventually able to fly the patterns within the accepted limits.

There was some speculation on whether or not Laurie Jones would recover from his knee operation in time for the Coronation and if he'd be relegated to 61 Entry. He returned from hospital soon afterwards, but was on light duties, off drill and restricted in flying to dual instruction only.

I heard that a Ceylonese chap in 61A had been hit by a cricket ball and received a fractured skull, and that another Flight Cadet had had a car accident and received not only a fractured skull, but two broken legs.

The College was advised that His Royal Highness The Duke of Edinburgh would be the reviewing officer at the next passing-out parade and would also attend the ball. As this would occur in Coronation Term, a meeting of the Senior Mess voted to buy a trumpet and banner for the College band – one of eight new instruments being purchased. More money than usual was voted for the ball to help make it a really grand affair. The College was later advised that the Duke would be coming only to the passing-out parade.

In discussions about the last ball, the general opinion was that it had been the best we'd experienced. I heard, however, that one of the Flight Cadets who'd been chopped by the CFI (Wg. Cdr. Peveler) and transferred to Digby, had got a little tipsy at the ball and slapped the CFI on the back and said, 'Had any more good chops lately?' I suppose the College officers took such incidents in good part and, hopefully, didn't remember them the next day.

Betty wrote to say she was uncertain about coming to the next passing-out parade and ball as she had to earn money for another term at University and an employer may not let her off work to attend. Later, I was much relieved when she wrote to say that she'd arranged suitable employment and would be coming to the passing-out parade and ball. Mrs Aitken, in her second letter to me, gave permission for Betty to go to Cranwell and then to London (as Betty and I both wanted some time together after the ball). I'd also invited Cousin Mabel to the passing-out, but she'd replied that she would try and come when I got my Wings. Miss Ronaldson, who was still in Britain, again asked if she could come to a passing-out parade.

On the first guest night of term, 60 Entry assembled in its own ante-room before going into 59 Entry's ante-room to await the arrival of the College officers and guests – an RAAF Group Captain, and a photographer and a reporter from *Illustrated* magazine. We then moved into the dining hall where the rest of the Flight Cadets were waiting, standing behind their chairs. 59

Figure 33. Guest night, College dining hall, May 1953.

Entry as Senior Entry sat at the Queen's Colour end of the hall, while 60 Entry sat at the other end below the band gallery. A Squadron, as Sovereign's Squadron, occupied the centre row of tables (Fig. 33). The band was so noisy that talking to Flt. Lt. Hall, who was sitting with 60A, was difficult.

Afterwards, the visitors from *Illustrated* were allowed to attend the initiation of 64 Entry as Flight Cadets − a rare event, as not even the College officers attended such occasions. One member of 64 Entry forced a needle through his cheek and was going to light something in his mouth when he was given the 'thumbs up'. A Pakistani member then extinguished lighted cigarettes by pushing them into his heel and leaving them there! The College had had enough and passed him without penalty.

The *Illustrated* visitors were then encouraged to go on stage and give an item. They weren't penalised, but some unfortunate members of 64 Entry were blindfolded and had to blow up the inner tube of a car tyre until it burst. Others had to run around the outside of the College naked, or go down a manhole in the College and find their way to another manhole. In the middle of the commotion, some fool let off a fire extinguisher and turned through 360 degrees. There were Flight Cadets diving for cover all over the place! I wasn't affected and was glad I didn't have to clean up the mess.

The *Illustrated* people were at the College for several days gathering information for two articles that were published about two months later. The three and seven page articles, 'RAF cradle of tomorrow's pilots', and 'Men who will run the Air Force', were all good stuff. Luckily, the photographs didn't include any from the initiation of 64 Entry! Though Ted and I were photographed several times on a ceremonial parade, our pictures didn't appear in *Illustrated*. I was also photographed running in a 100 yards race and as a member of the Fine Arts Section (having been press-ganged into this because insufficient members of the Section had turned up!), but none of these photographs were published. Selected photos were later put on the College notice-boards so that copies could be ordered.

The College had previously received good publicity through The *Royal Air Force Review* magazine in articles entitled, 'The first airmen of the Queen' and 'Cranwell'. *Sport and Country* had also published an article on the use of land at Cranwell, and in *New Elizabethans*, Sir Philip Gibbs, KBE, had recalled a visit he'd made to the College.

As soon as possible, Sqn. Ldr. Thomas made his views known to A Squadron about the guest night − he wasn't at all impressed by the fire extinguisher incident and various other matters that'd come to his attention. I felt the same way as he did.

At another dinner, the College entertained a few cadets from the RAF Technical College, Henlow, and then competed with them in a debate. Later,

Ted, Mal, Julian and I were detailed to show a party of farmers, retired Colonels and the like around the College.

I was rostered one Saturday as the A Squadron duty Senior Flight Cadet. The responsibilities included having to remain in uniform, not leaving the College, being responsible for the duty Flight Cadet in the Senior Mess, making out parade states (including sick parades), recording the 'crimes' of defaulters, turning off lights at night, checking that Flight Cadets were in their rooms and recording absentees in a book. In the dining hall, the duty Senior Flight Cadets sat at the eastern ends of the table lines. As A Squadron was Sovereign's Squadron, the A Squadron duty Senior Flight Cadet became 'Mr Vice'. After a formal dinner, Mr Vice moved to the western end of the dining hall and sat in the Mess President's chair when it became vacant, and waited until all the Flight Cadets had left the hall – presumably to ensure that nobody whipped the silver!

Then on the following Saturday, I was rostered as the duty Flight Cadet of Junior Entries. This meant signing on at 0625 hours, taking defaulters' drill from 0630–0645 hours, asking if there were any complaints during meals, inspecting the barracks while Cadets were away, taking the fire picket parade at 2130 hours, and checking that the mess was locked up, lights were out and everyone was in bed by 2230 hours. During the inspection of the barracks, the Junior Entries Flight Sergeant accompanied me while I left chits on the beds of Cadets whose bed spaces and kits I considered were not up to standard. I then completed a report and handed it in the next day. At meals in the Junior Mess, the duty Flight Cadet sat at the opposite end of a table to the Junior Entries duty NCO. Worst of all, the duty was for a week and meant sleeping in a room at Block 78. The only advantage of being the duty Flight Cadet of Junior Entries was that one got off drill at the Senior College!

On returning to Block 78 late one night, I found that a number of the doors were locked and the Flight Cadets were preparing to do battle as a result of some C Squadron chaps raiding the place. I soon had everyone back in bed. The newly appointed Junior Entries Adjutant, Flt. Lt. C. Fountain, and F/S Mitchell called briefly to say there was trouble brewing elsewhere. I returned to my temporary room and found that my pyjamas had been tied in knots, my bed had been apple-pied and my razor blade was missing (luckily I had a spare with me)! I was glad when my week of duty was over and I could return to the comfort of my room in the Senior College.

When Mal Dines was away with the Sailing Section the next Saturday, I was detailed to replace him as the duty Flight Cadet of Junior Entries. This being the third week in a row I'd been on duty, I began to suffer from a lack of sleep.

Paul Chamberlain of 59A showed me a confidential report form that he had to fill out on each member of 60A. This seemed to be the start of a new system whereby members of the Senior Entry got experience in assessing Flight Cadets of other entries.

The Senior Entry started throwing their weight around as was usual at the beginning of term and at one stage I counted fifty-one Flight Cadets on extra drill.

Among the masses of mail awaiting me when I returned to Cranwell was an iced twenty-first birthday cake from Mum. I invited all of 60A to my room to have a piece and gave other pieces to Ron and Jim. Betty gave me a very nice set of gold oval-shaped cuff-links that had 'R' engraved on them, so I sent her some of the cake. The last of the cake went to Cousin Mabel.

My sister Heather sent me the following amusing doggerel:

> Your birthday on the eighth of May
> I did remember all the day.
> Although I gave it every thought
> No birthday present had I bought.
> For I would not presume to buy
> Your socks and shirts and taste in tie.
> You very likely have your share
> Of chocolates, plants and things to wear.
> Until these plastic pegs did see
> (A product of the UEB)
> Which on the line should keep your shirt
> And save its blowing in the dirt.
> And if your car runs dry (alas)
> Just fill the tank with Mobilgas.
> I'm sorry they are sent so late
> But good things come to those who wait.
> P.S. If you do not like this verse
> Console yourself it could be worse.
> P.P.S. And if you think you could do better
> Reply by verse in your next letter.

With Laurie Jones unable to take up the Captaincy of the A Squadron Knocker Cup team, Denis Briggs of 61A replaced him and I was appointed his Deputy. On one occasion the circumstances were such that I had to conduct the Knocker Cup practice.

The RNZAF and RPAF members of the College were advised that Hastings aircraft from RAF Shawbury might be available during the next leave period to take us home for a visit. Ron, Jim and I were told that we were high on the priority list to travel, but we doubted there would be trips because of our previous experience of such things.

We weren't surprised when later advised that the planned flight home had been cancelled because of an expected lack of available aircraft. Sqn. Ldr. Thomas persisted in trying to get me a flight to New Zealand until I told him I'd made other plans for the leave.

An order was promulgated that in future, officer pattern raincoats were to be worn only with uniform – not with mufti.

Early in the term, I was able to visit Lincoln twice to do essential shopping (like buying a suitable civilian raincoat), prowl around a most interesting museum and have a more detailed look at the Castle and the commemorative window to New Zealand airmen in the Cathedral. On another occasion I joined in with some Flight Cadets on a rabbit shooting expedition using bows and arrows borrowed from the Archery Section. Needless to say, we didn't get any rabbits!

I had to attend a gliding meeting, as the Officer in charge of Gliding, Flt. Lt. 'Bud' Abbott, wanted to deliver a 'rocket' on various things, such as damage to the T21B glider when it had got away from a Flight Cadet holding a wing-tip and been blown on its back by the wind. I decided to give up gliding that term to concentrate on my thesis and athletics.

The athletics season began with a match against Jesus and Emmanuel Colleges, Cambridge. I won the high jump with a height of 5 feet 8 inches and just failed to clear the bar at 5 feet 10 inches. This was my best effort to date and helped Cranwell win the match. Afterwards, the visitors were entertained in the Fancy Goods Store as mess guests. Unfortunately I'd hurt a knee in my last jump so didn't accompany Ron and Jim that night to a dance at Kesteven Teachers' Training College.

Mr Watts, the AAA coach, visited Cranwell again and said that it was remarkable I'd jumped 5 feet 8 inches as I'd virtually no free leg swing. He considered that I'd an unusual amount of spring and would jump higher once I was able to develop my free leg swing. (He was right. I later easily jumped 5 feet 10 inches and just failed at 5 feet 11 inches.)

I was then involved in a series of Wednesday and Saturday athletics matches commencing with one against Carre's Grammar School, Sleaford. The College didn't enter its best team, but still won easily. I ran in the relay. We also won against Leicester College of Art and Technology. A thunderstorm drenched everyone and that affected performances. Then the Cranwell team went to Nottingham to compete against the University and Saltby Technical College on a very poorly prepared ground. The high jump bar was solid like a crowbar. Cranwell came second in that match.

When the team travelled to Leicester to compete against University College we had an excellent ground. I ran in the 100 yards using starting blocks for the first time, but only came third. The Cranwell team again won. Afterwards, we went into the city to view the gaudy Coronation decorations and see a Terry-Thomas variety show. (The show was apparently the origin of a common saying at that time, 'You're a shower, an absolute shower!') We ended up at a University College dance. A girl I danced with slipped over on the floor, much to her embarrassment as yards of her petticoat and legs were showing. A very tired team got back to Cranwell by 0100 hours. On a trip to Loughborough College, I won the high jump, but the Cranwell team was well beaten.

The athletics team had an evening match at Scunthorpe with athletics clubs from Appleby-Frodingham (against whom we'd previously competed), Don-caster, Grimsby, Lincoln and RAF Kirton. I was intrigued that adults were paying 1s and children 6d to watch us perform and wondered if this would affect our amateur status. I found myself high jumping off the grass of a cricket field onto soft earth piled on the grass, and running in the 4 x 110 yard relay. After Cranwell had won the match (which was in doubt right up to the end), the Officer in charge of Athletics, Fg. Off. Rickard, treated the team to drinks in the bar above the cricket pavilion changing rooms. Our return to Cranwell was again 0100 hours.

Ted and I found ourselves back on rifle drill practising for the Coronation. This only convinced us that we never wanted to do rifle drill again. We then had to train Alpin MacGregor of 62A as a reserve Commandant's Orderly so that he could stand in for Ted during a church parade when Ted was away with the Sailing Section. Later on, another reserve was trained to stand in for me when I was away on athletics.

There were further clothing parades and visits to the Clothing Store in East Camp. We found that the Store had been moved even further away from the College, and changing groundsheets to ones of a uniform colour was rather a chore. On the first rainy day we drilled with rifles while wearing groundsheets and got rather wet. Our webbing equipment was also a mess so, as the rainy days continued, some Flight Cadets went on parade without webbing belts and bayonets under their groundsheets. That was when the rain stopped and we were ordered to remove our groundsheets and fix bayonets! As a result, quite a few of us were on Under Officer's parades for a day.

Kit inspections began. Over several days, our uniforms were inspected, then webbing, boots and rifles (twice), and finally general inspections by Sqn. Ldr. Thomas and the Assistant Commandant. Our white webbing had to be scrubbed free of blanco, dried and handed in for coating with a white plastic to overcome the problem of blanco weeping onto uniforms in wet weather. Removing the plastic from our brasses (by using a suit cleaning liquid or by scraping) and then polishing the brasses was a difficult and time consuming job. We all had to buy new black Moss Bros. ties.

On my first lot of night flying in a Harvard, Flt. Lt. Reid talked me through circuits at RAF Barkston Heath. The blue flame of the engine exhaust near the starboard wing root necessitated a lookout mainly to the left of the engine cowling. On the approach to land, the large nose of the Harvard tended to restrict my view of the angle of approach lights at the end of the runway. I thought that Flt. Lt. Reid had an even more difficult job to see from the rear cockpit because of the low wings. The ultra-violet and red cockpit lighting intensity had to be adjusted to be just right – not too bright and not too dim. I found everything to be exaggerated at night – the engine noise, the intensity of lights and so on. The darkness was a tremendous stimulus in concentrating one's attention and more accurate flying usually resulted. My landings began to improve, but I had to wait till after the Coronation before going solo at night.

Of immediate concern were Intermediate Handling Tests. I was the first in 60 Entry to be tested. The E Flight Commander, Flt. Lt. Woods, took me flying and, in the heat of the moment, I did stupid things such as falling out of a stall turn, attempting to make a forced landing down wind and making a bumpy final landing. As a result, I was classed as above average in upper air work and average in lower air work. Overall I was average. I was a bit relieved when Ted told me he'd also been classed as average, and Mal (who'd done well in his Basic Test), said he'd fumbled his Intermediate Test.

Our flying was again interrupted by the Senior Entry taking our aircraft for bombing practices. Then an electrical storm and cloudburst caused flying to be cancelled.

One of the flying instructors, Flt. Lt. L.J. Day, DFC, told me he was from Auckland, New Zealand, and had been in the RAF for a number of years. He was slightly built and had sandy coloured hair. I was invited for a drink and chat in his caravan one evening at the caravan park near Daedalus House. On the appointed date and time, I arrived at the door of his caravan. There was no response to my knock though a light was on in the caravan. Further knocking brought noises from within and eventually the Flight Lieutenant opened the door. He'd forgotten about the appointment and was obviously very drunk. He insisted on me coming in and managed to find me a soft drink. We talked for a while about our home country, but as soon as I could reasonably leave, I bade him good night and returned to my room.

Once again, there were a series of tests in our academic subjects, relieved a little in War Studies by an Army exercise called Operation Ziegfried, named after an actual happening in Germany during World War II. I was a Section Commander in the exercise.

On another guest night, I seemed to be surrounded by flying instructors – Louis Maisonpierre, John Reid and others – so I had to maintain polite conversation during the meal and afterwards in the ante-room, until the Commandant and other officers departed. The College band had left Cranwell for pre-Coronation training, so the music was played that evening (and for parades immediately prior to the Coronation) by a voluntary band from RAF Hednesford.

There was now little time remaining to complete our preparations for the Coronation. A ceremonial parade was held at which about seven hundred officers and airmen from Flying Training Command were spectators. They were at Cranwell to be kitted and trained for the Coronation. The visitors also attended a combined pre-Coronation service on Whit Sunday in the Hangar Church at which there were special prayers for the Queen. The Queen's Colour was paraded in the march past after the service.

That afternoon, the College formed up with rifles in five flights on the new grass outside the College Headquarters building as if we were on Parliament Square, and stood there in hot sunshine for four and a half hours. I was in No. 3 Flight with the Queen's Colour nearby. We were told to fall out if feeling faint, and many Flight Cadets (including Ron) did so. Six people collapsed and had to be carried off parade, but most were back again a few minutes later. We were kept alert giving compliments to various 'dignitaries' who processed past us. NCOs banging dustbin lids were the bane of the Under Officers when they were giving orders.

Part way through the afternoon the order was given that one in four Flight Cadets could fall out for ten minutes and visit the toilets in the Headquarters building. We were told to leave our rifles by the foot of the Flight Cadet on our right so that he could stand on the rifle if someone tried to steal it. Officers attempted to do this, so the spit and polish finish of a number of rifles was ruined by the hobnails of somebody's boot.

Then we stood at attention for thirty minutes and more people fainted. A Flight Cadet collapsed beside me and almost hit me with his bayonet. Adjustments had to be periodically made in our ranks to allow 'Prince Charles' and other 'dignitaries' to come into 'Parliament Square' from 'Great George Street'. We were also briefed on what to do if a horse in the procession went mad and if the Police needed help with the crowd, but nothing was said on what to do if somebody threw a grenade.

Then the Flying Training Command airmen arrived and were spaced along a road. They stood there for two or three hours and had trouble standing for such a long time. The next day they left for the Coronation on a special train brought up the little used branch line between Sleaford and Cranwell.

The Assistant Commandant made a short speech before the College contingent boarded buses at 0830 hours to take us on the day long trip to Sandhurst. Two trucks carried our luggage. We were each allowed one suitcase and a service pack. Mine were crammed with the five different types of footwear and other gear that we were required to have with us. The Colour Party travelled in a shooting-brake with the pole of the Colour sticking out the rear window.

I was in an old bus that had seats so close together I was unable to sit squarely to the front. As a result, I welcomed stops at Baldock and Windsor in which to stretch my legs. On the way, I saw aircraft such as a Viscount, a Constellation, a DC6 and a Stratocruiser, and we passed Ascot racecourse and Denham and Pinewood film studios. The portable radio of a Flight Cadet helped relieve the boredom of the trip.

At Windsor, some of us crowded into Nell Gwynne's Café for refreshments. Ron and Jim went shopping and were delighted to be able to buy a New Zealand flag. Eton College boys walking along the crowded streets in their pin-striped trousers and tailed coats somehow seemed incongruous amongst the casually dressed tourists. The Cranwell contingent drove on to Camberley through park-like land. Sam Boyce declared we were 'deep in the heart of Pongo territory'.

Sandhurst was on the northern outskirts of Camberley. I was billeted in the Somme Company building of New College (built in 1907) with a member of the Sandhurst Senior Entry, Senior Cadet Peter Brown. Peter's room was small, so with a narrow folding bed in it for me, there was barely room to move. Compared with my room at Cranwell, Peter's room seemed primitive. The floor was of unpolished wood and the walls were poorly painted. Water for the hand basin had to be carried in a jug from a bathroom along the corridor, and waste water flowed into a bucket beneath the hand basin. There was no wall cabinet for shaving gear and no heating. The only window looked out onto rows of Quonset huts and a tall chimney that left smuts on the bedding when the window was open. As a result, the window was closed most of the time. Our rifles were kept in the room. When relaxing in a Victorian bath that night, I couldn't help wondering what distinguished Army officers had used the same bath.

The long corridors at Sandhurst had wooden or tiled floors, and the walls were tiled in places. The huge Cadet's Mess with its high barrel roof also had tiles on the walls, above which were armour, weapons, pictures of Queen Victoria, old Colours and the like. About six hundred people were seated in the Mess for a band night. I was seated directly in front of the band and, though the band played some stirring music, having a conversation was almost impossible. There was no choice in the meal (except to refuse) and the quality of the food was far below the Cranwell standard. Afterwards, we were shown the film, *The Browning Version*.

Peter told me that he'd had two months as an ordinary serviceman before going to Sandhurst. There were two terms a year and, as his entry had about three hundred Cadets in it, he didn't know all their names. The Sandhurst course was for eighteen months or so.

I thought the hats of the Sandhurst Cadets were most impressive as they were worn well forward on the head – Guards style. The Sandhurst gorgets, however, were blancoed (unlike those at Cranwell) and looked terrible close-up.

I ran into two former Cranwellians who, after being chopped from the College, had been selected for training at Sandhurst. They were full of stories about suicides at Sandhurst. One chap had shot himself in the mouth and the bullet had continued and hit a Cadet in bed upstairs! A few months earlier, a Cadet had blown his brains out and another had tried to hang himself with his rifle pull-through. There had also been some desertions. Such things didn't happen at Cranwell!

At breakfast the next day, I noticed that the Sandhurst Cadets could buy newspapers in the Mess and bring them into the dining hall. The tables were covered by rather worn, unattractive tablecloths. On parade, the Cranwell and Sandhurst Coronation contingents stood for three and a half hours and paid compliments to passing 'dignitaries' in much the same way as had been done at Cranwell.

That evening, Peter and I went by train to Reading to see a film, *Desperate Moment*, and go to the Oxford Dance Hall – a place that was often frequented by Sandhurst Cadets. The two dance floors were hot and crowded so when I could, I joined others in taking a taxi back to Sandhurst. I was told a joke about a taxi driver who, in dropping a Cadet in front of the sprawling buildings of Sandhurst late at night, said, 'Nice place you've got there, gov'ner.'

On Trinity Sunday, there was a pre-Coronation outdoor drum head service during which we had to stand for one and a half hours in hot sunshine. Afterwards, I did spit and polishing until Peter had completed fire picket duty and was able to join me for a meal in Camberley. Having meals out seemed to be quite common because of the standard of the Sandhurst meals and the lack of second helpings. Perhaps that was why the Fancy Goods Store at Sandhurst was better than the one at Cranwell and well patronised. As Peter and I walked through Camberley, I couldn't help noticing that it was full of Service outfitters. A number of the Sandhurst Cadets seemed to be well-heeled, had classy accents and spent weekends in London dressed in bowler hats, Edwardian sports coats, fawn coloured tight trousers, brown suede shoes and carrying black umbrellas. No doubt the Camberley shops helped them spend their money.

On the last day at Sandhurst, another parade was held in which we stood for two hours. I wasn't feeling the best having developed a bad cold or possibly hay fever.

(In the medical examination before joining the RNZAF, I'd been asked if I suffered from hay fever and had answered, 'No.' This was because Mum had always said I'd a propensity to colds and taken me as a child on a long journey from the South Island of New Zealand to Wanganui in the North Island to see Dr Ulrich Williams, who was renowned for his 'natural cures'.

He'd prescribed deep breathing exercises as the 'natural' way for me to overcome my problem. For years I'd done ten minutes of deep breathing on waking in the morning and ten minutes before sleeping at night without feeling any benefit. Since coming to Cranwell, I'd gradually become aware that my problem was really hay fever, and I'd inadvertently given an incorrect answer to the hay fever question in my recruitment medical!)

There was nothing that I could do as I stood on parade at Sandhurst, but suffer in silence and blow my nose when I could.

A lecture on the history of the Coronation followed the parade. The Cranwell and Sandhurst contingents sat in a huge hangar-like building whose walls were decorated with painted metal shields of World War II Army divisions. I found the lecture interesting, but my nose ran continually.

At 0215 hours the next morning, I was woken by fire alarms and loudspeakers in cars outside. The Sandhurst contingent (about half of the Academy) got up and left for the Coronation. At 0315 hours the Cranwell contingent was told to get up and, after tea and biscuits, was taken in buses to Camberley railway station where we waited forty-five minutes for a train to Vauxhall Station in London. In the early morning light, Brookwood Cemetery, reportedly the largest cemetery in the world, could be seen from the train.

On arrival at the station, we walked across the Thames at Vauxhall Bridge and marched to the Army barracks at Millbank. The Sandhurst contingent was already there. Five marquees were pitched on a small asphalt square in the centre of the dingy-looking barracks. Eventually breakfast was served in the marquees and we wolfed down barely warm bacon, reconstituted egg and fried bread, followed by sweet tea and bread and butter. The sky was overcast and rain began to fall, so groundsheets had to be worn. I began to wake up and notice the hundreds of cars going past the barracks carrying nobility, foreign dignitaries and other VIPs to Westminster Abbey. The people looked terrific in their best clothes, robes and regalia. Someone said that he'd never before seen so much 'peaches and cream'.

At about 0800 hours the Dartmouth contingent appeared and a large Army band led the Cranwell, Sandhurst and Dartmouth contingents on the one and a quarter mile march to Parliament Square. The rain had become drizzle, so we carried our groundsheets on our left arms with our rifles. I noticed the Dartmouth chaps were little more than young boys and didn't carry rifles. As I passed Westminster Abbey, I could see out of the corners of my eyes the impressive temporary foyer built in front of the Abbey and peers of the realm and others standing outside. Large temporary stands, packed with spectators, lined every available space along the route. The crowds cheered enthusiastically as we took up positions on our markers in Parliament Square. We laid our folded groundsheets behind us on the roadway. When ordered

Figure 34. ON THE DAY OF THE CORONATION
JUNE 1953

A squadron, the Sovereign's Squadron, with the Queen's Colour lining the route at attention on the Home Office side of Parliament Square, London. Author fifth from left.

to stand easy, we relaxed a little without moving, and took cautious glances around us as best as we could out of the corners of our eyes.

I was so thrilled about what was going on that I forgot about my hay fever. Across the road and behind me were stands with seats that cost £50 each (so I was told later). In front of the seats, spectators had been standing since 0600 hours. Between these people and the Cranwell contingent stood first aiders and Police.

Tension mounted and the noise from the crowd became greater when, thirty minutes later, the procession of heads of state and Royalty began. For one and a half hours, we stood in the drizzle and cold at 'attention', the 'slope', or the 'present' while the procession passed by to the Abbey. I just about seized up, but somehow managed to cope. There was so much to see on such a splendid occasion that I'm unable to do justice in trying to describe it. Suffice to say, amongst the dignitaries I recognised Sir Winston Churchill,

Queen Salote of Tonga, Queen Elizabeth the Queen Mother, the Royal children, the Duke of Edinburgh and, of course, Queen Elizabeth II. As she went by, we presented arms once again and the Colour was lowered in salute. The spectacle of bands, horses, gilded coaches and gorgeously dressed people was far beyond my expectations. The greyness of the day seemed to bring out the colour in everything.

Soon after 1100 hours, the Coronation ceremony began in the Abbey and a broadcast could be heard in the streets. Since I was facing the Abbey and having previously been inside, I could visualise the pageantry going on there. I was amongst the first detail to be allowed to fall out for ten minutes and go to the toilets at the Westminster underground railway station. Then we ate the Lyons boxed lunches given to us – two sandwiches, a bun, an apple, a bar of chocolate and barley sugar. In addition, we discreetly sucked sugary stuff and Horlicks tablets from time to time.

The long period of standing took its toll and several people in the crowd fainted and had to be carried or assisted from the area. I was aware of two Cranwell chaps fainting (one injured himself with his bayonet), and at least two Sandhurst chaps had to fall out.

Soon after, the Queen's words of self-dedication were clearly heard and she was crowned, the rain came down in earnest and we were ordered to put on our groundsheets. When the rain had reduced to drizzle, we again took off the groundsheets. As the service in the Abbey drew to a close, thousands of men and women of the British Commonwealth Armed Forces marched into Parliament Square through the gap we made in our ranks at the Great George Street corner. The variety of people and uniforms seemed endless – black, white, brown and yellow people, busbies, tartans, shorts, sandals, Gurkhas playing bagpipes, Canadian Mounties and so on. Our former Senior GCT Officer led the RAF Regiment group. Flt. Lt. W.J. (Bill) Bangay, MBE, the Director of Music at Cranwell, led the College Band. I felt a great moment of pride seeing members of the New Zealand Armed Forces march by. Every so often there were tall escorting guardsmen, resplendent in bearskin hats and medals, who acted as guides and 'continuity men' for the parade. They wore swords in long curved scabbards which were periodically dragged on the roadway to help the parade keep in step between one band and another. The crowd roared with delight when two old men came along the road cleaning up after the horses.

In the procession from the Abbey, most cheers, after Queen Elizabeth II, were for Queen Salote of Tonga. She'd refused to carry an umbrella and sat dripping wet in an open landau waving gaily to the crowd. Her impressive size, regal bearing and cheerful smile will long be remembered. I watched the procession fascinated until, suddenly, at 1530 hours it was all over.

The crowd stayed put while we formed up to march off. In spite of the noise, commands could be heard, but our limbs almost refused to respond. The soaked Colour and Colour Party were behind my Flight. A stentorian voice from the crowd shouted, 'Well done, Cranwell!' Dartmouth led the way around Parliament Square, followed by Sandhurst and Cranwell and, to much cheering from the crowds, we marched back to Millbank Barracks past VIPs waiting for their cars at the Abbey.

The Dartmouth contingent disappeared while the Cranwell and Sandhurst contingents had a rather miserable tea in the marquees. I noticed that white blanco had wept from the webbing of the Sandhurst contingent and made a mess of its dark uniforms, whereas the Cranwell contingent with the plastic finish to its white webbing looked smart in comparison. The Sandhurst contingent left to return to Sandhurst, but the Cranwell contingent had to wait in wet uniforms until 1730 hours before marching back to Vauxhall railway station. One compensation was that we saw the RAF formation fly past of Meteors and Sabres over London, led by a Meteor with a red tail.

Before boarding the train to Camberley, I bought a copy of the Coronation souvenir edition of the *Evening News*. I thought it amazing that photographs and details of the Coronation could be available just two hours after the end of the Coronation. I was also amazed and thrilled to read that an unknown New Zealand bee-keeper called Ed Hillary, and Sherpa Tensing, had just climbed the world's highest mountain, Mount Everest, the first to do so. The coincidence of this great event and the Coronation seemed remarkable, so I further rejoiced when the Queen recognised this by knighting Hillary.

When the Cranwell contingent arrived at Camberley, we found the Sandhurst contingent and band waiting so that together we could march the two miles to Sandhurst. Hundreds of people watched us, but I felt that, wet and dishevelled, we weren't worth watching. The Cranwell contingent was at the rear of the parade and had difficulty hearing the band at the front and keeping in step. A manoeuvre to change rifles from our left shoulders to our right and so relieve our aching left arms was a real shambles. At last we came to the Old College parade ground, marched off the Colours and dismissed.

As soon as possible, most of the Cranwell contingent changed into mufti, boarded buses for Camberley railway station and individually returned to London. On arrival at Waterloo railway station at about 2230 hours, I saw crowds watching a fireworks display from the South Bank Festival site. Searchlights swept the black sky. I was lucky to get a taxi to 120 Lexham Gardens, which I found was just off Earl's Court Road and not far from where Cousin Jennifer lived. The Scottish housekeeper showed me to a very comfortable double room and gave me some supper. A hot bath to relax my tired muscles ended a very long and memorable day.

For the next day and a half, I walked through milling crowds in the West End of London, admired the Coronation decorations, did mainly window-shopping and went to one of the new wide screen cinemas to see the excellent comedy, *Genevieve*. One of the shorts was a thirty minute documentary on the Coronation, but I didn't see myself on parade. The film makers must have been up all night producing the film. When taking a walk along The Mall I noticed crowds gathering, so I stopped and eventually saw the Queen go by. I didn't take any photographs or buy any Coronation souvenirs other than newspapers, as the latter were cheap and seemed to cover events in sufficient detail. I bought some hay fever pills and began experimenting with quarter pills so as not to become drowsy – this being an unfortunate side effect of such pills in those days. I called briefly on Sqn. Ldr. Gavin. He said Cranwell looked much better than Sandhurst at the Coronation, and he'd let me know when a decision was made on how Ron and I would be returning home after passing-out from Cranwell. Too soon, I had to leave for Sandhurst.

A gala day was being held at Sandhurst, comprising a parade (reviewed by the American General Mathew B. Ridgeway, Supreme Allied Commander Europe), activities on the lawns and a ball in the evening. Not being involved in this, I took the opportunity to have a quick look around some parts of Sandhurst such as the library, the outdoor confidence training area, two large lakes (on which yachts could sail) that'd been excavated by French prisoners of war, and the impressive collection of guns and cannons (some of which were highly polished).

For the return to Cranwell, the College buses were less crowded so I was able to spread out on a seat to myself. We passed Runnymede where the Magna Carta had been signed, and Eton College where cricket, picnics and other activities of a parents' day could easily be seen. One of the breaks on the way was an inexplicable hour long stop at Grantham. Some of us filled in the time by having a meal and then were annoyed to find on reaching Cranwell that dinner was awaiting us.

We were spared a parade the next day as much work had to be done on cleaning the rust off our rifles and bayonets, and generally spit and polishing our kit. A message was promulgated from the RAF Chief of the Air Staff congratulating the College on the 'splendid bearing' of Flight Cadets at the Coronation.

The weather was still bad over England, and a Lincoln, several Varsities and Ansons, a Gemini and some other light aircraft were forced to land at Cranwell and wait for the weather to clear. I heard that a Lincoln bomber had crashed on the south airfield while we'd been away, so I visited the wreck and watched it being disassembled.

A parade was held at which the Commandant awarded Coronation Medals to eighteen Flight Cadets including the two New Zealanders in 59 Entry, Jack Henderson and Colin Loveday, and 60 Entry members Dickie Hoare,

Laurie Jones, John Tucker and Tony Whitwam. Those Flight Cadets not already in the Senior Entry who got medals, seemed to have been earmarked as future Under Officers. There was some ill feeling in 60A, however, over Laurie Jones receiving a medal when he'd not been on the Coronation. Sqn. Ldr. Thomas got to hear of this and talked the matter through with 60A, excluding Laurie from the discussions.

There was also some dissatisfaction in the College over the Cadet Wing Adjutant being awarded a medal when he'd not been listed as a College officer officially on the Coronation, yet had stood near the Colour Party in Parliament Square.

Ron Chippindale and I learned some time later that the RAF hadn't considered us for medals because we were RNZAF, and that the RNZAF hadn't considered us for medals as we'd been seconded to the RAF! Apparently all the members of the New Zealand Armed Services contingent at the Coronation received medals.

Several Coronation films were shown at the College, but in only *A Queen is Crowned* could some of the Cranwell contingent be seen. I was pleased when the *Journal* later published a photo that showed me on parade amongst the Cranwell contingent in Parliament Square (Fig. 34).

We were soon back into normal routines again. Concentrated morning and evening practices were held for the Knocker Cup inter-squadron gymnastic competition. Laurie Jones took over as leader of the A Squadron team, but his late inclusion didn't help and, when the competition was held on the Orange, A Squadron came last.

The Orange was also the site for cricket matches by the First XI. I got a great view of them from my room. Ron was one of the scorers for such events. Occasionally the First XI was able to get off church parades because of all-day cricket matches.

South of the Orange across Camp Road, the old parade ground was torn up and replaced by a big new one directly in front of the Junior Mess. Another change was that the RAF Selection Board moved into Daedalus House.

The Queen's Birthday was celebrated by a parade of the whole of RAF Cranwell on the grass to the north of the College. Rain fell, so everyone got soaked as we formed a hollow square to salute the Queen and give her three cheers. Ted and I had been told before we formed up on either side of the Commandant's dais that the parade would be just like other ceremonial parades. Unfortunately a temporary flagpole had been placed behind us and we didn't see the Union Jack being raised on the flagpole. At the General Salute, we should have about turned, but neither of us moved. Then I saluted as the parade saluted, but Ted didn't. When the three cheers were given, Ted and I were uncoordinated in raising our hats. After such a performance in front of thousands of people, we were glad to escape back to the College, dry out and watch on television the 'Trooping of the Colour' at Horse Guard's Parade.

The early morning and evening peace at Cranwell began to be disturbed by a formation of sixteen Chipmunks flown by instructors practising for the Queen's Review of the Royal Air Force to be held at RAF Odiham. Later, the Home Command Prentice formation joined the training. I also saw a formation of twenty-two Canberra and eight Lincoln bombers fly overhead – presumably training for the same event.

While flying solo one day, Ted, Mal and I just happened to meet over Boston and decided to do a little unauthorised formation flying. This was the first time we'd done formation flying in Harvards. We took turns at leading and used all the approved visual signals. Luckily we weren't caught!

I was also back onto instrument flying and night flying. Bad weather forced flying to be cancelled one night just as I was about to start my Harvard.

On another night, there was a big flying programme on of Chipmunks and Harvards at Cranwell, Barkston Heath, Spitalgate and Digby, but the 'met. man' was again wrong in his forecast. When I got airborne at 2230 hours with Flt. Lt. Woods (Flt. Lt. Reid being away with influenza), the cloud base was quite low, but we pressed on and did circuits and bumps at Barkston Heath. The brilliant orange lead-in and lead-out lights to the runway could be clearly seen, but the Drem lighting along the runway was barely visible on the approach to land. Patches of cloud came down below normal circuit height at times and I found myself flying through cloud on instruments.

I'd almost finished flying at about midnight when I heard the air traffic controller calling 'King' – the code name being used by Mike Goodall of 60C that night. Contact had been lost with him after he'd called 'downwind' in the circuit. Some other people flying saw a flash amongst lights near Grantham, but thought it was just car headlights. I landed at Barkston Heath and sat with other Flight Cadets in the control tower crew room wondering what'd happened. The talk was that Mike might have had total electrics failure and gone back to Cranwell, which would have been normal in such circumstances. When word came through that he wasn't at Cranwell and he'd now be out of fuel, we feared the worst.

We were instructed to search for Mike using every available vehicle. I was in a bus that went almost to Sleaford and back using side roads. Mist was very close to ground level in the area. Radar hadn't picked up Mike's Harvard so full emergency procedures had been put into action including notification of the local Police. Night flying was cancelled. There was nothing else we Flight Cadets could do, but return to Cranwell for a dismal supper and bed at 0400 hours.

I was up again at 1000 hours and heard the sad news that Mike had been killed when he flew into a wood near Grantham. He could have been doing a low level circuit below the cloud and not realised he was so close to the ground, or have become disorientated in cloud, or had engine failure – I never heard the likely cause of the accident. The *Journal*, in recording Mike's death, reported that on entering the College, 'He quickly established himself as an athlete, as a promising member of his Entry and Squadron, and as a Flight Cadet of great promise.' Mike Goodall had consistently been one of the gen men. I remembered that he'd been a genial companion travelling in the same train compartment with me from London to Sandhurst. His family preferred to have a private rather than a military funeral, so only members of 60C attended his burial near London.

Sqn. Ldr. Derisley spoke to E and F Flights in Flying Wing about not getting the 'twitch' over what'd happened. I felt 60A thought this rather unnecessary – after all, we'd already experienced the trauma of Spike Heaney's death, though we were very much aware that with the loss of Mike Goodall, the original members of the Entry had fallen from 46 to 29 members.

Early that term, I qualified for a certificate that stated I'd received instruction in first-line servicing of Harvard aircraft and was considered proficient to carry out such servicing under supervision.

I made the first of two trips into Lincoln with Tony Whitwam in his car to get a folder and paper for my thesis and to see a film. Trying to find time to work on my thesis was difficult, so I was pleased when the lights out time in the Senior Mess was abolished. This enabled Flight Cadets to work all night if necessary (though I doubt that this happened). There was only a check after 2230 hours to ensure that Flight Cadets were in their rooms and not making unnecessary noise. I was also pleased when Flt. Lt. Dean told me that, having written over a third of my thesis, I'd done more on my thesis than most members of 60 Entry at that stage. Unfortunately, he was unable to get approval for me to visit the Avro works and get a practical insight into the design and construction of delta winged aircraft.

I found time to complete the delta winged Avro 707B model aeroplane and successfully fly it on a calm evening. The performance was rather sluggish, however, because the model was too heavy for the under powered Jetex engine.

One evening, Mal Dines found himself stranded in Boston without transport and spent much of the night walking the twenty-six or so miles back to Cranwell. Ted Reynolds was elected to replace me as House Member on the Mess Committee.

The main lecture hall was being redecorated in preparation for the end of term functions, so an after guest night film show had to be held in one of the ante-rooms. Though the Senior Mess and officers could barely move in the ante-room, we saw a most interesting colour film on Bomber Command wartime operations, made and presented by Air Cdre. H.I. Cozens, CB, AFC.

When the painting of the main lecture hall had been completed, meals were served there while the dining hall was redecorated. Dinner nights were cancelled until the dining hall could again be occupied. The dining hall walls were then resplendent in a delicate lime green colour with the beams and pillars in ivory. The ceiling panels were sky blue with the Tudor rosettes at the corners of each panel picked out in gold. Curtains and hangings were in maroon brocade edged with gold.

A new order stated that on supper nights, except for those on Wednesdays, Saturdays and Sundays when sports clothes were worn, lounge suits had to be worn in place of airman pattern best blue uniform. At dinner nights, the Mess President for the night (a member of the Senior Entry in the Sovereign's Squadron, standing below the Queen's Colour), had the task of saying grace before everybody sat down. Usually the grace was 'Thank God,' but on one occasion when there were no officers present, the grace was given in a rather bored voice as 'Thank Christ'. There was a stunned silence, then a buzz of discussion over this unusual event!

As a result of the Sandhurst experience, an order was promulgated that in future all members of the College would wear anklets with battledress at early morning drill. This seemed to be just another thing we had to remember to clean and wear. Laurie Jones adopted a Sandhurst way of giving rifles a brilliant shine by using methylated spirits and boot polish rather than spit and polish. He could polish his rifle in just ten minutes.

This method came in handy for the Ferris inter-squadron drill competition. There were the usual inspections and practices for the competition. Ted and I once more found ourselves doing rifle drill. The weather turned hot, so everyone changed into Short Sleeve Order. On the day of the competition, however, we were in full ceremonial dress and sweated as never before. A Squadron assembled at 0720 hours for an inspection by Sqn. Ldr. Thomas, then marched on parade at 0800 hours for another lengthy inspection by the visiting team from the RMA Sandhurst. When asked what tune the band was playing I said I didn't know. I was told it was a very famous tune and I ought to know it! (Perhaps it was the inspecting officer's regimental march past!) After all our efforts, A Squadron only came second in the competition. For a day or two afterwards, my hands were reddish with dye sweated from my unlined brown gloves.

Laurie Jones missed the Ferris because he'd been given additional light duties that kept him off drill and sport for the remainder of term, though he was able to resume flying solo. He was later to spend some of his next leave at the RAF Hospital Nocton Hall having further treatment for his knee injury.

After months of concentrated drill, the College relaxed a little with no drill for a week. I was glad of the break as a combination of drill and high jumping had given me a bruised right heel that was taking a long time to recover.

The AAA coach Mr Watt returned with more slow motion coaching films and tips. Gp. Capt. Nuttall also watched me high jumping and told me I needed to 'explode' more on take-off. My take-off was from my sore right foot, so I had difficulty in achieving heights that I knew I was capable of. I began to think that I'd miss out on the coming big athletics match against the RMA Sandhurst, the RNC Greenwich and the RNEC Manadon, particularly when told to practise the 4 x 110 yard relay for this match. Then the College athletics team played a game of basketball as a limbering up exercise, but we almost seized up from using a different set of muscles. The field events group beat the track group. We then played cricket. No scores were kept, but I bowled one of the track group and made one run! Though these activities were a great way to relax, I felt that they weren't suitable training for athletics.

A return athletics match was held with University College, Leicester, and again Cranwell won. In a match against RAF Spitalgate, I competed in the hop, step and jump for the first time. Cranwell won the match. Another return match with Loughborough College again resulted in Cranwell losing. As a spectator at the Flying Training Command sports at Cranwell Stadium, I was interested to see that the winning height in the high jump equalled my best jump.

In Law and Administration, each member of 60 Entry had to give a ten minute talk on an administration subject that'd been chosen for us. This was a way of checking what we'd absorbed before starting into the Manual of Air Force Law and Queen's Regulations. Then as part of our Weapons instruction, we harmonised the guns and camera of an old Tempest fighter at the rear of the Flight Cadets' Garage. We later moved on from fixed gun sighting to the gyro gunsight. In War Studies, we refought the Battle of the Atlantic. I was fascinated in Aerodynamics by a transparent supersonic wind tunnel about five inches long through which compressed air was passed. Shock waves could be seen forming on shapes placed in the tunnel. A hypodermic needle inserted in the tunnel acted as a pitot head. The air pressure forced mercury up a tube to record the airspeed. A cunning system enlarged the results and projected them on a screen.

While again duty Flight Cadet in Junior Entries, I caught some Cadets outside their Block after lights out in pyjamas and bare feet. They stood rigidly to attention when I approached and asked what they were doing. A Cadet replied lamely, 'I thought I'd heard a noise!' I then caught a Cadet using a torch while he wrote in bed and another on a toilet reading a logarithm book! Soon afterwards, I was also the duty Senior Flight Cadet in A Squadron. These duties seemed to come at the most awkward times.

I went to a dance at the School of Domestic Science at Leicester. There were a great variety of dances, and prizes were given in lucky spot competitions and the like. In one competition, my partner and I won packets of cigarettes. I gave mine away. On arriving back from Leicester in the early hours of the morning, I became aware that a party was still going on from an Old Cranwellians' Day at the College.

When the mid-term dance was held at the College, there was much discussion as to whether or not it was worth going to because former girlfriends could have accepted the blanket invitations sent to the local Teachers' Colleges. I decided to attend and found that Ann Maltby was also there, but we didn't dance together.

One Saturday afternoon, I was given the chance to have a ride in the College Meteor 7, but declined the offer because of a cold or hay fever. I felt sure I'd get another opportunity to fly in the College Meteor, but that never came.

The weather deteriorated and became foggy. I caught a glimpse through the murk of two huge American B36D aircraft flying slowly overhead at about 6,000 feet. Their long swept back wings had six pusher piston engines, and auxiliary jet engines were slung beneath their wings. When the Senior Entry deprived us of our aircraft once more, I found myself practising back beam standard beam approaches on the link trainers.

When airborne again, Flt. Lt. Reid had me doing Pattern Bs on instruments using a limited panel, i.e. there was no artificial horizon or direction indicator – only the altimeter, the air speed indicator, the turn and slip indicator, the vertical speed indicator, and the compass. I did ninety degree turns with two minutes between each turn, before trying loops and barrel rolls – all on limited panel. This type of flying soon became routine when we were not doing beam flying and controlled descents through cloud.

The College athletics team left Cranwell while a ceremonial parade was on and travelled by train from Grantham to Plymouth via London, Exeter and Teignmouth. A Royal Navy bus took us to a barrack block at the Royal Naval College Keyham where, from the third and top floor, we had a view along Plymouth Sound. The barrack beds were short and narrow with well tucked in bedding, so most of us had rather uncomfortable nights.

When the Sandhurst athletics team arrived, some of us joined them to go on a roundabout bus ride into the centre of Plymouth. The centre had been flattened by bombing in World War II and the large, modern and imposing buildings that'd since been built reminded me of those that I'd seen in the centre of Rotterdam. On entering a rather scruffy pub in Union Street, we were confronted by a lot of drunken sailors and women. They stopped their drinking and singing, turned and stared at us. We beat a hasty retreat, glad that we weren't in uniform. In an unofficial shooting contest at a games parlour, Cranwell beat Sandhurst. We eventually ended up in a large and modern NAAFI not far from Plymouth Hoe, and had supper before returning to Keyham.

Next morning, the Cranwell and Sandhurst teams were taken to the docks and shown over HMS *Roebuck*, a former destroyer that'd been converted into a modern anti-submarine ship. The operations room in the ship was particularly interesting as it incorporated many things that we'd heard about. We were shown how the interior of the ship could be sealed off in chemical warfare and how anti-aircraft guns could be trained and fired automatically.

The group I was in took so long on this tour that we missed going down a large modern submarine moored nearby. Those Flight Cadets who did see the interior of the submarine reported on the intricacies of the snorkel device, the cramped conditions and seeing sailors sleeping beside live torpedoes. I could see from the docks an old German submarine, ships under construction or repair and numerous small craft.

The Navy then took us to see RNEC *Manadon*, an imposing lot of buildings for some three hundred engineering officers, set in spacious grounds. Our tour missed out the educational rooms, but we were shown workshops, numerous machines and the things that the students had to make. In a hangar, Seafire, Sea Fury, Sea Hornet, Sea Hurricane, Swordfish and Wyvern aircraft were being worked upon. Stress machines, naval aero engines and propellers could also be seen.

With the weather rather warm and the tour somewhat tiring, we thought it was all a plot by the Navy to wear us out before the triangular athletics match that afternoon at the Brickfields sports ground in Devonport. When I got to the ground I complained that the high jump take-off area was very soft, but was told it was too late to do anything about it. Though two Cranwell records were broken at the meeting, I could only get third in the high jump. Two Sandhurst chaps both did 5 feet 10 inches. One of them, a slightly built Nigerian, jumped more than his own height and said he'd never before jumped higher than 5 foot 5 inches! I didn't have to run in the relay after all. Sandhurst won the match with Cranwell second and Manadon third.

After an excellent meal at a guest night that evening, the loyal toast was drunk in the Navy tradition sitting down. I think I was the only person to ask for water with which to drink the Queen's health. Waiters wearing white gloves offered everybody free cigars and cigarettes, and then apples and oranges before a padre pronounced an end of meal grace.

We moved to an ante-room where some fairly heavy drinking began. A member of the Cranwell team won the competition to drink three and a half pints of beer from a yard long glass horn. The Navy competitor was sick and the Army competitor gave up. Then some of the chaps climbed to an I-shaped beam holding up the roof, scrambled along it upside down to the centre of the room and wrote their names on the ceiling. Tiring of such antics and the ribald singing, a few of us changed into mufti and went into Plymouth to see the city lights. After going to bed that night, I was woken at 0200 hours by two Sandhurst chaps who were having trouble getting the Cranwell beer drinking champion into bed.

Needless to say, none of us was feeling too fit when we had to leave Plymouth in continuing warm weather later that morning and travel to London. RAF transport took us across London to King's Cross railway station, but we found that for some unknown reason, we'd been booked on a train that didn't leave for Grantham until 2235 hours. To fill in time, the 60 Entry members of the athletics team went to see *Malta Story* at the Odeon cinema. When we eventually left King's Cross, the Cranwell cricket and swimming teams were also on the train. On returning to Cranwell, I was told that during my absence a visiting Sandhurst sportsman had been sleeping in my bed.

With the Senior Entry away on a factory visit and all of 60A, except for me, on night flying, I had to call A Squadron on parade for the usual early morning drill. I also had to fill in for Mal as duty Senior Flight Cadet in A Squadron. There were so many of the College away for one reason or another the following Sunday that church parade had to be cancelled.

On the next night flying briefing, the weather was forecast as being clear all night. Flt. Lt. Reid, who was sitting beside me, looked out of the window and saw ground fog starting to creep up from surrounding valleys onto the south airfield. He tried unsuccessfully to attract the attention of the 'met. man', so told me to change into flying gear and wait for him in the crew room. Soon afterwards he arrived to say that night flying had been cancelled. This incident did little to give me confidence in the meteorological service.

In strong winds on another night, Flt. Lt. Reid checked me on circuits and bumps at RAF Barkston Heath before sending me solo for forty minutes of circuits – my first night solo in a Harvard.

There was some excitement in Flying Wing one day when we heard that the Duke of Edinburgh had landed a Devon on the south airfield, but he departed soon afterwards.

Then aircraft at Cranwell were grounded because a large formation of aircraft were reported to be in the vicinity. When the all-clear was given, there was a mad rush to get airborne. My Harvard wouldn't start. After an infuriating delay, Flt. Lt. Reid and I got it started and I began taxiing in the usual snake-like way towards the caravan at the take-off point. Flt. Lt. Reid said, 'I have control,' opened the throttle and, with the tail of the Harvard off the ground, headed straight for the caravan. 'Do as I say, not as I do,' he told me over the intercom. We only had time for one circuit before the next flying period began.

A cloud burst caused torrential rain to fall and hailstones covered the landscape. This didn't stop us from the next lot of night flying. I went to the night flying briefing at 2115 hours, dozed on my bed until 0030 hours, had some coffee, picked up my flying gear and caught the bus provided to take my detail to RAF Barkston Heath. I was given the responsibility of ensuring the safe arrival at Barkston of tea urns and sandwiches for the air and groundcrew on night flying duty there. I was airborne by 0200 hours with one of the E Flight instructors, Flt. Lt. J.P. Britton, and did dual circuits before being sent solo for more circuits. I then flew back to Cranwell and at 0400 hours, had my first experience of landing in the half-light of dawn.

During the night flying, Ron Edwards of 60B had a main undercarriage leg of his Harvard collapse on landing – apparently through structural failure. On two subsequent days, I returned from flying with wheel plate covers bent and half off because the retaining clips were unserviceable.

One weekend, Ron Chippindale got compassionate leave so that he could visit the parents of his girlfriend, June Spackman, and explain why she'd been sent down from Kesteven Teachers' Training College. Apparently he'd returned June to the College five minutes after the time she should have been in. On the way to see June's parents, Ron had the misfortune to drive into the back of a car that'd stopped suddenly ahead of him, so damaging both cars. June was later reinstated at Kesteven.

All the New Zealanders at the College were summoned to have tea in the guest room with Air Cdre. Wallingford (Geoff's father), who'd recently retired from being Air Member for Personnel in the RNZAF. I asked him if he knew what would happen to Ron and me on passing-out from the College. He replied that the original idea was for us to attend an Advanced Flying School in Britain before returning to New Zealand. He thought it more likely that we'd convert onto Vampires at an AFS, go to Cyprus for six months and fly Venoms with No. 14 Squadron of the RNZAF before returning home. This sounded pretty good to Ron and me.

Much of the discussion with Air Cdre. Wallingford, however, was on the possibility of the College First XV having a few games of rugby in New Zealand while on a visit to the RAAF College Point Cook during the coming leave period. (The team didn't get to New Zealand, but two members, Geoff Wallingford and Guy McLeod, were flown by the RNZAF from Australia to New Zealand so that they could see their families, later returning to Australia by commercial airliner.)

There was a lot of talk in 60 Entry as to where we'd be going when we did the customary overseas navigation flight on becoming the Senior Entry. Initially, we were told we'd be going to Greenland. When that was cancelled, the prospect was a trip to Cyprus via Malta or one to Egypt via Gibraltar. We'd be flying in Lincoln bombers from RAF Shawbury, a master airfield near Shrewsbury. On each aircraft, one Flight Cadet would be navigating, one operating the radar and one flying – under the supervision of the normal crew members, of course. The purpose of the trip included giving us some appreciation of the roles of other aircrew members. We had the first of two inoculations in preparation for going overseas. My arm became so sore I was given two days of light duties.

When 60 Entry was briefed on the overseas navigation flight, the route was confirmed as being from RAF Shawbury to Malta, Gibraltar and back to Shawbury, taking seven days. Ron, Jim and I would be in the first group of twelve Flight Cadets, flying in four Lincoln bombers. Others of 60 Entry would fly the route on our return. Tropical kit would be issued and we'd have to make arrangements for travellers cheques etc.

We were also told that we had to visit two of the British Armed Services in the leave period and our preferences were requested. I wanted to fly Vampires in the fighter/ground attack role on leaving Cranwell, so arrangements were made for me to have three days at the RAF operational fighter station of Horsham St Faith near Norwich. Similar arrangements were made for Tom Greenhill-Hooper of 60B. Ron Chippindale wanted to fly Sunderlands in the RNZAF so was told he'd be going to the Royal Naval Air Station at Culdrose where there were maritime reconnaissance and anti-submarine aircraft. Jim Brown was to accompany him. In addition to a visit to a flying station, Ron and I asked for one to the Royal Navy and were allocated three days at Portsmouth.

The timing of these trips made it difficult for us to participate in other activities during the leave, such as a survival camp in the Harz Mountains in Germany, caving in Yugoslavia, a visit to the Middlesex Regiment in Austria and a voyage in a minesweeper to Norway and the Arctic. I felt I was running out of time to do such interesting things.

When Mum read of what was planned for the next leave, she very kindly sent me another £50 to help me with my expenses.

At one of the ceremonial parades that term, Mick Armitage of 58C was awarded his Wings as he'd missed passing-out with his Entry through injuries sustained in a Harvard crash.

I heard that Tony Mallet of 61A had damaged the wing of his aircraft on a low level cross-country flight when he hit high tension power lines. Then Johnny Weaver of 59A broke his ankle in a motor bike accident, but was able to recover in time to pass-out with his Entry. Pete McKechnie of 60C survived a chop check with the new CFI (Wg. Cdr. MacDougall), but the Wing Commander took over as his flying instructor.

Laurie Jones became the first in 60 Entry to pass the flying and oral examinations for a White Instrument Rating. This meant that he could fly solo in certain weather conditions. Mal Dines also qualified, but most of 60 Entry had to wait until the next term to achieve a coveted 'White Ticket'.

The College athletics team competed against RAF Cranwell, the Appleby-Frodingham sports club and the Lincoln athletics club. I won the high jump, but Lincoln just pipped the College to win the match. The College also lost a return match with the Leicester College of Art and Technology because some of our best athletes were suffering from inoculations and couldn't compete. In rather wet conditions, I won the hop, step and jump and also the high jump. The Cranwell team members didn't have much money with them so returned to Cranwell straight after the match, stopping briefly on the way to buy some drinks and sweets.

In a return athletics match with Carre's Grammar School, the College team members were entered in events other than their normal events and still won the match. I won the long jump. The final match of the term was against the Milocarians, a team comprising officers and officer cadets from the three Armed Services. They'd come from all over Britain in a Viking aircraft. Ten of their members were Sandhurst Cadets, so the match developed into an unofficial Cranwell versus Sandhurst competition. I was beaten in the high jump by the Nigerian from Sandhurst who'd beaten me at Devonport. Though I did my best distance to date in the hop, step and jump, I only came second. Overall, the Milocarians easily beat the College. We then entertained our guests in the Fancy Goods Store until they had to head for their aircraft.

In sixteen athletic matches that term, I came first in the high jump on most occasions, and never below third. My main tactic was not to jump until I had to, so as to conserve energy and to get a psychological advantage over my opponents (who may have thought I was a good jumper!). At one meeting I jumped at only one height, winning on the third attempt after failing the first and second jumps. That was a bit too close for comfort! Sometimes I won on the count back, having had fewer jumps than my opponents. As a result, I was awarded Full Colours in Athletics by the College and invited to join the Milocarian Athletic Club.

There were three wet weather and three dry weather rehearsals for the passing-out parade at which the Duke of Edinburgh was to be the reviewing officer. We began dressed in battledress and anklets, then paraded in airman pattern best blue uniform and blue webbing, before finally rehearsing in full ceremonial dress and white webbing. I missed the first wet weather rehearsal because of night flying the previous night. In the second hangar rehearsal the USAF Exchange Officer, Major Charlson, acted as the reviewing officer. There were a few smirks in 60A after the Senior Entry had left the parade ground when the diminutive Sam Boyce was told to give the orders and march off the Cadet Wing. Ted and I were given additional coaching as

Commandant's Orderlies by the Chief GCT Instructor, Sqn. Ldr. D.G. Roberts, MM, and were issued with new aiguillettes.

Then the College and much of RAF Cranwell turned out to watch a squad of RAF Regiment airmen perform drill manoeuvres, many of which were new to the College. The squad had been on the Coronation and wore new uniforms made of officer-type material. They had their own band and performed on the new Junior College parade ground. Only about four commands were given, but we could just hear someone in their midst calling the time for each manoeuvre. Members of the College were a very critical audience, but we had to acknowledge that the squad was pretty good, even if the eyes of the squad members did tend to wander during the parade.

An announcement was made that as from the next term, the sixty members of the Equipment and Secretarial Wing of the College at RAF Digby would be merged into the three squadrons of the Cadet Wing at Cranwell. D Squadron at Digby would cease to exist. 60A would get Alan Bright and Robin Pringle, 60B Joe Vella and John Watts, and 60C Dave Woods.

Then the Commandant advised that Air Ministry approval had at last been given to each squadron having one Senior Under Officer and three Under Officers effective the next term. Thus, the rank of Flight Cadet Sergeant would follow that of Flight Cadet Corporal into oblivion.

59 and 60 Entries assembled in an ante-room to be told the 59 Entry Order of Merit and prize winners, and the 60 Entry promotions for next term.

I was thrilled to hear that the two New Zealanders in 59 Entry had done well – Jack Henderson coming second in the flying Order of Merit and first in the overall Order of Merit (winning the Queen's Medal, the Philip Sassoon Memorial Prize, the A.G. Fellowes Memorial Prize and the Air Ministry Prize for Imperial and War Studies), and Colin Loveday coming fourth in the flying Order of Merit and ninth in the overall Order of Merit. Colin later told me he was posted to RAF Worksop, a night fighter and all-weather fighter station.

In the 60 Entry promotions, Laurie Jones would become the A Squadron Senior Under Officer and Ted Reynolds, John Tucker and Robin Pringle the three Under Officers. The B Squadron Senior Under Officer would be Wally Close, and Tony Whitwam, Tom Greenhill-Hooper and John Watts the Under Officers. C Squadron would have Pete Anstee as Senior Under Officer and Alun Morgan, Dickie Hoare and Hammy Khan as the Under Officers. The promotions were about as expected except for Tom Greenhill-Hooper and Hammy Khan. The latter had received a lot of ragging all term that if he didn't pull up his socks in this and that, he'd never be promoted. The two Secretarial chaps, Pringle and Watts, were totally unknown to most of us. The remainder of 60 Entry would be promoted to the rank of Senior Flight Cadet.

Amongst the usual end of term postings, Flt. Lt. Sillars, my former flying instructor, was promoted to Squadron Leader on transfer, and the announcement was made that Sqn. Ldr. Thomas, the A Squadron Commander, would be replaced early in the next term by Sqn. Ldr. R.D.A. Smith, DFC, a member of the RAF rugby team.

The A Squadron senior year decided to hold a farewell party for Sqn. Ldr. Thomas in the Bristol Arms Hotel at Sleaford. Flt. Lt. Hall, the A Squadron Cadet Wing Officer, was also invited. The dinner wasn't up to much, probably because of the short notice given the Hotel. Sqn. Ldr. Thomas was presented with a silver plated covered dish, and two Coronation mugs for his children. For the first time, we found the doyen of the Squadron Commanders not knowing what to say!

As some solid drinking began a few home truths emerged, such as the nickname of 'Boo' for one of the Cadet Wing Officers – because he never said anything disapproving to Flight Cadets! Things became more boisterous with singing and the removal of Sqn. Ldr. Thomas's tweeds. Surprisingly, he didn't seem to mind! The party didn't get more out of hand as we all had to be back at Cranwell by 2300 hours.

With the term rapidly coming to a close, there were a thousand and one things that needed doing. I tried to swot for the end of term tests. Squadron, prize winner and sports team photos had to be taken. I borrowed a Full Colours blazer for the athletics team photo. The newly promoted Flt. Lt. Maisonpierre asked for an individual photo of me. There was my flying logbook to be made up for signature, my hair to be cut and money to be drawn from the College bank. The end of term was the busiest I'd experienced.

Ted wanted to show me the car he'd been building up from a chassis in the Flight Cadets' Garage. (The building of this Riley Special later featured in the *Journal*.) The car hadn't been painted, but Ted took me for a drive in it to see the E Flight Commander, Flt. Lt. Woods, at his home in the married patch. Ted knew Flt. Lt. Woods well, having been sailing with him, and as a result, Ted's girlfriend had been invited to stay with the Woods family for the passing-out parade and ball. Ted showed me an antique emerald ring and said he was going to get engaged at the ball. (I took this with a grain of salt as he'd been talking about getting engaged since Junior Entries.) Flt. Lt. Woods came for a ride in Ted's car, showed us the still visible foundations of the great airship hangar that once stood in the married patch area, let us admire his carefully restored former London taxi called 'Matilda', and very kindly invited us into his home for a drink.

As members of the Senior Entry were allowed to ride bicycles around Cranwell, I bought Paul Chamberlain's bike. A bike was considered essential because of the distances to be covered and the time saving involved. I called the bicycle 'Belinda', parked it in a stand at the rear of the College and later became adept at saluting when riding it.

In preparation for the passing-out parade, four Meteor 8s from No. 203 AFS practised formation aerobatics over the College, followed by the individual aerobatics of another Meteor 8. Large marquees were erected on the Orange and raised platforms were constructed by the parade ground to seat some of the expected 2,500 spectators. A saluting base for the reviewing officer and towers for film and television crews suddenly appeared.

At the final guest night there was an hour of speeches, welcoming and farewelling College staff. The new B Squadron Commander, Sqn. Ldr. E.H. Taylor, AFC, introduced himself to me as being a fellow New Zealander. Amongst the guests were eight Flight Cadets and two officers of the Luftkrigsskolen (the Royal Norwegian Air Force College).

When the 59 Entry review 'Mid Smoke at Midnight' began, that seemed to be the signal for toilet rolls to be thrown and the tweeds to be removed from some unfortunate Flight Cadets. One pair of trousers landed on the bank of lights above the stage and remained there for the rest of the evening. Several skits in the review were based on the Roman equivalent of Cranwell, 'Superna Cretinus', and included quips such as, 'Someone's being crucified down at Junior Entries – wacko, let's go and see the fun.' A rotund Adjutant (a Flight Lieutenant), complete with a large Coronation Medal, admired his reflection (dressed as a Squadron Leader) in a 'mirror' while apparently singing, 'No two people have ever been so in love'. Tears of laughter came to our eyes when the mime was repeated with the recording at half speed. On the Adjutant committing suicide, someone cried, 'There's another for the Tiber.' One of the most imaginative skits was about what it's like going instrument flying for the first time. The stage was in darkness, but a luminous control column and oxygen mask appeared in front of giant luminous instruments that floated around in a most alarming manner as a result of amusing instructor/pupil verbal exchanges.

Ron drove me in his car to the Grantham railway station to meet Betty. Heavy rain was falling and the weather prospects didn't look good for the passing-out parade the next morning. Block 78 had been cleared of Flight Cadets so that guests could be accommodated. We left Betty there and a WRAF Corporal showed her to a room. I rushed off to finish preparing my kit for the passing-out parade and do other essential jobs.

That evening, Air Chief Marshal Sir John Baker, KCB, MC, DFC, Vice-Chief of the Air Staff, presented Wings and squadron trophies to members of Nos. 59 GD(P) and 10 E & S Entries. He took particular pleasure in presenting his son Guy with his Wings.

Two hours before the passing-out parade started, people began to pour in through the main gates of the College and take up positions along the south

Figure 35. COMMANDANT´S ORDERLIES
MAY–AUGUST 1953
Flight Cadets E. (Ted) Reynolds and R.M. (Hank) Hancock (both 60A).

side of the parade ground. The weather was almost perfect. Never before had so distinguished a gathering assembled for a passing-out parade, including seven members of the Air Council and three former Chiefs of the Air Staff. The Cadet Wing was given an extra thorough inspection before marching onto the parade ground. Ted and I marched on later by the west flank to await the arrival of Marshal of the Royal Air Force His Royal Highness The Duke of Edinburgh, KG, PC, KT, GBE. The Duke had flown a Devon to Cranwell, then transferred to a Rolls-Royce limousine. He looked a distinguished figure as he stepped onto the parade ground resplendent in his RAF uniform, complete with 'scrambled egg' on the peak of his cap, aiguillettes, Wings, ribbon medals and rows of rank braid on his sleeves.

Ted and I preceded the official party to the saluting base for the fanfare and Royal Salute. During the inspection of the Cadet Wing, a photo was taken of Ted and me (Fig. 35). We'd been told that after the inspection, to go directly towards the crowd and then along to the saluting base so that the

Duke could be seen close-up by some of the spectators. When I turned to halt by a pennant at the eastern side of the saluting base, I was horrified to find that the Duke hadn't stopped at the base, but had continued to greet people and was intercepting my path! I slowed down while the official party speeded up, averting a collision. The Duke walked to the end of the seating and then returned to the saluting base. My hat was killing me and I couldn't wait for the parade to be over. After the march pasts, advance in review order and another Royal Salute, the Duke presented the 59 Entry recipients with the Sword of Honour, the Queen's Medal and the Medal of Honour before giving an inspiring address. The Queen's Colour was then marched off and the newly commissioned officers slow marched into the College. The 60 Entry Senior Under Officers took over to march off and dismiss the Cadet Wing.

As soon as Ted and I had taken our leave of the Duke, we rushed to join the remainder of 60 Entry in sewing Senior Entry gorgets onto the lapels of our uniforms. These were like our existing gorgets in that they were white with the coloured squadron stripe down the middle, but they also had gold braid on the left and right sides, and a small brass button inset near the top. I grabbed my hat and gloves and went out onto the Orange to meet my guests.

Betty was talking to my old Sunday School teacher, Miss Ronaldson! By coincidence, Miss Ronaldson, her brother and her sister-in-law, had been sitting behind Betty during the parade and when they heard Betty speaking in a Scottish accent to another spectator, they guessed they'd found Betty. Mum had obviously briefed Miss Ronaldson well! Betty looked stunning in an almost sleeveless, lemon coloured summery dress that had black buttons on the bodice. She also wore a black coloured necklace, belt and court shoes.

Miss Ronaldson leaned on a walking stick and appeared frail, but was in her usual good form. I suggested we have lunch in one of the marquees on the Orange. The NAAFI-provided lunch was cold, but of excellent quality. When someone said that Air Cdre. Kay was in the crowd and wanted to see all New Zealanders at 1400 hours, I decided to ignore the request as I wanted to show my guests around West Camp, and planned to call on the Air Commodore when next in London. Our progress around West Camp was slow. Betty listened very patiently to my commentary, having heard it all before. At 1500 hours I had to leave my guests to join 60 Entry on the parade ground.

Meantime, the Duke of Edinburgh had met College officers and their wives, planted a tree, inspected the Flying Wing, met NCOs and their wives, had lunch with other VIPs in the College, made a short tour of the library, hall of fame and memorial chapel, met the most long serving College servants and signed the visitors' book.

The Duke, accompanied by the most senior of the VIPs, then came onto the parade ground and the 60 Entry Senior Under Officers and Under Officers were presented to him. He then chatted with all of the Entry and told a few tall stories. We crowded around him while watching the Meteor aerobatic display and having our photographs taken. One of these photos, which included me, was later published in the *Journal*. We then gave him three cheers (plus an unofficial one for the Tiber!) as he departed for his Devon.

At the conclusion of the day's ceremonies a commemorative tree was planted by Marshal of the Royal Air Force The Viscount Trenchard, whose portrait hung in the main entrance hall of the College. I was interested to see this elderly retired officer, walking with the assistance of a cane, as he was well known as 'The father of the Royal Air Force'.

After the Ronaldsons had left, I took Betty to the billiard room for tea before returning her to Block 78. I changed into sports gear and helped 60 and 64 Entries put up the decorations for the ball that evening. I had the job of wiring up table lamps in the main lecture hall and converting the hall into a lounge. The lamps operated off one electrical connection. Luckily the fuse held when I switched the lamps on! On the stage of the main lecture hall an 'aircraft' was constructed out of all sorts of bits and pieces. At best, it could be called a beer barrel special!

The eastern end of the dining hall was covered with screens and painted to resemble a bridge. Water below the bridge cascaded down into a pool. Luminous paint and concealed lighting made it look quite realistic. A bandstand was built in the north-west corner of the hall and surrounded with flowers.

The Fancy Goods Store became a bar and was decorated with posters from current London shows. Suitable drawings and lighting were put into the Junior Ante-room to make it the Devil's Bar. The Senior Ante-room was filled with surrealist art work and wire models (including one of an unknown Flight Cadet on restrictions) on which one's imagination could run riot. The Senior Entry Ante-room and the billiard room were set up as supper places. After three hours of hard work, I had a bath and dressed for the ball.

Betty wore the same white gown as at the previous ball, but with a Chinese embroidered jacket. The jacket was soon abandoned as we danced the evening away. We ate some of the continuous supper and went outside to watch a fireworks display on the Orange. The display was similar to that of a year earlier and ended with '59 Entry' outlined in fire.

I eventually got to bed about 0400 hours, but was up again by 0730 hours to go with other members of 60 Entry and have a second inoculation for our overseas trip. Unfortunately, the doctor on duty was not the one who'd arranged the appointment, and he refused to give the inoculations as they'd be earlier than was normal. He gave us instead, notes explaining the situation so that we could get the inoculations from a local RAF station while we were on leave.

60 and 64 Entries then set about clearing up after the ball. This task had been done on previous occasions by College servants, but somebody had decided to change that. The job was finished by 1130 hours, so Betty and I caught a chartered bus for Grantham. We had time to have lunch in the café of the Granada cinema before boarding a train for London. I had so much kit with me that poor Betty had to cope with her own suitcase. I'd already got Charlie, my batman, to post my tropical kit and typewriter to Aberdeen. (I had the misguided idea that I'd have time during my leave to start typing my half finished thesis!)

I sank into a seat on the train, held Betty's hand, glad to be going on six weeks leave, and began to realise the implications of now being in the Senior Entry. I couldn't be chopped now – or could I? Little did I know the trials and tribulations that were still to confront me in my final term at Cranwell!

CHAPTER 17

Final Leave

BETTY HAD NEVER BEEN TO LONDON. I wanted to show her some of the sights before she had to return to Aberdeen University. Since we'd met, she'd missed quite a lot of lectures and study through visiting Cranwell and going out with me. We stayed at 120 Lexham Gardens.

In the two days we had together, we wandered beside the Serpentine in Hyde Park, explored the Science Museum and window-shopped along the main routes of the West End. A photographer took our pictures as we fed the pigeons in Trafalgar Square. We came upon the Billingsgate fish market and saw men wearing flat-topped hats carrying stacks of wicker baskets on their heads. Large blocks of ice lay melting amongst the trays of fish in the open warehouses. The smell of the place was discouraging, so we didn't linger.

Betty wore a tight fitting tartan dress that hindered our progress. I was used to striding about London and had to slow down to her pace. We looked in the visitors' book at New Zealand House to see if there was any name that I knew. I decided not to visit Air Cdre. Kay after all. We were tired and, as rain began to fall, went to see the film *Lili* at the Empire cinema and later our first 3-D film, *Sangaree*, at the Plaza cinema. Wearing wire and celluloid glasses to get the 3-D effect was certainly a new, though uncomfortable experience.

On arrival at King's Cross railway station, we were interested to see carriages of the new 'Elizabethan' train that had recently been in the news. Unfortunately, we couldn't get sleepers on 'The Aberdonian', so we sat and talked for most of the long journey north. Betty insisted on me having breakfast at her home before I went out to the Rundles' at Stoneywood.

Only Cousin Lella, Alice and Francis were at the Rundles' place as the rest of the family were away on holiday. Cousin Lella treated me as an honoured guest and wouldn't let me help in the kitchen, so I left her fussing there and assisted Francis in constructing his latest model aeroplane. We then went to see two control-line model aircraft having a dogfight, each trying to cut with its propeller a streamer trailing from the model in front.

I cycled to the RAF station at Dyce to have the second inoculation that was required before I went overseas. The RAF doctor wasn't available so I was included in a sick parade going to a civilian doctor at Bucksburn. The latter didn't have the right inoculation! I was then sent back to Dyce where the medical staff tried unsuccessfully to locate an NCO who was qualified to give inoculations. I was running out of time before my train left Aberdeen. A dash to one of the big hospitals in Aberdeen solved my problem and I caught the train with just minutes to spare.

The train seemed to be full of airmen and, without a seat, I had to sit on a suitcase in the corridor all the way to Perth. The inoculation began to hurt as I filled in time at Perth looking at a fair in a park near the railway station. The next train took me through Glasgow in the early hours of the morning – this not being the right time to see Glasgow! I arrived in Crewe and had another long wait before getting a train to Shrewsbury. A bus took me to RAF Shawbury by 0900 hours. After a late breakfast at the officers' mess, I fell asleep in my room.

At 1300 hours, I joined the first party of 60 Entry members for the briefing on our Mediterranean trip. The weather was very warm with a strong wind blowing, so having to wear battledress during the briefing rather than tropical kit made me feel most uncomfortable. John Maitland, John McEntegart and I would be flying in Lincoln 'V' for Victor. In addition to the pilot, engineer, signaller and three groundcrew, our navigation lecturer Flt. Lt. R. Colbeck would be flying with us. I was detailed as the navigator on the first leg to Malta, so had to draw from Stores a navigator's bag and equipment. Dinghies, Mae Wests and parachutes were issued and our oxygen masks were tested. We were then given numerous plotting, radio aids and general purpose maps for each leg of the trip, and told to record on the maps information such as direction finding stations along the routes.

Next day, we were shown over our Lincoln bomber, taken to a radar hut to see the latest Gee unit (called a universal indicator), and shown over the navigation museum. The latter contained hundreds of fascinating instruments from many countries of the world. We went to bed early as we had to be up by 0630 hours the following morning for our flight.

After the usual meteorological briefing, flight planning and passing through Customs, the engines of 'V' for Victor were started, but radio transmissions were found to be poor. The engines were shut down and the radio equipment was checked. The pilot, Flt. Lt. Richards, concluded that the control tower transmitters were the problem so we eventually got airborne and headed for Sète (on the southern coast of France) and then Malta.

The noise in the Lincoln was terrific and I wondered if I could navigate in such a din for over seven hours without getting a headache. The pilot climbed to 9,500 feet and levelled off, flying at an indicated airspeed of 160 knots. I was too busy with information from the signaller, Gee fixes and automatic air plots to think about the scenery we were flying over. Flt. Lt. Richards had 'George,' the automatic pilot, flying the aircraft and called me to look at a marvellous French chateau passing below. I didn't see anything more until we passed within a mile of Cape Teulada on the southern tip of Sardinia. At that time, we were out of Gee range and one of the signaller's bits of equipment went unserviceable. Flt. Lt. Colbeck then assisted in the navigation by taking sun fixes. I watched the coast of Sicily and the small island of Pantelleria pass by on the H2S radar.

We started letting down to 1,500 feet on the approach to Malta, but ran into cumulo-nimbus clouds, heavy rain and bumpy conditions. The wing tips and four engines of the Lincoln flexed alarmingly in the turbulence. When we were once more in clear air, everyone changed into khaki shirts, shorts and socks. The air was definitely humid. Flt. Lt. Richards took over from 'George' and entered the Malta approach lane. I was able to stand behind him in the cockpit and watch as we flew over the island of Gozo towards RAF Luqa on the island of Malta. The land was fascinating – terraced rocky ground with reddish soil, stone walled fields that appeared barren except for cactuses, and a few trees and limestone buildings. The landing at Luqa gave me the feeling that if we overshot the runway, we'd be in the Grand Harbour at Valletta.

Leaving our flying gear in the Lincoln, we stepped out onto the tarmac in scorching sunshine and sweated while waiting for the last two Lincolns

Figure 36. Author and Lincoln bomber at Luqa, Malta, August 1953.

containing members of 60 Entry. An airman photographed us (Fig. 36). At the control tower building we changed some of our money. I found that English coins were accepted on Malta, but English pound notes had to be exchanged for Maltese pound notes.

At the Transit Officers' Mess, we were just in time for dinner. The corrugated iron and stone building looked very temporary, little better than the Quonset huts of the airmen's quarters nearby. We looked at two souvenir and general goods shops in the Mess before moving outside into cooler air (Fig. 37). A few Flight Cadets went swimming in Valletta, but Tom Greenhill-Hooper and I decided to have a look at the aircraft on the tarmac – Viking airliners of British European Airways, Canberra and Lincoln bombers, Hastings transports and Shackleton Mks 1 and 2 and Neptune maritime reconnaissance aircraft. Having never seen the last before, we inspected the wing-tip tanks, the Leigh lights, radar scanners and other things of interest before climbing aboard one of them. A Sergeant appeared and asked who we were. Satisfied with our explanation, he went away. Night fell rapidly about 1930 hours. We watched a civilian York transport aircraft land on the flare-path and start refuelling. As we wandered back to the Mess, fireworks went off beyond the perimeter of the airfield.

Tom, John Gratton and I shared the same room. We tried to sleep under dusty mosquito nets, but the air was too humid. After midnight, some drunken

Figure 37. At Officers' Mess Luqa, Malta, August 1953: L-R: Ron Chippindale (60B), John Gratton (60B), John Maitland (60B) (Seated), Tony Whitwam (60B), Dave Vickers (60C), Chris Taylor (60C), 'Bulldog' Drummond (60C) (Behind), John McEntegart (60A), Jim Brown (60B), Ron Edwards (60B), and Tom Greenhill-Hooper (60B).

Flight Cadets arrived noisily in the room next door. Someone turned off the main electrical switch to quieten them down.

We woke to find rain falling – a most unusual occurrence in the middle of a Maltese summer. 60 Entry seemed to be jinxed by bad weather! We'd been looking forward to swimming at St Paul's Bay and touring the mainland.

Instead, we were taken by bus into Valletta and given a short time to look for bargains in the small shops that crowded the narrow streets. Then we were driven to see the air traffic control centre for the Malta area. I caught glimpses of the Grand Harbour, two huge floating docks and numerous ships of all sorts and sizes. The air traffic control centre was underground and similar to what we'd seen at RAF Langtoft. I was sweating in spite of the air conditioning and glad to get out into the fresh air again, even if we did emerge in the middle of a tropical rain shower. With no coats, we hurried onto our bus. Maltese people huddled in doorways and gazed at the muddy water cascading down the narrow, sloping, stony streets. Our bus driver lost his way and got the bus stuck between stone walls at a sharp bend in the road. Eventually we reached a gun emplacement on a headland near the entrance to the Grand Harbour. In light warm rain, we had a hurried look at a six inch gun and its radar, were shown how to load the gun and tried 'sinking' an aircraft carrier that happened to be passing.

Back at Luqa, we were briefed on the next leg of our flight to Gibraltar. An early start had to be made the following morning, as in summer almost everything at Gibraltar closed down by 1300 hours. The leg would take about 5½ hours. After the briefing, we were free to do as we liked.

Most of us caught a local bus into Valletta to go shopping again. Such buses appeared to be museum pieces that departed when full, or according to the opinion of the occupants. All the vehicles I saw seemed to have horrible sounding horns. When tired of shopping, we had a very nice dinner on the balcony of a hotel overlooking a square, and watched some British Army guards marching up and down in front of an important building. When we tried to board a local bus to return to Luqa, the bus was full, so eight of us crammed into a taxi, beat the driver down in the fare he was asking, turned up the volume of his radio and headed back to the Mess. We went straight to bed in preparation for an 0400 hours wake-up call the next morning.

I was the H2S radar operator on the leg to Gibraltar. This meant getting bearings and distances to pass on to the navigator. Flt. Lt. Colbeck kept a close eye on what each of us Flight Cadets was doing. We flew to Pantelleria then in a straight line over Tunisia and Algeria to Gibraltar. The barren hills along the North Africa coast were interspersed by the occasional green valley. Primitive huts could be seen, but on one hill were some very nice looking European-style mansions. When not operating the radar, I stood behind the pilot's seat and admired the view. Tunis and Algiers could be clearly seen.

Flt. Lt. Richards let me fly the Lincoln for twenty minutes from the co-pilot's seat. When trimmed, the aircraft handled very nicely, but turning required some strength and a slightly different technique to what I'd been used to in a Harvard. I was told to call up Algiers air traffic control and say that we were passing out of their zone. The Algiers reply was so distorted that we couldn't make out what was said. I had time on this leg to have my packed lunch – sandwiches, two packets of chocolate and sweet tea.

As we flew around the impressive 1,396 foot high rock of Gibraltar I took a photo of the water catchment side, and stared at the town and harbour on the other side and the enormous runway jutting out into the sea across the isthmus to Spain. We landed safely, changed our English and Maltese notes into Gibraltarian notes, went by bus to the airmen's mess for a late meal and then to the officers' mess at the edge of the harbour. Our accommodation in a multi-storeyed block was fairly basic. There were again three of us to a room. As soon as we could we had a swim in the tepid water of the harbour. Sunbathing proved to be our undoing, however, as most of us ended up getting rather sunburnt.

Then two Old Cranwellians, Fg. Offs. Jevons (formerly 54A) and Taylor, took us off to the bazaars in the main street of Gibraltar. New cars competed with pedestrians in the narrow streets. Shopkeepers, many waving fans to try and keep cool, accosted us on all sides to buy their wares. We were told that some 22,000 people lived within a small area on The Rock. They could speak English, but their native tongue was a Gibraltarian version of Spanish. I noticed that a lot of the older people wore black clothes. There seemed to be an extraordinary number of beautiful girls around, no doubt of mixed race descent.

Unfortunately we had to go to a cocktail party in the Mess that evening put on by the Air Officer Commanding RAF Gibraltar, Air Cdre. C.F. Chilton, CB (an Old Cranwellian), in honour of the British Permanent Under Secretary of State for Air. Our sunburn hurt and we were hot, even outside on a floodlit terrace sitting on the harbour sea-wall. Quite a number of us, including the ladies who were present, drank numerous glasses of iced orange juice.

Immediately after breakfast the next morning, three of us cadged a ride on a fire launch to go out of the harbour and have a look at the P&O liner *Orcades* and other big ships anchored in the roads. Gibraltarians in dinghies were trying to sell things to passengers on board the ships.

Then the British Army put us in VIP jeeps and gave us a guided tour of the restricted area of The Rock. We were driven up narrow, steep, winding roads above the town through trees singing with insects, before entering The Rock and driving along Fossway, the main road through The Rock. Our driver said there were about forty-five miles of roads in the The Rock, yet only two per cent of The Rock had been tunnelled. The air in the tunnels seemed pure with no draughts. We were shown enormous concrete-lined rooms, the largest excavated caverns in the world containing workshops that could make just about anything, and huge generators for the provision of electricity. Electric lighting in some parts of The Rock had only just been installed.

At Old St Michael's Cave, said to be one of the most beautiful natural caves in the world and unique in many ways, we were shown the hole to New St Michael's Cave – discovered when a workman doing some excavating fell eighty feet into the Cave. Old St Michael's Cave had a concrete floor and still contained the dripping remains of an emergency hospital built in World War I. The 2,000 year old caves were certainly awe inspiring. We heard the legend about how apes had come to Gibraltar through the caves when Gibraltar was an island, but no one had been able to find a passage from the caves to Spain.

We emerged from The Rock at Jock's Lookout and, over a sheer drop, could see the runway far below and La Linea just across the border in Spain. Then on a flat area called Princess Ann's near the top of The Rock, we were shown around a number of enormous 9.2 inch calibre guns. At the foot of a radio tower, we came upon the famous Gibraltarian apes. They were being fed carrots and plums (their individual food allowance being 4½d a day). Though we were melting with the heat, we watched the apes and listened to the story that if the apes left Gibraltar, the British would also leave. We looked down at the harbour and across to Algeciras in Spain, then down the very steep slope of the water catchment area and over the Strait of Gibraltar to Spanish Morocco. What a view!

We were keen to cross the border into Spain and visit La Linea, but our request was declined as some visitors from Gibraltar had recently caused trouble there.

In the afternoon, Fg. Off. Jevons and Taylor again took us in hand. They drove us around to Sandy Bay on the scarp side of The Rock for a swim. The Bay wasn't very sandy, but lots of families were there enjoying themselves. I took precautions not to get more sunburnt. The water catchment area towering above us looked very impressive.

After another dip in the harbour that evening, we went off rather late to the Assembly Rooms, the best night club in town. Unfortunately, the usual Spanish cabaret wasn't performing that night, but a very good band from Madrid played with great gusto. The dancing was outdoors under coloured lights, so I chose the prettiest girl I could find and danced to the tune, 'Blue Tango' – at least I tried to dance, since the crowded floor only permitted rhythm dancing. For the remainder of the time I tried to keep cool sipping cold drinks while watching the more exotic dances. Though most of the people there were about my own age, I was surprised by the number of quite old people (chaperons?) sitting around the edge of the dance floor.

We had a slow start the next morning – Sunday. Everybody, except Ron Edwards who somehow got left behind, went off for a cruise in a high speed RAF launch. After looking at a newly arrived ship surrounded by Gibraltarians in their dinghies, we sped around Europa Point to the far side of The Rock to look for a Lincoln bomber that had crashed into the sea at the end of the runway a year or so earlier. We didn't find it, but watched fishermen in small boats drawing in miles of nets to encircle tunny fish. A large liner could be seen approaching Gibraltar harbour, so we made a dash in the launch back to the harbour to see it. Salt spray wet us as we rounded Europa Point and came into wind. The liner was Italian – very rakish looking and modern.

After this outing, a siesta was called for. Later I walked to the tarmac area on the isthmus and photographed a British Overseas Airways Corporation Rapide used for flights to Morocco, and *Sir Walter Raleigh*, a British European Airways Elizabethan aircraft – said to be the most beautiful aircraft ever designed. In the evening, most of us went to the Naval Trust Cinema and saw *Five Stories* by O. Henry.

Breakfast and briefing were early the next morning as we had to be airborne by 0700 hours. I wasn't allocated any particular duties on the seven-hour flight back to England, so I went aft and sat in the rear gunner's turret. The position was certainly a lonely one. Occasionally I looked over my shoulders to make sure the tail of the Lincoln was still there. Vibrations in the aircraft seemed to be exaggerated so far behind the centre of gravity. There wasn't much to look at as we were above cloud most of the way and flew around the coast of Spain and Portugal. (We weren't allowed to fly over these countries at that time.) I saw Capes Roca and Finisterre, but spent much of the time reading just about anything readable on the aircraft.

I moved forward to the bomb aimer's position to do some aerial photography when we flew over the Scilly Isles at 5,000 feet. I then sat in the front gunner's turret as we passed over Lands End and Wales, before moving to a safer position by the wing main spar for the landing at RAF Shawbury. We were soon through Customs, handing in our safety and other equipment, enjoying a hot meal and answering the questions of a rather scruffy looking reporter from a news agency. (The only published article on 60 Entry's trip I saw was that by Nigel MacNicol, whose 'Popping down to the Med.' later appeared in the College *Journal*.)

Tom Greenhill-Hooper and I had got the permission of the Wing Commander Flying at Shawbury (while he travelled to the Mediterranean with us) to stay overnight at Shawbury and fly to RAF Horsham St Faith the next day in one of the Shawbury Anson aircraft. Several ATC cadets attending a camp at Shawbury came with us just for the experience. Tom and I did map reading during the flight.

On landing at Horsham St Faith, Tom and I were met by two Old Cranwellians – Fg. Off. John Parker (formerly 55C) and Plt. Off. Nigel Wickman (formerly 56B). They told us there were a number of Old Cranwellians at the station, some of whom we'd heard of or knew by sight. When we were introduced to the Wing Commander Flying, Wg. Cdr. R.D. Yule, DSO, DFC and Bar (formerly April 1938 Entry, A Squadron), I discovered that he was from Invercargill, New Zealand, had been a boarder at my secondary school, the Timaru Boys' High School, and had last visited the school when I'd been a pupil there. I remembered having read about him in Pierre Clostermann's book, *The Big Show*. He arranged for Tom and me to be attached to one of the two operational fighter squadrons at Horsham St Faith – Tom to No. 74 Squadron and me to No. 245 Squadron. We were then taken to the officers' mess. Though sharing a room in the mess, Tom and I considered ourselves lucky not to be in one of the temporary huts that were occupied by so many of the officers.

After the 0815 hours 'met.' briefing the next morning, John Parker introduced me to the twenty-five or so pilots of 245 Squadron. They were a cheerful bunch and swapped stories around the Coke and chocolate stocked bar in the crewroom before a briefing was held and they left to fly their Meteor 8 single-seater jet fighters.

I was then taken to where the order was given for the Meteors to scramble and watched formations of three aircraft take-off in quick succession. As one of John Parker's responsibilities was that of Intelligence Officer, he showed me around the intelligence hut. At the safety section, I watched dinghies and survival kits being packed and was fitted out with equipment for my first flight in a jet aircraft.

Flt. Lt. W.H. Cadamy, an exceptional pilot and a former Central Flying School instructor, showed me around a Meteor 7 before installing me in the rear cockpit. I noted there were no ejector seats – unlike the Meteor 8s. He kept talking to me so that I knew what was going on. We began using pure oxygen as soon as we started up and taxied to the end of the runway. The undercarriage was raised immediately on becoming airborne and we climbed steeply at 4,000 f.p.m. to 30,000 feet. I was given control and tried turning, stalling and a few simple aerobatics. Very little movement was required on the controls compared with a Harvard, so initially I over-controlled a lot. The Meteor was very nice to handle even though a moderate rate of turn required a lot of bank and the G forces were quite high. The rate of roll was phenomenal.

Flt. Lt. Cadamy asked me where Norfolk was as he wanted to divert my attention while throttling back one engine. I could see the Norfolk Broads like millponds far below and so replied promptly. We then flew asymmetrically and he showed me the critical speed and some related things. On full power again, he demonstrated maximum rate turns going in opposite directions, a high speed stall and a high speed run before doing some of the more difficult aerobatics.

I began feeling hot though I knew the cockpit temperature was at a comfortable level – well above the freezing temperatures outside. The whine of the engines seemed very remote. I was beginning to feel squeamish.

Flt. Lt. Cadamy realised I'd become rather quiet so made a maximum rate descent. With dive brakes out we came down almost vertically at Mach .82. The indicated air speed was about 300 knots, but our true airspeed was probably more like 500 to 600 knots. The altimeter unwound so fast that it was hardly worth looking at, so I concentrated on clearing my ears. In true fighter style, we beat up the runway at Horsham St Faith, peeled off in the circuit direction, lowered the undercarriage and continued the usual checks as we turned onto the final approach to land. The speed and height of approach was vastly different to what I was used to, and Flt. Lt. Cadamy didn't help my apprehension when he pointed out the wreckage of a Meteor 7 on farm land just short of the runway, in which two pilots from RAF Coltishall had died along with some two hundred chickens.

We touched down safely. Flt. Lt. Cadamy opened up the throttles again and we went around for another circuit. On the second and final landing he kept the nose of the Meteor high for as long as possible to let the aircraft act as an air brake. The fifty minutes of exhilarating flying I'd experienced just reinforced my desire to become a jet fighter pilot.

In the days that followed, I wasn't given the opportunity to fly again, but I participated as much as possible in the routine of 245 Squadron. The fighter pilots often 'bounced' other aircraft they came upon and took cine film of their 'attack'. The films were then viewed by everyone and assessed to determine whether or not the 'enemy' had been 'shot down'. USAF Sabres were often the victims of such attacks.

I also watched the procedures for air-to-air firing. A Meteor would take-off towing a banner about thirty feet long and six feet wide, with the banner width weighted so that it flew vertically. Pairs of Meteors would follow and, over the North Sea, fire their 20 mm bore cannons at the banner. The different coloured bullets of each aircraft left coloured holes in the banner, and these holes were later counted when the banner was dropped on the airfield. Flt. Lt. Nicholls, one of the Flight Commanders who'd shot down a Mig in Korea and damaged another, achieved a 31 per cent hit rate on one of these exercises. This was considered to be acceptable, as achieving a high score was quite difficult.

Classified documents were distributed before a briefing on Operation

Momentum. The Squadron was to be put on a high state of alert for an exercise during which the airfield could be attacked. I assisted in erecting tents on the airfield in which the Squadron would live during the exercise. Some of the Meteors were placed at runway readiness, i.e. the pilots sat in their aircraft on the runway plugged into starting equipment and the operational radio frequency waiting for last minute instructions before starting their engines and taking-off.

Tom and I were driven to Bawburgh just west of Norwich where there appeared to be a farm house amongst trees, but it turned out to be the guardhouse for the underground headquarters of the eastern sector of Fighter Command. The complex looked very similar to those we'd seen at RAF Langtoft and Malta. We were introduced to the Air Commodore in charge.

One evening, the Squadron decided to relax at a Folies Bergère-type show called *Peep-a-Boo* at the Hippodrome in Norwich. I was invited to be present, along with the wives and girlfriends of the Squadron members. I was amused by the remarks made by the latter about the partially clad showgirls.

All too soon, Tom and I had to leave Horsham St Faith. After making our farewells, we were driven to Norwich, caught a train to London and went our separate ways. I got a sleeper on 'The Aberdonian' to stay again with the Rundles.

Leslie Rundle, having attained second class honours in science at Aberdeen University, told me he'd been invited to continue his studies, but had decided to accept a position with ICI at Grangemouth. We walked several times to Dyce to see his friend Jimmy Donald who had just become a qualified doctor.

I wrote some more of my thesis and did research at Aberdeen Library, but my heart wasn't in the work. I wanted to be out with Betty. We took a bus to Oldmeldrum to see Barra Castle, once occupied by an ancestor of mine. The Castle was about a mile out of town on the road to Inverurie. We walked right past it as it didn't look like a castle. I'd expected to see imposing battlements and towers set on a hill. Instead, the Castle was a three storeyed, stone, U-shaped building that had steeply slated roofs, tall chimneys, and two low, circular towers with conical slated roofs at the corners of one wing of the building. Set amongst flat farm land, the Castle had obviously been a substantial defended farm house when it was built in the seventeenth century. If its driveway and garden were anything to go by, the Castle looked rather neglected.

As we entered the cobbled inner courtyard, the barking of a dog brought a woman out to see us. We introduced ourselves and I tried to explain my connection with the Castle. The woman said she hadn't been long there and didn't know much about the history of the place or former owners. As she was feeding a child, she offered to have a young girl show us over the Castle. We gratefully accepted this generous offer.

The girl showed us her room in which a ghost known as The Green Lady was thought to have appeared from time to time. Nearby was a room containing an ornate, four poster canopied bed. (Mum had always told me that her Aunt Mary Stuart Reid had once slept in such a bed at the Castle.) The interior walls of the Castle were of white plaster or had wooden panels with faded blue paint on them. One wall panel was locked and obviously led to something. The young girl thought it was the entrance to a tunnel that went to the top of a low hill. Old paintings, drawings and prints hung on the walls of a rather nice drawing room. The furniture looked antique. We were even shown the bathroom, then led up the spiral stone staircase of one of the towers to a bare, heavily beamed room at the top. The other wing of the Castle was closed off.

After thanking the young girl and the woman we'd met, Betty and I walked slowly back to Oldmeldrum, talking about this little bit of my family's history.

My remaining time in Aberdeen passed all too quickly. Betty and I went ice skating and swimming, danced at the Students' Union, dined out, walked and generally mooned around.

I travelled to London and then to Portsmouth, meeting on the train some of the other forty-three Flight Cadets who, like me, were on attachment to the Royal Navy. Ron Chippindale arrived at Portsmouth by car. He and I discovered that we were the only members of the Senior Entry in the Cranwell party. Ron was billeted in the Royal Marines' barracks, while I was given a cabin in HMS *Boxer* – a rather large, former tank landing-craft that'd been converted into a radar training ship. My cabin was below deck at the stern. A stretcher had been put into the limited floor space for another Flight Cadet, but luckily for me he didn't turn up. Though there was no porthole and the fresh air ventilator didn't work, I found the cabin comfortable enough.

On arrival, the Cranwell party changed into mufti, had dinner and went ashore to see the sights. We strolled past Nelson's *Victory* (all lit up in its own dry dock), the aircraft carrier *Indomitable*, and the most modern battleship in the fleet, the *Vanguard*. On leaving the dockyard I came across Ron, so went with him for a walk and supper.

Next morning the Cranwell party was taken to HMS *Vernon*, a land-based torpedo and anti-submarine school, for a naval exercise. I was put in charge of two submarines, two destroyers, two frigates, a convoy of transport ships and a Shackleton maritime reconnaissance aircraft. I was located on one of the destroyers and, with the captain of the destroyer, had to cope with whatever calamity the naval officer directing the exercise sent our way. A master plot of the action was shown on a translucent screen. From surrounding cabins fitted with plotting boards and other equipment, the Cranwell party did quite well – after allowance had been made for things that they were not expected to know. A post-mortem concluded a thoroughly enjoyable exercise.

After lunch, a launch took us across Portsmouth Harbour to Gosport. At the land-based submarine depot and navigation school, HMS *Dolphin*, we were shown a film on the principles of submarine warfare before splitting into groups and going down two submarines. The interior of the submarine I was in was very hot and, with little room in which to stand, I couldn't see much of what was being shown to us. Back on shore again, another film explained how submarines could be used in warfare. Then men in a water-filled tank demonstrated how to use submarine escape gear. Nearby, a 100 foot tower was about to be commissioned for more advanced underwater escape exercises.

We had tea and returned by launch to HMS *Boxer*. Every sort of ship seemed to be in the harbour – massive ocean-going tugs, scores of warships such as HMS *Jamaica*, and even an old paddle steamer tugboat. There were inlets everywhere with naval sheds, cocooned ships, dry docks, huge cranes and many other things of interest. A Skyraider, a Beaver and several helicopters flew overhead. During the evening, some of us went to Southsea Pier to have a look around.

That night a seaman slung his hammock outside the door of my cabin as he said it was the quietest place on the ship! I had difficulty agreeing with him when an engine that kept throbbing all the time changed pitch just as I was going off to sleep. I considered the seaman my personal bodyguard!

Next morning, the Captain of HMS *Boxer* and other officers lectured us on subjects such as the supply organisation of a ship. I had great difficulty in concentrating because of the dryness of the subjects and the constant noise of a motor in the lecture room blowing air down a tube to repairmen several decks below. I was glad when we began a tour of certain parts of the ship.

In the afternoon we were shown over the cruiser *Sheffield* along with a number of Wrens and ATC personnel. On being piped aboard, we saluted the quarterdeck and were then formally welcomed. There was little time to see the cruiser as we also had to make a visit to the frigate *Carisbrooke Castle*. Our tour of HMS *Victory* was more interesting, though we had to queue for ages with civilians to get aboard. Our sailor guide rattled off parrot-fashion, details about Lord Nelson and the Battle of Trafalgar, showing us the brass marker on the deck where Nelson had been wounded, and below decks the brass marker where he'd died. The sailor took off his cap and knelt reverently on one knee as he recounted Nelson's last moments and the famous words, 'Kiss me Hardy.' I had no difficulty imagining what life must have been like on the sailing ship – I was bent almost double between decks!

On our way back to HMS *Boxer*, we came upon a crowd watching a stretcher being lowered from the biggest hammer head crane in the area.

Apparently a painter had broken both legs and an ankle in machinery 130 feet above the ground.

In the evening, Robin Holmes of 61A and I went ice skating in Southampton. We had a most enjoyable time, but the slow train journeys caused us to arrive back at Plymouth after midnight.

The refit of HMS *Boxer* being complete, the ship went to sea for a day on engine and anchor trials. We had to line the decks while leaving and entering harbour, coming to attention when the bosun's whistle sounded while we passed other ships. The sea was choppy and some Flight Cadets became seasick. Most of us went to the square bow to be in the fresh air, but spray coming over the bow wet a number of the Flight Cadets. Unfortunately, more lectures and another tour of the ship had been scheduled for us. We were shown the radar training rooms and the officers' and crews' quarters. On returning to Portsmouth, the flat-bottomed *Boxer* was ignominiously towed backwards to its berth by three tugs – one being the paddle steamer I'd seen earlier.

Most of us rushed ashore to waiting buses and caught the train to London by the skin of our teeth. I was soon relaxing in the comfort of Overseas League House, glad that I'd chosen the Air Force for a career and not the Navy.

I'd four days to fill in before returning to Cranwell. Shopping was high on the priority list as I wanted to improve my wardrobe before returning home. After a good browse around men's shops, I ordered a tailor-made sports suit and a dinner jacket, and bought several things that were in fashion at the time including a Parachute Regiment tie, a corduroy cap and yellow knitted gloves. (When Jim Brown later saw me wearing the gloves, he looked me up and down and said disapprovingly, 'Spiv!') I also shopped in the bookshops along Charing Cross Road, including the aeronautical section of the famous Foyles Bookshop. One of my long walks around London took me through Horse Guard's Parade where various aircraft were being assembled for the coming Battle of Britain Day.

I relaxed by going to the Royal Festival Hall and saw excerpts from three ballets, one of which starred the well-known dancer, Anton Dolin. Then I joined a mile long queue at the Empire Pool at Wembley to see *Chu Chin Chow on Ice*. The show and supporting acts were most impressive with magnificent costumes and spectacular skating and lighting. I also thoroughly enjoyed seeing the films *Roman Holiday* and *The Sword and the Rose*.

During a brief call at RNZAF Headquarters in London, I found Sqn. Ldrs. Furlong and Gavin talking together, so I plied them with questions that Ron and I had compiled. There was still no word about what would happen to Ron and me after leaving Cranwell. I checked such things as, how we'd be paid the money that was being withheld while we were at Cranwell, and what pay we'd get as Pilot Officers including flying pay, clothing allowance and marriage allowance. I was advised to purchase one of the new RAF beltless greatcoats before leaving Britain.

When I rang Cousin Jennifer to invite her and Robert to my passing-out parade, she was still involved in the filming of *The Gay Dog* and couldn't be certain about what they would be doing in three to four months time.

I was able to attend another service at St Martin-in-the-Fields. The re-decoration of the church in cream, white and gilt gave the interior a clean, airy, spacious look and helped emphasise the beautiful plaster work rather than the dark woodwork.

On the spur of the moment I decided to go to the Farnborough Show. With thousands of other people, I left Waterloo railway station for Farnborough and walked a mile or more to the airfield. The day was very warm, so I felt tired by the time I began wandering through the huge marquees housing the 240 display stands of aeronautical manufacturers. I much admired the professionally made display models of the latest British aircraft. I picked up pamphlets, photos and the like that I thought might be of use for my thesis, and bought a copy of *The Times' Survey of British Aviation*.

The heat and the smoke laden air in the marquees drove me towards the open air static display of aircraft and equipment. Fifty different aircraft were on show, twelve being completely new types. Later, I was to see forty of the aircraft in a thrilling flying display. I was disappointed that, for security reasons, some of the new aircraft were in special enclosures so that the public couldn't get up close to them. I wandered around the static display observing as much as I could including attention getters such as the Martin-Baker ejector seat test rig and the retraction of a giant multi-wheeled undercarriage.

I wanted to sit down, but the restaurants were full and there was no seating at buffet counters. The catering staff could barely cope with the crowds of people. I managed to buy some food, but it was all very expensive. I envied the customers of aircraft firms being wined and dined in caravans behind the static display.

Though the flying display was further away from the crowd than the previous year (when the test pilot John Derry and his observer had been killed in a terrible accident), I was fascinated by the spectacular manoeuvres, the noise (including sonic booms and loudspeaker commentaries) and the sight of aircraft that I'd never seen before. I lost count of the new aircraft, but well remember the displays of the Hawker Hunter 2, de Havilland DH110 and Vickers-Supermarine Swift F4 jet fighters, the Short SB5 adjustable wing research aircraft, the Vickers Valiant and Handley Page Victor jet bombers, the Fairey Gannet anti-submarine aircraft, the Bristol Britannia and Vickers Viscount turbo-prop airliners, the enormous Blackburn Beverley freighter and the very impressive 140-ton ten-engined Saunders-Roe Princess flying boat.

I was most interested in the delta winged aircraft – the Sapphire and Olympus powered versions of the Avro Vulcan 2 bomber, the Boulton Paul P111A and Avro 707 aircraft used for aerodynamic research, and the Gloster Javelin all-weather day and night fighter. My camera worked overtime as I tried to record the two Vulcans flying in formation with two of the high-speed 707As, a low-speed 707B and a 707C trainer. Unfortunately, the closest I was able to get to the delta winged aircraft was when they were taking-off and landing. There were so many things to photograph in the air and on the ground!

I noticed some RNZAF officers and airmen amongst the crowd. When an RAF officer removed his sun-glasses, I recognised the Old Cranwellian, Gp. Capt. P.W. Townsend, CVO, DSO, DFC (romantically linked at that time to Princess Margaret). Judging from the strange languages I heard, many of the spectators were from overseas countries.

Rather weary, but elated by all that had happened that day, I dragged myself away from Farnborough, returned to London and, with a number of other Flight Cadets, journeyed back to Cranwell.

CHAPTER 18

The Answer is Yes

AS USUAL, there was a pile of mail awaiting me at Cranwell and a lot of news to catch up on.

I heard that John Jennings of 62C had safely parachuted from a Chipmunk when he'd got into trouble during inverted flight, and his aircraft had crashed setting a house on fire. Also, the New Zealander Wg. Cdr. Yule had died in hospital after his Meteor had crashed at Woolwich Arsenal. The newspapers were full of praise for his bravery in staying with his aircraft and guiding it away from the explosives dump. Apparently he'd been in a formation of Meteors practising for a Battle of Britain display when one of the Meteors had flown into the tail of his aircraft when only 1,200 feet above ground level. The Sergeant Pilot flying the other Meteor landed safely and had been taken to hospital suffering from shock. I felt very sad when I heard of this accident as I'd met both pilots at RAF Horsham St Faith.

Then the news came that Pete McKechnie of 60C had been relegated to 61 Entry and Ted Reynolds of 60A had been demoted from being an Under Officer! Apparently a senior officer had complained to the Commandant about Ted during a cruise on the English Channel and, though Sqn. Ldr. Thomas had taken a contrary view, Ted was relegated to being a Senior Flight Cadet. This meant that Ted had to move out of the Under Officers' rooms overlooking the College parade ground and U/O John Tucker moved in, so becoming second in command to Laurie Jones, the A Squadron Senior Under Officer. Sam Boyce was then promoted to be the second Under Officer in the Squadron.

Ted Reynolds announced that he'd become engaged. A number of other Flight Cadets in 60 Entry then mentioned that they'd also been thinking about getting married.

The word went around that Plt. Off. Chris Peile (formerly of 59A, who'd come third in the overall Order of Merit and won the Royal United Services Institution Award for his thesis on wind-tunnels) had designed a wind-tunnel that was theoretically more efficient and used less power than existing wind-tunnels. As a result, the de Havilland Aircraft Company was building a wind-tunnel to his design.

Ron Chippindale and Jim Brown returned to the College wearing the beginnings of moustaches. After a rather long struggle, Ron eventually managed to grow quite a bushy moustache.

I began to enjoy the additional privileges of being in the Senior Entry such as use of the Senior Entry ante-room and cloakroom, being able to go to the head of queues at the servery in the dining hall, riding a bike around the station, not having a curfew at night, wearing officer pattern shirts and collars with uniforms, not having to give an 'Eyes Right' (or 'Left') when passing officers in the College buildings, and making sure that everyone below me in the College stood to attention when addressing me and called me 'Sir'.

The 60 Entry GD(P) Autumn Term programme of instruction contained a lot of time for flying and private study, with only a limited number of formal lecture periods – these being: Air Force Law and Administration, Airmanship, Commonwealth History and International Affairs, War and Service Studies, and Weapons, plus the reintroduction of Navigation/Radio and Performance (a combination of Aerodynamics and Aircraft Structures).

Ron, Jim and I were in the same sets for lectures as in the previous term, except that in Humanistics Ron moved up to Set 2, as Sets 2 and 3 had been combined. The gen men remained the same, but since the death of Mike Goodall their number had fallen to seven.

With more private study time, I forged ahead in completing the writing of my thesis and then laboriously typing all 102 foolscap pages of it. During lectures, revision began for the final exams to be held just after the mid-term break.

I played squash with Ron, Laurie Jones, Mal Dines and John Gratton to try and restore my fitness. Then I beat D.C.E. (George) England of 61A to head the 'beginners' ladder' and so become eligible to be chosen for the College squash team.

At the first church parade of term, I was told (for some unknown reason) to carry the Queen's Colour. Fortunately, this honour was accomplished without any problems.

There were a number of A Squadron and Senior Entry meetings. In one of the latter, 60 Entry sorted out what penalties would be imposed on 66 Entry during their initiation as Flight Cadets.

At the first guest night of term, Sqn. Ldr. Thomas was officially farewelled. After the dinner, 66 Entry performed quite well at their initiation, two of them riding motor bikes up a ramp and through a burning ring on the Orange. One new Flight Cadet, wearing only underpants, had to report to the guest room where the officers in full mess kit were having a quiet after-dinner drink, and request that Sqn. Ldr. Thomas inspect the other Flight Cadets who'd been penalised. Sqn. Ldr. Thomas carried out his inspection with considerable aplomb, bearing in mind that the new Flight Cadets were wearing next to nothing and the rest of the College was just waiting for the Squadron Leader to burst out laughing. 'Haircut,' the Squadron Leader ordered without the glimmer of a smile, as he looked at one poor unfortunate's hairy anatomy. We all burst into roars of laughter.

60A decided to give Sqn. Ldr. Thomas a party in the Red Lion Hotel at Caythorpe before he left to take up his new posting. The A Squadron Cadet Wing Officer, Flt. Lt. Hall, was included in the invitation. We Flight Cadets dressed in the weirdest combination of clothes we could find, such as a pyjama top, gaudy tie, tartan waistcoat, sloppy corduroy trousers and 'brothel creeper' shoes. Sqn. Ldr. Thomas, always the epitome of sartorial elegance, couldn't believe his eyes when he saw us, but entered into the spirit of the occasion and was soon enjoying the plentiful food and drink.

I'd just finished drinking a glass of pineapple juice when one of my colleagues in 60A offered to buy me some more. The barman produced a filled glass from beneath the counter and I became suspicious. I took a sip and sure enough, the drink had something in it – probably gin. I told my colleague and refused to have any more of the drink. In front of a roomful of people, my colleague invited Sqn. Ldr. Thomas to take a sip and say if he thought there was anything in the drink. 'Nectar, pure nectar,' the Squadron Leader declared, 'Nothing but pineapple.' I felt that his taste buds had become impaired and turned away disgusted, leaving my colleague to finish the drink he'd bought. I was annoyed at being put in such a situation and by the view so many people seemed to take that drinking alcohol was necessary to have a good time. I felt that whatever the reasons people had for not drinking alcohol, friends would respect those reasons.

I came upon one of 60A sitting by himself and looking absolutely miserable. On enquiring what was wrong, he told me, 'I always get depressed when I drink too much!' When the time came to leave the hotel, we emerged into a completely black and starless night. I had difficulty in seeing where our cars had been parked. No doubt my somewhat inebriated colleagues had even greater problems, and I later heard that some had close shaves in driving back to the College. As the only sober person there, I was asked to drive one of the cars.

Before leaving the College, Sqn. Ldr. Thomas apparently wanted to make an impression as he made a thorough inspection of A Squadron rooms and, on his final church parade, conducted a detailed inspection of every member of the Squadron except for members of 60A. Thank goodness the Senior Entry was exempt from inspection on church parades!

When Sqn. Ldr. Thomas flew in one of the Cranwell Ansons to RAF Turnhouse where he'd been posted, Ted Reynolds got his permission to fly with him just for the experience. The flight was during private study time, but unfortunately for Ted, there was a change in the programme and 60A was scheduled for flying instruction. On his return, Ted was hauled before the CFI for not getting his permission to miss flying instruction! As a result, Ted was given two weeks of extra duties.

Nigel MacNicol was also in trouble as he'd been sleeping during the private study time and hadn't heard the Tannoy message announcing the change in programme!

I was put in charge of 64A and briefed about later making a report on each member. In order to achieve this, I began to have meals periodically with 64A in the Junior Mess.

The College paraded in airman pattern best blue uniform and blue webbing to celebrate the anniversary of the Battle of Britain. Our drill was awful, but it was a little better a few days later when a ceremonial parade was held. I heard that during a Battle of Britain flying display at RAF Coningsby, a Meteor from RAF Horsham St Faith had exploded and the pilot had been killed. A piece of the aircraft fell amongst the spectators, almost hitting the Commandant of the College. On Battle of Britain Sunday there was a printed order of service, but the OD padre went on so long that the ODs again missed out on the march past the Commandant.

When I reported to E Flight in Flying Wing, I found that only two of the former instructors remained. My Harvard flying instructor, Flt. Lt. Reid, had been transferred to a Chipmunk flight and I'd been allocated a new instructor, Fg. Off. J.A. Smith, who'd recently been flying fighter ground-attack Vampires at RAF Valley. There were other changes such as that Cranwell's code letters 'CP' had become 'CW', Harvards were being called 'Palmoil' and I'd been given the call-sign '502'.

Fg. Off. Smith and I began with general flying exercises and some simulated instrument flying.

E Flight was then briefed on mutual cross-country flights, i.e. one Flight Cadet flew from the front seat of a Harvard and another navigated from the rear seat. Ted and I did flight planning for the first of these flights. I flew while Ted navigated, but bad weather in the Bury St Edmunds area caused us to abandon our triangular route and practise diversions on the way back to Cranwell.

On the second flight, Mal Dines flew while I navigated to Leighton Buzzard and Bury St Edmonds. This was the first time that I'd been airborne in the rear cockpit of a Harvard. We began worrying when Mal noticed that there were only ten gallons of fuel in the starboard tank instead of forty. (He'd forgotten to note the contents of the starboard tank when doing the preflight checks.) He thought the fuel gauge had stuck, but halfway along the first leg the starboard tank ran dry and he hastily switched to the port tank. I did some rapid calculations and decided we'd just enough fuel to complete the flight. When we landed, there were only eight gallons left in the reserve tank. Needless to say, we learned a lesson from this incident!

Night flying began again with dual and solo circuits and bumps. As Senior Entry, we did night flying from Cranwell rather than Barkston Heath. There was a full moon and everything went smoothly. The next lot of night flying was cancelled because of fog.

I was one of the last in 60 Entry to have my final navigation test. Flt. Lt. Colbeck (the navigation instructor who'd flown with me on the Mediterranean trip) watched closely as I carefully flight planned, did the aircraft checks and headed for Leighton Buzzard. The navigation on the first leg had to be done using radio bearings. When a fix was required, Flt. Lt. Colbeck returned my maps to me. On passing Bedford, we saw two enormous black hangars at Cardington and two airships, one cruising above our height. Then we ran into cloud and had to descend. We emerged into clear air with Leighton Buzzard just two miles ahead.

The next leg was eastwards to a windmill! I wasn't allowed to use radio bearings and could only consult a map when told to use one. Then I had to do some mental dead reckoning for a short leg to where a creek joined a river. The final leg was at low level, navigating by map reading. I misunderstood what was expected of me at one point and missed a road going over a dried-up creek just north of Spalding. I was then asked to make a diversion to Barkston Heath. When this was successfully completed, Flt. Lt. Colbeck, who was a qualified pilot and somewhat out of practice, couldn't resist taking control of the Harvard for the return to Cranwell. His circuit and landing were terrible!

There was little time for a debriefing as I had to rush and have tea before attending a night flying briefing. Flt. Lt. Colbeck said, however, that my navigation wasn't too bad. A few weeks later when I thought Flt. Lt. Colbeck had forgotten about the oral part of the navigation test, he gave Ted Reynolds, John Tucker and me a written instead of an oral test on navigation subjects. Unprepared as we were, we all passed!

The navigation exercises were continued at night. The Flight Commander of E Flight, Flt. Lt. Woods, flew with me to Goole and Louth to accustom me to flying and navigating at the same time from the dimly lit cockpit of the Harvard. When the cockpit lights were turned up, they were too bright for flying purposes and not bright enough for map reading and log keeping. A torch used for the latter was too bright (unless masked in some way) and could easily be dropped into the black depths of the cockpit. The night was very dark, and I could see only the lights of towns and the occasional airfield pundit flashing red identification letters in Morse code.

Having survived that trip, I was immediately sent on a solo navigation exercise to Northampton and RAF Marham, an all-weather master airfield. Each aircraft was separated by a ten minute interval and 500 feet in height, and pilots had to call at the turning points. If an aircraft was late over a turning point, then the next had to circle the turning point and restore the ten minute interval. Strong winds had been forecast, but they died and backed, causing our flight plans to be well out. I was port of track on the first leg, but could see on the horizon the loom of lights at Northampton. An alteration of course soon brought me overhead the flashing neon signs of the city centre. The Cranwell air traffic controller called me for a weather report. I then made my way to RAF Marham with the aid of two radio bearings and looked down at the runway lights and aircraft parked on illuminated tarmac surrounding the black shapes of hangars. Back at Cranwell I started to think that night cross-country flights were a lot of fun!

Gunnery exercises began on Harvards. The aircraft didn't have guns, but a small movie camera recorded the view through the gunsight. We flew straight and level behind another Harvard and took film at various ranges. This was repeated during turns and, in progressively more difficult exercises, we developed full attack patterns and imagined ourselves fighter pilots. Two Harvards would fly in the same direction on a parallel track about 1,200 yards apart along a straight feature on the ground such as Ermine Street. The attacking Harvard went a little ahead of the other then turned ninety degrees towards the target Harvard and the camera was operated during a curve of pursuit. When this had been mastered it was repeated, but with the two Harvards flying in opposite directions. The exercises were with our instructors, then solo with other Flight Cadets. When the films had been processed, we saw the results on a screen and analysed where we'd gone wrong.

Flt. Lt. R.C. Hooper, DFC, took me for my air-to-air gunnery test when I was expecting another lot of solo gunnery. Sam Boyce of 60A in the other Harvard was also being tested by an instructor. The visibility was very poor. I wasn't at all happy with my parallel course attack, but my three opposite course attacks were reasonable. After Sam had made his attacks, the instructors took control and did some dogfighting. I was then told to do a flapless glide landing at Cranwell and succeeded in making a perfect approach and three-point landing, which I felt wasn't too bad on an almost windless day. When the gunnery film was available, I was told I'd passed my test.

For several days at Cranwell, I saw a team of surveyors on the grass of the south airfield obtaining data for the proposed runways and taxiways.

My oxygen mask had become uncomfortable as the rubber had wrinkled around the edges. Having got Flt. Lt. Woods to sign in triplicate the form for a replacement, and obtained the required certificate from the Flight Safety Section, I took the mask to the Stores Section only to be told that the Radio Servicing Section had first to attach a label stating what category the mask was in, e.g. salvageable (as the microphone still worked)! A frustrating thirty minutes later, the Radio Servicing Section issued me with a pre-used mask fitted with a new high altitude microphone, and I returned the unused form to Flt. Lt. Woods.

When detailed for another week of being the A Squadron duty Senior Flight Cadet, I missed dinner one night at the Junior Mess because the meal time had been changed. (I was pleased to note that I wasn't the only duty Senior Flight Cadet to miss the meal!) Unfortunately, Flt. Lt. Hall and the new A Squadron Commander, Sqn. Ldr. Smith, noticed my absence. Both spoke to me about it, but didn't penalise me.

Then, with the other duty Senior Flight Cadets, I dressed for a guest night at the Junior Mess. After we'd called our squadron rolls, 'Sorbo Bill', the Cadet Wing Adjutant, told us that seating in the Junior Mess was so acute for the guest night there was no room for us! He claimed that he'd told somebody about this a fortnight earlier. We could have strangled him as by then, we were too late for dinner at the Senior Mess.

After the guest night, I turned off the lights in Block 78 at 2315 hours, only to be rung a few minutes later by Flt. Lt. Hall wanting to know why the lights weren't out at 2300 hours. I said I understood the time for lights out after guest nights was 2315 hours, but he wasn't convinced. Flt. Lt. Hall also wanted to know who'd been shouting obscene language from a window at about 2300 hours, and asked me to report to him the next morning. I ran into Sqn. Ldr. Smith the next morning and he also questioned me about the lights out time. After that I heard nothing more about it. No one owned up to the obscene language, however, so Laurie Jones, the A Squadron Senior Under Officer, was called in to harangue the occupants of Block 78 and clag them if nobody admitted to the bad language.

I was again thankful when my week of being duty Senior Flight Cadet ended. At least, I'd been off drill all that week!

On returning to the Senior Mess, I found that a boiler had burst and there was no hot water for twenty-four hours.

I was in hot water of another sort in Weapons lectures, as the new Senior Tutor Science took over the instruction for a while to get to know the Senior Entry. He began by teaching us inductive and deductive logic, and then statistical methods in relationship to bombing. Using dice and cards to illustrate probability, he asked me how many hearts there were in a pack of cards. Not being a card player, I said I didn't know. He expressed great surprise and told me that I wouldn't be a social success if I didn't know that when asked to play cards with the Commanding Officer's wife. (I'm pleased to say that my lack of interest and knowledge about cards has never limited me socially!)

On another occasion, I had a difference of opinion with the Senior Tutor Science and, in effect, he called me a liar. (Certainly the rest of my set took his viewpoint, much to my embarrassment.) After the lecture I had it out with him. He backed down saying he'd just been joking and he praised me for raising the matter with him. Thereafter, we got on very well.

I decided to attend the 67 Entry boxing, not because I liked the sport, but the Senior Entry had to set an example and I didn't want to give anyone the opportunity of 'having a go' at me for being absent. I later attended the College boxing competition and a judo display.

Practice for the Knocker Cup inter-squadron gymnastics began. I preferred to participate in this rather than in rugby during my final term, not wanting to risk breaking any more bones.

During early morning drill, the Senior Entry was taken aside and given instruction on sword drill using very rudimentary wooden swords. Drill for the Senior Entry at ceremonial parades was a little different in that we were positioned in front of our squadrons as supernumerary officers without swords or rifles. Only the Senior Under Officers and Under Officers who acted as Parade Commander, Parade Adjutant and Squadron Commanders carried swords.

Surprisingly, there was no drill for the Senior Entry one morning, so we slept in and went to breakfast as late as possible. Our lives were so hectic that any break in the routine was welcomed.

At 0530 hours one day, the fire alarms rang and instructions over the Tannoy system ordered us to get out of bed, collect fire buckets and assemble on the Orange. After a roll call, 'Sorbo Bill' announced that the call-out was just a fire practice. There were mutterings amongst some Flight Cadets as to what they would do to 'Sorbo Bill', but we went back quietly to our rooms and tried to sleep before reveille at 0630 hours.

After flying until late in the afternoon, I rushed to have tea and then attend an Airmanship class. A Knocker Cup practice was followed by a guest night. Major Charlson of the USAF and the new Medical Officer, Sqn. Ldr. R.A. Riseley-Pritchard sat beside me. Our polite conversation over an unusually poor dinner was continued afterwards in the ante-room until all the officers had retired. Then I hastily prepared my kit for a ceremonial parade the next morning. Pete Anstee of 60C commanded the Cadet Wing for the ceremonial and had the misfortune when giving orders of having his voice break on several occasions.

When the Knocker competition was eventually held, A Squadron could only manage third place.

In order to relax a little, about half of 60 Entry decided to go to a formal dance at Kesteven Teachers' Training College. As the dinner jacket I'd ordered hadn't arrived, I wore interim mess dress to the dance. Pete Anstee took me and some other chaps in his car. Our main interest was to meet the seventy-six or so new female students! I danced with one of the newcomers, Monica Potter.

Sqn. Ldr. Gavin wrote to Ron and me saying that we'd be returning to New Zealand by sea, but he couldn't give any details as the passages were still to be booked. Air Cdre. Wallingford's statement that we might do an AFS course in Britain before flying with the RNZAF at Cyprus had seemingly come to naught. We hoped that we'd be sent via the Suez Canal, having already been through the Panama Canal. There was no word about what postings we'd have back in New Zealand. Sqn. Ldr. Gavin enclosed information on clothing allowances and what uniforms we'd require as officers. He also advised that new identification cards would be issued to us before we left Britain.

In preparation for my departure from Cranwell, I arranged for Gieves Limited to make me a new officer pattern hat, uniform and Crombie fleece greatcoat, and Burberrys Limited to make me a Cranwell Full Colours sports blazer. I also bought a Cranwell Full Colours tie and scarf, a wall shield with the Cranwell crest on it and a rather elegant set of cuff links. As the RNZAF was unlikely to pay me the money being held for me until after I'd been commissioned, Dad very thoughtfully sent me another £50 to cover these and other expected expenses. (I wanted to buy two model aeroplane engines and some modelling equipment.)

I'd invited Betty to the 60 Entry passing-out parade and ball, but she was unable to accept as she would have university exams at that time. This news left me at a loss as to what to do – I didn't feel like inviting another girl and yet it would be such a pity not to enjoy fully this culmination of my training.

Then Cousin Jennifer wrote to say that she and Robert wouldn't be able to accept my invitation to the passing-out parade. I booked Cousin Mabel into a Grantham hotel in anticipation of her being at the parade.

I realised one day that Robin Pringle of 60A was missing – he'd left at short notice to see his dying mother in America and had got a flight in a USAF B36D bomber.

Then Tony Whitwam of 60B reported his car had been stolen in Lincoln. He got it back a few days later in Newark with a flat tyre and minus the battery.

The Field Shooting and Wildfowling Section had a very successful meeting one day and carried into the Senior Mess a large number of rabbits, hares, widgeon and other birds that had been shot. The Mess staff obligingly prepared a banquet and I was fortunate to be one of the Flight Cadets invited to participate in the unusual feast.

Members of the Senior Entry were rostered to have a meal with the Commandant. Accordingly, Nigel MacNicol and I changed into lounge suits after church parade one Sunday and reported at The Lodge. Air Cdre. Eeles introduced us to Mrs Eeles and their guests, Canon and Mrs A.M. Cook of Lincoln Cathedral. The two Eeles children played with their dog, Jill. As sherry and then lunch were served, Nigel and I were on our best behaviour. The conversation, however, was mainly between the Eeles and the Cooks, with Nigel and me participating in it whenever we could. I felt that if an objective of the Commandant was to get to know Nigel and me, he made little attempt to do so. Nigel was probably as relieved as I was when the time came for us to thank our hosts and leave to watch an inter-squadron riding competition that all the College had to attend. That evening, six of 60B were given dinner at The Lodge.

Night navigation trips resumed, the last that 60 Entry were to do at the College. Navigation briefings were held at 1530 hours followed by night flying briefings at 1715 hours. The sky was dark enough for the first Harvard to be airborne soon afterwards. Flt. Lt. A.T. Williams flew with me to Doncaster and RAF Binbrook. The latter didn't have its pundit and runway lights operating, so all I could see from 4,500 feet were the dim lights of barrack blocks and streets. On our way back to Cranwell, we practised a diversion to RAF Coningsby. After landing at Cranwell I was to do a solo trip, but flying was cancelled when another pilot reported cloud starting to cover the proposed route.

The next lot of night flying was also cancelled because of bad weather. On the third night, the air was smooth and the weather forecast was accurate. I was sent solo (without first having a dual check) to RAF Feltwell and RAF Oakington. On the return leg to Cranwell, a diversion was made to RAF Cottesmore. Everything went very well for me, but Dickie Hoare of 60C in a Harvard behind me had radio failure and, in accordance with standard procedures, fired a red Very cartridge before joining the Cranwell circuit and landing.

On another day I was taxiing out for take-off when I came upon a Chipmunk and a Harvard that had collided head-on. I also heard that a member of 61A had foolishly done a slow roll while flying alongside a Dakota aircraft and had been given jankers and relegated to 62 Entry.

I was just getting used to Fg. Off. Smith as my flying instructor when he was transferred to become the C Squadron Cadet Wing Officer. He was replaced by Fg. Off. W. Bolton, a tall thin chap whose gingery hair was swept back from a receding hairline. Fg. Off. Bolton told me he'd been a wartime pilot and then become a civilian instructor at RAF Digby, flying Tiger Moths at a school that assessed the flying ability of pilot recruits. After some six years, he'd rejoined the RAF and was very pleased to be posted to Cranwell as his home was in Sleaford and he would have lost money on his house if he'd had to move in a depressed property market. I rather liked his quiet competence and easy manner.

Operation Husky began in War Studies. This study of the invasion of Sicily during World War II was most interesting as it included places such as

Pantelleria which I'd flown over during the Mediterranean flight. I was part of a 60 Entry team that gave a briefing on the air plan of the Operation. My role was to outline the air plan whereas other members of my team detailed the build-up, the assault etc. Other teams spoke on subjects such as the Army and Navy activities, plan coordination and so on. Much time was occupied in rehearsing our roles and preparing large wall maps to illustrate particular parts of the Operation. The Senior Tutor Humanistics, Squadron Commanders and other officers sat in on the 60 Entry presentation. Afterwards, comments were made on our individual performances. I was told that the information I'd imparted was good and showed a lot of preparation, but I was inclined to stick to my notes.

As part of our Air Force Law instruction, Sqn. Ldr. R. Bullen, GM, and Sqn. Ldr. G.C.T. Richards dressed as airmen and acted the parts of the accused in a series of charges. There was so much laughter that I'm sure many of the key points were overlooked by the audience.

When the College practised, for the second time, a full RAF ceremonial parade on the Junior College parade ground, we didn't perform very well, being much better on Cranwell versions of ceremonial parades. When practice for the Ferris inter-squadron drill competition began, 60 Entry was told that, as the competition had been changed to have a new test piece each term, we wouldn't be involved and there was no drill for us for a fortnight! This seemed too good to be true!

Rain and mist turned into fog, greatly restricting flying at Cranwell. I was most surprised to see a Hurricane fighter on the airfield one day – possibly the last one flying in Britain. When the weather cleared sufficiently, my Flying Wing Squadron Commander, Sqn. Ldr. Derisley, unexpectedly flew with me, saying he just wanted to get airborne for a while. Afterwards, he told me I had nothing to worry about with my flying, considering my experience to date. With more attention to detail, my flying would continue to improve.

I heard that F/C Reg Strevens of 64C had been killed in a Chipmunk prang during night flying at RAF Spitalgate. Then there was news that Plt. Off. Derek Reypert (formerly 59C) had been killed in a Vampire crash.

The rumour circulated that too many qualified pilots were failing to cope when converting onto jet aircraft, so in future, Wings wouldn't be awarded at Cranwell until Flight Cadets had completed advanced flying training. There were also rumours concerning the planned introduction of Balliols and Vampires, and the interim use of the north airfield and RAF Barkston Heath until the Cranwell runways had been completed.

Just before the mid-term break, Sqn. Ldr. Gavin again wrote to Ron and me saying that we'd be returning to New Zealand via the Panama Canal on the Shaw Savill 15,000 ton passenger ship *Akaroa*, departing from Liverpool a fortnight after our passing-out parade. Single berth cabins on A Deck had been reserved for us, there being only one class of cabin on the ship.

Sqn. Ldr. Gavin also mentioned that Ron and I could wear the RAF Wings that we would be presented with when we passed-out, but on our return to New Zealand we would have to wear RNZAF Wings. This disappointed us greatly as we felt that we'd be entitled to wear RAF Wings, having been trained in the RAF to RAF Wings standard. We were given permission, however, to wear New Zealand shoulder patches on our uniforms after the passing-out parade.

Ron was one of the few members of 60 Entry who took the mid-term break. Most of us remained at Cranwell and swotted for the final exams. When relief from swotting was required, some of us rode bicycles around the north airfield looking for mushrooms. The mushrooms were later cooked for us by the dining hall staff. Then we saw *Sword of d'Artagnan* at the Cranwell cinema.

Just before we sat our final exams, we had to spend precious time in preparing for a ceremonial parade.

For four days, the 60 Entry GD(P) group sweated in the main lecture hall over nine papers covering eleven subjects, including Meteorology and Thermodynamics for which there'd been no lectures that term. I thought the Meteorology paper was the worst of the lot, but when the marks were announced, I was surprised that I'd achieved the average mark of the Entry in that subject. Jim Brown easily beat Ron and me in the academic papers. We had to wait, however, for the academic marks to be combined with marks for flying, officer qualities and other things to make up the final Order of Merit.

After the exams, some of 60 Entry went off on a pub crawl, a few dressed up and went to the 'Per Ardua Beagles' Ball, and the remainder disappeared – probably to bed! Tony Whitwam drove me in his car to Grantham to see the film *By the Light of the Silvery Moon*.

60 Entry went onto a special programme for the remainder of the term. This began with a physical fitness officer lecturing us on PT in the RAF. Then we were told that there'd be some more ground combat training (which we thought we'd seen the last of in Junior Entries!), an aircraft factory visit and the remainder of our flying training. Everyone had to hand in his thesis and we were reminded that a navigation exercise on pressure pattern flying, issued the previous term, had to be completed. The last involved some feverish, late night work by certain members of the Entry!

The mid-term dance at the College was rather poorly organised so Julian Bowes appointed himself as the master of ceremonies and made up the programme during the evening. As before, there was a record player for music and we had to wear officer pattern uniform. Monica Potter from Kesteven

Teachers' Training College was there and we had quite a pleasant time together. I happened to be the A Squadron duty Senior Flight Cadet that night so had to wait until after the dance to turn off lights and do the other things required of me.

I almost lost my voice in shouting when A beat B in the inter-squadron rugby competition. Soon afterwards, I watched A beat C in the inter-squadron soccer competition and then C beat A (by one point!) in the Ferris inter-squadron drill competition on a cold and windy day.

At a combined service in the Hangar Church a Methodist lay-preacher, Professor T.E. Jessop of Hull University, preached a learned and at times witty sermon.

Ted Reynolds told me that his parents were emigrating to New Zealand and, as he was still keen to join the RNZAF, he planned to go to RNZAF Headquarters in London and enquire about a permanent commission.

I heard that Johnny Langley and Gordon Grierson of 61A had a lucky escape from injury when Johnny slow rolled his small Austin car and ended up in a ditch – fortunately the right way up. Mike Southgate of 62A, who'd taken over Spike Heaney's room after his death, was not so lucky as he broke a leg in a separate accident. Then a Pakistani Flight Cadet landed a Harvard on the south airfield wheels up. His story was that he'd raised the undercarriage when overshooting and the engine hadn't responded. The instructors thought that a more likely story was he'd forgotten to lower the undercarriage for landing!

60 Entry was measured for jet aircraft by sitting against a wall and having the distance taken between the wall and our knee caps.

Fog delayed me having my Instrument Rating Test. When the weather improved, Flt. Lt. J. McPhee, AFC, tested me on things such as a Pattern F, unusual positions, steep turns and limited panel work. My performance in the last wasn't too good. On calling for permission to join the radio beam for a let-down, the Cranwell controller told me to land within three minutes as flying was finishing for the day. This was a disappointment as a new ruling said that, for the issue of a White Rating, all IRT exercises had to be completed in one flight. I later heard that Ron, Jim and some other members of 60 Entry had failed their attempts at the flying part of the IRT.

Fg. Off. Bolton took me for some more dual instrument flying. He put me in the rear cockpit of a Harvard where a cloth hood prevented me from seeing outside the aircraft. Having natural light instead of blue goggles and amber screens was a great advantage, but the control column in the rear cockpit took some getting used to as it was different to that in the front cockpit.

When Flt. Lt. McPhee tested me again, he asked me to do only the limited panel work and beam let-down. Everything went well this time, though my overshoot from the beam approach could have been better. I did another approach and overshoot and passed the flying part of the IRT. A few days later, Flt. Lt. C.H. Atkin gave me the oral part of the IRT – questions on meteorology, aircraft instruments, air traffic control, principles of flight and so on. I passed! I finally had my 'White Ticket'!

Flt. Lt. J.P. Britton took me on my first bombing flight. We flew at 3,000 feet to the range at Bassingham Fen, which was just a little west of the midway point between Cranwell and Lincoln. Flt. Lt. Britton, who was in the front cockpit, put the Harvard into a sixty degree dive towards the target, sighted the 25 yard diameter target through the gunsight (since the Harvard didn't have a bomb-sight), and at 225 knots released one of the eight 10 lb practice bombs from racks fitted under the wings. He pulled out of the dive by 500 feet and turned to watch the puff of white smoke released when the bomb hit the ground. The range controller radioed the bearing and distance of the bomb from the centre of the target.

After another dual bombing flight, but with me in the front cockpit, I was authorised to do solo bombing. Getting the bombs in the target circle wasn't easy, but it was great fun! I got a real thrill on achieving an average error of 16 yards, equalling Laurie Jones's score which was the best to date in E Flight. During one of my solo bombing flights, two of the practice bombs failed to release when required, so after two more bombing runs, I had to jettison the bomb rack. I eventually came second in the Entry for solo bombing with an average error of 19.36 yards, Laurie Jones coming first with an 18.4 yard average.

Flt. Lt. J.P. Douglas took me for my bombing test. I felt afterwards that I hadn't performed very well as only two of the four bombs dropped were within the circular target, though the average error was 17 yards. The main thing as far as I was concerned was that I'd passed the test!

On the next guest night, I found myself sitting beside Gp. Capt. Nelson, the Assistant Commandant, so again had to watch my 'ps and qs'. Gp. Capt. Nuttall, who was also present, told me that an Old Cranwellian he knew, AVM W.H. Merton, CB, OBE, MID, RAF, had just been appointed RNZAF Chief of the Air Staff and could be sailing to New Zealand with Mrs Merton on the same ship that Ron and I would be on! When I told Ron this startling news, we thought of all sorts of advantages in this and also a lot of disadvantages!

On Remembrance Sunday, all of RAF Cranwell paraded in greatcoats for the first time that winter. I felt restricted when swinging my arms. The Queen's Colour was also paraded. I'd never before seen so many officers at the OD church.

Early one Monday morning, most of the 60 Entry GD(P) group (except for Nigel MacNicol, John Tucker and Andy Whitson who had to catch up on their flying hours) left Cranwell for the aircraft factory visit, accompanied by five of the College officers.

Our bus driver took us to Armstrong Siddeley Motors Ltd at Coventry in time for morning tea. We were shown through the vast factory where some 7,000 people were employed largely on development work. Hundreds of machines were producing items for development or the prototypes of new engines. The automatic milling machines were particularly fascinating. We watched the testing of Cheetah piston engines, Mamba, Double Mamba and Sapphire jet engine compressors and combustion chambers, and were shown the results of failures of various sorts. Finally, we were taken along the production line of the luxury Armstrong Siddeley Sapphire cars that were being produced at the rate of one an hour.

Just outside Coventry at Ansty, we were given lunch at another Armstrong Siddeley facility and shown the production lines of Mamba and Sapphire jet engines. We wandered through an apprentice school, looking at diagrams, working models and superbly finished showroom models of various engines, including the Snarler liquid fuel rocket motor. In the control room of one of several engine test houses, we saw a Python jet engine being tested. The engine had been running continuously for over a day. Our eyes were glued to the whirling fuel gauge! All the gauges in the test houses were periodically photographed so that they could be analysed at a later time.

After tea at Ansty, we were driven to RAF Wellesbourne Mountford, a training station just east of Stratford-upon-Avon, and given accommodation in the single rooms of prefab-type huts. That evening, Sir W.G. Armstrong Whitworth Aircraft Ltd (AWA) put on a magnificent dinner for us at a high class hotel. I was seated beside the Chief Aerodynamicist of AWA, Dr W.F. Hilton, whose book *High Speed Aerodynamics* was one of the references I'd used in my thesis. Dr Hilton was most interesting to talk to. I discovered he collected stamps. When I said my sister, Heather, was the stamp collector in my family, he expressed interest in exchanging stamps with her.

The next morning, AWA lectured us at their impressive factory on aircraft design, aerodynamics and factory organisation and methods. Dr Hilton told us about a supersonic wind-tunnel that he'd designed and was building. Questions were invited on anything except guided missiles. Since World War II, AWA hadn't been very successful in selling its designs to the Ministry of Supply, so the firm had taken in work from other organisations and prepared for expansion.

As a result, we saw production of the Supermarine Seahawk, the Hawker Hunter and the AWA NF11 (originally a Gloster Meteor that'd been developed by AWA as a night fighter). We were allowed to clamber over a partially completed Hunter, admire the beautifully laid out cockpit, and see the limiting Mach number on the Machmeter. The main spar of the Hunter was particularly impressive, looking rather like a complicated piece of steel railway line that required forty-three separate milling operations in its manufacture. The all-flying tail and other modern refinements of the Hunter weren't lost on us. Nearby was a Meteor with a modified nose so that a pilot could fly it from a prone position. In another area, cockpit canopies were being tested to destruction and plate glass was being developed that might crack, but not shatter. A large bubble canopy was being developed for Meteor 7 and NFI1 aircraft.

That evening we were driven to RAF Ringway, a master airfield just south of Manchester that was jointly run by civilian airlines and the RAF. The officers and Under Officers were accommodated at the Officers' Mess while the rest of the Cranwell party was quartered in barracks. After arrival, we went to a British Empire Airways restaurant and had another magnificent meal, this one being provided by A. V. Roe and Co. Ltd. Afterwards, drinking continued at the officers' mess. Some horseplay with the furniture resulted and thunderflashes were thrown. I managed to have a good conversation, however, with Jimmy Orrell, Avro's Chief Test Pilot. He looked more like a rugby front row forward than an exceptional pilot. In the early hours of the morning, I returned to the barrack and came upon some officers who'd just thrown a thunderflash into the building. Ron and Jim were amongst my colleagues who had a rude awakening!

Rather tired, we were taken later that morning to Avro's Headquarters at Chadderton in Manchester. Over coffee, Mr Ewans, the Chief Aerodynamicist of Avro, spoke informally to us and invited questions. I'd drawn heavily on the work of Mr Ewans for my thesis and was pleased to meet him. We were shown how new ideas in aircraft structures were tested. For example, a wing tip of cellular construction with bullet holes in it was being distorted in a rig. Strain gauges seemed to be everywhere. In one enormous room that seemed full of draft boards, we were shown the machine that produced blueprints and whiteprints. Other huge rooms had desks and machines filling every available space. Parts for the English Electric Canberra were being manufactured, but the aircraft were being assembled at RAF Woodford to the south of Manchester.

We travelled to Woodford and spent the remainder of the day in another vast factory. Large aircraft parts were being made and Canberra, Shackleton and Vulcan aircraft were being assembled. We had a look inside a newly finished Shackleton and noticed how much more comfortable it appeared compared with the inside of a Lincoln bomber. We were shown a wind-tunnel with a square nine foot test section in which a model of the delta winged Gloster Javelin was being tested. Test models of various aircraft lay around. They were four to five feet in wing-span, beautifully made in wood and French-polished to a dark red colour. Everywhere we went there seemed to be electroplating baths, hot salt baths, huge presses, machines that stretched flat sheet over curved moulds and rolling mills that transformed flat rod into intricate straight and curved shapes.

As far as I was concerned, the *pièce de résistance* was the Vulcan production line, although at that time it hadn't been advanced very far. The jigs for this super priority delta winged bomber were gigantic to prevent flexing and achieve very fine tolerances in the construction of the aircraft. I saw mock-ups of the Vulcan flying controls, undercarriage and airbrakes systems.

We were taken across the airfield to the flight section where a scarlet painted, delta winged Avro 707A was being serviced on the tarmac. I was able to inspect it closely and have a look in the cockpit. The prototype Vulcan was being serviced in a hangar and we were allowed to climb scaffolding and look into various exposed parts of the aircraft. Seeing such a huge and complicated machine close-up was truly awe inspiring. The second Vulcan to be produced was parked on another part of the tarmac. In a separate building, an Olympus powered Vulcan was undergoing pressurisation and other tests.

There was so much to see! I could have taken weeks to wander around the aircraft factories rather than just three days. Reluctantly I boarded the bus to go back to Cranwell, armed with photographs, pamphlets and booklets that I'd been given by the aircraft companies. Somehow, the cold supper awaiting us at Cranwell seemed rather a let-down after what we'd been experiencing.

During the factory trip, some of my colleagues adopted a new line in trying to get me and Hammy Khan to drink alcohol. They spread around that we'd been drinking orange and sherry, the latter having been put in our glasses when we weren't looking. Then members of 60 Entry came and congratulated us on starting to drink alcohol! I found this infantile behaviour annoying and felt that it once again showed the lack of tolerance that many of my colleagues had to something slightly out of the ordinary.

At GCT, we dressed in denims, blue belts and boots to revise rifle, Sten and other drills that we'd learned in Junior Entries. The RAF Regiment instructors seemed to delight in having us lie on muddy wet grass or sit in a small, stuffy room while they lectured and tested us on airfield defence. They loved tearing covers off a blackboard to reveal key words such as Flexibility, Concentration and Co-operation, or turning over the blackboard to reveal a summary they considered to be vital. I think most of 60 Entry found all this rather boring.

The firing of rifles, Stens, Brens, pistols, mortars and smoke bombs on the range was of greater interest. We travelled to the Beckingham Range, eight miles west of Cranwell, for some of the firing. Our instructors had told us that mortars were easy to construct out of a piece of drainpipe, so when something was found to be wrong with the mortars to be fired, we reminded them of what they'd said. We got only dirty looks in reply!

The weather deteriorated rapidly at the range making the targets difficult to see. While we waited for the weather to clear, we tried to keep warm by making a fire out of packing from ammunition boxes. Chris Taylor found a rabbit that'd been recently killed by a bite to the back of the head. Ron skinned it. Then Bulldog Drummond beheaded and gutted the rabbit, and we all stood around watching it roast over the fire. After much discussion, a few of the Entry tried eating the rabbit before we left the range. I don't think they came to any harm!

Unfortunately, I had a ringing sound in my left ear after one lot of rifle firing. When the sound didn't go away in a few days, I reported sick. The College Medical Officer, Sqn. Ldr. Riseley-Pritchard, said there was no damage to my eardrum, but it might have a slight dent in it. A few days later, the MO thought that the ear mechanism might be sticking so gave me some menthol to inhale. He also gave me a chit excusing me from further range firing. When the menthol didn't have any effect on my ear, the MO sent me to a specialist at the RAF Hospital Nocton Hall. I began to be alarmed, thinking that I could be taken off flying, I wouldn't pass-out from the College – I might even be thrown out of the Air Force!

Much to my relief, the specialist told me that my ear problem wouldn't affect my passing-out, but he wanted me to go to the Central Medical Establishment in London for a further examination. I had to travel at short notice to London and, after a difficult bus and train journey, managed to get overnight accommodation at Overseas League House. I reported to the CME near Oxford Circus next morning, had an ear examination and an audiogram, and was told that I had some high tone deafness in my left ear that wouldn't affect my flying. No treatment was required. My tinnitus would decrease a little, but I would have to learn to live with it.

I arrived back at Cranwell during a ceremonial parade, having missed, through a change in programme, two of the rehearsals for the passing-out parade.

After a general flying trip with Fg. Off. Bolton, I went on my Final Handling Test with Flt. Lt. R. Griffin, one of the Flying Wing Flight Commanders. Such things always seemed to be sprung on us and I was rather nervous, but managed to fly quite well. Flt. Lt. Griffin said afterwards there was nothing really wrong with my flying – only small points – and he would rate me as being a high average. Needless to say I was greatly relieved to hear this.

I completed an instrument landing system approach at the Link Trainer Section, so finishing all the required exercises in the College syllabus. Altogether, I'd spent 28 hours in link trainers.

I decided to relax with Ron and Jim at an informal dance at the Kesteven Teachers' Training College. We wore lounge suits and thoroughly enjoyed dancing to music from an old gramophone. Then we went outside to see some fireworks and the burning of a Guy before trying our hand at cooking potatoes in the embers of the fire.

60 Entry met to sort out the format of the end of course review. There were so many funny things we wanted to incorporate in the review that I ended up not being sure what we actually would be doing. Presumably someone knew! Later, we spent most of one day and an evening rehearsing for the review.

My former flying instructor, Fg. Off. Smith, spoke to 60 Entry about what it was like converting onto jet aircraft at an Advanced Flying School. Then the A Squadron Commander, Sqn. Ldr. Smith, continued with additional useful advice. We were shown films on ejector seats and investigations into air accidents.

Ron told me that a Central Flying School instructor had flown with him. Unfortunately, their Harvard's tail wheel tyre had burst on landing through fair wear and tear. I saw the results of another Harvard accident – dents and tears in the cowling and wings made by a flock of birds during a low flying exercise. I heard that a drunken Corporal had tried to take-off in a Chipmunk during night flying, only to crash into a hangar, extensively damaging the aircraft.

CFS instructors also flew with Laurie Jones of 60A, Wally Close of 60B and Mal Dines of 60A, as all three had been nominated for the R.M. Groves Memorial Prize for flying.

The flying Order of Merit was then promulgated. As expected, Laurie topped the list, followed by Wally and Mal. I was fourteenth equal out of the thirty-one GD(P) members, but Ron and Jim were well down the list.

At a guest night attended by several Naval Captains, Hammy Khan of 60C presented a cup on behalf of the Pakistanis at the College for inter-squadron badminton competition. Then an Old Cranwellian, Gp. Capt. J.H. Lapsley, OBE, DFC, AFC, MID, of Fighter Command Headquarters, gave a first rate lecture on fighter operations. He was largely responsible for the fighter tactics used at that time in the RAF and spoke with authority about modern fighter performance. Much of what he said was right up to date and highly classified. He concluded by showing a film on fighter tactics in which Meteors made spectacular head-on attacks on Superfortresses. This was what I wanted to do!

Ron again took me in his car to Kesteven Teachers' Training College. He told me that he and June would announce their engagement before the end of term and they'd already chosen a ring. 'Well done – I hope you'll be very happy,' I said. At Kesteven I thought I'd meet up with Monica Potter, but she'd missed a note I'd sent and wasn't there, so I joined up with some other visiting Flight Cadets and went into Grantham. We saw a film and attended a dance, meeting a number of Kesteven girls at the dance. Eight of us squeezed into a taxi for the return to Kesteven. The girls very kindly gave us supper of tea and biscuits before we had to return to Cranwell.

I heard that, for some reason, girls from the local Teachers' Training Colleges would not be permitted to attend the 60 Entry passing-out ball, even though their terms finished on the same day as the ball. This was hard to understand and affected a number of Flight Cadets who had girlfriends at the Colleges. An exception was made for June Spackman, however, as she was about to announce her engagement and Ron would be leaving for New Zealand soon afterwards.

As Laurie Jones had been detailed as the parade commander for the passing-out parade, John Tucker became the A Squadron commander. John had his first experience of this at a routine ceremonial parade and caused some confusion by being a little out in the timing of two or three orders.

When A Squadron became the duty squadron, John and I were told to inspect the Junior Entry Cadets and march them to church. I had again to take the reading at the OD church.

Late in the term, Joe Vella, one of the Equipment and Secretarial chaps who'd been integrated into 60B, was relegated to 61B. I'd only known him about two months so didn't feel his departure as keenly as other colleagues I'd known longer. He was to be the last to leave 60 Entry before the passing-out parade.

Of the forty-six original GD(P) members of the Entry, eighteen had been killed, relegated, transferred or suspended, giving a chop rate of 39.1 per cent – well above what was understood to be the College average of some 23.5 per cent. Of the nine additions to the Entry from No. 59 GD(P) Entry and No. 11 E & S Entry, two had been relegated or transferred. Thus, with only thirty-five of us left, the final chop rate became 36.4 percent.

The Assistant Commandant summoned 60 Entry and told us the final Order of Merit and the prize winners.

I was twenty-second out of the thirty-one members of the GD(P) group! I'd beaten Ron (who was twenty-sixth), but Jim was well ahead at sixteenth. I hardly expected to beat Ron – I was just filled with relief to be graduating from the best air academy in the world, Ron and I being the first from the RNZAF to do so. Laurie Jones, of course, topped the list winning not only the Sword of Honour, but the Queen's Medal and four other prizes – a unique achievement and almost a clean sweep of the major prizes.

There were still three weeks to go, however, before we could pass-out from the College on 15 December.

My tutor, Flt. Lt. Dean, challenged me to a game of squash. He was a member of the RAF Cranwell team that'd won the last RAF Squash Team

Championships, so easily beat me. He told me that my thesis had come second in the science section to that of Pete Anstee, who'd won the thesis prize – The Royal United Services Institution Award. I was greatly encouraged on hearing this. Flt. Lt. Dean also mentioned that the Senior Tutor Humanistics had incorporated in his lecture notes some ideas on air power that'd come from a few of the humanistics section theses.

Fg. Off. Bolton took me on my first official formation flight in a Harvard, with Mal and Sam solo in two other Harvards. On another day, I did solo formation flying with other Harvards in rather bumpy conditions. Each pilot took turns at leading and we all ended up sweating profusely. We continued to fly on solo formation flights whenever we could until fog brought them to an end.

Ted Reynolds, Nigel MacNicol and I flew with our instructors to RAF Upper Heyford to practise ground controlled approaches. As the station was occupied by the USAF, our radios had to be recrystallised so that we could talk on American frequencies. We flew above cloud most of the way, but the American radar easily located us and a controller talked us down with incredible accuracy to safe landings – 'You are ten feet above the glide path . . . turn one degree to starboard . . . steady . . . you are now below the overcast, on the centre line, on glide path . . . look ahead and land.' I looked ahead, closed the throttle and landed.

A jeep with a 'Follow Me' sign on it appeared in front of us. We taxied behind it to the dispersal area. Identification labels were given to us and we were taken to the officers' mess for lunch – shredded chicken, hash browns, salad and coke. The Americans looked at us with some curiosity. We were then taken to the control tower to meet the GCA controller and have the GCA system explained to us. A jeep again guided us to the take-off point. The other two Harvards flew in formation on me as we returned to Cranwell.

The RAF Regiment instructors briefed 60 Entry for a night exercise. Half of us were to 'attack and destroy' an aircraft in a hangar at RAF Barkston Heath, while the other half defended the airfield. We were all issued with twenty blank cartridges for our rifles, and thunderflashes were issued to the Under Officers. I was one of the attackers. The night was pitch black so recognition of leaders, signals and landmarks was virtually impossible. Night flying at Cranwell prevented us from using Very cartridges to help us see in the dark.

As a result, we attackers wandered across the airfield unopposed and were about to enter the hangar when a referee prematurely sounded the withdrawal signal. Somewhat frustrated by this, we started firing blank cartridges and throwing thunderflashes as we withdrew, scaring a few civilians on Ermine Street. The rifle magazines wouldn't feed the blanks properly, so each blank had to be manually loaded. We still had a lot of blanks left when we climbed aboard trucks and returned to Cranwell for a hot meal. A debriefing the next morning tried to make something of this rather futile exercise. We attackers were even blamed for firing during the withdrawal and scaring civilians!

Our last GCT exercise was a tactical exercise without troops (TEWT) at Byard's Leap. We were divided into syndicates and each had to decide where to place squadrons, flights and sections to defend the area. We got so cold and muddy tramping about the countryside that, at a break in proceedings, we rushed to a local café and filled up on eggs, chips, coffee and the like. Having such an exercise so late in our training was hard to take seriously.

The RAF Regiment instructors then tried to asphyxiate us. After lectures on atomic, bacteriological and chemical (ABC) warfare, 60 Entry was told to put on gas masks, enter a hut full of tear gas, do some exercises and then remove the masks for about half a minute. We were a sorry sight when we emerged from the hut, gasping for breath, tears streaming from our eyes and feeling stinging on our necks where we'd shaved.

Cranwell became hosts once again to officers and Cadets of the RMA Sandhurst for the annual boxing, cross-country running, fencing, rugby, shooting and squash contests. A guest night showed an extraordinary variety of uniform, including those of the Royal Navy and Royal Marine arbiters of the contests. An Army officer in a dark green uniform with chain mail on the shoulders sat to one side of me, while on the other side in his dinner jacket sat the College Director of Studies.

We then moved to the gymnasium to watch the boxing. The band played and cigar, pipe and cigarette smoke rose above the floodlit ring as we all screamed ourselves hoarse urging on the contestants. Unfortunately, that weekend the College only won the rugby and the cross-country running.

The instructors of E Flight in Flying Wing decided to hold a farewell dinner for the 60 Entry members of the Flight. They took us in their cars to the Sleaford Golf Club and gave us a very pleasant evening. When the Club closed we continued with party games at Flt. Lt. E.J.A. Patterson's married quarter. His Canadian wife didn't seem to mind! Laurie Jones went back to the College because he had to be up early for a parade the next morning, so when the rest of us returned to the College, we rather unkindly tipped him out of bed.

On another night, I went with a number of Flight Cadets to a formal dance at Eaton Hall Teachers' Training College. I wore my dinner jacket for the first time. There were lots of girls there I hadn't met before, so I got to know a few of them.

Ron drove Tony Whitwam and me to Kesteven Teachers' Training College for another night out. He told us that he and June were now officially engaged. We congratulated him warmly. He also said that Jim Brown was going to buy his share of the car. At Kesteven, I met up with Monica Potter again. We hitchhiked the four miles to Grantham, had a meal, saw a film, hitchhiked back to Kesteven and drank coffee until Ron was ready to return to Cranwell.

Ron and I also went to the Kesteven end of term dance. The hired band was hopeless, so many of the dancers went into another room and danced to loud music from a radiogram until someone came to say that the band had left and visitors should also be going home.

Ted Reynolds and I decided to exercise one of the Senior Entry privileges by getting permission to go to the station cinema on a Thursday night. We needed something to occupy the unaccustomed spare time that we now had! On other nights, few of 60 Entry seemed to be around. Presumably they were at parties!

As a final act of authority while still the Senior Entry, 60 Entry conducted a kit check of everyone in the College.

60 Entry members had their own kit problems, however, as we were given a list of equipment that had to be returned and another list of equipment that would be issued to us. In addition, we were given a clearance form that required twenty-four signatures in a certain order! Ron and I were unsure as to whether we should accept the equipment issued to RAF officers (e.g. the battledress design was different and the RNZAF didn't wear berets), and asked for advice from RNZAF Headquarters in London. We were told to accept what was issued to us and our kit would be reviewed on arrival back in New Zealand.

A bus took 60 Entry to the Clothing Store, together with the equipment we had to return. We retained our airman pattern boots as they were to be used during the passing-out parade. I was very pleased to be issued with a metal trunk in which to pack my accumulation of books.

I heard that Plt. Off. Tony Pugh (an Old Etonian, formerly in 59A) had been killed in an aircraft accident – the second of his Entry to lose his life. Soon afterwards two former members of 60 Entry, Pete McKechnie and Sabre McLelland-Brown, were suspended from 61 Entry. When Ramsay Brown of 60C was charged with the theft of a generator from the Flight Cadets' Garage, there was considerable speculation as to whether he'd be the last to be chopped from the Entry. Fortunately, a summary of evidence cleared him of the charge just prior to the passing-out parade. For some unknown reason, Bulldog Drummond of 60C didn't go on parade one day so he was put on jankers for the rest of term. I was detailed to take early morning Under Officers' parades and found it strange having to drill one of my own Entry!

60 Entry waited anxiously for the end of term interviews. The Commandant wanted to see us individually, dressed in officer pattern uniform.

Air Cdre. Eeles told me that, on the whole, my report was a good one. My flying had improved tremendously during the last term and I was a high average pilot with plenty of initiative. My academic work was just below average. I'd tried hard and had absorbed the basic stuff. I was smart, conscientious, considerate, mature etc., but (I was wondering when he'd come to this!) tended to stay in the background, lacked drive and sparkle. He thought I'd do better in a squadron and said I should make a conscious effort. He concluded by saying how the RAF and the Dominion Air Forces must stick together. When he asked if I had any comments, I said that I thought there needed to be more co-ordination between the College and RNZAF Headquarters in London, and I mentioned one or two examples. The Commandant then shook my hand and wished me luck.

Ron told me after his interview, the Commandant had said much the same as he'd said to me – but that Ron remained in the background, lacked assertiveness and polish. In flying, he said Ron should develop into a good average pilot suitable for heavy aircraft. Jim told me that the Commandant said he (Jim) treated GCT and drill far too lightly.

My interview with the A Squadron Commander, Sqn. Ldr. Smith, went along much the same lines as that of the Commandant.

Then the Assistant Commandant, Gp. Capt. Nelson, addressed 60 Entry after a Sunday lunch and made it clear that he didn't think much of us as an Entry. We hadn't worked well together – it had something to do with our attitude – and he warned us about this in our future careers.

I felt that Gp. Capt. Nelson had made a good point and remembered an earlier comment directed at 60A that we were always cutting each other's throats. Perhaps there were too many individualists in 60 Entry and we could have done better. There was a view in the Entry, however, that we were as good as if not better than previous entries we'd known. I was a little aggrieved that the Group Captain's criticism (if justified) hadn't been made much earlier so that the Entry could have done something to improve its performance.

60 Entry practised the slow marching into the College that would be done at the end of the passing-out parade. Then in Hangar 30 we slow marched off at the end of a wet weather rehearsal.

For the last ten days of term, there was an almost unprecedented spell of foggy weather that prevented many of 60 Entry completing their flying. I still had thirty minutes of formation flying to do, but that was insufficient reason to retain me after the passing-out parade. During my time at Cranwell, I'd flown dual and solo a total of 292 hours and 20 minutes, plus 48 hours as a passenger. Ron and Jim had less flying time and were told they had to complete their flying after passing-out from the College.

At the final guest night, 60 Entry had sherry with the officers and guests before entering the dining hall. I found myself sitting beside the Rev. E. Davies, who promptly talked me into reading one of the lessons at the final church service of term. The usual speeches were made welcoming and farewelling staff before the Commandant rose to address 60 Entry. He began by saying that the best way of getting out of making the speech, having a graduation and all it entails would have been to chop the Entry – and that is what had been tried! He put it very politely that he thought we were a 'shower', but eventually proposed a toast to 60 Entry. Laurie Jones replied and proposed a toast to the College. For once the band played quietly (seeming to reflect the depressing tenor of the Commandant's speech), until the familiar strains of the 'Post Horn Gallop' sounded. This cheered me up a little.

60 Entry then went on to present the review, 'Hell's a Choppin' or The One in Sixty Yule'. A programme was issued marked CONFIDENTIAL (burn before reading) on which readers could use their imagination:

   I INTRODUCTION

  II HMS *DEADLOSS*
     (Selection team: Grizzly Strickhard, Robertson, No. 21, Ivor Crasnovitch and Intruder)

 III THREE JUVENILE UNDER OFFICERS
     (S/U/Os Bones, Pansy, Closet and one Cadet)

 IV PASSING OFF THE SQUARE
     (W/O Basters and sundry Cadets)

  V MESSY MEETINGS
     (Flt. Lt. Crawl, Gp. Capt. Belson, Gp. Capt. F . . . all and Cadets Qweer, Pharter and Others)

 VI A SQUADRON LEADER BIDS ADIEU
     (An unknown Sqn. Ldr. and his CWO)

 VII NIGHT FLYING BRIEFING
     (Met. Man, Duty Air Traffic Controller, Squadron Commander, Corporals and odd Cadets)

VIII A LECTURE ON THE REGIMENT
     (An Instructor and interested Cadets)

 IX WHAT IS A FLIGHT CADET?
     (Your guess is as good as ours)

  X THE KNACKER CLAP

 XI PASSING-OUT PARADE

 XII FINALE

Considering the small amount of time we'd spent in preparing the review, it all went very well and was rated by many of the people I spoke to as being the next best review after that of 57 Entry. Even the Assistant Commandant said it was very good – except in one or two places where it was bad enough to cause the C of E Padre to walk out! I think most of 60 Entry considered the review to be quite mild compared with that of 58 Entry which was downright rude. Afterwards, the officers bought us drinks in the Senior Entry ante-room and we talked well into the next morning. As a final prank, some of 60 Entry captured the hall porter and sang Christmas carols over the Tannoy system at 0200 hours!

The postings for the RAF members of 60 Entry were announced. Jim Brown was delighted that he'd be flying Meteors at RAF Driffield.

Robin Pringle had the misfortune to fall ill, but was let out of dock just in time to pass-out from the College.

Our College bank and mess accounts were closed and all transactions after that had to be in cash. We were each given a copy of the Rules of the Old Cranwellian Association and invited to join. I was disappointed, however, that British Commonwealth graduates were excluded from joining. 'Sorbo Bill' issued flat RAF Wings to be later sewn onto our battledress uniforms. Flying log books had to be made up for the signature of the CFI.

I returned my flying equipment to Stores and sold my bike. 'Henrietta', the ex-London taxi, which had been little used during the term because of its unreliability, was left with Mal Dines to sell. Laurie and I played our last game of squash. The final photographs of term were taken including that of 60 Entry (Fig. 38s361
).

There were numerous letters that had to be written before I left Cranwell. I received a very nice personal letter from Gieves Limited (just before they sent me a bill for £53 4s 7d!):

Pilot Officer R.M. Hancock, RNZAF,
Royal Air force College,
Cranwell, Lincs.

Sir,
    The achievement of a Commission concludes the initial stage of your career in the Royal New Zealand Air Force.
    This is an occasion, therefore, when I hope that I may be permitted to send you my most respectful and sincere congratulations, and to include the good wishes of all those in 'Gieves' whose pleasure it has been to look after your requirements.

I am, Sir,
Yours obediently,

(R. W. Gieve),

Figure 38. NO. 60 ENTRY DECEMBER 1953

Back Row

L-R: S/F/Cs Colin P. Field; J.C. (Jim) Brown; E.H. (Ted) Moors; M.J. (Mal) Dines; John E. Maitland; Julian M.B. Bowes; John B. Gratton; R.A. (Ron) Edwards; U/O T.S.B. (Sam) Boyce; S/F/C John R. McEntegart.

Second Row

L-R: S/F/Cs D.J. (Dave) Woods★★; J.M. (Bulldog) Drummond; Duncan Allison; Ron Chippindale, RNZAF; D.D. (Dave) Vickers; M.M. (Mike) Marsh; A.C. (Andy) Whitson; R.M. (Hank) Hancock, RNZAF; Alan Bright★★; Nigel R. MacNicol.

Front Row

L-R: U/O M.H. (Hammy) Khan, RPAF; U/O John R. Watts★; U/O T.J. (Tom) Greenhill-Hooper; U/O A.S.J. (Tony) Whitwam; S/U/O W.E. (Wally) Close; S/U/O L.A. (Laurie) Jones; S/U/O/ P.J. (Pete) Anstee; U/O .J. Alun Morgan; U/O R. (Dickie) Hoare; U/O Robin B. Pringle★; U/O John A. Tucker.

Absent: S/F/Cs Ramsay McN. Brown; Armand K. Coleman; E. (Ted) Reynolds; C.C. (Chris) Taylor.

All General Duties (Pilot) Branch except:

★Secretarial Branch,

★★ Equipment Branch.

Managing Director.

When the final church service of term was held, there were prayers for 60 Entry before we marched away from the Hangar Church with the College band playing the usual tune for such occasions, 'Wish me luck as you wave me goodbye'. Rain then forced the band to retire.

When the presentation of Wings ceremony began in the main lecture hall, Air Vice Marshal L.F. Pendred, CB, MBE, DFC (Air Officer Commanding-in-Chief, Flying Training Command), the Commandant, the Assistant Commandant, the Director of Studies and 'Sorbo Bill' took their seats on the stage. The audience comprised 60 Entry and their guests. Gp. Capt. D.W. Baird, AFC, and Sqn. Ldr. Gavin were present, representing the RNZAF. 'Sorbo Bill' called the GD(P) members of 60 Entry onto the stage in alphabetical order to receive their Wings from the Commandant. The padded Wings were temporarily attached to our best blue uniforms. We each shook hands with the Commandant and returned to our seats. The Commandant then presented the squadron trophies, individual prizes and awards, and congratulated the prizewinners, particularly Laurie Jones on his remarkable record of prizes won. He said that Laurie showed an extremely wide range of ability in all types of technical subjects, flying skill and other aspects of the College training.

When the Commandant addressed 60 Entry (Appendix V), he offered the usual good advice, but I felt that he need not have repeated on this rather public occasion the adverse comments the Assistant Commandant had earlier made privately to us. Also, he referred to our two years of training, when in fact it had been almost two years and eight months.

When the formalities were over, Julian Bowes asked me to look after his guests, Mrs Woods and daughter Rosemary, while he changed into mufti. I was pleased to see them again and catch up on their news. Then Ron and I chatted with Gp. Capt. Baird and Sqn. Ldr. Gavin. Ron left to meet his fiancée, June, so the Group Captain invited me to have dinner with him and Sqn. Ldr. Gavin at Grantham. I changed into mufti and an airman drove us to the George Hotel. I was surprised to find Ron, June and her parents also having a meal at the Hotel. The Group Captain told me over dinner that he'd trained at RAF Spitalgate, but had forgotten the area. We then walked to the Red Lion hotel to meet Cousin Mabel, but she'd just gone to the cinema. I left a message for her. There seemed to be an awful lot of Cranwell people in Grantham that evening! The Group Captain's driver returned me to Cranwell in time for me to catch up on some much needed sleep.

A telegram from my parents arrived the next morning just before the passing-out parade, congratulating Ron and me on graduating from Cranwell.

Thick fog covered much of Britain on 15 December, but Cranwell had uninterrupted sunshine and mild temperatures for the passing-out parade.

Unfortunately, we still had to wear greatcoats! Pools of water on the parade ground from early rain reflected the glistening green roof, red brick and white stone of the College.

At 1110 hours, the three squadrons of the Cadet Wing marched onto the parade ground and formed up in line in review order while the College band played (as shown on the programme) the 'Royal Air Force College Quick March'. U/O Dickie Hoare, the Queen's Colour Ensign, then marched on parade accompanied by the Colour escorts. Spectators stood, saluted or uncovered their heads while 'The Point of War' was played followed by 'The Lincolnshire Poacher'. During the intermission that followed, the band played 'Greensleeves'. As usual, my hat was killing me and the strong light from the sun, low on the horizon, at times made my eyes water. I felt that I never wanted to hear 'Greensleeves' again!

The newly appointed Chief of the Air Staff, Air Chief Marshal Sir William F. Dickson, GCB, KBE, DSO, AFC, had difficulty in travelling from London in the fog to review the parade, but he arrived right on time. The Commandant escorted him to the saluting base. Spectators stood and those in uniform saluted as he passed. The band played 'Fanfare'.

S/U/O Laurie Jones, the parade commander, then ordered a General Salute and the band played 'The Royal Air Force General Salute'.

The rather short Air Chief Marshal made a surprisingly quick inspection of the Cadet Wing, much to my relief, while the band played 'The Regimental Colour' and 'The Skye Boat Song'.

When the Cadet Wing had formed close column on the west flank to the tune 'The British Grenadiers', Laurie Jones and the parade adjutant, U/O Tony Whitwam, led the slow march past to the east flank while the band played another well known tune, 'Scipio'. C Squadron, the Sovereign's Squadron, commanded by S/U/O Pete Anstee was followed by A Squadron commanded by U/O John Tucker (Fig. 39), and then B Squadron commanded by S/U/O Wally Close. After halting and turning about, the Cadet Wing

---

Opposite page: Figure 39. NO. 60 ENTRY PASSING-OUT PARADE DECEMBER 1953

A Squadron slow marching in open order past the saluting base.

No. 60 Entry A Squadron members
(except for S/F/C D.D. (Dave) Vickers, C Squadron, who was filling a gap left by S/U/O L. A. (Laurie) Jones, A Squadron, the Parade Commander) –
Squadron Commander: U/O John A. Tucker
Supernumeraries:
L-R: U/O Robin B. Pringle; S/F/C R.M. (Hank) Hancock; S/F/C Alan Bright; S/F/C Nigel R. MacNicol; U/O T.S.B. (Sam) Boyce; S/F/C M.J. (Mal) Dines; S/F/C E. (Ted) Reynolds; S/F/C D.D. (Dave) Vickers (obscured); S/F/C/ Julian M.B. Bowes (obscured)

made a quick march past to the west flank to the tune 'Highland Laddie'. As the Colour passed, spectators saluted or uncovered.

The Cadet Wing then reformed in line as the band played 'Hearts of Oak'. When an advance in review order was made to the tune 'The Royal Air Force Advance', there was another General Salute – the band once again playing 'The Royal Air Force General Salute'.

ACM Dickson presented the Sword of Honour and the Queen's Medal to Laurie Jones before delivering his address (Appendix VI). The Air Chief Marshal directed his remarks to the RAF members on parade and didn't mention that the RNZAF and RPAF were also represented in 60 Entry. I felt this was an unfortunate oversight – or he'd been poorly briefed.

Laurie requested permission to march off the Colour and the Senior Entry. As the Colour Party and 60 Entry slow marched up the steps into the College, the band played 'Auld Lang Syne'.

At last I could remove my hat and wipe my brow – Yes, I'd made it – I'd graduated and was now a Pilot Officer! There were congratulations all round amongst the newly commissioned members of 60 Entry.

I watched from the main entrance foyer as the Cadet Wing, under the command of the new Senior Entry, marched off the parade ground to the stirring sound of 'The Royal Air Force March Past'.

(The *Journal* later reported that, 'The parade and the attendant ceremonies reached as near perfection as is possible in human affairs . . . but the experts could find some points which they resolved should be yet better done next time.')

I quickly changed into my new officer pattern uniform, complete with Pilot Officer's braid, padded New Zealand Wings and shoulder patches. Out on the Orange, I located Cousin Mabel and found that she'd been sitting almost opposite me while the parade was formed up in line. I was delighted she was able to be there, particularly when my parents and Betty couldn't be present. Gp. Capt. Baird and Sqn. Ldr. Gavin congratulated Ron and me and photographs were taken of us all.

Cousin Mabel and I then went on a tour of the College, except for the library where sherry was being served to the VIPs. 60 Entry and guests then had a formal lunch with the VIPs in the dining hall. The band played tunes as on a guest night such as 'Do you ken John Peel', making conversation a little difficult. After a thoroughly enjoyable meal, Cousin Mabel and I walked slowly around West Camp while I gave her a running commentary. All too soon, her bus arrived and she had to depart for Grantham and catch a train to Aberdeen.

Late in the day, thick fog returned to Cranwell causing the cancellation of buses and other means of transportation. This, and the decisions of the local Teachers' Training Colleges not to allow their female students to go to the ball that evening, resulted in a shortage of girls for the ball. Some Flight Cadets decided to drown their sorrows at the bars.

I took the opportunity to speak with most of my former flying instructors, including Sqn. Ldr. Sillars who'd returned to Cranwell for the occasion. Jim and I had supper with his flying instructor and wife. Then I danced with an attractive girl who'd been standing by herself in the ballroom. She was part of a group from Sleaford and RAF Scampton who were guests of a Flying Officer stationed at Cranwell. We all got on very well and many remarks were made about my New Zealand Wings and shoulder patches. The graduation ball eventually came to an end and I wearily made my way to bed at 0300 hours.

I was up again at 0730 hours to get the last two signatures on my clearance form. My good intentions of saying goodbye to members of my Entry didn't happen as I'd hoped – there was so much to do at the last minute. I made a special effort to see Jim and wish him well as we'd been through so much together since leaving New Zealand, but he'd developed influenza and was feeling sick after some heavy drinking at the ball. I said goodbye to Charlie my batman, threw the last of my things into my cases and, with a fleeting look back at the College, left at 1100 hours in a taxi with Laurie for Grantham railway station.

I was just getting settled in the train to Aberdeen when Zoë Sinton and a girlfriend came to speak to me. What a coincidence! Zoë had seen me get onto the train. We talked much of the way to Newcastle (where she was going for a holiday), and I discovered she'd just got a Government bursary that would allow her to continue ballet dancing in Britain for another two years. At Newcastle, I helped get her cases off the train and we wished each other the best of luck for the future.

I had to change trains at Edinburgh and wait for the connection as it had been delayed by fog. Thick frost covered everything when I arrived at Aberdeen late in the evening. I called briefly on Betty to wish her well for an exam the next day. When I reached the Rundles' place, Cousin Mabel was waiting up for me with a snack. I was soon asleep in bed.

After a long lie-in, the Rundles told me that Cousin Lella hadn't been too well, Alice had a poisoned leg, Francis's voice had broken, Alice and Leslie wouldn't be home for Christmas, the piano had been sold and Peter the cat had died.

I began sorting my things in preparation for the voyage home. My surplus clothing went to Mr Rundle, my model aeroplanes to Francis and my heavy luggage to the shipping agents at Liverpool. I had a photograph taken of me in my Pilot Officer's uniform (Fig. 40), bought Christmas presents for the Rundles and Aitkens, and also a Boxing Day birthday present for Betty.

Figure 40: PILOT OFFICER RUTHERFORD M. HANCOCK
DECEMBER 1953

Needless to say, I spent most of my leave with Betty. We had a great time at the end of year dance in Aberdeen University's Mitchell Hall where we'd met. This rather made up for Betty not being able to come to my passing-out ball. Then we went ice skating twice, saw the comedy film *Scared Stiff*, had supper at Betty's home and attended a Christmas carol service. Cousin Mabel invited Betty to dinner and I tried teaching Betty how to use a slide rule. I was looking for a suitable opportunity to propose to her (as I was in love and felt sure she was the one the fortune-teller had referred to), but everywhere we went seemed too public. Betty suggested we go for a late afternoon walk in snowy conditions and freezing temperatures at Hazelhead Park. There were not many people around, and our dallying only resulted in us getting locked in the Park and having to climb over a fence to escape!

Then we went to the Christmas Day dance at the Students' Union. As usual, the dance was scheduled to begin at 8 p.m., but few people did any dancing until about 10 p.m. We danced, had supper, danced again and looked for a lounge in which to cool down and talk. The lounge we went to was in darkness. I was about to switch on the light when a man with a thick Scottish accent said, 'Leave the bloody light alone.' (Where had I heard something like that before?) Betty and I groped our way to a settee and became aware that several unseen couples were in the lounge. I felt sure that noises across the room were coming from a couple having intercourse! Somebody came into the lounge, switched the light on and off quickly and departed leaving me temporarily blinded.

At last the other people departed and Betty and I were alone. I wasted no time and proposed to her. To my delight, she said 'Yes.' My fears that she would want to continue living in Scotland and marry a university graduate who was not in the Air Force proved to be groundless. (I'm also pleased to say that the comment made by the French entertainer Maurice Chevalier, that 'Many a man has fallen in love with a girl in light so dim he would not have chosen a suit by it' didn't apply in my case!)

We could hear the band playing the National Anthem so knew that the dance was over. Arm-in-arm, we walked slowly to Betty's home.

By a strange coincidence, we arrived there at 2.50 a.m., the time that Betty had been born exactly twenty-one years previously. Mrs Aitken was still up and expressed surprise when Betty and I told her of our engagement! 'Betty has always thought of herself as a career girl, but you've changed all that,' she told me. Fortunately, Mrs Aitken gave us her blessing and I didn't have to mention that when she was at the same age as Betty, she'd got married! 'You remind me of my late husband, Harry,' she added. I felt that she was trying to pay me a compliment. Betty woke her younger sister, Hazel, and told her the news. Hazel wasn't at all surprised! She'd guessed that Betty and I would become engaged. Reluctantly I said goodnight and made my way back to the Rundles' place.

I was up in time for lunch and told the Rundles about my engagement. They were only mildly surprised as I'd forewarned Cousin Mabel that I might be getting engaged. I sent my parents a cryptic telegram ('The answer is Yes') as I didn't want the girl at the Post Office counter to read wording that was more direct. (Luckily, Mum and Dad interpreted the telegram correctly.)

Later on Boxing Day, I went to the Aitkens' for Betty's birthday tea. Betty showed me her presents and told me that her pet aversion was getting Christmas and birthday presents rolled into one! She wondered what her friends would say when they heard about our engagement and dreaded having to tell Professor Barrow that, when she got her BSc in six months time, she wouldn't be continuing for Honours! I left my photo albums with the Aitkens so they could show them to relatives.

Betty and I spent ages looking for an engagement ring. Eventually we bought one made of platinum that had an emerald and two diamonds held in a delicate mounting. Leslie claimed full credit in choosing the ring because we'd bought it at a jewellery shop he'd recommended!

Betty had the opportunity to flash her engagement ring at two functions – one by Billie and Mary Reid (old friends of the Aitkens) and the other by Mrs Aitken. With about twenty people at the latter, I got rather confused as to who everyone was, let alone names such as Mary Reid, her daughter Mary Massie ('Little Mary') and husband Sandy Massie, Sandy Anderson ('Big Sandy') and son ('Little Sandy'). With everyone talking at once in strong Scottish accents, I could have been excused at times for missing what was said. Everyone was very generous in giving Betty and me lovely engagement gifts and cards.

As I'd promised Mrs Killoh and Mrs Alexander that I'd try and see them again before I returned to New Zealand, I took Betty with me to Oldmeldrum and we had tea with them. Though Mrs Killoh was suffering from arthritis, she and her sister seemed very glad that we'd come, and said they were most impressed with Betty.

The Rundles invited the Aitkens to dinner one evening and a good time was had by all. Mr Rundle taught us some party tricks and we played a card game called Cheat.

The time had come for me to leave. Cousin Mabel and Cousin Lella were in tears as they stood on their doorstep and bade me *au revoir*, not knowing when we'd meet again. I just didn't know how to thank them for all they'd done for me and felt as if I was leaving home again. We promised to keep in touch.

I had a last meal with the Aitkens and they all came to see me off at the railway station. What could I say to Betty? We knew that at least six months would go by before she completed her degree and we could be married. Should she get an assisted immigrant passage to New Zealand? If I was sent to Cyprus, should she join me there? I comforted her as best as I could and departed for London, heavy in heart.

I didn't want to go to London, but the Bank of New Zealand had said that I needed to call at their London office to close my account. Also, I was so short of money that I hoped RNZAF Headquarters would give me the pay they'd been withholding from me while I was at Cranwell.

Though I had a sleeper on the train, I didn't sleep much and arrived in London tired and resentful. RNZAF Headquarters had booked me into the Regent Palace Hotel near Piccadilly Circus and, though I was impressed by the facilities and opulent style of the place, I'd have given anything to have been with Betty that New Year's Eve.

I joined the thousands of people in Piccadilly Circus and never felt more lonely. The statue of Eros had been barricaded up for the New Year celebrations and was surrounded by policemen. Several people climbed lamp-posts that had been greased to prevent them from being climbed. Policemen who intervened lost their helmets in the scuffles. Half-hearted attempts were made at community singing. (Newspapers later reported that it had been an unusually quiet New Year's Eve in London.) Cameras and a BBC announcer recorded the occasion. The traffic was stopped at 11.30 p.m. and eventually a countdown began and cheering broke out as clock chimes rang in the New Year. People kissed, linked hands and sang 'Auld Lang Syne'. I wondered what Betty was doing. Slowly, I forced my way through the crowds to Trafalgar Square to see the huge Norwegian illuminated Christmas tree. After supper in a Soho restaurant, I made my way back to the hotel and listened on the radio to Jimmy Shand and his band playing Scottish tunes from Glasgow.

Later on New Year's Day, I went to the Odeon to see *The Robe*, the first cinemascope film I'd seen, where sound came from speakers around the cinema. I had tea with Cousin Jennifer and some of her friends. Robert was at Brighton preparing for another play and Jennifer said she'd soon be joining him. I felt that Jennifer was rather preoccupied, so I didn't stay and said goodbye.

As soon as the Bank of New Zealand was open again, I withdrew my money and closed the account.

Then at RNZAF Headquarters, I was given a travel warrant for the train to Liverpool and told to pay my hotel bill and claim a refund in New Zealand. The aircrew watch I was wearing was taken from me to be returned to the RAF. (This was most inconvenient as my own watch was in a suitcase in the hold of the *Akaroa* at Liverpool.) I was also told that the pay owed me would be handed over in New Zealand after my RAF kit had been reviewed and financial adjustments had been made. This was a blow, as I was down to my last £7 and still had to pay the hotel, shipping agents and shipboard expenses.

I telegrammed my parents to have some money waiting for me when I arrived at Auckland. (I was later to step ashore at Auckland with just 1s 6d in my pocket – never have I been so broke! This was just enough to telephone home if money wasn't waiting for me. Luckily, my parents had sent money to get me to Timaru.)

I filled in the remainder of the day by going to the Bertram Mills Circus at Olympia. The show was excellent, though I was disappointed there was no flying trapeze act. Then I had supper with the Thomson family at Finchley and said I'd pass on their best wishes to their relations in Timaru.

Early next morning, I left Euston railway station on the boat train for Liverpool. There was thick fog all the way. Sqn. Ldr. Free, the recently promoted Movements Officer at RNZAF Headquarters, came into my carriage looking for the new RNZAF Chief of the Air Staff, AVM Merton. The train slowed as it went through a long tunnel under Liverpool before arriving at the docks. I boarded the *Akaroa* and joined Ron Chippindale on the deck.

'Did you get engaged?'

'Yes,' I answered.

'Congratulations – well done.' Ron shook my hand hard.

We resumed leaning on the rail of the *Akaroa* gloomily looking at the Liverpool docks and lapsed into silence. We'd both left a fiancée behind and were uncertain as to when we'd see them again. We each had our private thoughts.

Ron interrupted me with, 'I suppose we'd better find Mert and introduce ourselves to him.' I nodded.

Our odyssey in Britain was over.

Epilogue

EIGHT YEARS AFTER PASSING-OUT FROM CRANWELL, I was a Squadron Leader serving as New Zealand Military Liaison Officer in Korea and Member of the United Nations Command Military Advisory Group in the Common- wealth Liaison Mission at Panmunjom, when I was asked to go to Kimpo Airport at Seoul and meet an RAF Hastings aircraft that was bringing supplies and replacement members for the 17th and 25th Lancers based in Korea. A young RAF Pilot Officer was on the aircraft. When we discovered that we were both Old Cranwellians, he said that at his passing-out, his Entry had been told they may never meet each other again, but if they went to the ends of the earth they'd find an Old Cranwellian. He felt that in coming to an out-of-the-way place like Korea and meeting me, he'd arrived at the ends of the earth!

I regret that since leaving the College, I've had little contact with Old Cranwellians. While I was flying Vampires on No. 75 Squadron at RNZAF Ohakea, a Flight Cadet (whose name I forget) visited the Squadron. Then Flt. Lt. Sammy Salmond, formerly of No. 58 Entry, stayed briefly with me during the time I was a flying instructor at RNZAF Wigram. In five short visits to Britain over the years (three being at the end of business trips), I've been fortunate to attend two graduations – that of No. 91 Initial Officer Training Course (at which a New Zealander in the RAF was awarded the Sword of Merit) and that of No. 158 Initial Officer Training Course. I've also been able to visit the grave of Spike Heaney at Wakes Colne.

So what happened to the thirty-five members of No. 60 Entry after they'd passed-out from the College? Appendix VII, compiled from a number of publicly available sources, gives some indication of the Service careers of my former colleagues. I was fascinated to find that Duncan Allison, Laurie Jones and Alun Morgan reached Air rank, yet other members of 60 Entry who'd been high on the Order of Merit didn't achieve such high rank, retired early or served for many years in relatively junior ranks. I wonder why? As could be expected, Laurie Jones, winner of the Sword of Honour, Queen's Medal and other prizes, had a brilliant RAF career, became Air Member for Personnel, was knighted and, after retirement, was appointed Lieutenant-Gov- ernor of the Isle of Man. Unfortunately, he died of lung cancer before completing his term as Lieutenant-Governor. What happened to the rest of the thirty-five after they'd left the Service, to those members of 60 Entry relegated to other Entries, and to the other members of 60 Entry who didn't pass-out? I imagine I'm not the only one who'd like to know.

Ron Chippindale, Jim Brown and I all resigned our commissions when Squadron Leaders. Ron married June, became the Chief Inspector of Air Accidents in New Zealand and has been a target of media attention over the years, particularly during his investigation into the crash of an Air New Zealand DC10 airliner near Mt. Erebus in Antarctica. Jim married Llanis, flew Hunter fighters in the air force of the Sheik of Abu Dhabi and then Boeing 737 jets of Gulf Airways until retirement in New Zealand. I married Betty (but not without many difficulties – as foreseen by the fortune-teller), became a training consultant and then joined a multinational oil company as Personnel Manager – but that's another story.

The RNZAF continued to send officer Cadets to Cranwell until a university cadetship scheme was introduced in New Zealand. In all, fifteen members of the RNZAF went to Cranwell and graduated from the College (Appendix VIII), five of them winning the Sword of Honour and three the Queen's Medal. Three reached Air rank in the RNZAF, one becoming the Chief of the Air Staff. This was a good record by anyone's standards.

Then there were the New Zealanders in the RAF. Ron Parfitt resigned when a Flight Lieutenant, four years after winning the Sword of Honour at Cranwell. Colin Loveday became a Squadron Leader before resigning some fifteen years after leaving Cranwell. Jack Henderson became a test pilot, was awarded an OBE and AFC and Bar, before retiring as a Wing Commander almost twenty-seven years after winning the Queen's Medal at the College. Unfortunately, Jack died ten years later. Since then other New Zealanders have done well in the RAF such as Ken Hayr of No. 69 Entry who won the R.M. Groves Memorial Prize and one other prize and retired as AM Sir Kenneth Hayr, KCB, KBE, AFC, and Dmitri Zotov of No. 80 Entry, a navigator who won the Queen's Medal and four other prizes. Dmitri resigned from the RAF and worked for Ron Chippindale as an Inspector of Air Accidents.

My flying instructors also had chequered careers. Fourteen years after I'd left Cranwell my Prentice/Chipmunk instructor, Fg. Off. H.McC. Vincent, resigned from the RAF as a Flight Lieutenant. Flt. Lt. R.B. Sillars, who took over as my Chipmunk instructor, retired when a Group Captain over twenty years later. My other instructor on Chipmunks, Flt. Lt. L.J.A. Maisonpierre, retired as a Squadron Leader some twenty years later. Three of my Harvard instructors became Squadron Leaders – Flt. Lt. A.J. Thompson retired almost nineteen years later with the Honorary rank of Squadron Leader, Flt. Lt. J.P.M. Reid transferred into the Engineering Branch and retired almost fifteen years after I'd left the College, and Fg. Off. J.A. Smith retired over twenty-six years later. My last Harvard instructor, Fg. Off. W. Bolton, retired as a Flight Lieutenant fourteen years after I'd returned to New Zealand.

Perhaps some comment would be appropriate about the two Cadet Wing Officers with whom I was most associated. The A Squadron Commander, Sqn. Ldr. P.E.H. Thomas, retired as a Wing Commander about eleven years after I'd been commissioned. Flt. Lt. H.D. Hall, the A Squadron Cadet Wing Officer, retired twenty-nine years later as AVM H.D. Hall, CB, CBE, AFC. Sqn. Ldr. Thomas was right about the odds of reaching high rank being slim!

And what happened to the fourteen apprentices who went with me to Britain? One of them, Tom Enright, topped his course at Halton and went on to Cranwell where, in No. 70 Entry, he won the Sword of Honour, the Queen's Medal and other prizes. Eight of the apprentices were eventually commissioned in the RNZAF.

A few words about the College may also be pertinent. After I left the College, the fourth residential wing of the College (D Squadron) was built and sealed runways and taxiways were laid on the south airfield. The Hangar Church was replaced by a new Church of St Michael and All Angels and the Memorial Chapel in the College was transferred to it. Offices for the College Secretariat filled the space left by the Chapel. The Cadets' Garage and the Science and Weapons Block were demolished and replaced by trees. The old hangar that housed the Museum also disappeared. A new instructional building known as Whittle Hall was constructed in the field of poppies near the stadium, a new gymnasium and swimming pool replaced the A Site lecture rooms and an engineering block called Trenchard Hall was built in East Camp. The short cut from the west end of the College to Camp Road was closed and the old post office was demolished to make way for 'The Queen's Walk' from opposite the College gates to the Junior College parade ground. A new post office and shop was built across the road from the guard room in East Camp, and a new officers' mess was constructed on the north airfield to the east of the College. The marbled floors of the College corridors were carpeted and the heavy leather covered furniture in the ante-rooms was replaced by fabric covered settees and chairs. The individual rooms in the residential wings were completely refurnished. In the dining hall, the seating was rearranged and the huge National Gallery oil paintings were replaced by new ones of well known Old Cranwellians, such as His Royal Highness the Prince of Wales, Sir Frank Whittle, Gp. Capt. Sir Douglas Bader and the Earl of Bandon.

Two years after I left Cranwell, Junior Entries ceased to exist. Navigator and then RAF Regiment Cadets were introduced to the College, followed by Technical Cadets when the RAF Technical College at Henlow merged with Cranwell. No. 101 Entry was the last of the Flight Cadet entries. A Graduate Entry Scheme was introduced and Student Officers were often older, more mature and sometimes had wives and families. Women students appeared in the College with No. 1 Graduate Entry and were totally integrated with their male counterparts. The decision was then made to have all RAF officer training undertaken at Cranwell. The College syllabus, which was in some cases as long as three years under the old Flight Cadet system, was reduced initially to eighteen months and then became two years for Initial Officer Training Courses. Chaplains, lawyers, nurses, doctors, dentists and some re-entrant officers had a course length of eight weeks. The old nomenclature for A, B and C Squadrons gave way to a numerical system of squadrons and flights. Foreign and Commonwealth students were permitted to wear the uniforms of their countries.

One thing is certain, changes will continue at the College as every endeavour is made to increase the high standards set in its seventy-five year history, or at least maintain them.

I now look back at my time at Cranwell with some nostalgia, tending to remember the good times rather than the bad. Passing through the College wasn't easy, but I feel that I greatly benefited from being a Flight Cadet. In the three years I was overseas I probably did and experienced things that many people wouldn't do or experience in a lifetime.

As people tend to do, I wonder what would have happened if . . . if my cousin Keith Skinner hadn't given me a model aeroplane, if my family hadn't moved to Timaru, if Mr Pickard hadn't taught me at school and been my ATC officer, if I hadn't been selected for Cranwell, if I hadn't met Betty, if I hadn't passed-out from Cranwell, if . . .?

Appendices

Appendix I

ABBREVIATIONS AND EXPRESSIONS

Abbreviations

<u>Ranks</u>

AC2	Aircraftman 2
AC1	Aircraftman 1
Cpl.	Corporal
Sgt.	Sergeant
F/S	Flight Sergeant
W/O	Warrant Officer
Cdt.	Cadet
F/C	Flight Cadet
S/F/C	Senior Flight Cadet
U/O	Under Officer
S/U/O	Senior Under Officer
Plt. Off.	Pilot Officer
Fg. Off.	Flying Officer
Flt. Lt.	Flight Lieutenant
Sqn. Ldr.	Squadron Leader
Wg. Cdr.	Wing Commander
Gp. Capt.	Group Captain
Air Cdre.	Air Commodore
AVM	Air Vice Marshal
AM	Air Marshal
MRAF	Marshal of the Royal Air Force

Organisations

AAA	Amateur Athletics Association
ANS	Air Navigation School
ATC	Air Training Corps
AFS	Advanced Flying School
BBC	British Broadcasting Corporation
FTS	Flying Training School
GS	Grammar School
ITS	Initial Training School
NAAFI	Navy, Army and Air Force Institute
RAAF	Royal Australian Air Force
RAF	Royal Air Force
RMA	Royal Military Academy (Sandhurst)
RN	Royal Navy
RNAS	Royal Naval Air Service
RNC	Royal Naval College (Greenwich)
RNEC	Royal Naval Engineering College (Manadon)
RNZAF	Royal New Zealand Air Force
RPAF	Royal Pakistan Air Force
TTS	Technical Training School
USAF	United States Air Force
WRAF	Women's Royal Air Force
YMCA	Young Men's Christian Association

Other

ANZAC	Australian and New Zealand Army Corps
CAO	Cadets' Activities Organisation
CFI	Chief Flying Instructor
C-in-C	Commander-in-Chief
E & S	Equipment and Secretarial Branch
G	Gravity
GCA	Ground controlled approach
GCI	Ground controlled interceptions
GCT	Ground combat training

GD(N)	General Duties (Navigator) Branch
GD(P)	General Duties (Pilot) Branch
HMS	Her Majesty's Ship
IRT	Instrument Rating Test
MO	Medical Officer
NCO	Non Commissioned Officer
OD	Other Denomination
PT	Physical training
QGH	Controlled descent through cloud
VIPs	Very important persons

Expressions

Blanco	White or blue substance for colouring web equipment
Blood wagon	Ambulance
Bogs	Ablutions
Bollocking	Severe reprimand
Bolshie	Rebellious, uncooperative
Bull/Bulling	Unnecessary routine tasks or discipline
Chiefee	Flight Sergeant
Chop/Chopped	Dismissed, suspended, killed
Clag/Clagged	Penalised
Creased	Tired out
De-digitate	Remove finger, get cracking
Dock	Sick quarters/hospital
Erks	Airmen
Finger boy	Someone who does too much spit and polishing
Frog	An attachment to a waist-belt to support a bayonet etc.
Gen/Genned up	Brainy, information
Get skids on	Hurry up
Irons	Cutlery
Jankers	Punishment for defaulters
Mentioned in despatches	Mentioned in daily orders as having committed some misdemeanour
Pit/Sack	Bed

Pommy	English-born person
Pongo	English/Army person
Prang	Crash or accident
Set	Group of students of similar abilities
Shambolic	Chaotic
Skive/Skiving	Evade a duty, shirking
Shower	Contemptible or unpleasant person(s)
Slush	The town of Sleaford
Stick	A number of paratroopers
Thunderflash	Explosive device intended for training exercises
Tweeds	Trousers
Whipped	Took, stole, removed
Wizard	Wonderful, excellent
Wrap up	Be quiet, shut up

Appendix II

PERMANENT COMMISSIONS IN THE GENERAL DUTIES (FLYING) BRANCH OF THE ROYAL NEW ZEALAND AIR FORCE VIA THE ROYAL AIR FORCE COLLEGE CRANWELL

Introduction:

The Royal Air Force College, Cranwell, England, was established after the first World War with the aim of training suitable youths for Permanent Commissions in the Flying Branch of the Royal Air Force. Over the years, Cranwell has built up a tradition which remains unequalled – a tradition which those who enter the College can be proud to follow.

By agreement with the British Government the facilities of Cranwell are now available to New Zealand youths and each year two selected applicants may be nominated for entry as General Duties Branch Cadets for subsequent Permanent Commissions in the R.N.Z.A.F.

The Cadetship is regarded as an excellent opportunity for youths who are interested in an Air Force career, since entry through Cranwell offers prospects for promotion to the highest ranks of the Royal New Zealand Air Force. For this reason, only youths of the highest calibre and possessing potential qualities of leadership will be selected.

2. Conditions of Entry:

Applicants must fulfil the following conditions:

(a) Have attained the age of 17½ years but not have reached the age of 19 years on 1st January 1951.

(b) Have passed University Entrance examination <u>including mathematics and physics.</u>

(c) Be members of families resident in New Zealand.

(d) Comply with the medical standards laid down for admission to the General Duties Branch of the Royal Air Force.

3. Cadetship:

The duration of the cadetship is 2 years 7 months made up of three terms a year and eight terms in all. Flying training will normally commence towards the end of the first year's training.

On graduation, cadets should have reached the standard of the second year's work for a University Pass Degree, should be qualified as pilots and in navigation, and should have gained an adequate understanding of the duties of other categories of aircrew and of the functions of all classes of squadrons.

During the tenure of the cadetship no fees are payable nor is there any charge for books, etc., required in connection with studies. Cadets will, however, live in a Mess run on model Officer Mess lines and will be called upon to pay normal Mess fees.

The major items are:

	per month
Extra Messing	£1/10/-
Mess Maintenance	15/-
Sports	12/6
College Societies	2/-
Library	6d.
	£2/15/-

In addition there are certain other incidental expenses, some of which may be limited by individual taste, but it is customary to 'tip' college servants and to pay them for the pressing of clothes.

4. Rates of Pay:

During training, Cadets will be entitled to a daily rate of 11/8d. per day. In addition, on commencement of flying training towards the end of the first year, flying instructional pay at the rate of 3/-d. per day will be paid.

During service in the United Kingdom, R.N.Z.A.F. Cadets will be paid by the R.A.F. according to the rates provided for R.A.F. Cadets. The difference between the R.A.F. and the substantially higher R.N.Z.A.F. rates of pay will accrue at R.N.Z.A.F. Headquarters, London. Advances from accrued pay will be made for any reasonable purpose, on application to the Air Officer Commanding, R.N.Z.A.F. Headquarters, London. On return to New Zealand, personnel will receive the balance of all accrued pay.

R.A.F. Cadets are paid at the rate of 7/-d. per day, plus flying instructional pay when applicable.

Attached are the present rates of pay and allowances of permanent officers of the Royal New Zealand Air Force. Social Security and Income Tax are payable. Contributions are made to a Superannuation Fund from which a retiring allowance is payable on completion of service.

5. Commissions:

On successfully completing the course of training, Cadets will be appointed, subject to continued physical fitness, to permanent commissions in the General Duties Branch of the Royal New Zealand Air Force in the rank of Pilot Officer. Cadets who fail to qualify for entry to the General Duties Branch owing to lack of aptitude or a deterioration in physical fitness will be considered for alternative cadet training with a view to the grant of a permanent commission in one of the ground branches of the Service.

6. Passages to United Kingdom:

Free return passages to the United Kingdom will be provided for suitable applicants.

7. Guardianship:

Parents of successful applicants will be requested to nominate relations or friends in the United Kingdom as temporary guardians. Where this is not possible, the High Commissioner for N.Z. in London will act as official Guardian with the Air Officer Commanding, R.N.Z.A.F. Headquarters, London, keeping a close watch on the progress of the boys.

8. Selections:

All suitable candidates will be interviewed by a Selection Committee and those selected will be required to enter Cranwell towards the end of April 1951.

9. How to Apply:

All applications must be made on the prescribed form which may be obtained from the Air Secretary, Air Department, Wellington (for attention P3).

Attachment 'A' to Air Pamphlet 10

Pay and Allowances:

The following tables set out the rate of pay at present authorised for officers of the General Duties Branch.

		per day
Pilot Officer		24/4
Flying Officer		
	1st year	26/10
	2nd year	27/10
	3rd year	29/4
	4th year	31/10
Flight Lieutenant		
	1st year	35/10
	3rd year	37/10
	5th year	39/10
Squadron Leader		
	1st year	44/4
	3rd year	46/4
	5th year	48/4
	7th year	50/4
Wing Commander		
	1st year	50/10
	3rd year	53/4
	5th year	55/10
Group Captain		
	1st year	60/10
	3rd year	63/4
	5th year	65/10
Air Commodore		
	1st year	68/10
	3rd year	73/10

Allowances as under are issuable in conjunction with these rates of pay:

(a) Quarters and Rations Allowance: Where quarters and rations are not provided in kind an allowance of 4/6d per day is payable.

(b) Marriage Allowance: There is a marriage allowance of 3/-d per day.

(c) Separation Allowance: Where a married member is required to be separated from his family owing to exigencies of the Service and has to 'live in' on Station a separation allowance of 3/3d per day is payable.

(d) Uniform Upkeep Allowance: An allowance of £16 per annum is payable
to enable members to make necessary replacements to uniforms.

Uniform Grant:

Cadets on appointment to commissioned rank, receive a uniform outfit grant
of £70 and will be required to purchase all necessary articles of uniform.

Acknowledgement:

Air Pamphlet 10 was originally issued by the RAF and modified by the
RNZAF for the purpose of RNZAF Cadetships at the RAF College,
Cranwell.

Appendix III

From:-Headquarters, Royal Air Force College.

To:- Distribution List 'R'.

Date:- 25th April, 1951.

Ref:- RAF. COLL/JE/2526.

EARLY TRAINING
PROGRAMME – NO. 60 ENTRY

1. Herewith the Early Training Programme for No. 60 Entry, reporting to the Royal Air Force College on 2nd May, 1951.

		NO. 60 ENTRY PROGRAMME FOR PERIOD 2ND MAY 1951, TO 14 MAY 1951.		
Ser. No.	(a) Date and Time	(b) Event	(c) Place	(d) Action By
1.	2nd May	Arrival of Entry, issue of knife, fork, spoon, mug and pyjamas. Meal.	Sleaford. Block 77. Cdts Mess.	J.N.C.O. S.N.C.O. N.C.O. i/c Cdts Mess.
2.	3rd May 08.15	Reception talk and arrival report.	Hut 198.	Adjutant (J.E.)
3.	09.30	Kit inspection for serving airmen and ex-apprentices.	Block 77.	Adjutant (J.E.)
4.	09.30	Measurements taken for O.P. Uniforms.	Block 77.	College Tailors.
5.	11.00	Talk by College M.O. and F.F.I.	S.S.Q.	College M.O.

6.	11.30	Civilians hand in documents.	Hut 198.	Attestation Team.
7.	13.30	Vaccinations. Digby and Cranwell in separate parties.	S.S.Q.	College M.O.
8.	14.30	Attestation papers filled in for civilians.	Hut 198.	Attestation Team.
9.	14.30	Clothing parade for serving airmen, ex-apprentices, and civilians who have completed their documentation.	Clothing Stores.	Officer i/c Clothing Stores. Camp Tailor is to attend all clothing parades.
10.	4th May 08.30	Civilians clothing parade after their attestation papers are completed. Serving airmen and ex-apprentices clean and mark kit.	Hut 198. Clothing Stores. Hut 198.	Attestation Team. Officer i/c Clothing Stores J.N.C.O.
11.	14.00	Conducted tour of Cranwell.		S.N.C.O.
12.	5th May 08.30	Attestation.	College.	Squadron Commanders.
13.	10.15	Break.		
14.	10.45	Security talk and films.	College.	Adjutant (J.E.)
15.	11.30	Vaccination Inspection.	S.S.Q.	College M.O.
16.	14.30	Transport to Digby for Cadets of the E&S Wing.		Adjutant E&S Wing.
17.	14.30	Organised Games.		Cdt Wg P.F.O.
18.	6th May 09.30	Inspection.	Block 77.	Adjutant (J.E.)
	09.45	March to College and watch Church Parade. Attend church and watch the march past.		S.N.C.O.

19.	7th May 08.15	Inspection of Entry.	Block 77.	Adjutant (J.E.)
20.	09.00	Introductory talk by the Director of Studies.	College Main Hall.	Director of Studies.
21.	10.00	Maths or Science Test.	Room 206 'A' Site.	Senior Tutor (ASE).
22.	11.15	I&W or English Test.	Room 206 'A' Site.	Senior Tutor (E).
23.	14.00	Outstanding issue of kit.	Clothing Stores.	Officer i/c Cloth. Stores.
24.	15.30	Drill.	Square.	S.N.C.O.
25.	8th May 08.30	Maths or Science Test.	Room 206 'A' Site.	Senior Tutor (ASE).
26.	09.45	I&W or English Test.	Room 206 'A' Site.	Senior Tutor (E).
27.	11.00	Group photograph.	College steps.	N.C.O. i/c Photo Section.
28.	11.30	Drill.	Square.	S.N.C.O.
29.	14.00	1) Issue of flying clothing (parties of 8). 2) Marking of clothing.	Clothing Stores.	Officer i/c Cloth. Stores.
30.	16.00	Interviews with the Director of Studies and two Senior Tutors.		Adjutant (J.E.)
31.	9th May 08.30	Placing flying clothing in lockers.	Anson Flight.	Officer i/c Nav. Flight.
32.	09.40	Drawing parachute harness.	Parachute Section.	NCO i/c Para. Section.
		Description of Anson Aircraft.	Anson Flight.	Officer i/c Nav. Flight.
33.	11.30	Drill.	Square.	S.N.C.O.

34.	14.00	1) Interviews with the Director of Studies and two Senior Tutors. 2) Sport.		Adjutant (J.E.) Cdt Wg P.F.O.
35.	10th May 08.15	Flying Wing Documentation.	Briefing Room.	Flying Wing Adjutant.
36.	09.45	Issue of rifles.	Armoury	Arm. Officer.
37.	11.00	Individual photographs.	Photo Section.	N.C.O. i/c Photo Sect.
38.	11.30	Drill.	Square.	S.N.C.O.
39.	14.00	Drill.	Square.	S.N.C.O.
40.	15.15	Interview with Squadron Commanders.	College.	OCs 'A', 'B' & 'C' Sqns.
41.	16.10	Interviews with the Director of Studies and two Senior Tutors.		D of Studies and two Senior Tutors.
42.	11th May 08.30	Drill.	Square.	S.N.C.O.
43.	09.30	Inspection of vaccinations.	S.S.Q.	College M.O.
44.	11.00	G.C.T. lecture.	Hut 308.	S.G.C.T.I.
45.	14.00	Interviews with Padres.	1. C/E 2. O.D. 3. R.C.	St Christophers Holy Trinity St Mary's
46.	15.30	Drill	Square.	S.N.C.O.
47.	16.30	Interviews with Director of Studies and two Senior Tutors.		D of Studies and two Senior Tutors.
48.	12th May 09.00	Inspection of Block 77. Cadets standing by their beds.	Block 77.	Adjutant (J.E.)
49.	10.00	Drill.	Square.	S.N.C.O.
50.	11.00	Squadron Commanders disposal.		Adjutant (J.E.)

51.	14.00	Organised games.		Cdt Wg P.F.O.
52.	13th May 09.45	Inspection.	Block 77.	Adjutant (J.E.)
53.	10.00	March to the church, attend the service and watch the march past after church.		S.N.C.O.

2. With effect from 07.30 hours on 14th May, the normal programme of instruction will operate.

3. Dental inspection for the Entry will take place at 14.00 hours on 18th May, 1951. The Adjutant (J.E.) will contact the Senior Dental Officer for instructions.

Group Captain J.C. Woods
for Assistant Commandant
Royal Air Force College

Appendix IV

DS/101/1

R. A. F. COLLEGE – NO. 60 ENTRY
WEEKLY PROGRAMME OF COLLEGE
INSTRUCTION SUMMER TERM 1951

DAY	TIME	SECT. 1		SECT. 2		SECT. 3	
Mon	0830 – 0920	Aeroscience	B	Meteorology	E	Workshops	
	0930 – 1020	Meteorology	E	Mathematics	H	Workshops	
	1040 – 1130	Mathematics	J	Workshops		Flying	
	1140 – 1230	Electricity	L	Workshops		Flying	
	★1400 – 1600	Workshops		Flying		Navigation	6
	1610 – 1700	——————— P. T. ———————					
Tue	0830 – 0920	Mathematics	J	Meteorology	E	Aeroscience	B
	0930 – 1020	English	Z	English	U	Geography	T
	1040 – 1130	Geography	Z	Geography	T	English	U
	1140 – 1230	——————— P. T. ———————					
	1400 – 1600	—— Sqn Cdrs or Ground Combat Training ——					
	1610 – 1700	——————— Private Study ———————					
Wed	0830 – 0920	English	Z	English	U	Geography	W
	0930 – 1020	Geography	Z	Geography	T	English	U
	1040 – 1130	Mathematics	J	Electricity	K	Meteorology	E
	1140 – 1230	Electricity	K	Mathematics	H	Private Study	
Thu	0830 – 0920	Navigation	7	Aeroscience	B	Electricity	K
	0930 – 1020	Navigation	7	Workshops		Mathematics	J
	1040 – 1130	Meteorology	F	Workshops		Aeroscience	B
	1140 – 1230	——————— P. T. ———————					
	★1400 – 1600	Flying		Navigation	6	Workshops	
	1610 – 1700	——————— Private Study ———————					
Fri	0930 – 1020	English	Z	Geography	T	English	U
	1040 – 1130	Aeroscience	B	Electricity	L	Mathematics	J
	1140 – 1230	Private Study		Private Study		Electricity	L
	1400 – 1600	—— Sqn Cdrs or Ground Combat Training ——					
	1610 – 1700	——————— P. T. ———————					
Sat	0830 – 0920	Geography	Z	English	U	Geography	T

| 0930 — 1020 | Workshops | Mathematics | H Mathematics J |
| 1040 — 1130 | Workshops | Aeroscience | A Meteorology E |

*Flying periods commence at 1330 hours.

Note:1. Rooms A to F Science Block, Rooms G.1 and G.2 Weapons Block, Rooms H to Z 'A' Site, Rooms 1 to 7 College.

2. Grading of Classes in ASE and H subjects shown at Annex 'A'.

Annex 'A' To Appendix IV

NO. 60 ENTRY
GRADING OF CLASSES IN A.S.E. AND H SUBJECTS

Grading of Classes in A. S. E. Subjects

60 Sc.1	60 Sc.2	60 Sc.3
ALLISON	BAILEY	BROWN R. MCN.
ANSTEE	BOYCE	CARTWRIGHT
BEDFORD-ROBERTS	BROWN J.C.	CLOSE
BOWES	CHEDGEY	DA SILVA
DRUMMOND	CHIPPINDALE	EDWARDS
GOODALL	DINES	ELLIOTT
GRATTON	FIELD	GRIERSON
HEANEY	GREENHILL-HOOPER	HANCOCK
HOARE	LEWIS	HINTON
JONES	MARTIN	KHAN
LANGLEY	MARSH	MCKECHNIE
MAITLAND	MCENTEGART	MOORS
MCLELLAND-BROWN	MORGAN	QURESHI
MacNICOL	PURSE	WHITSON
WHITWAM	REYNOLDS	WOODS
	TAYLOR	

Grading of Classes in H Subjects

60 H.1	60 H.2	60 H.3
ANSTEE	ALLISON	BAILEY
BOYCE	BEDFORD-ROBERTS	CARTWRIGHT
BROWN R. MCN.	BOWES	CHEDGEY

CLOSE	BROWN J.C.	CHIPPINDALE
DA SILVA	GREENHILL-HOOPER	ELLIOTT
DINES	HANCOCK	DRUMMOND
EDWARDS	JONES	FIELD
GOODALL	LANGLEY	KHAN
GRATTON	LEWIS	HINTON
GRIERSON	MAITLAND	MCLELLAND-BROWN
HEANEY	MARSH	QURESHI
HOARE	MCENTEGART	WHITSON
MacNICOL	MCKECHNIE	WOODS
MARTIN	PURSE	
MOORS	REYNOLDS	
MORGAN	TAYLOR	
	WHITWAM	

Cranwell
2nd May 1951

Distribution – List A

50 to Adjutant (J.E.) for 60 Entry
20 Spare.

Appendix V

ADDRESS BY THE COMMANDANT, AIR COMMODORE H. EELES, CBE, MID, AT THE PRESENTATION OF WINGS, PRIZES AND AWARDS TO NO. 60 ENTRY

14 December 1953

C–in–C, Members of 60 Entry, Ladies and Gentlemen.

Before I say a few words to the members of 60 Entry, I would like to extend a very cordial welcome to our visitors – we are pleased to see you all here tonight, and I do hope that you will find your stay at Cranwell interesting, enjoyable and impressive.

I must, of course, begin my short talk this evening by offering my congratulations to the Flight Cadets of 60 Entry who have just been awarded their Wings. This is a great moment of achievement for you people who have been on the platform just now and I am sure, at this moment, you are feeling that the arduous and busy training that you have had during the last two years is more than worthwhile.

You have now acquired what I might call flying speed, but although you may have flying speed, you have by no means yet reached your operational ceiling, at least I hope you have not. From now on you still have a great deal of hard work to do if you really wish to become a first class RAF pilot. You are, of course, going on to a further stage of training, but after that further stage of training you will still have a great deal to learn.

Your entry into the RAF as Pilot Officers has come at a most exciting and progressive time as you all know only too well. The RAF is now rapidly being equipped with the most advanced types of aircraft, and it will be your duty and responsibility very shortly to fly these new types. They will be a very heavy responsibility and I do ask you to continue your training and your endeavours to become really first class pilots who are worthy of flying these first class machines.

Now a word to the Equipment and Secretarial Flight Cadets who are also passing-out tomorrow, but who do not earn their Wings. Their responsibilities on leaving Cranwell are going to be no less exacting and no less responsible than those of their colleagues who are in the General Duties Branch. You will leave here and will be plunged straight away into responsible positions at whatever unit you are being posted to. They will be positions full of trust and with a wide scope for initiative. The other chaps, at this stage are still going on to be taught something, but you are leaving here to take on your job right from the word go. You will find it interesting, you will find it responsible, but be confident in your own powers; I am sure that the training that you have received here has fully equipped you to carry out the tasks which you are going to meet so soon. I would remind you of the fact that your training here has been a joint training with the General Duties Branch; always remember in the future that you are colleagues together and that the officers of the Equipment and Secretarial Branches are in no way different and in no way less responsible than the General Duties officers.

I would also like to congratulate our prize winners – I nearly said, on looking at the programme, our prize winner. I think that everybody would agree with me that the prizes that have been won by Senior Under Officer Jones represent a remarkable record and constitute virtually a clean sweep. This shows an extremely wide range of ability in all types of technical subjects, flying skill and other aspects of the College training. It is no disparagement, I think, to Senior Under Officer Jones if I say that his individual successes are possibly hardly flattering to the remainder of his Entry. The competition perhaps has not been so keen as it might.

The Sovereign's Squadron is, for the second term running, C Squadron. There again this is a most creditable performance on the part of C Squadron, but at the same time I do hope that next term the other Squadrons will redouble their efforts in trying to wrest that most privileged honour from what is a jolly good squadron.

Now, gentlemen, that is all for congratulations. On similar occasions to this, we have had the privilege of listening to advice and guidance from many distinguished officers, and I would like to remind you for a moment of the advice that was given to you, or perhaps I should say to the last passing-out Entry, last term. That advice came from Air Chief Marshal Sir John Baker who was then VCAS. On that occasion Sir John made a suggestion that an officer's life and conduct should be guided by what he called the ABC code, and he enumerated to you what the ABC code was. A – Ability. B – Bearing. C – Courage. D – Discipline. E – Enthusiasm. All these qualities are undoubtedly required by an officer who wishes to make his mark, but I think myself that that is only half the battle and I would like to project Sir John's theory slightly beyond the arguments that he gave. I would like to draw your attention to some of the less virtuous characteristics which may, in fact, destroy the latent good that may be in you, and I would like to warn you of certain characteristics which, if they develop, will prevent you or anybody else from becoming a good officer. I would list first of these Irresponsibility in word or deed, second I would list a disregard for any moral values in this world of ours. Thirdly I would suggest a contempt for authority and fourthly I would suggest any deterioration in the standards which have been put up as your goal.

Your training at Cranwell during the last two years has admittedly been on what I would call a corporate basis. Your interests and your enthusiasm have been largely subordinated to the interests and well-being of your own particular Entry and also to the Squadron to which you have been nominated during your time here, and therefore the individual side of character development has been possibly subjugated to these mass loyalties to Squadron or Entry at the expense of the individual character training. I must say quite frankly that in certain matters the record of your Entry, both in the collective sphere and in some cases in the individual sphere, has been rather disappointing, and that is why I have enumerated, for your edification, those characteristics which I would ask you to avoid in the future.

Remember that personal example by the individual is one of the most important things in any officer in any service. The individual is watched constantly although he may not know it, not only by his superiors but more particularly by his subordinates, and an officer's standard of behaviour, provided it achieves a right and good standard, can be followed with justification by any subordinate; but if it does not reach the required standard, then the subordinates, human nature being what it is, will always delight in taking the easy path to a break down in standards, and will make the excuse the example of the officer whom he is watching and following.

I would like to use some words which I quoted the other evening, and some of you may have heard me use them, and that is that your example and behaviour will make or mar, not only your own career, but the reputation of the Service as a whole. I personally am quite confident that you can accept the responsibilities that you are about to be given, and that you are quite capable of achieving the highest possible standards in everything you do.

I shall not be surprised at all, or upset, if you forget what I am telling you tonight. Neither shall I be upset at all, but I may be very surprised, if you forget about Cranwell, particularly the tutors who have taught you, or the instructors who have tried to make you fly, and many other members of the Cranwell staff. But I will be sincerely grieved and upset if you, in any way, in the future, attempt to discard the standards of training that this College has tried to give you. I repeat, that I am fully confident of your ability to do well. Each one of you here has got it in you to do really well and I wish you every possible success in your future careers.

Tomorrow, gentlemen, after the Parade, you will be marched off by the Senior Under Officer and as you go into the College you will see two flags flying from the College tower. The right hand flag will be the Standard of the RAF College and the left hand flag will be the RAF Ensign. As you pass into the College on the completion of the Parade, you will transfer your allegiance from the Standard of the College to the Ensign of the RAF and from that moment you will have finally and irrevocably dedicated yourself to your Queen and your country; but having done that I would still like you to think of the College.

What of the College in the future? The RAF College and all those who serve the College will watch your achievements and what you do for the RAF and for yourselves with pride and satisfaction, provided you maintain our tradition and reputation.

Appendix VI

ADDRESS BY THE CHIEF OF THE AIR STAFF, AIR CHIEF MARSHAL SIR WILLIAM DICKSON, GCB, KBE, DSO, AFC, AT THE PASSING-OUT PARADE OF NO. 60 ENTRY

15 December 1953

I would first like to congratulate you on a parade which is in keeping with the high standards of Cranwell. I would also congratulate No. 60 Entry on completing the first stage of your careers as permanent officers of the Royal Air Force.

You are, I think, fortunate to be going out into the Royal Air Force at this time. In the first place it is good for you to feel that the career you have chosen is important and worthwhile. You can know with all humility that it is upon the fighting capability and flying efficiency and the high morale of our Air Force, and those of our allies that the peace of the world at this critical period of history depends. To contribute to that end is certainly worthwhile.

You are also going out into a Service that, because of these responsibilities, offers a wide field of interest. At this time, it is a particularly wide field, and full of all the same kind of fascinating problems which has always made Air Force service such fun and so full of opportunity for the individual.

You are also lucky that throughout your whole career you will be leaders of a Service whose primary role will be the flying and directing of aircraft piloted by General Duties officers. The fact that aircraft are developing in capability just like ships did in the last century, and the fact that the Royal Air Force has new weapons like guided missiles to develop, so that they may be complementary to the operation of aircraft, are matters of added interest and opportunity in your future careers, and not otherwise. I feel confident that what has been built into your characters here at Cranwell will serve you and the Service in good stead in the future. In your very proper keenness and enjoyment of flying, do keep in the back of your minds that you have been given this unique training and opportunity to fit you to be leaders of men – leaders of airmen. Man is more important than the machine. So, quietly and unobtrusively, study the art of leading men; and do remember (however dull it may sound) that operational efficiency depends on very good administration and maintenance. It was not the tactics, but attention to the preparations which lay behind nearly every victory in the history of warfare.

My final word of advice is: Keep your Cranwell standards! All eyes will be on you out in the Service. There will be some envy. There will be many temptations to fall in with the stream. But, I am sure that with good manners – especially good manners – and tact, and with cheerfulness and keenness, you will survive and be respected. But let nothing destroy that aim which you have set yourself here. Much has been given to you, and much is expected.

I wish each of you of No. 60 Entry, individually, all success and happiness in your future lives.

Appendix VII

NO. 60 ENTRY, RAF COLLEGE CRANWELL
3 MAY 1951 – 15 DECEMBER 1953

General Duties (Pilot) Branch   **Order of Merit**

Allison, Duncan   (Duncan)   9GD(P)
>   Coleshill GS and No. 1 TTS, RAF Halton.
>   B Squadron; Senior Flight Cadet; Athletics
>   (Full Colours), Rugby, Association Football,
>   Bridge (President).
>   Retired from RAF August 1985, an Air Commodore.
>   Honours and Awards: CBE.

Anstee, Peter John   (Pete)   5GD(P)
>   Dulwich and No. 2 ANS, RAF Thorney Island.
>   C Squadron; Senior Under Officer; Phillip
>   Sassoon Memorial Prize; The Royal United
>   Services Institution Award; Rugby (Secretary,
>   Half Colours), Debating.
>   Retired from RAF July 1987, a Wing Commander.

Bailey, Reginald Graham   (Reg or Reggie)
>   Liverpool Institute.
>   A Squadron; Flight Cadet. Suspended December 1952.

Bedford-Roberts, Alan Gordon (Alan)
>   Wellington and No. 1 ITS, RAF Jurby.
>   C Squadron; Cadet. Suspended January 1952.

Bowes, Julian Martyn Belaye   (Julian)   10GD(P)
>   Douai and Millfield.
>   A Squadron; Senior Flight Cadet; Languages
>   Award; Fencing (Captain, Full Colours),
>   Pentathlon, Dramatics (President).
>   Retired from RAF March 1956, a Flying Officer.

Boyce, Timothy Simon Baron (Sam)   6GD(P)
    Stowe.
    A Squadron; Under Officer; Shooting (Full Colours).
    Retired from RAF December 1985, a Wing Commander.

Brown, James Cardow   (Jim)   16GD(P)
    Otago Boys' High School, Dunedin, New Zealand.
    New Zealander in RAF.
    B Squadron; Senior Flight Cadet; Rugby.
    Retired from RAF March 1970, a Squadron Leader.

Brown, Ramsay McNair   (Ramsay)   25GD(P)
    Kirkham School.
    C Squadron; Senior Flight Cadet; Camping.
    Retired from RAF May 1985, a Wing Commander.

Cartwright, Robert Lawrence   (Bob)
    Bedford.
    A Squadron; Flight Cadet. Suspended April 1953.

Chedgey, Ronald Ivor   (Ron)
    Woolwich Polytechnic.
    B Squadron; Flight Cadet. Suspended September
    1952.

Chippindale, Ronald   (Ron or Chips)   26GD(P)
    Rangiora High School, Rangiora, New Zealand.
    Royal New Zealand Air Force.
    B Squadron; Senior Flight Cadet; Rugby.
    Retired from RNZAF November 1974, a Squadron
    Leader.

Close, Walter Ernest   (Wally)   2GD(P)
    Wimbledon College.
    B Squadron; Senior Under Officer; Cricket
    (Captain, Full Colours), Rugby, Tennis.
    Retired from RAF December 1984, a Wing
    Commander.

Da Silva, Cecil Evan Victor   (Cecil)
    St Thomas's College, Mount Lavinia, Ceylon.
    Royal Ceylon Air Force.
    B Squadron; Cadet. Suspended January 1952.

Dines, Malcolm James   (Malcolm or Mal)   21GD(P)
    Christ's Hospital.
    A Squadron; Senior Flight Cadet; Sailing
    (Secretary).
    Resigned from RAF April 1957, a Flight
    Lieutenant.

Drummond, James Michael   (Bulldog)   29GD(P)
    Wellington.
    C Squadron; Senior Flight Cadet; Engineering
    (President), Choral (President).
    Retired from RAF January 1968, a Flight
    Lieutenant in the Secretarial Branch.

Edwards, Ronald Alfred   (Ron)   15GD(P)
    Chichester High School.
    B Squadron; Senior Flight Cadet; Cricket (Full
    Colours), Association Football (Secretary, Full Colours).
    Retired from RAF January 1987, a Group Captain.
    Honours and Awards: OBE.

Elliott, Michael Anthony Charles (Mike)
    Westminster T. I.
    C Squadron; Flight Cadet. Suspended April 1953.

Field, Colin Patrick   (Colin)   30GD(P)
    Caterham School.
    C Squadron; Senior Flight Cadet; Cricket.
    Retired from RAF November 1959, a Flying Officer.

Goodall, Michael John   (Mike, Sal or Salvador)
    Chislehurst and Sidcup County GS, Kent.
    C Squadron; Flight Cadet. Killed in Cranwell
    flying accident, June 1953.

Gratton, John Breton   (John)   17GD(P)
    Kingswood School, Bath.
    B Squadron; Senior Flight Cadet; Photography.
    Retired from RAF February 1971, a Squadron Leader.

Greenhill-Hooper, Terry John (Tom)   11GD(P)
    Hele's School, Exeter.
    B Squadron; Under Officer; Shooting, Photography.
    Retired from RAF November 1970, a Squadron Leader.

Grierson, Gordon Stewart   (Gordon or Graggers)
>   Caldy Grange GS.
>   A Squadron; Flight Cadet. Relegated to No. 61
>   Entry, December 1952 and graduated April 1954.
>   Resigned from RAF August 1956, a Flying Officer.

Hancock, Rutherford Moncrieff (Rutherford or Hank)   22GD(P)
>   Timaru Boys' High School, Timaru, New Zealand.
>   Royal New Zealand Air Force.
>   A Squadron; Senior Flight Cadet; Athletics (Full Colours).
>   Retired from RNZAF December 1971, a Squadron Leader.

Heaney, Michael Robert Hammersley (Michael or Spike)
>   Marlborough.
>   A Squadron; Flight Cadet. Killed in motor cycle
>   accident returning to Cranwell from leave, January 1953.

Hinton, Bernard Keith   (Dick)
>   Cheltenham GS.
>   B Squadron; Flight Cadet. Suspended April 1953.

Hoare, Richard   (Dickie)   18GD(P)
>   Isleworth County School.
>   C Squadron; Under Officer; Fencing, Debating.
>   Retired from RAF August 1970, a Flight Lieutenant.
>   Honours and Awards: Coronation Medal.

Jones, Laurence Alfred   (Laurie)   1GD(P)
>   Whitgift Middle School, Croydon.
>   A Squadron; Senior Under Officer; Sword of Honour;
>   Queen's Medal; R.M. Groves Memorial Prize and
>   Kinkead Trophy; Dickson Trophy; A.G. Fellowes
>   Memorial Prize; J.A. Chance Memorial Prize; Rugby
>   (Full Colours), Athletics (Captain, Full Colours).
>   Retired from RAF after being Air Member for Personnel
>   January 1990 as Air Marshal Sir Laurence Jones. Became
>   Lieutenant-Governor of the Isle of Man. Died September
>   1995.
>   Honours and Awards: KCB, AFC, Coronation Medal.

Khan, Muhammad Hamidullah (Hammy)   19GD(P)
>   D.J.S.G. Science College, Pakistan.
>   Royal Pakistan Air Force.
>   C Squadron; Under Officer; Hockey, Boxing,
>   Dancing (Secretary).
>   Killed when a Flying Officer in an RPAF flying
>   accident March 1955.

Langley, John Douglas   (Johnny)
>   Rochester Junior Technical School and No. 1 TTS,
>   RAF Halton.
>   A Squadron; Flight Cadet. Relegated to No. 61
>   Entry, March 1953 and graduated April 1954.
>   Retired from RAF April 1991, a Flight Lieutenant.

Lewis, James Thomas Campbell (Tiny)
>   Goldhurst School, Kent, and No. 1 ITS, RAF Jurby.
>   B Squadron; Flight Cadet. Suspended February 1953.

MacNicol, Nigel Ramsay   (Nigel)   4GD(P)
>   Framlingham and No. 7 FTS, RAF Cottesmore.
>   A Squadron; Senior Flight Cadet; Languages Award;
>   Boxing (Captain, Full Colours), *Journal*
>   (Committee and Editor).
>   Retired from RAF January 1976, a Flight Lieutenant.

Maitland, John Edmund   (John)   3GD(P)
>   Clifton.
>   B Squadron; Senior Flight Cadet; The Air
>   Ministry Prize for Imperial and War Studies;
>   Rugby, Hockey, Angling (Captain).
>   Transferred to National Air Traffic Services
>   January 1986.
>   Retired from RAF May 1993, a Group Captain.

Marsh, Michael Martin   (Mike)   12GD(P)
>   Gillingham County GS and No. 1 TTS, RAF Halton.
>   C Squadron; Senior Flight Cadet; Hockey.
>   Resigned from RAF February 1956, a Flying Officer.

Martin, Walter Raymond   (Wally)
>   Harvey GS, Folkstone, and No. 6 FTS, RAF Ternhill.
>   A Squadron; Flight Cadet. Suspended June 1952.

McEntegart, John Roxburgh   (John or Mac)   13GD(P)
    Felsted.
    B Squadron; Senior Flight Cadet; Beagling
    (Flight Cadet Whip).
    Killed when a Flying Officer in an RAF flying
    accident in Germany May 1955.

McKechnie, Peter   (Pete)
    Portsmouth GS.
    C Squadron; Flight Cadet. Relegated to No. 61
    Entry, September 1953. Suspended December 1953.

McLelland-Brown, Alan John   (Alan or Sabre)
    Kent College.
    A Squadron; Flight Cadet. Suspended February
    1953 and transferred to Equipment Branch, No.
    14 Entry, RAF Digby. After integration of
    E & S Wing with Cranwell, suspended from No.
    63 Entry December 1953.

Moors, Edward Henry   (Ted)   24GD(P)
    Burford GS.
    C Squadron; Senior Flight Cadet; Rugby, Cricket.
    Retired from RAF May 1969, a Squadron Leader.

Morgan, Jenkin Alun   (Alun)   8GD(P)
    Holloway GS.
    C Squadron; Under Officer; Association Football
    (Half Colours), Debating (President), *Journal*
    (Committee and Assistant Editor).
    Retired from RAF January 1987, an Air Commodore.
    Honours and Awards: CBE.

Purse, David Charles   (Dave)
    HMS *Conway*.
    C Squadron; Flight Cadet. Suspended March 1952
    and transferred to Equipment Branch, No. 12
    Entry, RAF Digby. After integration of E & S
    Wing with Cranwell, graduated in No. 61 Entry
    April 1954.
    Left RAF October 1964, a Flight Lieutenant, after
    being cashiered by sentence of a Court Martial.

Qureshi, Ijaz Ahmed (Joe)
> Islamia College, Karachi.
> Royal Pakistan Air Force.
> A Squadron; Flight Cadet. Relegated to No. 61
> Entry, March 1953 and graduated April 1954.
> Relinquished RPAF commission January 1955, a
> Pilot Officer.

Reynolds, Edward (Ted) 14GD(P)
> Portsmouth Municipal College.
> A Squadron; Senior Flight Cadet; Athletics,
> Sailing (Captain).
> Retired from RAF July 1958, a Flight Lieutenant.

Taylor, Christopher Churton (Chris or Kit) 27GD(P)
> Clifton.
> C Squadron; Senior Flight Cadet; Hockey (Half
> Colours), Swimming, Gliding (Secretary).
> Retired from RAF March 1988, a Wing Commander
> in Administrative Branch.

Whitson, Andrew Cameron (Andy) 23GD(P)
> Ashton-under-Lyne GS.
> B Squadron; Senior Flight Cadet; Athletics.
> Retired from RAF January 1971, a Squadron Leader.

Whitwam, Anthony Stuart Jabez (Tony) 7GD(P)
> Denstone.
> B Squadron; Under Officer; Athletics (Captain,
> Full Colours).
> Retired from RAF August 1975, a Temporary
> Squadron Leader.
> Honours and Awards: Coronation Medal.

Woods, Christopher Cardew (Chris)
> Sevenoaks School.
> C Squadron; Cadet. Suspended December 1951.

From No. 59 GD(P) Entry

Coleman, Armand Knowles (Armand) 28GD(P)
> Dover County GS.
> Relegated to No. 60 Entry, April 1953.
> C Squadron; Senior Flight Cadet; Athletics

(Full Colours).
Resigned from RAF April 1974, a Flying Officer
in Equipment Branch.

Scroggs, Timothy William Murray (Tim)
    Brighton College.
    Relegated to No. 60 Entry, September 1952.
    B Squadron; Flight Cadet. Suspended December
    1952 and transferred to Equipment Branch, No.
    14 Entry, RAF Digby. After integration of E & S
    Wing with Cranwell, graduated in No. 63 Entry
    December 1954.
    Retired from RAF November 1987, a Flight
    Lieutenant in Administrative Branch.

Tucker, John Arthur   (John or Tuck)   20GD(P)
    Taunton School and No. 1 TTS, RAF Halton.
    Relegated to No. 60 Entry, January 1952.
    A Squadron; Under Officer; Swimming (Captain,
    Full Colours), Boxing (Half Colours).
    Retired from RAF October 1967, a Flight
    Lieutenant.
    Honours and Awards: Coronation Medal.

Vickers, David Duncan   (Dave or Vic)   31GD(P)
    Rossall School.
    Relegated to No. 60 Entry, April 1953.
    C Squadron; Senior Flight Cadet; Swimming
    (Half Colours), Chess (Captain).
    Killed when a Pilot Officer in an RAF flying
    accident in Germany December 1954.

From No. 11 E & S Entry, RAF Digby, August 1953

Bright, Alan   (Alan)   2EQP
    King's School, Peterborough.
    A Squadron; Senior Flight Cadet; Pot-holing.
    Retired from RAF January 1971, a Squadron
    Leader in Supply Branch.

Pringle, Robin Bryan   (Robin)   1SEC
    St Peter's, York.
    A Squadron; Under Officer; The Air Ministry
    Prize for Secretarial Studies; Hockey, Rowing,

Rugby.
Resigned from RAF March 1960, a Flying Officer.

Vella, Joseph Francis (Joe)
The Lyceum, Malta.
B Squadron; Senior Flight Cadet. Relegated
to No. 61 Entry, November 1953 and graduated
April 1954.
Retired from RAF November 1984, a Wing
Commander in Supply Branch.

Watts, John Richard (John) 2SEC
Ranelagh GS.
B Squadron; Under Officer; Association Football
(Full Colours), Cricket (Half Colours).
Retired from RAF May 1984, a Wing Commander in
Administrative Branch.

Woods, David James (Dave) 2EQP
Portsmouth GS.
C Squadron; Senior Flight Cadet; The Air
Ministry Prize for Equipment Studies;
Cross-country, *Journal* (Committee and
Assistant Editor), Dramatics.
Retired from RAF September 1987, a Group
Captain in Supply Branch.

Analysis

No. 60 GD(P) Entry numbers 3 May 1951 46
  Less 2 killed, 4 relegations to No. 61 Entry, 2
  transfers (1 to No. 12 E & S Entry, 1 to No. 14
  E & S Entry), and 10 suspensions, i.e. a 'chop'
  rate of 39.1% 18
Plus 4 relegations from No. 59 GD(P) Entry 4
Less 1 transfer ex No. 59 GD(P) Entry to No. 14
  E & S Entry 1
Plus 5 transfers from No. 11 E & S Entry, RAF Digby,
  August 1953 5
Less 1 relegation ex No. 11 E & S Entry to No. 61
  Entry 1

Graduated 15 December 1953:

31 GD(P)   (28 original members of No. 60 GD(P) Entry
                   plus 3 ex No. 59 GD(P) Entry),
4 E & S   (Ex No. 11 E & S Entry)   35

On leaving Service:

Rank of the 35 graduates –

AM	1	Sqn. Ldr.	9
Air Cdre.	2	Flt. Lt.	6
Gp. Capt.	3	Fg. Off.	7
Wg. Cdr.	6	Plt. Off.	1

Honours and Awards of the 35 graduates –

KCB	1	AFC	1
CBE	2	Coronation Medal	4
OBE	1		

Appendix VIII

ROYAL NEW ZEALAND AIR FORCE GRADUATES OF THE ROYAL AIR FORCE COLLEGE CRANWELL 1951 – 1964

Entry General Duties Branch   **Order of Merit**

No.

60   **3 May 1951 – 15 December 1953**

Chippindale, Ronald   (Ron or Chips)   26GD(P)
>Rangiora High School, Rangiora, New Zealand.
>B Squadron; Senior Flight Cadet; Rugby.
>Retired from RNZAF November 1974, a Squadron Leader.

Hancock, Rutherford Moncrieff (Rutherford or Hank)   22GD(P)
>Timaru Boys' High School, Timaru, New Zealand.
>A Squadron; Senior Flight Cadet; Athletics
>(Full Colours).
>Retired from RNZAF December 1971, a Squadron Leader.

63   **1 May 1952 – 14 December 1954**

McLeod, Guy Xavier Edwin   (Guy)   5GD(P)
>King's College, Auckland, New Zealand.
>B Squadron; Senior Under Officer; Phillip Sassoon
>Memorial Prize; Rugby (Half Colours), Swimming,
>Tennis, Wild Fowling, Photography (Secretary),
>Jazz (Secretary), Classical Music, Debating.
>Left RNZAF January 1962, a Flight Lieutenant.

Wallingford, Geoffrey   (Geoff)   6GD(P)
>Hailbury and I.S.C.; Wanganui Collegiate School,
>Wanganui, New Zealand.
>C Squadron; Senior Under Officer; Sword of Honour;
>Shooting (Vice-Captain, Full Colours), Rugby
>(Full Colours), Swimming, Tennis, Athletics,
>Sailing, Skiing.

Retired from RNZAF September 1986, a Group Captain.
Honours and Awards: LVO, AFC.

66   29 April 1953 – 13 December 1955

Derby, Graham Colin   (Graham)   15GD(P)
New Plymouth Boys' High School, New Plymouth,
New Zealand.
B Squadron; Senior Flight Cadet; Shooting
(Full Colours), Rugby, Mountaineering, *Journal*.
Retired from RNZAF September 1977, a Wing Commander.

Hubbard, Geoffrey Charles   (Geoff)   1GD(P)
Marlborough College, Blenheim, New Zealand.
A Squadron; Senior Under Officer; Queen's Medal;
R.M. Groves Memorial Prize; Dickson Trophy and
Michael Hill Memorial Prize; Hicks Memorial Prize;
J.A. Chance Memorial Prize; Shooting (Full
Colours), Parachuting, Film Society.
Retired from RNZAF February 1990, an Air Commodore.
Honours and Awards: OBE.

69   28 April 1954 – 9 April 1957

Bevan, Peter Granville   (Pete)   15GD(P)
Nelson College, Nelson, New Zealand.
A Squadron; Senior Flight Cadet; Pot-holing,
Archery, Film Society.
Retired from RNZAF January 1975, a Squadron Leader.

70   8 September 1954 – 30 July 1957

Enright, Thomas Esmond   (Tom)   1GD(P)
Christian Brothers' High School, Dunedin, New
Zealand, and No. 1 TTS, RAF Halton.
B Squadron; Senior Under Officer; Sword of Honour;
Queen's Medal; A.G. Fellowes Memorial Prize;
R.M. Groves Memorial Prize; J.A. Chance Memorial
Prize; The Air Ministry Prize for Commonwealth
War Studies; Shooting (Captain, Full Colours),
Rugby, Gliding, Pot-holing, Fine Arts, Film Society.
Left RNZAF January 1971, a Squadron Leader.

72 **27 April 1955 – 1 April 1958**

Adamson, Peter Raymond   (Pete)   1GD(P)
> John McGlashan College, Dunedin, New Zealand.
> B Squadron; Senior Flight Cadet; Queen's Medal;
> A.G. Fellowes Memorial Prize; The Royal New
> Zealand Air Force Trophy; The Air Ministry Prize
> for Commonwealth and War Studies; Athletics,
> Soccer, Riding, Skiing, Photography, Aeromodelling,
> Film Society.
> Retired from RNZAF September 1992, an Air Vice
> Marshal (Chief of the Air Staff 1988–92).
> Honours and Awards: CB, OBE.

73 **7 September 1955 – 29 July 1958**

Thomson, Albert Edward   (Tommy)   2GD(P)
> Christchurch Boys' High School, Christchurch,
> New Zealand.
> B Squadron; Senior Under Officer; Sword of Honour;
> The Royal New Zealand Air Force Trophy; The Air
> Ministry Prize for Commonwealth and War Studies;
> Rugby, Athletics, Skiing, Gliding, Mountaineering,
> Motor Club, Film Society.
> Retired from RNZAF December 1989, an Air Vice
> Marshal.
> Honours and Awards: CBE, AFC.

75 **11 September 1956 – 28 July 1959**

Donaldson, William Ross   (Ross)   2GD(P)
> Palmerston North Boys' High School, Palmerston
> North, New Zealand.
> C Squadron; Senior Flight Cadet; R.M. Groves
> Memorial Prize; Kinkead Trophy; The Royal New
> Zealand Air Force Trophy; Hockey (Full Colours),
> Swimming (Half Colours), Photography, *Journal*,
> Bridge (Secretary).
> Retired from RNZAF July 1987, a Group Captain.
> Honours and Awards: OBE.
> Died in London, February 1992.

77   11 September 1957 – 25 July 1960

Edwards, Kenneth James   (Ken)   12GD(N)

Hutt Valley High School, Lower Hutt, New Zealand.
C Squadron; Under Officer; Rugby (Full Colours),
Tennis (Captain, Full Colours), Golf, Mountaineering
(Captain), Pot-holing, Photography (Secretary).
Retired from RNZAF December 1978, a Wing Commander.

81   9 September 1959 – 31 July 1962

Thomson, Russell Bennett   (Russ)   5GD(P)

Brother of AVM Tommy Thomson.
Cathedral GS, Christchurch, New Zealand.
C Squadron; Senior Under Officer; Sword of Honour;
J.A. Chance Memorial Prize; Fencing (Captain,
Full Colours), Modern Pentathlon, Pot-holing,
Jazz, *Journal* (Editor), Photography, Skiing,
Geographical, Choral, Film Society.
Killed when a Flying Officer in an accident
flying a Canberra off China Rock, Singapore,
November 1964.

84   11 January 1961 – 17 December 1963

Lamb, Kenneth Ross Forbes   (Ken)   15GD(P)

Whangarei High School, Whangarei, New Zealand.
D Squadron; Senior Flight Cadet; Rugby,
Cross-country, Badminton, Tennis, Aeromodelling,
Film Society.
Left RNZAF November 1975, a Squadron Leader.

86   7 January 1962 – 17 December 1964

Lanham, John Willis   (John)   8GD(P)

Christian Brothers' High School, Dunedin, New Zealand.
B Squadron; Senior Under Officer; Sword of Honour;
R.S. May Memorial Prize; Skiing (Captain, Full
Colours), Ocean Sailing, Canoeing.
Retired from RNZAF December 1987, a Wing Commander.

Analysis

Total RNZAF graduates 1951 – 1964	15
Sword of Honour	5
Queen's Medal	3

On leaving Service:

Rank –

AVM	2	Sqn. Ldr.	5
Air Cdre.	1	Flt. Lt.	1
Gp. Capt.	2	Fg. Off.	1
Wg. Cdr.	3		

Honours and Awards –

CB	1	OBE	3
CBE	1	AFC	2
LVO	1		

Index